PI

Jesus Chı
Ancient Cosmology an

"In this inspired work Fideler ma ... on number and geometry by the anci... philosophers, artists, architects, and seers whose ideals are at the foundation of modern Western civilization. In their grand but now lost science the ancients recognized identical archetypal principles recurring in mathematics, music, nature, art, architecture, science, cosmology, language, and religion, interweaving them into a symbolic whole which is known today only in fragments. Mythic exploits and relationships of the Egyptian and Greek deities were studied in mystery schools using geometric diagrams and musical harmonies. Fideler's careful scholarship and eye for geometry shed light on long-obscured but profound teachings. It can only increase our respect for the depth of ancient understanding and transform the way we look at our cultural inheritance."

— **Michael Schneider**, author of *A Beginner's Guide to Constructing the Universe*

"This book makes a convincing case for the continuity of the European tradition through detailed and original research on Pythagorean number theory and Hellenistic gematria. It is a brilliant achievement, literally thrilling, and a definitive text on Greek and Christian gematria and sacred geometry."

— **Ralph Abraham**, Professor of Mathematics,
University of California at Santa Cruz

"This scholarly but immensely readable work represents a truly remarkable accomplishment. To understand the world of antiquity, notably Christianity and Gnosis, we must first appreciate that the ancient genius was far from naive. In this path-making book, David Fideler systematically reveals just how sophisticated the cosmology of the early philosophers was and to what degree they were inspired by mathematics and the ideal of symmetry and harmony."

— **Georg Feuerstein**, Ph.D., author of *The Encyclopedic Dictionary of Yoga*, *Voices on the Threshold of Tomorrow*, and *Sacred Paths*

"The most convincing argument I have ever read for the historical significance of gematria as the literary embodiment of geometric formulas. This study is comprehensive, articulate, and beautifully illustrated."

— **Ernest G. McClain**, Professor Emeritus of Music, Brooklyn College; author of *The Pythagorean Plato: Prelude to the Song Itself*

"This book is essential reading for everyone seeking spirituality in our modern, materialistic age. Fideler's presentation of pre-Christian philosophy is truly moving, as is his analysis of how these ancient teachings could reinvigorate modern life. After reading this book, you will never look at the world, or Christianity, or yourself, the same."

— **Lance deHaven-Smith**, Professor of Political Science,
Florida Atlantic University

"This work is clearly an advance towards better understanding about the wide range of possibilities available to interpreters in the ancient Mediterranean worlds."

— **Robert A. Kraft**, Professor of Religious Studies,
University of Pennsylvania

"With the approach of the next millennium, there is renewed interest in the purpose and future of humanity. *Jesus Christ, Sun of God* puts Christianity back on the agenda. This book is important both as a work of meticulous scholarship on hitherto neglected Christian and gnostic texts and for the fresh light it throws on the Greek sources of Christian theology and spirituality. With David Fideler we glimpse anew the cosmic universalism at the heart of Christianity. This is a text for our own times which can yet reinherit and restore the inspiration of the West."

— **Dr. Nicholas Goodrick-Clarke**,
EUROPAEUM, University of Oxford

"Like an archeologist, Fideler digs beneath the surface of the Christian story to uncover the universal myths on which it is based. Then he goes further, into the bedrock of culture, by showing that these universal myths are themselves founded on a system of musically significant numbers."

— **Joscelyn Godwin**, Professor of Music, Colgate University;
author of *Mystery Religions in the Ancient World*; *Music, Mysticism, and Magic: A Sourcebook*; and *Harmony of the Spheres: A Sourcebook of the Pythagorean Tradition in Music*

"An essential book for understanding the ways ancient Christianity incorporated the timeless wisdom of antiquity, David Fideler's *Jesus Christ, Sun of God* allows us to see the Western traditions in a new light. This is a book for all those interested in philosophy, culture, science, geometry, language, and above all, religious studies. I highly recommend it."

— **Arthur Versluis**, Professor of English and Fulbright Scholar;
author of *American Transcendentalism and Asian Religions*

Jesus Christ, Sun of God

Ancient Cosmology and Early Christian Symbolism

David Fideler

A publication supported by
THE KERN FOUNDATION

Wheaton, Illinois ♦ Chennai (Madras), India

The Theosophical Publishing House
P.O. Box 270
Wheaton, IL 60189-0270

A publication of the Theosophical Publishing House, a department of the Theosophical Society in America.

This publication made possible with the assistance of the Kern Foundation.

Library of Congress Cataloging-in-Publication Data

Fideler, David R., 1961–
Jesus Christ, sun of God : ancient cosmology and early Christian symbolism / David Fideler
p. cm.
Includes bibliographical references and index.
ISBN 0-8356-0698-8 (alk. paper) : $24.00. — ISBN 0-8356-0696-1 (pbk. : alk. paper) : $16.00
1. Jesus Christ—Person and offices—History of doctrines—Early church, ca. 30–600. 2. Logos—History of doctrines—Early church, ca. 30–600. 3. Christianity and other religions. 4. Gnosticism—Relations—Christianity. 5. Paganism—Relations—Christianity. 6. Cosmology, Ancient. I. Title.
BT205.F53 1993
299'.934—dc20 93-2153
CIP

6 5 4 3 * 02 03 04 05 06 07 08

This edition is printed on acid-free paper that meets the American National Standards Institute Z39.48 Standard.

Printed in the United States of America.

For Diana

For Orpheus, whose head still
softly sings,

for Kronos, lord of Time, Eternity,
and weighty concerns,

and for Harmonia, who ever
weaves the veil
of this divinely beautiful world.

May they smile upon this work.

Table of Contents

Documentary Illustrations

List of Figures

No one after lighting a lamp covers it with a vessel, or puts it under a bed, but puts it on a stand, that those who enter may see the light. For nothing is hid that shall not be made manifest, nor anything secret that shall not be known and come to light.

—Jesus, Luke 8.16

The Pharisees and the scribes have taken the keys of knowledge and hidden them. They themselves have not entered, nor have they allowed to enter those who wish to. You, however, be as wise as serpents and as innocent as doves.

—Jesus, *Gospel of Thomas* 39

Truth did not come into the world naked, but it came in types and images. One will not receive truth in any other way.

—*Gospel of Philip* 67.9–11

Let him who seeks continue seeking until he finds. When he finds, he will become troubled. When he becomes troubled, he will be astonished, and he will rule over the All.

—Jesus, *Gospel of Thomas* 2

Preface

THIS BOOK throws light on some long-overlooked aspects of cosmological symbolism that were important both to ancient Greek philosophers and early Christian writers. The study focuses on the pre-Christian idea of the Logos, the pattern of Harmony which was seen as underlying the order of the universe, and which some of the earliest Christians identified with the figure of Jesus, the avatar of the Christian faith. As such, this is not a book about the historical Jesus, but shows how, in antiquity, Jesus and other divine figures were represented as symbolic personifications of cosmic principles.

If we want to understand the cosmological ideas of antiquity, it is necessary to suspend belief in our modern fragmentary approaches to the universe, for cosmology is an inclusive study, unifying all forms of human knowledge. It is also necessary to transcend the artificial boundaries of academic specialization, for it is not possible to understand ancient religious thought, mysticism, philosophy, cosmology, or metaphysics taken in isolation.

This book is an outgrowth of fifteen years of research. During that period, my approach has been to take the ancient Greek philosophers and mystics, whether pagan or Christian, seriously and at their word. When Plato states that "geometry is the knowledge of the eternally existent" and that it is not possible to understand his philosophy without first studying the Pythagorean sciences of arithmetic, geometry, musical harmonics, and astronomy, it is necessary to consider these statements in a serious light. Similarly, when the pagan theologians claim that the nature of the gods is related to Number, and the early Christian gnostics use a system of number symbolism to interpret the inner meanings of the new faith, a true scholar will approach such statements with curiosity, an open mind, and a willingness to investigate. It has always seemed to me that if you want to understand another person you need to take his or her statements seriously, and the same holds true if you wish to understand the thinkers of antiquity.

In my personal orientation, I have always been a philosopher first, a historian of religions second. Despite my preoccupation with historical information and raw data, my fundamental interest lies in acquiring insight, the spark of understanding. Hence, in addition to being an historical exploration of ancient forms of spiritual knowledge or gnosis, this book is something of a "gnostic" work itself. That is unavoidable, for if we wish to understand ancient cosmology we must first enter into the ancient world of thought through the use of historical imagination: to understand Plato, it is necessary, at least for a while, to think as a Platonist. Likewise, in terms of methodology, I have earnestly sought to understand Pythagorean thought *from the inside* as a potentially valid perspective. I have approached the Greek myths as would an Orphic theologian, and have tried to understand the gnostic dimension of early Christianity as did some of the ancient scholars and cosmologists. At its deeper levels, the human mind has changed little over the last 2,500 years, and only by entering sympathetically into the intellectual and spiritual world of antiquity can we ever hope to understand it.

This book is written both for the general reader and for scholars of Hellenistic religions and cosmology. Keeping in mind that some of the material will be unfamiliar even to specialists, I have provided complete documentation for anyone interested in studying the primary sources. The documentary illustrations at the end amplify themes touched upon in the chapters and stimulate the mythic imagination; full citations for the accompanying text are presented in the endnotes, but I decided not to use note numbers in this section for aesthetic reasons. Bibliographical references to classical sources are often abbreviated in scholarly publications and incomprehensible to noninitiates, a practice I have consciously avoided. Because of the problems associated with the modern concept of "Gnosticism" discussed in chapter 6, I do not capitalize gnostic, and envision the term as an adjective rather than a noun. The capitalized term *Gnosis* refers to the general patterns and myths that various gnostic teachings have in common, while the capitalized term *Gnosticism* refers only to the scholarly concept that has evolved in the last two centuries which is critiqued in chapter 6 as being inadequate. The dating system is that used by most scholars of early Christianity: C.E. (common era) and B.C.E. (before common era). In my citations, numbers directly following a classical source refer to the appropriate section of the text; however, if there is a comma between the title and the number, the page number of a particular edition is referred to.

Because ancient cosmological thought was concerned with the nature of cosmic principles, capitalized terms refer to Platonic Ideas or universal archetypes: for example, the word *sun* refers to the physical sun, while *Spiritual Sun* refers to the principle of Divine Unity and Being of which the physical sun was seen as a lower manifestation. At times this use of capitalization may seem excessive, but it is necessary for precision. In the index I have indicated the long vowels of *all* Greek words so that it also serves as pronunciation guide, but have refrained from indicating these vowels in the text except in the case of Greek words that are transliterated and given in italics. When referring to the numerical values of Greek words in the text, I always give the word in large and small capital letters: for example, the value of APOLLO is 1061.

While this work and the conclusions are my own, there are many friends and correspondents who have helped me along the way, and I would like to thank them here.

I owe a debt of gratitude to my friend John Michell whose book *City of Revelation* led me to the study of Greek gematria and its pre-Christian origins. It was musicologist Joscelyn Godwin who introduced me to the monochord—and hence the ancient science of harmonics—which also marked an important turning point in my research. This experience led me to notice the fundamental relationship between Greek gematria and the Pythagorean theory of Means. Siemen Terpstra, another servant of the Muses, also came along at the right time; his monograph on *Means and Music* helped lead me to recognize that the ratios of the Means *themselves* define the central values of Greek gematria, a topic explored in the last part of chapter 4 (and summarized in "The Music of the Sun II," in the documentary illustrations).

I am grateful to Robert A. Kraft of the University of Pennsylvania, not only for his excellent seminars on early Christian literature, which sharpened my analytical skills and exposed me to many of the sources here cited, but also for encouraging my research into the relations between early Christianity, ancient cosmology, and gnostic symbolism, in an atmosphere that was otherwise more congenial to computer-aided textual analysis.

Anne Macaulay commented on my analysis of the feeding of the five thousand and pointed out a more elegant way to represent the figure of the five loaves. Brenda Rosen, my editor at Quest Books, Joscelyn Godwin, Ron Hogart, Richard Smoley, Bob Tarte, and Arthur Versluis read the manuscript and made many valuable suggestions. I am also grateful for the many useful comments made by Bob Kraft who read the chapters on early Christian literature and to Marilyn Perkins for proofreading help.

Finally, I'd like to express my thanks to some other friends for their support and interest in my work over the years: Christopher Bamford, Diana Barruéco, Cynthia Weber-Brownell, Deborah Belle Forman, Heather Halstead, John Henry, Alvin Holm, Michael Hornum, Mark Kindt, Jay Kinney, Ruth McMahon, Steve Miller, Kathleen Raine, Christine Rhone, and Becky Wilson.

—DAVID FIDELER

INTRODUCTION

Cosmology and the Search for Unity

This sense of wonder is the mark of the philosopher. Philosophy indeed has no other origin.

—Socrates

THE GREEK PHILOSOPHERS maintained that the world is a wonderful and beautiful place. The natural world alone contains enough marvels to reward our contemplation and appreciation without end. That is to say nothing of the spiritual world, which is revealed to us not only by the history of ideas and civilizations, but is also omnipresently revealed within each and every person by the nature of consciousness itself. We are constantly surrounded on all sides by a remarkable tapestry of natural forms and ideas. Yet, despite the wonders of the universe and our unique powers to survey the realms of both mind and matter, we have been socially trained to concern ourselves only with the smallest fragments of a larger reality.

While our modern approach in both science and commerce is toward ever-increasing specialization and toward conceptually rending the fabric of Nature into ever smaller fragments, the approach in the ancient world was different. Then, science, philosophy, learning—even culture itself—developed from a spontaneous recognition of the beauty of the natural order and from the realization that the universe, of which we all are a part, is a living whole: in some elusive way, all the parts of creation are united within a greater unity, and this is something we tangibly sense whenever we are confronted with the experience of beauty. This realization of unity in diversity was one of the central concerns of the early Greek philosophers, and culminated in the Hellenistic idea of "the Logos," which drew on the earlier Pythagorean views of harmony and proportion. As is well known, in the first centuries of the common era, Jesus was widely perceived and represented as the Logos—the cosmic power of Harmony, which was seen as underlying the order of the universe by some of the earliest Christians.

In antiquity, the nature of the Logos was represented in many ways, but its most central emblem was the Sun, symbolizing the source of Reality, the source of Light and Life. Yet, in addition to the mystical approach, which is well documented in many surviving texts, the nature of the Logos was also studied in a scientific sense, long before the appearance of Christianity. One of the meanings of *Logos* is "ratio," as in mathematical ratio: "the pattern which connects," the principle of mediation between extremes, the conceptual link between one and many, unity and multiplicity. As the Pythagoreans realized, the principle of Logos underlies the manifestation of harmony at its very core. It is through the principle of mathematical ratio that the natural harmony of music arises, and it is through the principles of harmonic mediation—expressed mathematically—that the musical scale is created.

This study shows for the first time in the modern era how the ancient, scientific understanding of the Logos underlies the names and attributes of Apollo and Hermes, the Greek gods of music, harmony, and geometry. This mathematical symbolism originated in the Pythagorean and Orphic schools, which maintained that "the nature of the gods"—or the first principles of creation—"is defined by Number." This symbolism resulted from a quest for a universal language and from the realization that, in matters of both scientific and spiritual concern, the ultimate nature of reality transcends the limitations of our common, day-to-day language.

Remarkably, some of the earliest Christians took over this pre-existing symbolism of the Logos—the symbolism of Apollo—and used it as the underlying basis on which certain New Testament allegories were based. In 1972, John Michell showed how the New Testament allegory of "the 153 fish in the unbroken net" is really a geometrical "story problem" of the early gnostic Christians. In this work, I show how the same holds true for the New Testament account of the "miraculous feeding of the five thousand." I also demonstrate that the central values of the ancient number canon are actually codifications of the primary ratios that underlie the genesis of harmony—and were therefore seen as underlying the harmony of the universe itself.

Despite the importance of this material for anyone who wishes to understand the cosmological, spiritual, and philosophical thought of antiquity, the study of harmony, as the Pythagoreans taught, is a matter of perennial concern. Therefore, in the final chapter, I have tried to show how this historical material is important in a larger philosophical context as we strive for a more inclusive understanding of our place in the world today.

The study of cosmology shows how our relationship to the universe and our fellow humans is inextricably conditioned by our underlying belief systems and mythologies. As every thoughtful person realizes, the life of each civilization—and every individual—is influenced by underlying mythologies, whether sacred, scientific, secular, or profane. In our century, psychology has shown that those who do not believe that their lives are shaped by an underlying mythology are always those who are the most captivated by its spell. The question is not how to get rid of mythology—for myth, as the ancients realized, is the very stuff of life—but how to find the most beautiful and rewarding mythology so we can live our lives on the highest possible level, while honoring the people and the world around us.

The underlying mythology of the present age is based on the ideology of materialism, the notion that physical matter is the ultimate reality. This unstated yet dominant premise gives birth to a cultural ethos which is devoted to creating, for the most part, efficient workers and consumers, rather than encouraging the quest for deeper insight and enjoyment in every area of life. Due to the inherent inadequacy of materialist cosmology—and the harm it inflicts on both the environment and the human spirit—many people are now being drawn back to the perennial understanding that the universe itself reflects the nonmaterial principles of harmony, and that we can only be happy when our lives and culture acknowledge every level of reality. As the effects of our contemporary mythology are continually revealed in the symptoms of dis-ease which afflict nearly every sphere of human experience, and as we search for a more adequate view—"the best possible account"—perhaps it is time to see where we have been in order see where we are going.

CHAPTER ONE

In the Beginning: Philosophy and Initiation in the Ancient World

CHRISTIANITY, as a world religion, is a Greek religion. The New Testament is written entirely in Greek, and Greek was the primary language of Paul, the first New Testament writer. Paul was influenced by Jewish ideas already expressed in Greek, and his letters reveal an equally profound debt to Greek philosophical and religious thought. Similarly, the Jews of Alexandria had become so thoroughly Greek that the Old Testament and other scriptures had been translated into Greek, presumably because most had forgotten how to read the original Hebrew.

Christianity arose during a time of remarkable cultural and intellectual fusion which has been unparalleled in the history of the West, at least up until the present time. Christianity originated in the Hellenistic age when the streams of Greek, Judaic, Egyptian, and Eastern cultures flowed together to create powerful new social, spiritual, and philosophical syntheses.

Three hundred years before the appearance of the Christian movement, Alexander the Great's explorations and conquests of the known world prepared the way for cultural exchange and the development of a truly cosmopolitan perspective. Shortly thereafter, the famous library at Alexandria in Egypt became the largest repository of information in the ancient world. The environment at Alexandria, still the supreme archetype of the university town, was one of ongoing intellectual and philosophical fusion, and the collection of the library, which fueled the process, is known to have exceeded 400,000 papyrus scrolls.[1] Of course, the genius of the Alexandrian renaissance lay not so much in the accumulation of raw information as in the brilliant work which was undertaken in geometry, mathematics, music, astronomy, literature, philosophy, and theology.[2]

Countless religious and philosophical systems flourished both in Alexandria and throughout the Hellenistic world. Many of these traditions—philosophic, gnostic, and the teachings and rites of the mystery guilds—had their origins in ancient cultures which were based on the oral transmission of sacred lore: stories of the gods, or the divine principles behind creation which control the structure of the universe and the seasonal flow of life. Because of the visionary, life-bestowing forms of consciousness from which they sprang, the teachings of the mystery religions were characteristically embodied in allegory, myth, and symbolic imagery, both as "teaching stories" and as basic paradigms of human experience.[3] Certain philosophic schools, especially the Platonists and Stoics, drew upon traditional myths to illustrate insights which transcend merely logical description. Moreover, many held that the interpretation of the traditional myths, like the pursuit of philosophy itself, constituted, at its core, a process of initiation.[4]

Philosophy as Initiation: The Platonic Theory of Knowledge

Socrates said that the beginning of philosophy is a sense of wonder. The universe and nature evoke wonder in anyone who is in the least bit thoughtful, yet this sense of wonder is based upon an implicit understanding that there is more to the nature of reality than what we can merely touch and see. Both mystics and rationalists claim that there are more levels to creation than can be perceived exclusively through the physical senses. Mystics describe a world of spiritual essences which both informs and animates the physical universe, while scientists proclaim that mathematical and physical laws underlie the fabric of nature. Ultimately, these laws of the physical universe exist in the world of pure principles. In other words, though "the laws of physics" shape the universe, they themselves are not physical, nor do they have their existence in time or space—they just *are*. Interestingly, "they just are" is the ancient philosophical definition of *Being*, "that which is," the level of reality which is not subject to birth, generation, or decay.

According to ancient philosophical and religious teachings, we inhabit a world of external appearances, yet also a world of inner understanding. There any many paths which lead from superficial appearances to true understanding—science, art, philosophy, and religion are examples—but the movement itself, from appearance to insight, represents the path of initiation. For as the soul progresses along the path of initiation, it attains greater levels of insight into its own nature, that of the universe, and the laws which govern the creative process. *Initiation* is a process of awakening, a movement from darkness to light, and ancient philosophy often borrowed metaphors and analogies from the mystery religions when alluding to this process of deepening insight. Of these descriptions, one of the most powerful and memorable is Plato's allegory of the cave, which is a philosophical model of the phenomenal world.[5]

Plato likens us to prisoners who have been chained in a subterranean cave from birth, facing a dark wall. Only a tiny amount of light enters the cavern through a small opening high overhead, but the prisoners, who are chained facing the opposite direction, only observe dark shadows flitting about on the wall that they face, cast by the men and phenomena of the upper world.

The question is then posed, "What would happen if one of the prisoners could escape?"

Socrates answers that, at first, the prisoner would be blinded by the light and would continue, at least for a while, to attribute a greater reality to the illusory shadows of the cave:

> He would need, then, to grow accustomed before he could see things in that upper world. At first it would be easiest to make out shadows, and then the images of men and things reflected in water, and later on the things themselves. After that, it would be easier to watch the heavenly bodies and the sky itself by night, looking at the light of the moon and stars rather than the Sun and the Sun's light in the day-time. . . . Last of all, he would be able to look at the Sun and contemplate its nature, not as it appears when reflected in water or any alien medium, but as it is in itself in its own domain. . . . And now he would begin to draw the conclusion that it is the Sun that produces the seasons and the course of the year and controls everything in the visible world, and moreover is in a way the cause of all that he and his companions used to see.[6]

Such, Plato states, is the typical situation of humanity. The realm of the cave corresponds to the world of appearances, the realm of "Becoming" or Change. According to Plato, the perception of this lower world is dominated by mere assumption and human opinion. The upper realm, the source of the light, is the world of reality or Being. According to the Platonic tradition, the world of Being comprehends within itself all those principles and causes of which the world of phenomenal shadows reflects as an after-image. Finally, Plato uses the image of the Sun to represent the idea of the One, the Good, and the Beautiful, the source of Reality.

While there is no evidence to suggest that Plato was some sort of "pagan sun-worshipper," he was initiated into the ancient mysteries and is said to have studied at Heliopolis, the city of the sun, a great center of scientific and priestly learning in ancient Egypt. Conversely, he certainly did acknowledge the divinity of the natural world and the celestial bodies, for he experienced the universe as a theophany, a manifestation of the divine—the very "image" of the universal principles. In Egypt as well, many hundreds of years before Plato, the physical sun had been seen, at least by the learned, as a lower manifestation of a higher principle. Likewise, Plato uses the symbol of the Sun to denote a higher principle, itself the source of the physical sun and, indeed, the source of the All.

Following Plato and before the birth of Christianity, the sun came to be regarded as the doorway between the sensible and intelligible realms, between the manifest world of nature and the extratemporal world of first principles. Helios represented the heart of the celestial pattern, and his physical aspect was considered as the theophanic manifestation of a higher principle—the "Solar Logos"—a topic explored in chapter 3.

Plato depicted the path of philosophy as an upward "ascent" from the shifting world of appearances to the stable world of first principles. In his theory of knowledge and learning described in the *Republic*, Plato delineates four major pathways to knowledge: sensation, opinion, scientific reason, and direct knowledge in itself. The philosophical ascent is thus also a movement toward progressively higher states of cognition.[7]

The faculty of sensation, or what our senses reveal to us, is clearly not always reliable, as demonstrated by optical illusions and similar instances.

In Greek, the word *pistis* means opinion as well as belief or faith. Opinion can be either true or false, but even a true opinion is not equivalent to scientific knowledge. Popular opinion is based on "common sense," accepted beliefs, and outward appearances. According to outward appearances, the earth is stationary and the sun rises in the east. However, according to the next higher level of cognition, scientific analysis, we can see that the earth and the other planets really orbit around the sun.

Scientific reason depends upon the principles of discursive, rational analysis. This approach is necessarily divisive in nature, for it compares and contrasts, differentiating between this and that, subject and object. Reality is broken into parts and the parts are analyzed for relationships.

Many scientists, technicians, and "number crunchers" are content to extend their work no further than the level of rational analysis. But, as Plato forcefully argued, there is yet a higher level of cognition—direct knowledge or *gnôsis*, in which the mind becomes unified with the object of knowledge. Sensation, opinion, and scientific reason represent the preparatory stages leading to the higher insight of direct knowledge. Interestingly, careful examination reveals that most significant scientific discoveries actually spring from levels of insight higher than what is available to merely discursive analysis.[8]

The Celestial Hierarchy: Time and Eternity Personified

Plato discussed two fundamental levels of universal expression: the Intelligible Realm, or "upper world" of the cave allegory, the eternal world of first principles (the *Platonic Forms* or *Ideas*); second, the Sensible Realm, the interior of the cave, which is informed and shaped by the principles of the Intelligible Realm, even if the higher principles are unknown to its inhabitants. The upper world is identified as that of Being, or eternal principles, "that which is," while the lower world is that of Becoming or Change. Becoming, for Plato, is an image of Being, in the same way that "time is a moving image of eternity."[9] This simplistic sketch might give the impression that Plato was a dualist, pitting spirit against matter, but his views are more subtle than that: in actuality, the two poles of manifestation represent ideal extremes, with a variety of principles and levels mediating between these two polarities of creation.

However, before the beginning of the Christian era, Plato's insights into the relationship between the levels of Being and Change had been elaborated in popular cosmological speculation and incorporated into the structure of an Earth-centered cosmos. According to then current belief, the Earth exists at the center of the universe, surrounded by the orbits of the heavenly spheres. From antiquity until Copernicus, the universe was popularly believed to consist of a great celestial hierarchy reaching from the Earth, up through the spheres of the seven planetary gods (Moon,

Mercury, Venus, Sun, Mars, Jupiter, and Saturn), to the fixed sphere of the timeless and unchanging stars. (*Figure 1.*) The outermost sphere of the stars—or an even more transcendent sphere which existed behind it—was identified with the realm of eternal Being, free from change, and was seen as the habitation of the High God who holds within its Intellect the universal Forms on which all of creation is based. This highest sphere clearly corresponds to the nature of the Spiritual Sun, the source of all reality in Plato's myth of the cave.

Below the sphere of the moon, however, all is not so tranquil, for the sublunar sphere is the realm of profound change and flux, the lower world of the cave. As Heraclitus recognized, man exists in a world of change where "All is flow" and where "It is impossible to step into the same river twice."[10]

Obviously humanity, as a microcosmic reflection of all the principles which comprise the universe, participates in both Being and Change, Spirit and Matter. Human beings possess a transcendent spirit capable of knowing eternal principles, while the body is of a transitory nature, destined to dissolve within the confines of time and space. Hence the words of the Orphic initiate:

> I am a child of earth and starry heaven
> But my race is of heaven.[11]

Many of Plato's ideas about the relations of Being and Change were codified and given expression in a cosmological sense by the teachings of the highly influential Stoic philosopher, Posidonius of Apamea, who flourished *circa* 151–35 B.C.E. Since the earliest Christian theology was elaborated against the canvas of Posidonius' far-reaching and well known speculations, it is worth taking a brief look at his cosmology and some related ideas.

Posidonius, a student of Panaetius, was educated in Athens and has been called "the most universal mind that Greece had seen since the time of Aristotle."[12] He travelled widely, visiting Egypt and Spain, and in the year 97 B.C.E. established a philosophical school on the Greek island of Rhodes, the place where, according to legend, Helios, the sun, was born. Both a rationalist and a mystic, Posidonius' great achievement consisted in unifying the data of astronomy, mathematics, and the other sciences

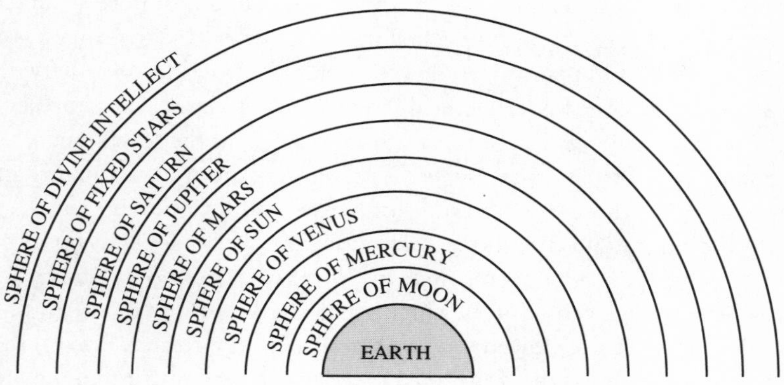

Figure 1. The Celestial Spheres

In ancient cosmology the universe was conceived as existing between the ideal extremes of the eternal and temporal spheres. In Hellenistic times the outermost sphere, the sphere of the Divine Intellect, was equated with the Intelligible Realm of Plato, the "repository" of the universal principles on which creation is based. The sphere of the earth, while informed by universal principles, is the realm of the greatest temporal change. The sun, which occupies the middle sphere on the planetary ladder, was regarded as both the mediator between heaven and earth and the central orchestrator of the planetary dance.

into a philosophical system which presupposed the underlying harmony of different classes of phenomena.

He observed, for instance, the fact that the tides of the sea correspond with the phases of the moon. This led Posidonius to his central idea that a principle of universal sympathy linked various celestial and terrestrial phenomena together, a presupposition which was to influence his entire philosophy. His view of the cosmos was strictly hierarchical: "The world is a hierarchy of grades of being, from inorganic entities, as in the mineral kingdom, through plants and animals up to man, and so to the super-organic sphere of the Divine, the whole being bound together in one great system and every detail being arranged by Divine Providence. This universal harmony and structural ordering of the universe postulates Absolute Reason, God, at the summit of the hierarchy and as the all-pervading Rational Activity."[13]

According to Posidonius, the realm above the moon is imperishable and heavenly, while the realm below the moon, the sublunar sphere, is subject to change and decay. The two realms are, however, bound together by the phenomenon of humanity, which represents the bond (*desmos*) between the spiritual and the material, the divine and terrestrial.[14] Man represents the highest manifestation of the material realm, but the lowest manifestation of the spiritual realm. (*Figure 2.*) Therefore, between humanity and the High God there exist the souls of heroes and lesser divinities.

Posidonius taught that the second, sublunary world depends upon the upper world for its vital sustenance; the lower world "is nourished by and lives from the heavenly forces which are poured into it from the first."[15] While earlier Stoics viewed God as a rational, fiery spirit (*pneuma*) that permeated the substrate of the universe, Posidonius contributed the idea that the world is permeated by a Life Power (*zôdikê dynamis*) which originates from the sun—an idea which, besides being based on scientific thought, would be heavily influential in later Hellenistic mysticism and theology. We can, for example, see this idea expressed very clearly in the pagan Hermetic writings, where the sun is portrayed as the sower and reaper of souls, indeed of all life:

> The Sun is the savior and the nurse of every class.
>
> And just as the Intelligible World, holding the Sensible in its embrace, fills it (all) full, distending it with forms of every kind and every shape—so, too, the Sun distendeth all in the Cosmos, affording births to all, and strengthening them.
>
> When they are weary or they fail, He takes them in His arms again.[16]

It is difficult to stress adequately how much the idea of the hierarchy of being—and the related idea of the celestial ascent and descent of the soul—permeated the cosmological and spiritual outlook of the Hellenistic period. According to a view at least as old as Plato, the pre-existing soul drinks from the stream of *Lêthê* (Forgetfulness) and descends into the world of change through the planetary spheres, forgetting its celestial origin; through philosophy, however, it may recall its origin in the world of first principles and regain its seat amongst the blessed. Posidonius believed that souls come from the sun, the source of all life, and descend to earth via the sphere of the moon. According to Plutarch, a priest of Apollo and a contemporary of Jesus, man is composed of *sôma* (body),

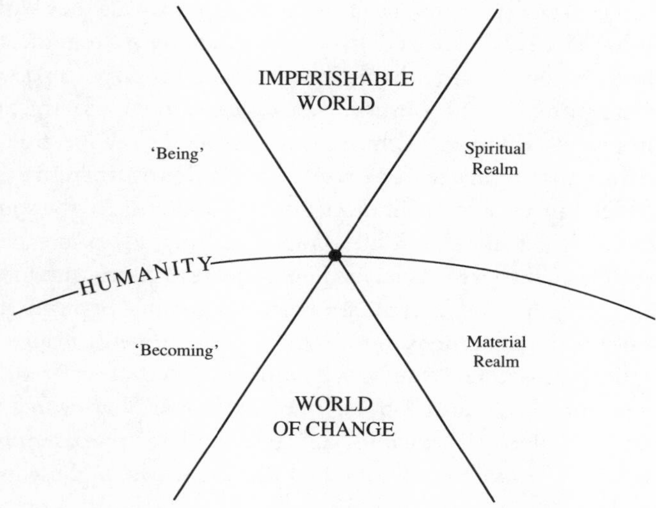

Figure 2. Humanity as the Bond between Spirit and Matter

As the living image of all the principles which comprise the universe, humanity was seen as the bond which links together the eternal and temporal spheres. This view, which sees humanity as microcosm, the mediator between spirit and matter, was held both by Greek philosophers and by the early fathers of the Christian church.

psychê (soul), and *Nous* (divine intellect), derived from the earth, moon, and sun respectively. As he explains in his essay *On the Face which Appears on the Moon*, at death the soul and intellect ascend to the moon, leaving the outer shell of the body behind on the earth. After a period, Nous or divine intellect leaves the soul behind on the moon and rises to the sphere of the sun. In the Hermetic writings, the soul descending into incarnation acquires a negative propensity at each planetary station, while after death it casts off each vice at the appropriate sphere in its reascent to the divine and eternal realm. In fully developed mythological gnosticism of the pessimist variety, the planets become archons, astrological rulers of Fate. In order to ascend through their spheres toward liberation, the initiate needs to have a magical number, password, and symbol. In one gnostic gospel, *The Books of Ieou*, Jesus, as revealer of saving knowledge, imparts to his disciples the very symbols, numbers, and passwords they will need for the celestial ascent. (*Figure 3.*)

Philosophers, on the other hand, have no need for magical passwords in order to accomplish the journey toward Being. For Plato, the pursuit of philosophy itself was enough to assure the soul's recollection of its origin and ultimate return to its native star. Nonetheless, there are certain studies which can assist in the illumination and liberation of the soul. For those who wish to make this "philosophical ascent," Plato suggests that training in the Pythagorean sciences of number, geometry, and harmonics is prerequisite, for through these studies it is possible to purify the eye of the soul for the apprehension of Reality.[17] Moreover, through these studies, the philosopher comes into intimate contact with the first harmonic principles of creation itself. According to Plato, while direct knowledge of universal principles demands a bit of preparation, this faculty is implicit within every soul and represents the highest form of genuine insight.

Platonism and Gnosis: Some Similarities

Naturally, not everyone is suited for the study of geometry, so providentially, it is not the only way to experience first-hand those principles on which the universe is based. That is because, whether we seriously decide to study it or not, Reality cannot be avoided. For example, even though the musical scale is based upon certain universal ratios of harmonic mediation which are capable of precise mathematical expression, it is not necessary to grasp these mathematical laws in order to be a great musician or to enjoy a musical work. Likewise, in the modern world one need not be an electromechanical engineer in order to appreciate the benefits of an electric toaster. Nonetheless, knowledge in all forms offers both power and safety. By recognizing the nature of electricity we can reduce our likelihood of getting shocked, and by recognizing the nature of the gods and goddesses who inhabit the human psyche we can learn to get along with them, rather than always falling victim to their multifarious promptings.

Conversely, as the gods and muses remind us, the rational intellect does not itself provide the only legitimate pathway to knowledge. In addition to being rational creatures, we are dreamers, mythic and poetic beings, as is perhaps the universe itself: that art copies nature is a truism, but there

Figure 3.
Gnostic Diagrams, Numbers, and Names from *The Books of Ieou*

In the Coptic gnostic gospel *The Books of Ieou*, several diagrams are given relating to *Ieou*, "the true God," such as the following:

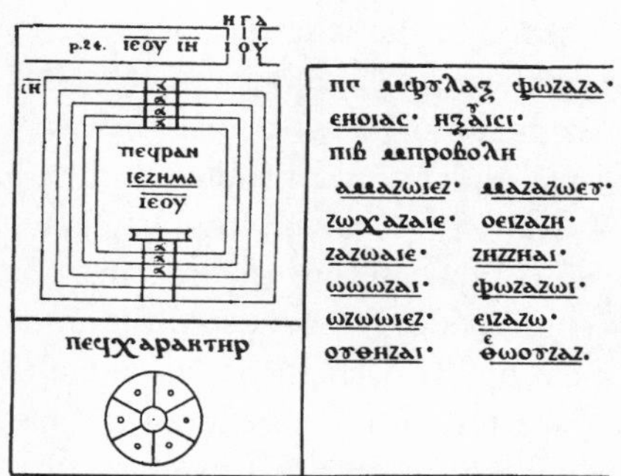

In the center of the squares is the inscription "His Name, *Iezêma Ieou*," while below is shown "His Character." On the right are the names of "The Three Watchers" and "The Twelve Emanations."

Elsewhere in *The Books of Ieou*, Jesus reveals to his disciples the magical names, numbers, and seals they will need in the afterlife ascent to the realm of light. Here is an example of Jesus' instructions:

> When you reach the fourth aeon, *Samaêlô* and *Chôchôchoucha* will come before you. Seal yourself with this seal:
>
> This is its name: *Azôzêô*.
>
> Say it once only. Hold this cipher: 4555 in your hands. When you have finished sealing yourself with this seal and you have said its name once only, say these defences also: "Withdraw yourselves *Samaêlô* and *Chôchôchoucha*, you archons of the fourth aeon, because I call upon *Zôzêza*, *Chôzôzazza*, *Zazêzô*." When you have finished saying these defences the archons of the fourth aeon will withdraw to the left. But you [will] proceed upwards.

The Books of Ieou is one the most unusual and least studied manuscripts of early Christianity. Consequently, it has not been ascertained whether there is an underlying mathematical structure to this enigmatic Christian gospel.

are also many interesting examples of nature copying art.[18] Within the leading spiritual and philosophical traditions of the ancient world, emphasis was placed on the education of the whole person, on developing an inclusive view of the individual soul in its relation to humanity and cosmos, art and science. Like the ancient Pythagoreans, we can express our higher insights through the language of mathematics; or, like the Orphic bards, through myth, symbol, song, and fable. And within the context of ancient cosmology, the two approaches were often combined.

The inadequacy of language is a problem which has beset creative thinkers of all types—artists, poets, philosophers, and scientists. It also occupied the attention of the ancient "theologians." For if we accept the existence of higher cognitive and creative states, it follows that our normal day-to-day language can only partially describe them.[19]

For example, the word *tree* is not a tree, nor is the same word used in different languages. Plato, noting this inadequacy of language, once observed that there are at least five things relating to the knowledge of any given thing. Using the example of *circle*, Plato explains that there is 1) the name; 2) the definition; 3) the circle which can be drawn (yet does not contain nor effect the properties of the true Circle); 4) the knowledge of the circle which exists in the soul; and finally 5) the pure reality and essence of the Circle in itself, with only this being the object of true knowledge.

Words, then, often separate us from the things they refer to as much as they unite us. Can love really be summed up in a word, and how can you be certain that the depth of your experience corresponds to the depth of my experience? Poets, who are most painfully aware of the inadequacy of verbal expression, are driven to use common language in an uncommon way, for this is the only way they have to transmit the content of experience through the confines of form. Likewise, when scientists see into the heart of physical reality, they are often forced to express their insights in terms of mathematical formulae. In the case of both poet and scientist, however, no matter how fine the expression, the description usually falls short of the actual experience or cognitive insight.

This fundamental, frustrating experience gives rise to both the beauty and inadequacy of poetic expression, scientific theory, and mystical cosmology. It underlies the genesis of mystical expression, for the word *mystic* is from the Greek word *muô*, which means "to be silent." The true mystic realizes that the highest level of insight is realized and honored in the nature of Silence, for the fullness of reality as it exists and as it is experienced can never be fully expressed by descriptive utterance. As Lao Tzu said, "Those who know do not speak; those who speak do not know." After Silence, the purest scientific expression is mathematical harmony, while the purest artistic expression is music and song.

Plato has been described as the world's greatest rationalist, but also as the world's greatest mystic. As we can see from the discussion above, the two positions are not incompatible. While Plato fully reaps the fruit of rational analysis, his most important works often culminate with a myth, illustrating a realization beyond formal, syllogistic description. As he states in his seventh *Letter*, matters of ultimate concern are best not discussed in writing but, after a long period of study, true insight, "like a blaze kindled by a leaping spark is generated in the soul and at once becomes self-sustaining."[20]

Most great philosophers and cosmologists have felt that rational knowledge and spiritual insight are not mutually exclusive. The Pythagoreans and Platonists believed that scientific inquiry and research into mathematical principles was essentially a spiritual pursuit. Many modern scientists have expressed similar sentiments, and by so doing they are rightly placing their work within a larger cosmological framework which affirms the underlying principles of beauty and value in the quest for knowledge. Likewise, the early Christian gnostics felt that knowledge, personal experience, and spiritual insight were inherently complementary.

At face value there are many unreasonable things about the beliefs of early Christianity, and, as the organized church developed, those individuals who possessed the key of interpretation, the gnostics, were forced out by the ecclesiastical authorities. Historically speaking, as Christianity developed, it *could* have both embraced and sanctified the classical quest for knowledge and learning, and several of the early church fathers actively worked toward this end. However, as things turned out, the developing church, as a political body, found it more expedient to emphasize unquestioning belief in dogma rather than the principles of open inquiry. One church father proclaimed that he believed in the teachings of the church *for the very reason that they were absurd.*[21] Irenaeus, a bishop who wrote against the gnostics, claimed that bread and wine were *literally* transformed into the body and and blood of Jesus, and that by feasting upon this substance our own physical bodies would be miraculously transformed into an immortal state.[22] Paul's belief in an entirely spiritual afterlife stood in sharp distinction to the materialistic views of some later church fathers who insisted on a literal, physical resurrection of the dead.[23]

As for the gnostics, Plato first stated that "Geometry is the knowledge (*gnôsis*) of the eternally existent,"[24] and the early Christian gnostics used the symbolic geometry of the earlier Greek mysteries to demonstrate the inner validity of the Christian legend, which Clement of Alexandria referred to as "the New Song" of the Celestial Order (Logos).[25] Like Plato and the teachers of the earlier mysteries, the gnostics made use of mythology and symbolism to say things about the nature of reality which transcend shallow, one-dimensional expression.[26] The gnostics claimed to have inherited from the past a code of spiritual knowledge, which they used in setting forth the mysteries of the new faith. Like Plato, the gnostics proposed that the actual source of the cosmos was a simple, transcendental principle that could not be expressed in words. This transcendental principle gives rise to the first principles of Being, called *aeons* or "eternities" by the gnostics, which make up the *plêrôma* or "fullness" of being, an analogue to the Intelligible Realm of the Platonists. Just as Plato criticized the amorous exploits of Zeus as inappropriate behavior for a god, so the gnostics blasted the popular Jewish conception of Jehovah as a jealous and wrathful divinity. This they did by identifying him in their myths with the Demiurge, the ignorant fabricator of the universe who stupidly proclaimed "I am the only true God," without realizing that there were many higher levels of reality above him.[27] In so doing, the gnostics also offered an effective critique of the human ego, which often pompously imagines itself as the true center of the soul.

Interestingly, while the matter is not capable of proof, it is likely that the historical Jesus was himself some sort of gnostic teacher; indeed, if this was the case, it would help account, at least in part, for his personification as the "Gnostic Revealer" in early Christian texts. Jesus was certainly a religious reformer, as were the gnostics in general, and he bitterly complained about those who elevated the letter of the law while not grasping its spirit: "The Pharisees and the scribes have taken the keys of Knowledge (*gnôsis*) and hidden them. They themselves have not entered, nor have they allowed to enter those who wish to. You, however, be as wise as serpents and as innocent as doves."[28] Jesus clearly taught the first principle of initiation in all its forms, simply, "He who seeks will find, and [he who knocks] will be let in."[29] Like other initiates of the ancient world, Jesus made extensive use of parables and symbolic teachings, as when he said that "The Kingdom of Heaven is like a grain of mustard seed"[30] or "The seed is the word (*logos*) of God."[31] According to New Testament accounts, he had a small group of followers to whom he explained the mysteries of the kingdom, but Jesus cloaked his teachings to others in parables: "With many such parables he spoke the word to them, as they were able to hear it; he did not speak to them without a parable, but privately to his own disciples he explained everything;"[32] moreover, speaking to his students he said, "To you it has been given to know the secrets of the kingdom of God; but for others they are in parables, so that seeing they may not see, and hearing they may not understand."[33] Jesus thus followed a model similar to that of the Greek bards and the Pythagorean philosophers, who used symbolism, mythology, parables, and other entertainments, while simultaneously transmitting a higher message for those who had ears to hear. Interestingly, some of the earliest and most important Christian writings—including one used by the authors of the New Testament—portray Jesus *exclusively* as a teacher of heavenly wisdom, with no mention whatsoever of his fate by crucifixion nor of belief in his subsequent resurrection.[34] In any event, Jesus actively encouraged his followers to search deeply for those hidden mysteries which would some day be revealed, "For nothing is hid that shall not be made manifest, nor anything secret that shall not come to light."[35]

As for the known gnostics themselves, like Jesus they did not call themselves such, but the term was applied to them. The word *gnôsis* means knowledge, and they claimed to be the heirs of an earlier teaching which emphasized direct knowledge of the higher realities on which the structure of the universe is based. According to the author of Matthew, Jesus, as "Gnostic Revealer," fulfilled the prophecy that "I will open my mouth in parables, I will utter what has been hidden since the foundation of the world."[36] Similarly, Paul insisted that "Among the initiates (*teleioi*) we do impart wisdom, although it is not a wisdom of this age or of the rulers of this age, who are doomed to pass away. But we impart a secret and hidden wisdom of God, which God decreed before the ages for our glorification."[37] Like the initiated composers and transmitters of the Greek myths, the Christian gnostics expressed the insights of esoteric cosmology—that "hidden pattern of creation which underlies the foundation of the world"—in the myths and legends of the new religion. One primary tool was the language of Greek gematria, discussed in chapter 2, itself based on the faculty of *analogia* or "hieroglyphic insight" into nature of the universal order.

Reading the Symbolism of Nature's Book: Hieroglyphic Insight as the Basis of Sacred Symbolism

Galileo, following in the footsteps of the ancients, wrote that "Philosophy is written in the great book which is ever before our eyes—I mean the universe—but we cannot understand it if we do not learn the language and grasp the symbols in which it is written."[38] Traditionally, the Book of Nature is read through the faculty of *analogia* or proportional insight, the formal expression of which is the Hermetic science of correspondences. Analogical thinking is rooted in the ability to intuit directly the essence of a thing, and, through the looking glass of analogia, phenomena are read hieroglyphically rather than literally.

As we have seen, a description, by necessity ever incomplete, always deals with the most superficial dimension; it is, to use the phrase, "only skin deep." To think analogically, on the other hand, is to discover the hidden soul of things, the invisible yet dynamic chain which binds a variety of phenomena together on the different levels of manifestation. As the later Platonist Proclus wrote, "Just as [true] lovers move on beyond the beauty perceived through the senses until they reach the Sole Cause of all beauty and all perception, so too, the experts in sacred matters, starting with the Sympathy connecting visible things both to one another and to the Invisible Powers, and having understood that all things are to be found in all things, established the Sacred Science. They marvelled at seeing those things which come last in those which come first, and vice-versa; earthly things in the heavens in a causal and celestial manner, and heavenly things on the earth in a terrestrial way."[39] Through the sacred science of correspondences, and especially through the science of gematria, it was possible for traditional cosmology to overcome the limitations of our day-to-day language. A very simple example is found in the name of the gnostic divinity ABRASAX ('ΑΒΡΑΣΑΞ), who represents an aspect of the Sun. As is shown in the next chapter, if the number-values of the Greek letters comprising his name are totalled, the sum is 365, the number of days in a solar year. His name, therefore, *at its very core*, has something inherently in common with what it seeks to express—the relation of the sun to the earth—in the same way that a physicist's equation precisely describes an aspect of the universal fabric.

The relationship between the hieroglyphic mode of thought—which for all intents and purposes underlies the natural symbolism of the Greek mysteries and Hellenistic theology—and the divisive ratiocinations of the analytic intellect, might be illustrated in the following way:

Hieroglyphic	**Analytic**
Analogia	Equality
A : B : C	A + B = C
(1 : √3 : 3)	(1 + 2 = 3)
Transcendental	Rational
Continuity	Discrete states
Interdependence	Independence
Unity	Units
Quality	Quantity
Logos	Logic

The actual basis of these two modes of cognition lies in the structure of the universe itself, the only enduring source of orthodoxy, which presents itself as both One and Many. In the hieroglyphic mode of perception, phenomena relate proportionally to one another: A, B, and C are but different aspects of one underlying, continuous proportion. In the analytic or quantitative model, however, A and B lose their qualitative individuality and relatedness. One and two evaporate into three; the phenomena of nature become mere statistics. From the perspective of analogia, dumping chemicals into the environment is ecologically hazardous; from the perspective of corporate accounting, pollution may sadly be seen as economically expedient.

The fact that the universe presents itself as both a unity and multiplicity suggests that it really *is* both One and Many at the same time. If such is the case, the most accurate and inclusive way of thought will necessarily approach the cosmos on its own terms, blending both modes of perception into an integrated whole, as effortlessly as the universe achieves the same end: at one moment developing first principles to plurality, and relating manifold phenomena to their first principles the next. Interestingly, this cosmological approach is implicitly reflected in the sacred symbolism of Delphi, the central Greek shrine where both Apollo and Dionysus have "an equal share."[40] That is because, in Greek theology, Apollo represents the principle of unity and Dionysus represents the principle of multiplicity. Apollo is "recollection," the return movement of multiplicity towards divine unity, while Dionysus is "manifestation," the first movement of unity towards divine multiplicity.[41] As one philosopher neatly summed up the matter, "When Dionysus had projected his reflection in the mirror, he followed it and was thus scattered over the universe. Apollo gathers him and brings him back to heaven, for he is the purifying God and truly the Saviour of Dionysus."[42]

The Nature of the Gods in Hellenistic Thought

The idea of a single, High God is old in Greece. "Half a millennium before Christ, Xenophanes spoke of the *one* God, the greatest of gods and men, neither in form nor in mind like mortals."[43] Both Plato and Aristotle accepted the existence of a high, transcendent divinity. Nonetheless, as we have observed, the universe is both One and Many. The same applies to the nature of the divine as well as to the nature of the human soul: God is one, yet there are many divine powers; the soul is one, yet it is composed of a variety of faculties. Writing around the time of Jesus, Maximus of Tyre explains that "The one doctrine upon which all the world is united is that one God is king of all and father, and that there are many gods, sons of God, who rule together with God. This is believed by both the Greek and the barbarian."[44]

The soul, as archetypal psychologist James Hillman has repeatedly pointed out, reveals itself through images.[45] This process occurs on both an individual and transpersonal level, and C. G. Jung's insights regarding the archetypes of the "collective unconscious" has done much to confirm the autonomous nature of the gods, manifest within the soul as patterns of psychic energy. The stumbling block of modern psychology (and many scholars) has been to underestimate the intelligence of the ancients, who, as we shall see, rather than being the unwitting victims of "unconscious projections," developed their knowledge of the gods into a sublime theological, cosmological, and psychological science.

Like the Egyptians, for whom the physical sun was a symbol of the one transcendent God of which the other gods were attributes, the Greeks were aware of the fact that in order for creation to exist, the principle of Unity must necessarily express itself in Diversity. As it is with the universe, so it is with the soul; as archetypal psychology has shown, the soul is a differentiated unity, populated by a variety of principles and archetypes. When these principles become harmonically balanced in the song of life, then the soul attains the power of unified expression. But without a diversity of notes the unity of melody becomes impossible. That is why the Greeks (and their later admirers in the Renaissance) recognized the reality of the various divinities who are subordinate to the One.

The transmission and interpretation of myths constituted not only one of the highest arts of the ancient world, but also, as the theological canon of Greek gematria shows, a sacred science as well. It is sadly representative of our time that the word *myth*, in common usage, denotes an untruth, as in the phrase, "It's just a myth." In antiquity, the word *mythos* had just the opposite meaning and denoted a traditional narrative designed to entertain, to educate, and to transmit the very soul and gnosis of the culture.[46] The great scholar-initiates of antiquity such as Plutarch and the later Platonists stressed the fact that reality is hierarchical, consisting of different levels. Mythology, it was held, refers to many levels of reality simultaneously. Therefore, if we are to gain insight into the nature of the gods—the divine principles which underlie creation—a particularly instructive approach involves the philosophical interpretation of myth.

Concerning this study the wise pagan Sallustius, in his treatise *On the Gods and the Universe*, succinctly observed that "myth represents the active operations of the gods."[47] Moreover, he notes, there is a distinctly esoteric dimension to the structure of the Greek myths. One might say that the outward circumstances of the story serves both to protect and transport the living, initiatic transmission, in the same way that the outer husk encloses the vital germ of a seed. This is accounted for by both necessity and design, because "to wish to teach all men the truth about the gods causes the foolish to despise, because they cannot learn, and the good to be slothful, whereas to conceal the truth by myths prevents the former from despising philosophy and compels the latter to study it."[48]

As Sallustius notes, some myths are theological, some scientific, others psychological, and others material. Some of the greatest myths refer to and integrate the spiritual, intellectual, psychic, and physical levels of creation.

Now, even the most cursory investigation will show that the ancients were aware that the stories about the gods are associated with the cycles and phenomena of nature and that they developed this recognition within their theology. However, this is quite different from the modern anthropological view, popularized by Sir James Frazer in *The Golden Bough*, that the gods are merely personifications of natural phenomena such as the vegetation cycle.

Writing in the 1920s, Frazer noted many fascinating parallels between the myths, rites, and symbols of the Greek divinity Dionysus, the Egyptian Osiris, and the Syrian Adonis. He could not help but observe that these divinities were associated with fertility, the vegetation cycle, and the power of resurrection and reanimation. To be sure, the ancients themselves recognized the essential unity of these divinities: the Greeks identified Dionysus with Osiris, and these with Adonis. As his myths reveal, Dionysus is the indestructible stream of life which undergoes countless transformations. The hieroglyphs often associated with Osiris in this capacity translate simply as "Life-Power." We must, therefore, take the ancients at their word. Rather than assuming Dionysus to be merely the personification of the vegetation cycle, perhaps we should, like those intelligent minds of antiquity, recognize that the vegetation cycle is merely one manifestation of that force which is Dionysus. Only then will our insight be purified for the sublime and timeless realization of the learned theologians that "The universe itself can be called a myth, since bodies and material objects are apparent in it, while souls and intellects are concealed."[49]

CHAPTER TWO

Gematria: The Secret Language of the Christian Mysteries

Accurate computation. The gateway to knowledge of all things and dark mysteries.

—Rhind Mathematical Papyrus
Egypt, *circa* 2500 B.C.E.

. . . numbers are the thoughts of God . . . The Divine Wisdom is reflected in the numbers impressed on all things . . . the construction of the physical and moral world alike is based on eternal numbers.

—Augustine

It is the mark of the divine intellect to be always calculating something noble.

—Democritus of Abdera

PYTHAGORAS, the first Greek to call himself a *philosopher*, "a lover of wisdom," taught that all things are arranged and defined by Number. For the Pythagoreans, Number represents a celestial power working in the divine sphere, a veritable blueprint of creation. Consequently, Number is itself divine and associated with the divinities.[1]

Whence Pythagoras derived this notion is uncertain. It could well be that his experiments on the monochord, a one-stringed musical instrument, revealed to him the basic numerical ratios which underlie the structure of harmony and music. It could be that the idea of the divine primacy of Number is a doctrine which Pythagoras received during his sojourns among the Babylonian and Egyptian priests. According to Iamblichus, Pythagoras received the doctrine from his initiation into the mysteries of Orphism. According to a Pythagorean writing, Orpheus taught that "the eternal essence of number is the most providential principle of the universe, of heaven and earth, and the intermediate nature; and farther still . . . it is the root of permanency of divine nature, of gods and divinities."[2] From this, Iamblichus concludes that Pythagoras "learnt from the Orphic writers that the essence of the gods is defined by Number."[3]

Whatever the case might be, we know that earlier cultures possessed similar ideas and doctrines. For example, the Babylonians represented each superior god as a whole number, assigning fractions to the inferior spirits. The number 20 stood for Shamash, Sin was represented by 30, Ea by 40, Bel by 50, and Anu by 60.[4]

Around the year 800 B.C.E., on the coasts of Asia Minor, the Greek alphabet was adapted from the alphabet of the Phoenicians. Earlier in the Mycenaen period the Greeks possessed another form of writing, Linear B. But some type of social upheaval occurred which was associated with the Dorian invasion; a dark age ensued and the art of writing was lost in Greece, at least according to available evidence. Despite the fact that writing was forgotten, Greek culture did not stop developing. As in other traditional cultures, the bards sang the ways of the gods and heroes. Therefore, when the new alphabet was introduced, Greek literature sprang into being, fully developed in all its glory. In "prehistoric" times the bards, priests, and poets had refined the telling of the sacred myths and Homeric epics; as soon as the alphabet was introduced, the fully perfected literature could be recorded on papyrus.

What is curious from the modern perspective is that the letters of the Greek and Hebrew alphabets also stood for numbers: there was no separate notational system for numbers as we have today. The way it worked is as follows: the first group of letters in the alphabet represented units, the next group of letters represented tens, and the last group of letters represented hundreds. (*Figure 4.*) One consequence of this alphabetic notation is that words can be represented as numbers and that numbers can be represented as words. The earliest known usage of this

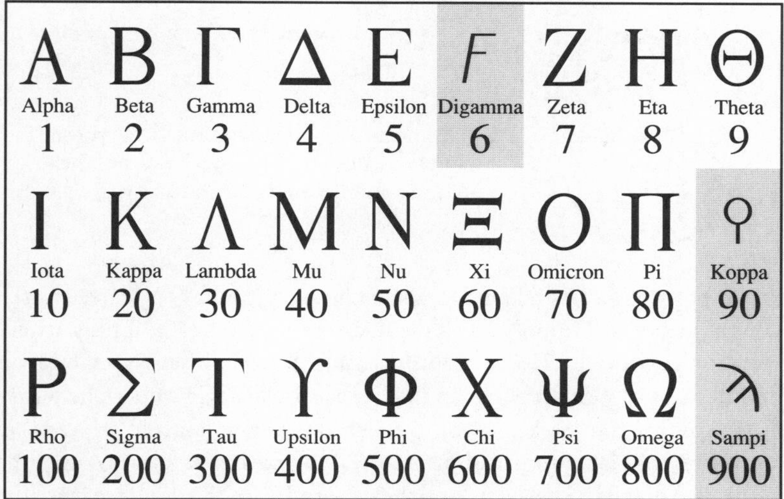

Α Β Γ Δ Ε F Ζ Η Θ
Alpha 1
Beta 2
Gamma 3
Delta 4
Epsilon 5
Digamma 6
Zeta 7
Eta 8
Theta 9
Ι Κ Λ Μ Ν Ξ Ο Π Ϙ
Iota 10
Kappa 20
Lambda 30
Mu 40
Nu 50
Xi 60
Omicron 70
Pi 80
Koppa 90
Ρ Σ Τ Υ Φ Χ Ψ Ω Ϡ
Rho 100
Sigma 200
Tau 300
Upsilon 400
Phi 500
Chi 600
Psi 700
Omega 800
Sampi 900

Figure 4. The Greek Alphabet

The Ionic alphabet of Miletus was officially adopted at Athens in the year 403 B.C.E. Shown above are the number values of the letters. The three shaded signs, *Digamma*, *Koppa*, and *Sampi*, were only used to designate numbers and are not considered actual letters of the alphabet.

practice, known as *gematria*, is recorded on a Babylonian clay tablet. It states that the ruler Sargon II (*fl.* 720 B.C.E) ordered that the wall of Khorsabad be constructed to have a length of 16,283 cubits, the numerical value of his name.[5]

From the Greeks, the Jewish kabbalists adopted the practice of gematria, interpreting the meaning of sacred words and phrases by their numerical values.[6] Words or phrases with the same numerical value were taken as having the same meaning, opening the door for a unique form of scriptural interpretation. The word *gematria*, however, is based on the Greek word *geômetria* or geometry, and, as we shall see in chapter 4, there exists definitive evidence that gematria constituted a sacred language of Greek theology and was used before the time of Plato.[7]

It is well known that the Christian gnostics, who claimed to possess a form of secret knowledge (*gnôsis*), employed the gematria and mathemati-

Figure 5. Abraxas

The gnostic solar divinity ABRAXAS, whose name was designed to equal the number 365, the number of days in a solar year.

cal symbolism in their teachings, for such is reported by the early church fathers Irenaeus, Hippolytus, Tertullian, and Jerome.[8] Hippolytus accuses the gnostic teachers Valentinus and Marcus of having taken over their numerical symbolism from the Pythagoreans.[9] Elsewhere he writes of Monoimus the Arabian whose teaching encompassed Pythagorean number symbolism, musical harmony, emanationist cosmology, the symbolism of the Primal Man, and the generation of the universe from the Platonic solids,[10] concluding that "the assertions advanced by these heretics evidently derive their origin from geometrical and arithmetical art."[11] Hippolytus also refers to another early Christian teacher, Colarbasus, "who attempts to explain religion by measures and numbers."[12]

Gematria appears in the system of Basilides, a gnostic teacher of the Alexandrian school, where the ruler of the "365 heavens" is identified as ABRAXAS or ABRASAX ('ABPAΣAΞ), and is represented on magical amulets from the time period as something of a solar divinity.[13] (See *figure 5* and "Abraxas: The Demiurgic Sun"). By adding up the number values of the Greek letters which comprise his name, we obtain the number 365, the number of days in a solar year, and we may safely conclude that the name was *designed* to equal this value. (A=1, B=2, P=100, A=1, Σ=200, A=1, Ξ=60; 1+2+100+1+200+1+60 = 365)

Likewise, St. Jerome reports that the name of the solar divinity MITHRAS (ΜΕΙΘΡΑΣ)—whose worship in many ways paralleled that of the early Christians—is also equivalent to 365, the number of the solar year.[14]

The Christian gnostics made much of the fact that the name JESUS ('ΙΗΣΟΥΣ) is equivalent to the number 888 (*figure 6*), and it is well known that the so-called "number of the beast," 666, in the book of Revelation is a reference to gematria: "Here is wisdom. He who has understanding,

$$\begin{aligned} \mathrm{I} &= 10 \\ \mathrm{H} &= 8 \\ \Sigma &= 200 \\ \mathrm{O} &= 70 \\ \Upsilon &= 400 \\ \Sigma &= \underline{200} \\ & 888 \end{aligned}$$

Figure 6. The Name "Jesus"

Shown above is the Greek spelling of the name JESUS which amounts to the number 888. The Christian gnostics identified Jesus as the Logos and the Spiritual Sun; they taught that his number, 888, symbolized the perfection and harmony of the spiritual realm.

Clement of Alexandria, an early church father, also referred to Jesus as the Spiritual Sun and explained how the power of the Logos tuned the disparate elements of creation into musical harmony. In view of his statements, it is interesting to observe first that 888 is mathematically related to the so-called "magic square of the sun"; secondly, in music tuning theory, with which Clement was well acquainted, .888 is the ratio (*logos*) of the whole tone, the mediating bond between the two tetrachords of the octave. Consistent with these facts, Clement referred to the then recent manifestation of Christianity as "the New Song" of the eternal Logos: a new spiritual expression of the pre-existing pattern of harmony on which all of creation is based.

let him count the number of the beast: for it is the number of a man, and its number is 666."[15]

The number 666, which we will discuss later, is associated with the figure of traditional cosmology known as "the magic square of the sun." (*Figure* 7.) It contains the first 36 numbers, arranged in a 6x6 grid, so that each line of numbers, whether added vertically, horizontally, or diagonally from corner to corner, equals the number 111. The value of the entire square is therefore 666. In the magical branch of the Jewish kabbalistic tradition, each planet is associated with a particular Intelligence and Spirit. The name of the spirit is numerically derived from all of the numbers comprising the magic square of the planet, while the name of the intelligence is derived from the sum of any line. Therefore, in the Hebrew Kabbalah, the name of the Spirit of the Sun is SORATH (סורת = 666), while the Intelligence of the Sun is NAKIEL (נכיאל = 111).

888, the number of Jesus, the Spiritual Sun of the early Christians, like 666 and other "triple numbers," may be derived from the magic square of the sun, and for this reason "triple numbers" were apparently thought to have a solar significance. These repeating numbers—666 and 888—are also the ratios that underlie the formation of the musical scale and have thus been revered since the time of Pythagoras or before. Another triple number appears in the magical formula ΧΑΒΡΑΧΝΕΣΗΡΦΙ ΧΡΟΦΝ-ΥΡΩΦΩΧΩΒΩΧ which is inscribed on a number of solar amulets from the Hellenistic period.[16] It has no literal meaning, but is equivalent to the number 9999, while in an address to Apollo from a Greek magical papyrus, the devotee states, "I am he . . . who have presented myself to you, and you have given me as a gift the knowledge (*gnôsis*) of your most great name, of which the number is 9999."[17]

Because of the fact that the Greek name Jesus is equivalent to 888, the early Christian gnostics refered to his name as "the Plenitude of Ogdoads," in other words, "the Fullness of Eights."[18] Reporting on gnostic doctrines, the church father Irenaeus states "Jesus is a name arithmetically symbolical, consisting of six letters, and is known by all those that belong to the called."[19] The gnostics refered to Jesus as the Ogdoad, because he "contained in himself the entire number of the 'elements' [*stoicheia* = letters], which the descent of the dove (who is Alpha and Omega) made clearly manifest, when he came to be baptized; for the number of the dove is eight hundred and one."[20] The meaning of this statement is fairly simple: The name Jesus, 888, is a perfect name encompassing the whole of creation, and is reflected in the perfection of the 24 letters of the classical Greek alphabet which, numerically, contains 8 letters denoting hundreds, 8 denoting tens, and 8 denoting units.[21] Jesus is therefore Alpha and Omega, the all-encompassing spiritual plenitude, which was made manifest by the descent of the dove at his baptism. This is because the Greek word for DOVE (ΠΕΡΙ ΣΤΕΡΑ) is equivalent to 801, which is also the value of ΑΩ. This type of symbolism was developed within certain circles of the early church, and the Alexandrian father Origen seems to

6	32	3	34	35	1
7	11	27	28	8	30
19	14	16	15	23	24
18	20	22	21	17	13
25	29	10	9	26	12
36	5	33	4	2	31

Figure 7. The Magic Square of the Sun

The 6x6 magic square of the sun contains the first 36 numbers arranged in such a fashion so that each line of numbers, whether added horizontally, vertically, or diagonally from corner to corner, will yield the "solar number" 111. The entire magic square therefore equals 666, a number which was significant to early Christian mystics. In Hebrew Kabbalah, the names of the Intelligence of the Sun and the Spirit of the Sun were designed to equal 111 and 666 respectively. Like 888, 666 is an important musical number, for .666 is the ratio of the perfect fifth, the most powerful harmonic interval.

refer to gematria when he writes, "A man who has been adorned with the spiritual gift called 'the word of wisdom' will also explain the reason for the opening of the heavens and the form of the dove, and why the Holy Spirit did not appear to Jesus in the form of any other living being but this."[22] Perhaps this was also why Paul, the earliest New Testament writer, maintained that Jesus possesses a "name which is above every name."[23]

The relationship between Jesus and the symbolism of the Ogdoad was developed a great deal in the teachings of the early church. One reason for this was that "Christ arose from the dead on the eighth day, the day of Helios" and "this had been the first day of Creation and for the Christians it became again the first day."[24] In other words, the creation of the world commenced on Sunday, while God completed the process on Saturday, the Sabbath, the Jewish day of rest. Jesus, the Spiritual Sun, rises from the grave on Sunday, now considered the eighth day because it ushers in a new phase of creation. A hymn by Origen celebrates the mystery of the Ogdoad, and the conception was further developed by the other fathers. Moreover, the so-called Christian Sibyllines, which purport to be pre-Christian prophecies, predict the coming of the new religion in the following way, clearly referring to the mystic number of Jesus:

> When the maid shall give birth to the Logos of God the Most High,
> But as wedded wife shall give to the Logos a name,
> Then from the east shall a star shine forth in the midst of the day
> Radiant and gleaming down from the heaven above,
> Proclaiming a great sign to poor mortal men.
> Yea, then shall the Son of the great God come to men,
> Clothed in flesh, like unto mortals on earth.
> Four vowels he has, twofold the consonants in him,
> And now will I declare to thee also the whole number:
> Eight monads, and to these as many decads,
> And eight hundreds also his name will show . . .[25]

One other aspect of gematria, which is examined throughout the course of this study, is its connection with the ratios of geometry, from which the term is derived in the first place. To cite a simple yet elegant example, a circle with the perimeter of 891 has a diameter of 284 units. The gematria value of 'ΟΥΡΑΝΟΣ, HEAVEN, is 891 while the value of ΘΕΟΣ, GOD, is 284. (*Figure 8.*) The arrangement nicely illustrates the conception that the abode of divinity is in the heavenly sphere. More importantly, according to the Pythagorean philosophers of Greece, the ratios of the fundamental geometry underlie the structure of the *kosmos* or world-order; furthermore, the most central numbers of Greek gematria were derived from the number values of these very same ratios that were seen as underlying the universal fabric.

Both orthodox "gnostics" (like Clement of Alexandria and Origen) and the so-called "heretical gnostics" taught, like the earlier mystery religions of Greece, that the Christian church, while open to all, nonetheless possessed secret doctrines. As Origen states in his work *Against Celsus*, "The existence of certain doctrines, which are beyond those which are

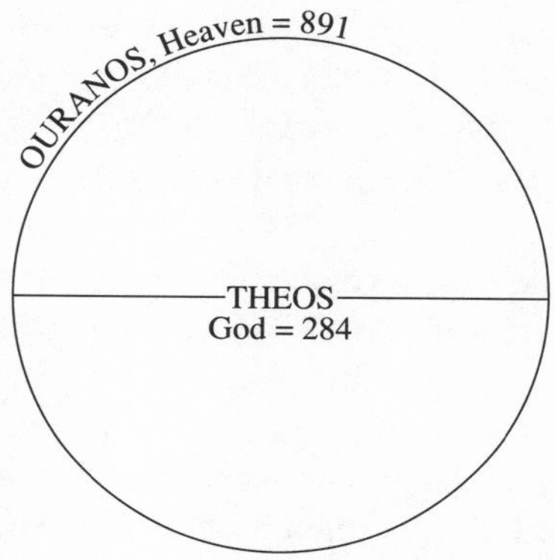

Figure 8. Gematria and Geometry

At the heart of Greek symbolic cosmology, gematria and geometry go together hand in hand. The simple example shown above demonstrates that a circle with a circumference of 891 has a diameter of 284. 891 is the number of the Greek word OURANOS, "Heaven," while the diameter, 284, is the number of THEOS, "God" or "Divinity."

exoteric and do not reach the multitude, is not a peculiarity of Christian doctrine only, but is shared by the philosophers. For they had some doctrines which were exoteric and some esoteric."[26] Clement of Alexandria refers to "the secret traditions of true knowledge"[27] possessed by the early church, while elsewhere he states that "it is not wished that all things should be exposed indiscriminately to all and sundry, or the benefits of wisdom communicated to those who have not even in a dream been purified in soul . . . nor are the mysteries of the Word (Logos) to be expounded to the profane."[28] Moreover, "knowing that the Saviour teaches nothing in a merely human way, but teaches all things to his own with divine and mystic wisdom, we must not listen to His utterances carnally; but with due investigation and intelligence must search out and learn the meaning hidden in them."[29] Clement also taught that scientific knowledge (*gnôsis*) is indispensable to a true understanding of the Christian faith, and, as he notes in a chapter on mathematical symbolism, the true Christian—the "gnostic"—"understands the involutions of words and the solutions of enigmas."[30] Moreover, the proper "distinction of names . . . produces great light in men's souls."[31] Origen writes that the Logos appears in many forms, always appropriate to an individual's present level of understanding;[32] yet the highest symbolic expression of the Logos is related to the gnostic use of mathematical symbolism, based on those first principles of harmony which underlie the structure of the universe itself.

The use of gematria stretches from the earliest Christian writings to the latest gnostic gospels. Ancient Christian manuscripts often terminate with the number 99 (ϘΘ) to signify the conclusion, for 99 is the numerical value of AMEN ('AMHN).[33] In the New Testament, the story of the feeding of the five thousand is based on the earlier Greek gematria of Apollo; so too is the story of the 153 fish caught in the unbroken net (for the feeding of the five thousand see chapter 5; for the 153 fish in the net see Appendix 1). Gematria is employed throughout the cryptic book of Revelation,[34] and it is likely that gematria underlies the structure of other New Testament stories and parables. Paul, who was influenced by the mystery religions, makes a simple reference to gematria in Galatians 3.17: there he refers to the Mosaic Law which came 430 years after God's covenant with Abraham. The chronology is incorrect, but 430 is the value of ΝΟΜΟΣ, the Greek word for LAW. Paul's writings were highly regarded by the gnostics and contain instances of more sophisticated gematria. In one of the earliest Christian writings, the *Epistle of Barnabas*, the author sees Moses' circumcision of 318 men as anticipating the saving grace of Jesus on the cross, for the cross is symbolized by the letter T (= 300), and Jesus by the first two letters of his name, IH (= 18). He concludes by saying that "No one has been admitted by me to a more excellent piece of knowledge (*gnôsis*) than this, but I know that you are worthy."[35] What he fails to explicitly mention is that 318 is also the value of HELIOS, the sun, with whom Jesus, "the light of the world,"[36] was symbolically identified by some. Finally, still within the sphere of Hellenistic Christianity, there is fascinating evidence that two esoteric gospels springing from the latest forms of Christian gnosis—*Pistis Sophia* and *The Books of Ieou*—employ a very sophisticated form of gematria. These ancient works purport to be the post-resurrection teachings of Jesus and deal with, among other things, "the 24 great mysteries" (that is, the letters of the Greek alphabet), encompassed within the confines of the First Mystery (Alpha) and the Last or 24th Mystery (Omega):

> But it happened that after Jesus had risen from the dead he spent eleven years speaking with his disciples. And he taught them only as far as the place of the first ordinance and as far as the places of the First Mystery which is within the veil which is within the first ordinance, which the 24th mystery outside and below, these which are in the second space of the First Mystery which is before all mysteries—the Father in the form of a dove. And Jesus said to his disciples: "I have come forth from that First Mystery which is the last mystery, namely the 24th." And the disciples did not know and understand that there was anything within that mystery. . . .[37]

We can see in the quotation above the reference to the mystery of "the father in the form of a dove" to which we have already alluded (ΠΕΡΙ ΣΤΕΡΑ, DOVE = 801 = ΑΩ). However, there appears to have existed in antiquity a more advanced gematria relating to the mysteries of the Alpha and the Omega which we can only briefly allude to in the present volume (see "Alpha and Omega"). It was the conclusion of Bligh Bond and Simcox Lea, in their pioneering study *Gematria*, that the teachings of *Pistis Sophia* and the *Books of Ieou*, rather than being compendiums of nonsensical mystagogery, are based on a sophisticated form of mathematical symbolism designed to unfold to the gnostic initiate the "aeonial" relationships of the higher world which transcends time and space.[38]

In summary, we have seen thus far that gematria was clearly used by some early Christians; moreover, it was especially favored by the gnostics. The celebrated gnostics described by the heresy-hunters such as Irenaeus, however, were certainly not the only Christians to allude to a secret tradition of gnosis within Christianity or to show knowledge of gematria. Most significantly, the fact that some New Testament stories—like the feeding of the five thousand—are based on gematria raises important questions which will have to be dealt with by any serious student of early Christianity. In order to find the answers, we must look back to the pre-Christian gematria of ancient Greece, a topic which is explored in chapter 4, "The Harmony of Apollo."

The examples of gematria given by the early church fathers and touched upon in this chapter are for the most part simplistic and only give a hint of gematria's true significance within the sphere of early Christianity and Hellenistic cosmology. Gematria obviously represents a symbolic *language*, but, if we pursue the subject to its pre-Christian roots, we will discover that gematria represents a scientific language as well, in the same way that a physicist's equation purports to throw light on the structure of reality itself. In both cases the ultimate goal is identical, to express mathematically the order of the universe. In the next chapter we will see how this order of the universe was symbolized and personified in Hellenistic philosophy, religion, and cosmology—a topic which has important consequences for anyone interested in glimpsing the long-eclipsed inner dimensions of the early Christian revelation.

CHAPTER THREE

The Solar Logos: The "Word of the Sun" in Hellenistic Mysticism and Cosmology

In the beginning was the Logos . . . In him was Life, and the Life was the Light of men.

—Prologue to the Fourth Gospel

That Light, He said, am I . . . the Light-Word (Logos) that appeared from Mind is Son of God.

—Corpus Hermeticum

All-Father Mind, being Life and Light, did bring forth the Archetypal Man co-equal to Himself . . . And Man from Life and Light changed into soul and mind—Life to soul, from Light to mind.

—Corpus Hermeticum

The Meanings of *Logos*

THE PROLOGUE to the Fourth Gospel, the Gospel of John, which begins with the unforgettable line "In the beginning was the Word," is instinctively recognized by many readers as one of the most beautiful passages in all the sacred texts of humanity. This writing describes the nature of the "Word" as a cosmic forming principle, its mission, and the manifestation of the Word in the figure of Jesus, the avatar of the Christian faith. Unfortunately, despite the beauty and profundity of the Prologue, most modern readers have not been able to unlock its inner meaning, for they have never been given the necessary key.

Central to the Prologue is the concept of "Word," a very inadequate rendering of the original Greek term *Logos*, one of the most important concepts of the Hellenistic world. In ancient Greek, *Logos* has many meanings, but none of them is "Word," which is based on a translation of a translation. When the Greek New Testament was translated into Latin, *Logos* became *Verbum*; and when the English King James translation was made from the Latin version, *Verbum* became "Word," twice removed from the original text.

Since *Logos* has so many meanings in ancient Greek, ranging from the scientific to the mystical, it is best left untranslated, as its nuances resound on many levels. Indeed, as E. R. Goodenough once noted, any student of Greek religion and cosmology "must first of all wipe that meaning ["Word"] from his mind and use the untranslated term Logos as he would use a new term in chemistry."[1]

Among its many meanings, *Logos* designates the power of "reason," the pattern or order of things, the principle of relationship, and an organized articulation of something. In general, it has the following meanings:

1) Order or pattern
2) *Ratio* or proportion
3) *Oratio*, a discourse, articulation or account, even a "sermon"
4) Reason, both in the sense of rationality and in the sense of an articulation of the cause of something
5) Principle or cause (*logoi* = "principles," "ratios," "reasons")
6) A principle of mediation and harmony between extremes

Logos has the same meaning as both the Latin words *ratio* and *oratio*. *Ratio* is the principle of Reason in its many senses, yet it is also ratio in a mathematical sense, as in continued geometrical proportion. *Oratio* is a discourse, an articulation, a setting forth of the "ratio" or nature of things. *Logos*, as a principle, is the natural order of things, the principle of reason, relation, and harmony, which exists both within the natural fabric of the universe and within the human mind. It is the faculty whereby one thing is related to another through *analogy*, or the power of "proportional insight."[2] Finally, in Greek mystical and cosmological thought, including early Christian thought, the idea of *The Logos* in a cosmic sense encompassed *all* of these meanings and refers to the underlying Order of the Universe, the blueprint on which all creation is based. If we are to appreciate the Prologue to the Fourth Gospel and other Greek mystical writings, all of these meanings must be simultaneously held in mind.

The Spiritual Sun

> I am the light of the world; he who follows me will not walk in darkness, but will have the light of life.
>
> —Jesus (John 8.12)

Since the Logos represents the heart of the cosmic pattern and the source of existence, its emblem is the sun, the source of life and light. Where this symbolism originated in a historical sense is difficult to ascertain for, as an ancient cosmologist might state, it is eternally revealed by the nature of the universe itself. Nonetheless, as we have seen in chapter 2, Plato used the image of the Sun to represent the idea of the One, the Good, and the Beautiful, seen as the source of existence and Being.[3]

One thing we know for certain is that, in the Pythagorean and Platonic schools of Hellenistic Alexandria, the sun came to be regarded as the doorway linking together the sensible and intelligible spheres, the material and spiritual orders of existence.[4] Helios was seen as the heart of the celestial pattern, and his physical aspect was considered as the lower manifestation of a higher principle which we may characterize as the Idea of the Solar Logos. This particular doctrine came to permeate the whole of Hellenistic cosmology in one form or another, influencing scientific, metaphysical, and theological thought. As Franz Cumont observes in his *Astrology and Religion Among the Greeks and Romans*,

> From astronomical speculations the Chaldeans had deduced a whole system of religious dogmas. The sun, set in the midst of the superimposed planets, regulates their harmonious movements. As its heat impels them forward, then draws them back, it is constantly influencing, according to its various aspects, the direction of their course and their action upon the earth. Fiery heart of the world, it vivifies the whole of this great organism, and as the stars obey its command, it reigns supreme over the universe. The radiance of its splendour illumines the divine immensity of the heavens, but at the same time in its brilliance there is intelligence; it is the origin of all reason, and, as a

> tireless sower it scatters unceasingly on the world below the seeds of a harvest of souls. Our brief life is but a particular form of the universal life. . . . This coherent and magnificent theology, founded upon the discoveries of ancient astronomy in its zenith, gradually imposed on mankind the cult of the "Invincible Sun" as the master of all nature, creator and preserver of men.[5]

Like God, the sun eternally gives forth from itself without ever being diminished, thus establishing itself as the most perfect symbol of the ineffable First Cause. Yet, as we have noted, among the learned, the sun itself was never taken to represent the First Cause, and was merely seen as its image and manifestation on a lower level of being, within the confines of space and time.[6] In a poetic sense, however, no one could quarrel with the assertion that the sun is, in a material fashion, the god of the physical universe. Along these lines, the Hermetic writings suggest that one should regard the sun "as the second God, ruling all things, and giving light to all things living in the Cosmos, whether ensouled or unensouled."[7] Likewise, in a scientific sense, few would question the Orphic *Hymn to Helios*, which identifies the sun as the "the light of life,"[8] an epithet which directly parallels the opening lines of the Fourth Gospel.

If the sun can be seen as the material reflection of the First Cause, by analogy the First Cause can be represented as the Spiritual or Intelligible Sun. This was a symbolic commonplace in the Hellenistic period in pagan, Jewish, and early Christian thought. The notion is clearly set forth in the important writings of Philo of Alexandria, a Jewish philosopher who sought to reconcile the spiritual traditions of Judaism with the light of Greek learning. Born around 30 B.C.E., Philo describes in his many works a comprehensive worldview based on the central idea of the Logos. In this emanationist cosmology, Philo refers to God as the Intelligible or Spiritual Sun,[9] and the Logos, his offspring, as "the Son of God."[10] This theology, which is independently found in the Egyptian Hermetica from the same time period and the writings of Plutarch, was chosen by the first Christian intellectuals as the vehicle for their own spiritual expression. As an expositor of the Logos doctrine, Philo's writings are appropriately filled with hundreds of examples of number symbolism, for Number was seen as an ordering principle at work in the cosmos; Number is thus allied with the ordering principle of Logos, which was also studied in a mathematical sense. For this reason, in one revealing passage, Clement of

Alexandria refers to his predecessor as simply Philo "the Pythagorean."[11] As is shown elsewhere in this volume, some early Christians were themselves interested in the scientific portrayal of the Logos, which they expressed through the numerical language of Greek gematria.

Despite his prolific output, Philo was a synthesizer and not an "original thinker," and the value of his work resides in this simple fact. While learned in the traditions of the day, the ideas and symbolism which Philo employs were "in the air," and he was not an innovator; as one scholar notes, "anything philosophical to be found in his writings can confidently be taken as genuine teaching of his environment."[12] In this respect, Philo's work sheds an especially important light on the ancient Logos teaching, for it is possible to infer from his writings, and those of his contemporaries, the central patterns of Hellenistic cosmology.

The Logos Teaching

> . . . the Logos is God's Likeness, by whom the whole *kosmos* was fashioned.
>
> —Philo Judaeus

> We speak of God, of the Son, his Word, and of the holy Spirit; and we say that the Father, the Son, and the Spirit are united in power. For the Son is the intelligence, reason, and wisdom of the Father, and the Spirit is an effluence, as light from fire. In the same way we recognize that there are other powers which surround matter and pervade it.
>
> —Athenagoras, early Christian apologist

In Hellenistic cosmology, the First Cause was envisioned as transcending human understanding. In the *Republic*, Plato suggested that it was even "beyond Being," a notion which was to have considerable influence for well over a millennium.[13] The Pythagoreans portrayed the first principle as the Monad, indicating that it is both a primeval Unity and apart (*monas*) from all other things, transcending time, space, and the multiplicity of the phenomenal world.[14] While all things have a relation to it, this primeval Source (*archê*) was never envisioned as a "personal God," or as a thinking and planning divinity like Yahweh, the God of the Old Testament, who consciously decided to create the universe. For the Greeks, the Supreme Principle is utterly simple, and superior to conscious thought and decision-making, even though it is symbolically identified with the power of Cosmic Mind in some writings.[15]

Because of its abundant perfection, the Source unconditionally gives forth a secondary principle, the Logos, in the same way that the sun gives forth rays of light. The Logos is not the First Cause, any more than rays of light "are" the sun, but nonetheless the two are very intimately related. In this ancient teaching, the Logos is the first, harmonically differentiated "image" of the First Cause. The Logos represents the first level of real manifestation or Being, for it encompasses within itself all the laws and relations which are later articulated in the phenomenal universe. Since the Logos is the emanation of the Transcendent Absolute, it may be poetically described as "the Son of God," as we see in the works of Philo, the Hermetic writings, and early Christianity. Underlying the source of all reality, the Logos is related to the principle of *Nous* or Universal Intellect, the "repository" of all the cosmic Forms and principles on which creation is based. And as the rational image of Divine Intellect, humanity is itself the living, incarnate image of the Logos. According to Clement of Alexandria,

> the image of God is His Word, the genuine Son of Mind, the Divine Word, the archetypal light of light; and the image of the Word is the true man, the mind which is in man, who is therefore said to have been made "in the image and likeness of God."[16]

Invariably, the powers of Light and Life were associated with the nature of the Logos in Hellenistic thought, for these are among the most central principles in all of creation. Like the early Christians, the pagan cosmologists held that humanity was created in the "image" of God. To illustrate this, the Hermetic writings present several schemas; in one of the more attractive versions, Eternity (Aeon) is said to be the image of God, Cosmos is the image of Eternity, the Sun is the image of Cosmos, and Man is the image of the Sun.[17] Because of these factors, the Logos has often been pictured in various cosmologies as Anthropos, the figure of the Perfect Man, the archetype and examplar of humanity. (See "The Celestial Man of Light.")

The nature of the Logos was also represented by the natural principle of musical harmony. Mathematically, harmony depends upon the nature of *logos* or ratio, a topic explored in chapter 4. Both pagans and Christians alike expressed the nature of the Logos in these terms, for it is through the power of harmony that all the parts of creation are reconciled into a greater whole. The great philosopher Plotinus, drawing on an ancient and perhaps eternal idea, put it this way:

> The being we are considering is a living unity and, therefore, necessarily self-sympathetic: it is under a law of reason (*logos*) and therefore the unfolding process of its life must be self-accordant: that life has no haphazard, but knows only harmony and ordinance: all the groupings follow reason (*logos*): all single beings within it, all the members of this living whole in their choral dance are under a rule of Number.[18]

Maximus of Tyre, an earlier Greek philosopher and rhetorician, expressed the matter in these terms, personifying the Harmony of the Universe as the Coryphaeus, the leader of a choir:

> Consider this Universe as constituting the harmony of a musical instrument, which harmony, having begun from God its maker, proceeds through the air and earth and sea and all that is animate or vegetative. Thereupon it sinks into divers unlike natures, the discord which it reduces to concord—just as the harmony of the Coryphaeus, when it has fallen upon the many voices in a choral dance, reduces to order their clamour.[19]

Finally, Clement of Alexandria, who disseminated the light of Christianity, the "New Song," exhorted his readers in the following fashion:

> Let us who are many haste that we may be brought together into one love, according to the union of the essential unity; and let us, by being made good, conformably follow after union, seeking after the good Monad. The union of many in one, issuing in the production of divine harmony out of a medley of sounds and division, becomes one symphony, following one Coryphaeus and teacher, the Logos.[20]

From this we can also surmise that the early Christian ideal of the *church* or assembly (*ekklêsia*), the mystical body of Christ, was itself seen by some as a social manifestation of the celestial harmony, whereby all individuals might be unified and uplifted into a greater whole.[21]

The Prologue to the Fourth Gospel

Having surveyed some common ideas regarding the Logos during the Hellenistic period, it would be useful to study the Prologue to the Fourth Gospel to see how it relates to this model. It is reproduced below, where the terms *Word* and *world* have been replaced with the Greek originals, *Logos* and *kosmos* respectively:[22]

The Logos in Himself

IN THE BEGINNING was the Logos,
 and the Logos was with God;
 and the Logos was God.
He was in the beginning with God.
All things were made through him,
 and without him was made
 nothing that has been made.
In him was life,
 and the life was the light of men.
And the light shines in the darkness;
 and the darkness grasped it not.

The Mission of the Logos

There was a man,
 one sent from God
 whose name was John.
This man came as a witness,
 to bear witness concerning the light,
 that all might believe through him.
He was not himself the light,
 but was to bear witness to the light.
It was the true light
 that enlightens every man
 who comes into the kosmos.
He was in the kosmos,
 and the kosmos was made through him,
 and the kosmos knew him not.
He came unto his own,
 and his own received him not.
But as many as received him
 he gave power of becoming sons of God,
 to those who believe in his name:

Who were born not of blood,
  nor of the will of the flesh,
  nor of the will of man,
  but of God.

The Logos Incarnate

And the Logos was made flesh,
  and manifested among us.
And we saw his glory—
  glory as the only-begotten of the Father—
  full of grace and truth.
John bore witness concerning him,
  and cried, "This was he of whom I said,
'He who is to come after me
  has been set above me,
  because he was before me.' "
And of his fullness
  we have all received,
  grace for grace.
For the Law was given through Moses;
  grace and truth came through Jesus Christ.
No one has at any time seen God.
The only-begotten Son,
  who is in the bosom of the Father,
  he has revealed him.

It is easy to see how the Prologue to the Fourth Gospel reflects the ideas of the Hellenistic Logos teaching, set forth here in its Christian version. The Logos is in the *archê*, the Beginning, Source, or Fount of existence. As the underlying harmonic pattern of creation, all things were made through the Logos, which contains the principles of Life and Light. The light of the Logos shines out, illuminating the darkness of matter, forgetfulness, and our unawakened spiritual nature, yet "the darkness" grasps it not: the darkness cannot understand the Light, nor can it destroy it. But by turning back toward the Logos and the world of first principles, humanity discovers what it means to truly live, and is illuminated by the spiritual source of creation.

John the Baptizer—perhaps a member of an Essene community[23]—bears witness concerning the Light. The *kosmos* itself is a reflection of the

Logos, which exists here-and-now in the manifest world; yet, without the power of Mind—the power of Light—the created world is unaware of the higher realities, even though it mirrors them. The Logos came unto its own, humanity, but not everyone recognized its nature. Yet those who received the Logos, "the dayspring from on high,"[24] and believed in its divine name, experienced a spiritual regeneration—referred to elsewhere in this gospel as "the birth from above"—and, like the Logos itself, became Sons of God.

The Logos was made flesh—it became incarnate in the universe via the principle of Humanity—and was "manifest" among us. This word, *manifest*, is usually translated as "dwelt." But the original Greek term is ambiguous and means, literally, "tented" or "tabernacled," referring to the tent in which the tablets of the Mosaic Law were kept. The meaning here is that the revelation of the New Law, the Logos, has now been made manifest among humanity as was the Law of old. The old Law was given through Moses, but grace and truth come through the Logos, Jesus the Christ, the anointed one. According to some early Christians, the human Jesus became the vehicle for the Divine Logos only at his baptism by John, signified by the descent of the dove, while developing orthodoxy decided that he had been the incarnation of the Logos from the start.

No one has at any time seen the ineffable, High God. But the only-begotten Son—the Logos—who is in the bosom of the Father, has revealed to humanity the nature of the transcendent Source, both through consciousness—the Light of Life[25]—and through the structure of the universe itself.

The Logos Personified

While the early Christians personified the Logos in the figure of Jesus, the Greeks had represented the Logos in the figure of Apollo, the god of geometry and music, a subject explored in chapter 4. Another favorite representation was Hermes, who, as the church fathers acknowledge, was actually called "the Logos" by the Greeks.[26] For example, according to the gnostic sect of the Naassenes, "Hermes is the Word who has expressed and fashioned the things that have been, that are and that will be."[27]

In ancient Egypt, where the Logos theology appears at an early date, the Greek god Hermes was identified with the Egyptian divinity Thoth. Thoth was the personification of the universal order, the "heart and tongue" of the sun god Rā who "spoke the words" which resulted in the creation of the heavens and the earth.[28] According to Iamblichus, Thoth was the author of 36,525 books (equal to the number of days in one hundred solar years).[29] He was represented as the "scribe of the gods," the revealer of mathematics, geometry, and priestly knowledge. As E. A. Wallis Budge points out:

> His knowledge and powers of calculation measured out the heavens, and planned the earth, and everything which is in them; his will and power kept the forces in heaven and earth in equilibirum; it was his great skill in celestial mathematics which made proper use of the laws (*maāt*) upon which the foundation and maintenance of the universe rested; it was he who directed the motions of the heavenly bodies and their times and seasons; and without his words the gods, whose existence depended on them, could not have kept their place among the followers of Rā.[30]

As "the reason and mental powers" of the sun god Rā, Thoth was "also the means by which their will was translated into speech."[31] As the revealer of celestial knowledge, the attributes of Thoth are later reflected in the figure Hermes Trismegistos (Thrice-Great Hermes), the reputed author of the Egyptian Hermetic writings. While the actual authors of these important works are unknown, like the unknown authors of the Christian gospels, Iamblichus repeats the tradition that "Hermes, the god who presides over language, was formerly very properly considered as common to all priests; and the power who presides over the true science concerning the gods is one and the same in the whole of things. Hence our ancestors dedicated the inventions of their wisdom to this deity, inscribing all their own writings with the name of Hermes."[32]

The Greek Hermetic tractates were written and used in Egypt during a period stretching from perhaps 100 B.C.E. to 350 C.E. by members of Hermetic spiritual communities which were active in synthesizing native Egyptian teachings with the expressions of Greek philosophy.[33] The ideas of this "pagan gnosticism" were certainly "in the air" during the formative days of early Christianity, and while "no direct literary relationship can be traced . . . it seems clear that [the person who wrote the Gospel of] John was working with similar presuppositions and along similar lines to those of the Hermetic authors."[34]

The Hermetic writings are cast as revelation discourses between Hermes Trismegistos, the spiritual "father," and Tat, his "son," the aspiring initiate. In an esoteric sense, "Hermes" and "Tat" may represent two aspects of an individual's soul, the higher and lower natures respectively. Through "his" writings and discourse with his disciples, Hermes Trismegistos reveals teachings of a spiritual and cosmological nature, concerning the nature of God, the soul, the origin and structure of the cosmos, and the path through which the soul may experience its divinizing rebirth in the divine principle of Mind or *Nous*. Common to all of these writings are parallels to the Hellenistic Logos doctrine as it has been summarized in this chapter.

According to the underlying myth of Gnosis, humanity is asleep, forgetful of its celestial origin and true nature. It is the task of the "Gnostic Revealer" to descend through the heavenly spheres and fan the slumbering sparks of spiritual knowledge which lie dormant within the soul, leading to the recognition of one's authentic nature and spiritual destiny. In Christianity, Jesus is personified as the Gnostic Revealer, the teacher of saving knowledge, especially in such works as the Gospel of John and the *Gospel of Thomas*. In the Hermetic writings, Hermes Trismegistos represents another Hellenistic manifestation of the Logos, also personified as the Gnostic Revealer. While one may have many teachers in life, Clement of Alexandria states that the ultimate spiritual teacher is the Logos itself, "the Teacher from whom all instruction comes."[35] According to the ancients, the Logos exists without, yet also within. We can never be separated from the harmony of the universe because we are its living reflection, even if, in our slumber, this recognition has been temporarily obscured.

Like the teachings of the early Christians, the Hermetic writings focus upon the mystery of the soul's "rebirth" and transfiguration, the discovery of "the inner man," which results in a divinization of the personality. Through this existential realization, the gnostic—the true initiate—discovers who he is, where he has been, and where he is going. The gnostic realization is that awakened, transfigured humanity is a manifestation of *Nous*, the Divine Intellect, the first emanation of the unknowable Source. In one of the Hermetic writings, *The Cup or the Monad*, the story is told of how the world creator, while giving each person a share of reason (*logos*), did not bestow on every soul an equal portion of Mind. Rather, Mind was "set up in the midst for souls, just as it were a prize."[36] In language which strongly parallels that of early Christianity, Hermes explains the liberating baptism in the Cup of Mind. The world creator, he says

> filled a mighty cup with it, and sent it down, joining a Herald to it, to whom He gave command to make this proclamation to the hearts of men:
>
> Baptize thyself with this Cup's baptism, what heart can do so; you who have faith can ascend to Him who sent down the cup, you who know why you have come into being!
>
> As many then as understood the Herald's tiding and doused themselves in Mind, became partakers in the Gnosis; and when they had "received the Mind" they were made "perfect men."
>
> But they who do not understand the tidings, these, since they possess the aid of Reason (*Logos*) only and not Mind (*Nous*), are ignorant of why and how they have come into being.[37]

Elsewhere, in another work, *The Secret Discourse Concerning Rebirth*, Hermes explains the process through which this divinization is experienced. Recalling the passage in the Fourth Gospel where Nicodemus asks, "How can a man be born when he is old? Can he enter a second time into his mother's womb and be born?", Tat proclaims "I know not, thrice-greatest one, from what womb a man can be born again, nor from what seed."[38] Hermes explains that the womb of rebirth is Wisdom and that the Will of God is the begetter. The mystery of rebirth—the race of the Divine Sonship—cannot be taught, but, when the time is right, God recalls the knowledge of the spiritual realities to one's awareness, the knowledge the soul possessed before being born into a body. As Walter Scott summarizes the teaching of this tractate:

> The man whom the Rebirth brings into being is a son of God; he belongs to the world of Mind; he is composed of divine Powers. He who has been born again has become an incorporeal being; he is no longer a thing visible to bodily eyes. . . .
>
> He sees things no longer by bodily sense; he sees with the eye of Mind. And thus seeing, he finds himself to be one with all that exists; he feels himself to be omnipresent and eternal.
>
> The new self which has thus come into being is imperishable. He who has once become a god, and son of God, can never cease to be that which he has become.[39]

In this ecstatic, transcendent state, both Christian and Hermetic mystics entered into divine union with the Logos, the Divine Intellect, the source of Life and Light. Instructed by the Logos itself, they became its mouthpiece, and could thus honestly proclaim that the realizations they experienced were the direct teachings of Christ or Hermes. It is no doubt from such ecstatic, heightened states of consciousness that many of the inspired *logia* or "sayings of the Lord" originated that later found their way into the early Christian literature. That is why Jesus—the Logos personified as the "Gnostic Revealer"—can accurately say in the *Gospel of Thomas*, "He who will drink from My mouth will become like Me. I myself shall become he, and the things that are hidden will be revealed to him."[40]

Generally speaking, the ancient gnostics primarily viewed Christ as an eternal, celestial power, the Logos, with which it is possible to have an intimate, personal relation, since our higher consciousness is made in its image. For this reason, gnostics stressed the experiential union with the divine, and showed little interest in the historical Jesus, whom it has always been impossible to know in a concrete sense, or even accurately in a historical sense. Because of this, gnostic speculation has always possessed a very strong ahistorical, cosmological tendency and dimension, preferring to concentrate on the liberating realization of Christ within.

This realization, of which the mystics speak, is the secret of initiation, and was referred to by the early Christians in a number of ways. The Prologue to the Fourth Gospel makes it clear that those who "received" the Logos experienced a divinizing energy, thus "becoming Sons of God," a transformation also referred to in the Hermetic writings. Elsewhere in the Fourth Gospel, this is referred to in Greek as "the birth from above."[41] Origen, in his work *Against Celsus*, states that those who follow the example of "the Sun of Righteousness," who sent forth His rays from Judaea, become not only followers of Christ, but Christs in their own right.[42] An even more appealing analogy is offered by Clement, who writes that not even the sun can show us the true God. That is because:

> The healthful Word or Reason, who is the Sun of the soul, alone can do that; through Him alone, when He has risen within in the depth of the mind, the soul's eye is illuminated.[43]

One of the primary roles of the Logos in Greek thought is its function as celestial mediator, the "geometric mean" between extremes. That is why Jesus proclaims, in the Gospel of John, "I am the Way" and "I am the Door." As the Prologue to the Fourth Gospel states, "No one has at any time seen God." However, "The only-begotten Son, who is in the bosom of the Father, he has revealed him." Not only is the Logos the image and manifestation of the otherwise transcendent Source, but it is the connecting principle through which we are joined back to the One, and that is why Jesus is represented as the mediator between heaven and earth in Christian symbolism.

As Christianity evolved into a collective belief system, it developed a political structure and creeds, teaching that Jesus came and left at a particular point in time, and that it was only possible to achieve salvation by joining the ranks of the organized church. At the same time, it outlawed other forms of religious expression, and confiscated the property of prominent individuals who resisted conversion to the new faith.[44] The church thereby proclaimed *itself* the official mediator between man and God, thus usurping the original function of Christ the Logos. However, according to the gnostic approach, the Logos is an ever-present celestial power, not limited by time, space, or political boundaries—nor to a single appearance. It underlies the structure of the universe and consciousness, and, for those attuned to its nature, the Logos illuminates the inner recesses of the heart with eternal, spiritual knowledge. That is why Jesus, in the ancient *Gospel of Thomas*, can accurately say "It is I who am the light which is above them all. It is I who am the All. From Me did the All come forth, and unto Me did the All extend. Split a piece of wood and I am there. . . ."[45]

CHAPTER FOUR

The Harmony of Apollo: The Origins of Gematria in Ancient Greece

To the man who pursues his studies in the proper way, all geometric constructions, all systems of numbers, all duly constituted melodic progressions, the single ordered scheme of all celestial revolutions, should disclose themselves, and disclose themselves they will, if, as I say, a man pursues his studies aright with his mind's eye fixed on their single end. As such a man reflects, he will receive the revelation of a single bond of natural interconnection between all these problems.

—Plato, *Epinomis* 991E–992

Mathematics in Antiquity

EVERYONE AGREES that the ancient Greeks possessed an affinity for the principles of harmony and proportion. This is evident in all the artifacts of Greek civilization, ranging from vases to architecture, from household items to temples and statuary. Given this innate awareness and love of harmony, proportion, and symmetry, it is not surprising that the Greeks perfected the study of these principles in the realms of science and philosophy.

The remarkable Greek accomplishments in the study of geometry are well known; and while we today boast the technological results of experimental science, ancient Greek science was not experimental: it was mathematical. Like scientists today, the Greek thinkers realized that mathematics provides a means of insight into the universal laws and principles which shape the phenomena of nature. Whether we appreciate the delicate geometries of snowflakes and flowers, the harmonies of music, or the vast spiral patterns of distant galaxies, we can see the effect of mathematical forming principles at work.

While the Greek geometers produced works which remain astounding for their brilliance and clarity to this day, it is known that the study of geometry and mathematics was vigorously pursued in remote antiquity by other civilizations, such as the Babylonians and the Egyptians. Historians also realize that the Greeks were, at least in part, the heirs of these earlier cultures. A cuneiform tablet at Yale University shows that, as of 1800 B.C.E., the Babylonians had calculated the value of $\sqrt{2}$—an "irrational number"—to an astounding degree of accuracy, "off" from the actual value by about 1 part in 100,000.[1] (*Figure 9.*) The Pythagorean theorem was known to both the Babylonians and megalithic builders of prehistoric England.[2] The Egyptians were also fabled for their extensive knowledge of geometry and mathematics, which is more reflected in their art and architecture than in the surviving mathematical papyri.[3] Plato, who is said to have studied with the Egyptian priests at Heliopolis, refers in his *Laws* to the Egyptian canon of music and proportion which maintained the integrity of that civilization for literally thousands of years.[4]

What we know from Greek philosophy is that the study of mathematics and geometry was viewed as the preeminent path leading to the knowledge of universal Forms, those ultimate principles which were held to underlie the structure of the cosmos and life itself. Plato sums this up clearly in the *Republic* when he writes that "geometry is the knowledge of the eternally existent."[5] Consequently, the study of geometry and mathematics formed a preliminary core of instruction at Plato's Academy, above the door of which was posted the famous notice, "Let no one ignorant of geometry enter here."[6]

In the *Republic*, Plato sets forth a course of study necessary for all philosophers, and all individuals qualified to act as guardians of his ideal state.[7] Because the health of both the individual soul and society at large depend upon the principles of harmony and justice (which may be studied in a mathematical sense), Plato maintains that all philosophers should study the Pythagorean sciences of arithmetic, geometry, harmonics (musical tuning theory), and astronomy. These four subjects make up the *quadrivium* of the earlier Pythagorean school, and were traditionally analyzed in the following way:

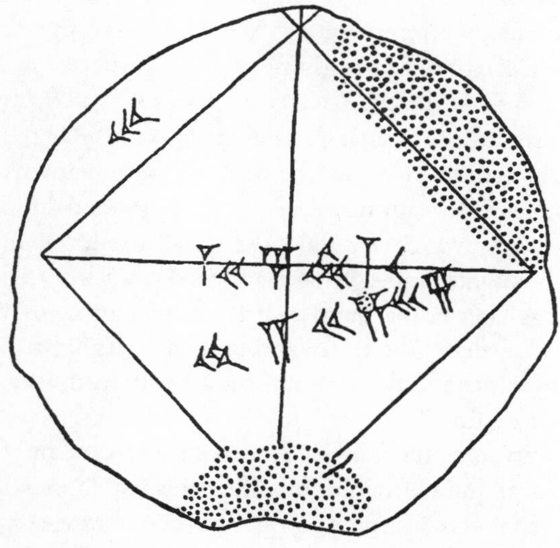

Figure 9. High Mathematics in Antiquity

This Old-Babylonian tablet (*circa* 1800 B.C.E.) in the collection of Yale University gives a value of √2 which is correct to five decimal places. Expressed in decimal terms, this Babylonian approximation is 1.414213 which, if squared, equals 1.9999983, "off" from the value of 2 by about 1 part in 100,000. This Babylonian value passed to Greece and was still used by the mathematician Ptolemy nearly two thousand years later.

Arithmetic: Number in itself
Geometry: Number in space
Harmonics (or Music): Number in time
Astronomy (or Cosmology): Number in space and time

Because geometry represents the knowledge of eternal principles, according to Plato the study of mathematics "will tend to draw the soul towards truth and to direct upwards the philosophic intelligence which is now wrongly turned earthwards."[8] Moreover, since number can only be conceived of through the use of intellect, "this study [arithmetic] is really indispensible for our purposes, since it forces the mind to arrive at pure truth by the exercise of pure thought."[9] Needless to say, this is a statement with which a modern physicist might well agree. It is necessary for the true philosopher, as well as the true scientist, to ascend intellectually to the comprehension of those universal principles on which the cosmos is based. In this philosophical ascent, the study of mathematics is invaluable, for it provides the inner training necessary to apprehend directly the laws of celestial harmony which are reflected on all the levels of being and manifestation. As Plato states, "It is quite hard to realize that every soul possesses an organ better worth saving than a thousand eyes, because it is our only means of seeing the truth; and that when its light is dimmed or extinguished by other interests, these studies will purify the hearth and rekindle the sacred fire."[10]

Plato stands firmly within the Pythagorean tradition and his writings abound in musical and mathematical allegories which, amazingly, have been ignored by most modern philosophers. The purpose of the *Republic* is to define the principle of justice and see how it operates in both the soul and society at large. This was a major focus of the earlier Pythagoreans who were also interested in political theory. What emerges in the *Republic* is the classic Pythagorean definition of *justice*: it is that "ideal state" in which each part receives its just and proper due, according to the principle of proportion.[11] Like the earlier Pythagoreans, Plato describes the principle of justice in the soul using the metaphor of the musical scale, itself based on the mathematical laws of proportion and mediation:

> The just man does not allow the several elements in his soul to usurp one another's functions; he is indeed one who sets his house in order, by self-mastery and discipline coming to be at peace with himself, and *bringing into tune those three parts, like the terms in the proportion of a musical scale, the highest and the lowest notes and the mean between them, with all the intermediate intervals.* Only when he has linked these parts together in *well-tempered harmony* and has made himself one man instead of many, will he be ready to go about whatever he may have to do, whether it be making money and satisfying bodily wants, or business transactions, or the affairs of state. In all these fields when he speaks of just and honourable conduct, he will mean the behaviour that helps to produce and preserve this habit of mind; and by wisdom he will mean the knowledge which presides over such conduct. Any action which

> tends to break down this habit will be for him unjust; and the notions governing it he will call ignorance and folly. (My emphasis.)[12]

As the musicologist Ernest McClain has shown, in setting forth his "ideal cities," Plato is also describing musical tuning systems.[13] Plato was looking for the best possible model for society, as well as the best possible way to represent ultimate reality. As a scientist, he saw that ultimate reality is best described through the agency of Number, viewed in both a quantitative and a qualitative sense. As a Pythagorean, he saw that the study of harmonics was invaluable in preparing the philosopher for handling the affairs of state.

Harmonics, the science of musical tuning systems, is—like human behavior and the phenomena of nature—based on certain laws.[14] These principles may be studied directly and experienced on the monochord, a one-stringed musical instrument used by the Pythagoreans. (See *figure 10*, next page.) The study of harmonics provides direct access to those principles of harmony, justice, proportion, and mediation which underlie different classes of natural phenomena. That, in itself, would provide sufficient reason to perceive a relation between harmonic theory and political theory. However, the pure harmonic principles and their practical application are two different things. As Ernest McClain points out, this is why the study of tuning systems is invaluable. Each tuning system requires a varying degree of sacrifice of the pure harmonic principles. For example, in our modern twelve-tone equal-tempered scale, the ratio between each semitone is exactly the same, which does give a perfect octave, but sacrifices the pure concords of the perfect fourth and perfect fifth.[15]

Likewise, in the affairs of state, one must search for the most perfect model, but realize that a certain degree of sacrifice is necessary in the terrestrial world of day-to-day affairs. Plato was aware of this dilemma and saw that tuning theory represented the most perfect metaphor of this vexing situation. By training the prospective leaders of state in tuning theory, Plato realized that the greatest possible benefit would be derived by exposing their minds to the principles of harmony, proportion, and mediation;[16] such exposure would also have the effect of separating the best qualified individuals from the chaff of mere political opportunists, who would have little patience for the subject, and who are never

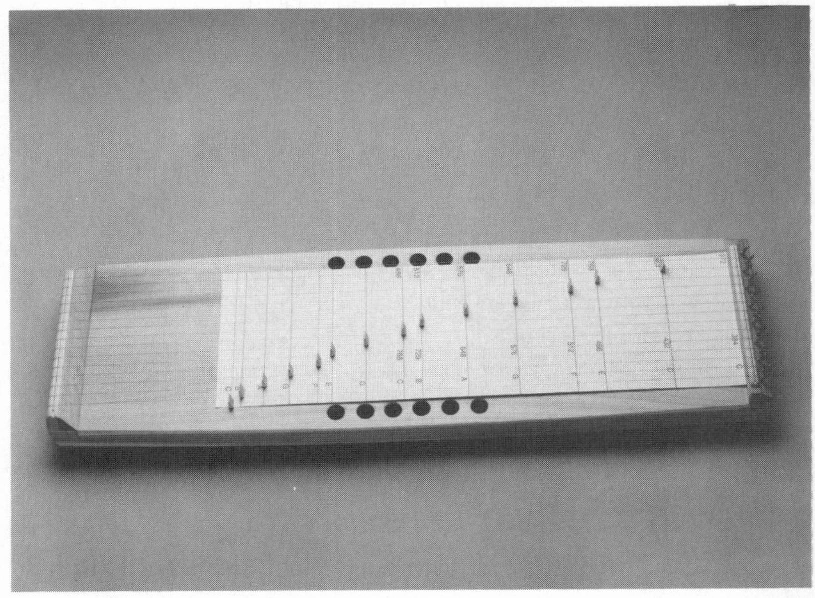

Figure 10. A Fifteen-stringed Monochord or Polychord

The monochord, a one-stringed instrument with a movable bridge, was used by ancient Greek philosophers and scientists to study the principles of harmony which underlie musical tuning systems. Pythagoras discovered that the concordant, harmonious ratios of music reflect simple numerical proportions, which may be demonstrated mathematically and audibly on the monochord.

On a polychord, as shown above, all the strings are adjusted to the same tension and pitch. The harmonic ratios are brought out through the use of movable bridges, arranged according to numerical proportions. Concordant intervals and musical tuning systems are thereby shown to represent mathematical patterns of harmonic relation.

The Greek astronomer and mathematician Ptolemy describes the fifteen-stringed polychord shown above in his treatise *On Harmonics*. This polychord allows the researcher to set up a tuning system covering two octaves, the range of the ancient Greek "Greater Perfect System." It also allows one to set up two different tuning systems side-by-side, for purposes of comparison. The tuning shown above is the classic Pythagorean diatonic scale, first described in Plato's *Timaeus*, here spanning two octaves. This is the same musical scale that we use today.

ultimately interested in the nature of reality or the welfare of others. Not everyone is fit to rule the state; nor is every mind "destined to take its full part in the apprehension of reality."[17] By encouraging the study of harmonics, Plato was both an idealist and a practical thinker. He realized that there is an ideal pattern "set up in the heavens,"[18] the standard against which we judge our accomplishments and failures; yet he was always aware that it would never be possible to fully realize heaven on earth in a collective sense, only "the best possible image."[19] Plato was also realistic about the inherent qualities we should look for in our prospective leaders, noting that "there is in some natures a crudity and awkwardness that can only tend to a lack of measure and proportion; and there is a close affinity between proportion and truth. Hence, besides our other requirements, we shall look for a mind endowed with measure and grace, which will be instinctively drawn to see every reality in its true light."[20]

The Pythagorean Definition of Harmony

According to the Pythagoreans, the cosmos is made up of a dynamic harmony of opposites or complementary forces. In the same way that the year encompasses both winter and summer, night and day, so too is the universe a living harmony of opposing tendencies and forces.

The starting point of Pythagorean science was to recognize the beauty of the universe. According to traditional account, Pythagoras was the first person to apply the word *kosmos* to the universe. This word, in Greek, means something like "ornament" or "adornment" (cf. "cosmetic"), and by applying the word *kosmos* to the universe, Pythagoras was saying that the earth and the heavens are adorned and ornamented by beauty. It implies that there is an order to the universe, an order which inspires delight and aesthetic appreciation.

Second, Pythagoras said that the *kosmos* is a *harmonia*, a "fitting together." Developed in a mathematical sense by the Pythagoreans, the root concept of *harmonia* is truly primordial; the term *harmony* springs from the prehistoric (*circa* 5000 B.C.E) Indo-European root **ar-**, "to fit together," which is the root of the words ARM, HARMONY, ART, ORDER, ORNAMENT, ADORN, RATIO, REASON, READ, RITE, ARITHMOS (number), and RHYME.[21] Through the principle of harmony, the parts fit together into the whole. Even though the universe contains an unlimited number of things, phenomena, and forces, they are all miraculously and beautifully reconciled into the greater whole. This is the law of "unity in multiplicity" which fascinates every careful observer of the natural world.

In their philosophy, the Pythagoreans expressed these relationships through the natural language of number and geometry. Number is a natural language because, like the harmonic ratios in music, it is not invented, but discovered. However, the Pythagorean vision of Number is quite different from the way we imagine it today. While we use numbers to count things in a quantitative sense, the Pythagoreans saw Number as a *qualitative* essence, a principle of relationship or *logos*.

For example, the Pythagoreans said that the number *One*—in Greek, the Monad—is not a number at all,[22] but the principle of Unity, and the underlying continuum out of which other numbers emerge. Hence, they called the *One* "Apollo," for in Greek *Apollo* (α-πολλων) means literally "not of many." According to Theon of Smyrna in his work on *Mathematics Useful for Understanding Plato*:

> Unity is the principle of all things and the most dominant of all that is: all things emanate from it and it emanates from nothing. It is indivisible and it is everything in power. It is immutable and never departs from its own nature through multiplication (1x1 = 1). Everything that is intelligible and not yet created exists in it; the nature of ideas, God himself, the soul, the beautiful and the good, and every intelligible essence, such as beauty itself, justice itself, equality itself, for we conceive each of these things as being one as existing in itself.[23]

In the same way that One represents the principle of Unity, *Two*—the Dyad—represents the principle of duality, multiplicity, and the movement away from divine unity toward manifestation. For this reason, the Dyad was called "Unlimited," "Birth," "Growth," "Matter," "Nature," and "Anguish," among other titles. As Theon of Smyrna notes,

> The first increase, the first change from unity, is made by the doubling of unity which becomes 2, in which are seen matter and all that is perceptible, the generation of motion, multiplication and addition, composition and the relationship of one thing to another.[24]

As Theon observes, the Dyad represents the beginning of manifestation and hence the beginning of strife. With the Dyad arises the duality of subject and object, the knower and the known. Nonetheless, the Dyad also signals the possibility of *logos*, the relation of one thing to another. This possibility of relation is consummated in *Three*, the Triad, where the gulf of dualism is bridged, for it is through the third term that a relation or *harmonia* is obtained between the two extremes. For this reason, the Pythagoreans called the Triad "Proportion" (*analogia*), "Marriage," "Peace," "The Mean Between Two Extremes," "Oneness of Mind," "The All," "Perfection," "Friendship," and "Purpose." The Triad is also called "Knowledge" or gnosis, because it is through the principle of knowledge that subject and object, knower and known, are brought together, reflecting a higher unity.

It is possible to illustrate these basic Pythagorean ideas and relations in geometric form, as indeed the ancients would have done (*figure 11*):

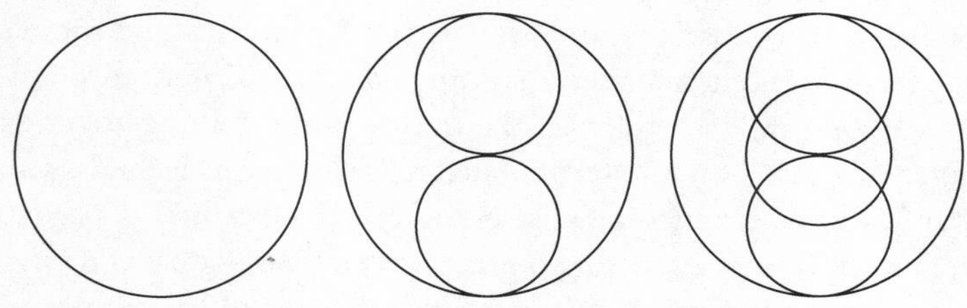

Figure 11. Unity, Duality, and Harmony

In this illustration, we can see that the Triad not only binds together the Two, but also, in the process, centrally reflects the nature of the One in a "microcosmic" and balanced fashion. Moving from unity, to duality, we arrive at a subsequent unification of duality, which results in a dynamic, differentiated image of the One in three parts: a continuum of beginning, middle and end; or of two extreme terms bound together, in *harmonia*, with a mean term.

Interestingly, this Pythagorean picture of the emergence of harmony from an initial unity reflects a common pattern in ancient Greek cosmology. As F. M. Cornford, the great scholar of Greek philosophy, has observed:

> The abstract formula which is common to the early cosmogonies is as follows: (1) There is an undifferentiated unity. (2) From this unity two opposite powers are separated out to form the world order. (3) The two opposites unite again to generate life.[25]

Indeed, one of the most widespread cosmological ideas at the beginning of the common era, entertained by both pagan and Christian philosophers alike, is that humanity represents the living harmony and synthesis of all the forces which make up the cosmos. A child of earth and heaven, humanity is the living bridge between matter and spirit, a living, harmonic image of the entire universe. As Clement of Alexandria says, man, composed of body and soul, is "a universe in miniature," an image of "the Celestial Logos," itself "the all-harmonious, melodious, holy instrument of God."[26]

In this passage, Clement brings together several closely related topics in Pythagorean cosmology: the function of the Logos, the place of humanity in the cosmos, and the nature of musical harmony. In Pythagorean thought, a state of harmony is achieved only through the power of *logos*, ratio or relation. Harmony is the joining together of extremes through a middle term. This middle term, as we have seen in chapter 3, was personified in a cosmological sense as the Logos, and its emblem is the Sun, the meeting point between the spiritual and physical orders of existence. Humanity, as the living image of the Logos, is the microcosm, the harmonic blueprint of the universe reflected in miniature. These Pythagorean ideas were taken over by the first Christian intellectuals and formed the basis of the earliest Christian cosmology: Jesus, as the Logos, was conceived of as a cosmological agent; not only is he the Logos, the cosmic pattern behind creation, but the Logos is also the mean between extremes—the divine mediator between heaven and earth, between transcendent God and incarnate humanity.

Apollo, the God of Harmony

> Now to Delphi I come, where
> Apollo, enthroned on earth's mid-navel
> over all the world,
> weaves in eternal song
> all that is and what shall be.
>
> —Euripides, *Ion* 5–7

In earlier Greek theology, the Logos was personified in the shining figure of Apollo, the god of light, music, geometry, and harmony, whose nature most closely reflects the highest realizations of the Greek spirit. (*Figure 12.*) As the god of harmony, he is said to have invented all music.[27]

Apollo was the god of reason (*logos*), yet he was also a god of prophecy. He is a personification of the celestial harmony, which is reflected in his favorite instrument and emblem, the Greek lyre: according to Plutarch, Apollo carries the lyre because "no work is so like that of the gods as concord (*harmonia*) and consonance (*symphonia*)."[28] He was the leader of the nine Muses, the goddesses of inspiration and the arts, who delight in their bright dancing places, spinning about the peak of the cosmic mountain.[29]

Apollo was worshipped at many sites and his spirit of divine harmony was invoked on many occasions, but his most famous seat of worship was at the Greek town of Delphi, located on the flank of Mount Parnassus, itself a favorite haunt of the Muses.[30] Poised beneath the craggy peaks above, known as the Shining Ones, and the olive-lined valley below, Apollo's temple at Delphi was the national sanctuary of the Greeks, situated at the very center of the world. According to legend, Zeus released a couple of eagles from the two ends of the earth. Flying toward the center of the world, they met at Delphi, the exact spot being marked by the *omphalos* (*umbilicus* or "navel") stone, located inside the temple of Apollo, which marked the navel of the earth. The omphalos stone, Apollo's sacred seat, is commonly represented on coins, vase paintings, and reliefs. (*Figure 13.*) It is oftentimes shown covered by an unusual net-like pattern, while in other instances it is shown with the twin eagles of Zeus perched on either side. While the actual omphalos was inside the temple, hidden away from public view, a replica was placed outside for the

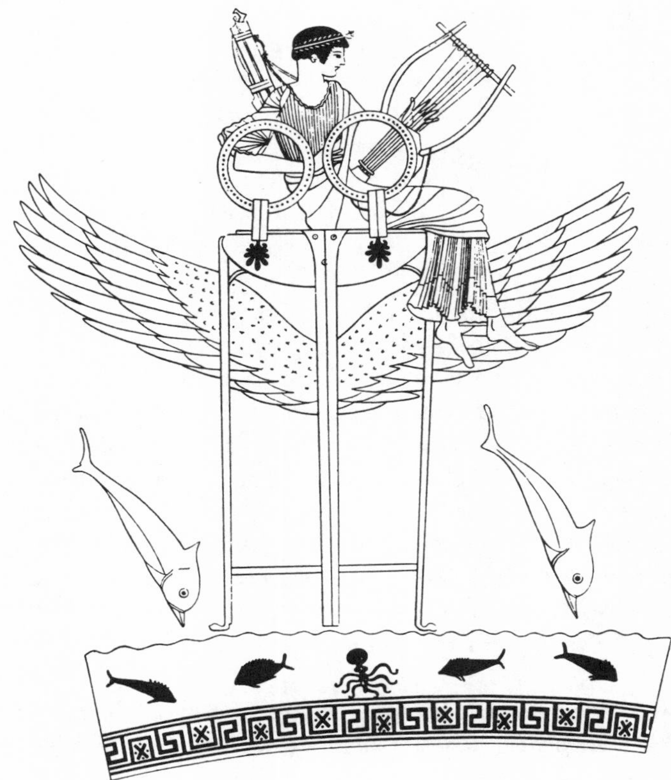

Figure 12. Apollo, the God of Harmony

Apollo, the Greek god of light and harmony, was associated with musical and mathematical symbolism in ancient cosmology. In the fanciful illustration above, he is shown seated with his lyre and quiver upon a winged mantic tripod, representing the sacred Tripod at Delphi. According to A. B. Cook, "The tripod itself, for those that know its history, is tantamount to a celestial seat. The god seated upon it is for the time being in heaven, released from the limitations of terrestrial life and free to range in thought over land and sea." Here, the diving dolphins identify him as *Apollôn Delphinios*.

Apollo was a god of sea-farers and fishermen. As a number of old writers have recorded, some of Apollo's temple precincts contained decorative fish ponds. The fishes would leap to the surface of the water when music was played, for that signalled their feeding time.

Figure 13. Apollo Seated on the Omphalos

This coin, issued in the time of Antiochus (246–227 B.C.E.), shows Far-Shooting Apollo with his silver bow, seated upon the net-covered omphalos stone at Delphi.

benefit of pilgrims and tourists, which can now be viewed in the Delphi Museum.

As the center of the universe, and the meeting place between heaven and earth, Delphi is naturally associated with the principle of regeneration and the renewal of time. This is most clearly seen in the story of Deukalion, "the Greek Noah." In a remarkable myth, which strongly parallels the Old Testament account, Zeus became angered at humanity because of its iniquities, and decided to destroy the men of the Bronze Age. By the advice of Prometheus, Deukalion constructed an ark, which he embarked upon with Pyrrah, his wife. Zeus unleashed a terrible rain which flooded and destroyed the population of Greece. Floating in the ark for nine days and nights, the pair drifted to Mount Parnassus, where the boat landed. After offering sacrifice to Zeus, Deukalion and Pyrrah were bid by the god to toss rocks, "the bones of Mother Earth," over their shoulders. These became men and women respectively, thus ushering in a new generation of humanity, a renewed cycle of civilization following an evil and decadent age.[31]

Delphi was also known as Pytho, because, before the coming of Apollo, the site was haunted by a monstrous serpent or dragon, the Python. In the Homeric *Hymn to Apollo*, the story is told of how Apollo came to Delphi, like a medieval dragon slayer, and vanquished the serpent from the land.

Apollo impaled the Python with his arrows, a deed which was to later influence the symbolism of the Christian saints, Michael and George. To commemorate the slaying of the Python, or simply because of his relation to the site, Apollo was also known as *Pythios* (sometimes spelt *Pytios*[32]), or in the more complete form as Apollo Pythios.

Apollo's temple was the site of the Delphic oracle, famed throughout the ancient world. Seated on his sacred Tripod, Apollo's priestess, the Pythia, would deliver oracles of the god under the influence of divine inspiration, after completing preparatory rituals of purification and drinking from the sacred spring. These oracles, often relating to matters of state and the foundation of Greek colonies, were put into hexameter verse, presumably by the priests. According to Plutarch, a priest of Apollo at Delphi around the time of Jesus, it was beneath the dignity of the god to speak directly through the priestess, for "the voice is not that of a god, nor the utterance of it, nor the diction, nor the metre, but all these are the woman's; he puts into her mind only the visions, and creates a light in her soul in regard to the future; for inspiration is precisely this."[33]

How it was that Apollo came to Delphi remains a mystery. Scholars realize that the site was previously an oracle, sacred to the Earth or some other goddess. According to a Homeric Hymn, Apollo was born on the sacred island of Delos, and after establishing his temple at Delphi, was in need of some priests to attend to it. Transforming himself into a dolphin (*delphis*), he overtook a shipload of Cretan sailors, leading them on to Delphi, where they became his first servants and attendants.[34] By another account, Apollo's temple at Delphi was founded by individuals from Hyperborea, a mythical land beyond the North Wind, sometimes identified with the British Isles and a host of other sites. According to Pausanius and other Greek writers, among these Hyperboreans was *Ôlên*, an ancient bard who lived even before the time of Orpheus. Olen was Apollo's first prophet, the first to sing the oracles of the god at Delphi in hexameter verse.[35]

As the god of harmony, Apollo is the personification of "the golden mean." Hence, his temple at Delphi carried the famous inscription which read "Avoid extremes" or "Nothing to excess," an exhortation to moderation, to follow the middle path; the temple also bore the god's primary commandment, "Know thyself."[36] He was known as the Healer, and as the god of light and piercing clarity, Apollo was depicted as an archer. In this capacity, he was known as the Far-Shooter and "He who Works from Afar."[37]

While it might be possible to elaborate Apollo's nature and deeds in endless fashion, we are here mainly interested in his cosmological symbolism and how it relates to the Greek ideas of *logos* and harmony. Toward this end, we will need to explore the realm of ancient mathematics, the principles of geometry, music, and harmony.

Apollo and Mathematical Symbolism

As we have noted, Apollo figures in the form of Pythagorean number symbolism known as arithmology, in which simple numbers between one and ten are related to various principles and divinities.[38] Both Plutarch and Plotinus connect Apollo with the symbolism of the divine Monad, the source of the cosmos, through the etymology of his name *A-pollôn*, which means "unity," or literally "not many."[39] And as A. B. Cook suggests in his study *Zeus*, Delphi, "As the veritable earth-centre . . . furnished the starting-point of later arithmology. In the mystic language of the Pythagoreans, who are known to have been deeply interested in Delphoi, the 'axle,' the 'tower of Zan [Zeus],' and 'Apollon' were all synonymous descriptions of the monad."[40]

Regarding the Pythagorean interest in Delphi or Pytho, ancient commentators link the name of Pythagoras himself with the place. Pythagoras' birth was predicted by the Delphic oracle, and, according to Aristippus of Cyrene, Pythagoras derived his name from his speaking (*agoreuein*) truth no less than *Pythios*, Apollo at Delphi.[41]

On another count, Apollo was associated with the number seven.[42] He was born on the seventh day[43] of the Greek month Bysios, the day on which his festivals were held. His lyre had seven strings, each one of which was associated with one of the seven planets[44]—the Pythagorean "music of the spheres"—and the seven vowels of the Greek alphabet.[45] The number seven is also related to Apollo's omphalos at Delphi, for the seventh "direction" represents the sacred center, after up, down, north, south, east, and west.[46]

A further suggestion that Apollo is associated with geometrical symbolism is his relationship with one of the three great problems of Greek mathematics, the so-called doubling of the cube.[47]

According to the account preserved by the ancient Greek scientist

Eratosthenes, who accurately measured the dimensions of the Earth, a plague had befallen the citizens of Delos, the island where Apollo was born. The oracle of Apollo was consulted, in the hope that a solution for the malady would be found. The response was that the situation would resolve itself if the Delians would simply construct a cubic altar exactly twice the volume of the existing one.[48] However, the Delian craftsmen were confounded by the problem, which is far more complex than it initially seems; "they therefore went to ask Plato about it, and he replied that the oracle meant, not that the god wanted an altar of double the size, but that he wished, in setting them the task, to shame the Greeks for their neglect of mathematics and their contempt for geometry."[49]

This is just the type of response one might expect from Plato, who is said to have held that "God geometrizes always"![50] Plato himself, however, was no stranger to Delphic lore and tradition; popular legend even held that he was a son of Apollo. In the *Laws* Plato writes that "no man of sense—whether he be framing a new State or re-forming an old one that has been corrupted—will attempt to alter the advice from Delphi" relating to religious concerns.[51] Likewise, in the *Republic*, after the structure of the ideal state has been articulated, all matters of religious importance and custom are left for Apollo at Delphi to decide, "who from his seat in the middle and at the very navel of the earth delivers his interpretation."[52]

According to Plutarch, however, there was another important reason why Apollo exhorted the Greeks to "double the cube," and hence study geometry. Namely, "he was ordering the entire Greek nation to give up war and its miseries and cultivate the Muses, and by calming their passions through the practice of discussion and study of mathematics, so to live with one another that their intercourse should be not injurious, but profitable."[53]

The "Geometrical Equality" of the Gods

> Pythagoras, therefore, in *The Sacred Discourse*, clearly says that "number is the ruler of forms and ideas, and is the cause of gods and intelligences." He also supposes, that "to the most ancient and artificially ruling deity, number is the canon, the artificial reason (*logos technikos*), the intellect also, and the most undeviating balance of the composition and generation of all things."
>
> —Syrianus in his *Commentary on the Metaphysics of Aristotle*

As we have seen, *harmonia* represents the fitting together of extremes via the principle of *logos* or proportion.

While there are several types of proportion, according to the Pythagoreans the most perfect form is continued geometrical proportion, because each term in the proportion is related to the next term through the same, continuous ratio.[54] As Plato notes in the *Timaeus*,

> two things alone cannot be satisfactorily united without a third; for there must be some bond between them drawing them together. And of all bonds the best is that which makes itself and the terms it connects a unity in the fullest sense; and it is of the nature of a continued geometrical proportion to effect this most perfectly.[55]

For example, in the proportion A:B:C, A is to B in exactly the same ratio as B is to C. In this proportion, the middle term B is the so-called Geometric Mean, the point of mediation between A and C. The mathematical formula for finding the Geometric Mean between any two numbers is a simple one: take the two extremes, multiply them together, and find their square root.

Thus, in the continued geometrical proportion

$$A:B:C$$

the Geometric Mean is B, because

$$B = \sqrt{A \text{x} C}$$

To use a specific example, the Geometric Mean between 1 and 3 is $\sqrt{3}$, because

$$\sqrt{3} = \sqrt{1 \times 3}$$

and the resulting continuous proportion is $1:\sqrt{3}:3$.

$\sqrt{3}$ is an irrational number, approximately 1.7320508... in decimal form, which, like the nature of God, love, beauty, and other important things in the universe, can never be precisely defined. Despite the fact that $\sqrt{3}$ can never be *exactly* defined either as a whole number fraction or in decimal form, it is, nonetheless, one of the most important mathematical constants in natural geometry, for it is the essential pattern of relation embodied in the perfect equilateral triangle (*figure 14*):

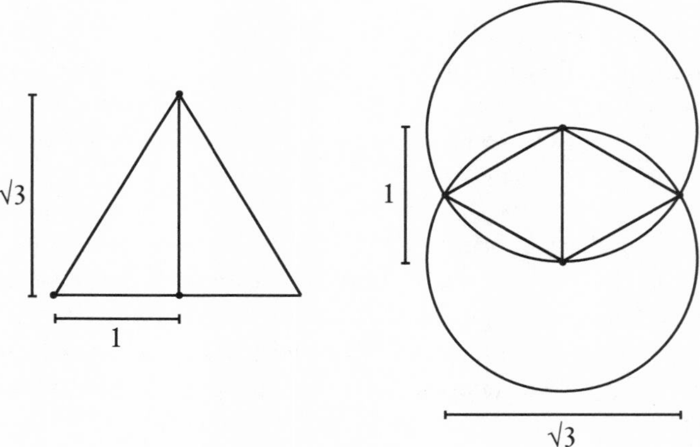

Figure 14. √3, the Ratio of the Equilateral Triangle

The "irrational" value of root three ($\sqrt{3} = 1.7320508...$) is the controlling ratio of the perfect equilateral triangle. On the left we see that an equilaterial triangle with a half-base of 1 has a height of $\sqrt{3}$. Therefore, as is shown on the right, a rhombus with a width of 1 has a length of $\sqrt{3}$. Geometrically, both triangle and rhombus emerge from the *vesica piscis*, the "fish" shape described by two perfectly interpenetrating circles of the same size.

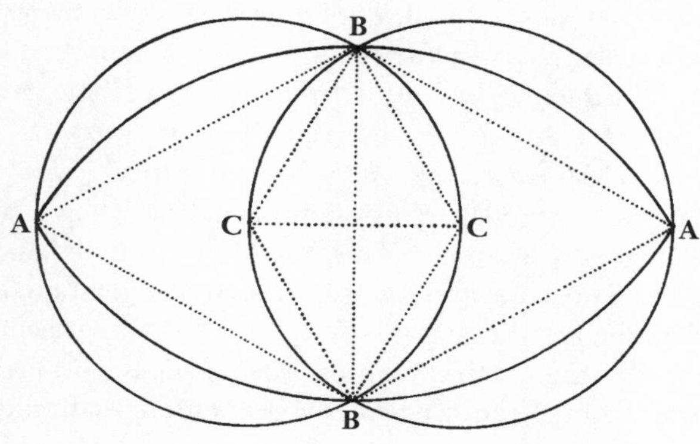

Actual Value • Gematria Value
AA = 1061 • 1061 = APOLLO
BB = 612.568 • 612 = ZEUS
CC = 353.666 • 353 = HERMES

Figure 15. The "Geometrical Equality" of the Gods

William Stirling, in his book *The Canon*, observed that the number values of APOLLO, ZEUS, and HERMES precisely relate to one another through the ratio of $\sqrt{3}$. This is shown above, with the exact mathematical values, taking 1061, the number of Apollo, as the starting point.

In 1897 a British writer, William Stirling, published an important book, the first ever study of Greek gematria written in modern times. It was entitled *The Canon: An Exposition of the Pagan Mystery Perpetuated in the Cabala as the Rule of All the Arts*. The argument of the book is that gematria constitutes a symbolic, pre-Christian language of ancient theology and symbolic cosmology, the immutable standard or canon on which ancient culture was based. This numerical canon of harmonies was a universal synthesis of ancient learning, the most important key to the knowledge of antiquity; it was maintained by the priests and formed the ultimate basis for the arts and sciences, including the art and science of initiation. However, because the nature of the canon was esoteric, one could employ it, and even vaguely allude to it in print, but was forbidden to explicitly reveal its secrets to the profane.

While the main thesis is sound, *The Canon* is flawed in many places by extravagant speculation. Nonetheless, it remains an important work, for Stirling did reveal the key which leads to the recovery of the ancient Greek science of gematria. As Stirling observed, *the primary numbers of Greek gematria relate to one another through the ratios of natural geometry.*

The most important and startling example which Stirling relates is the fact that the numbers of Apollo, Zeus, and Hermes are linked together through $\sqrt{3}$, the ratio of the *vesica piscis* and the equilateral triangle, shown in *figure 15* on the previous page.

In other words, the number values of Apollo, Zeus, and Hermes are linked together through the principle of *logos* or ratio, specifically through continued geometrical proportion.[56]

Stirling's discovery of the relationship between Apollo, Zeus, and Hermes is important. But if he had a deeper background in the study of Pythagorean science and mathematics, he would have stressed two things, which he does not:

1) The significance of this relationship is that the names of the divinities are not united through just *any* ratio, but through $\sqrt{3}$. This particular ratio, which is reflected in the geometrical division of space and the structure of living things, is one of the First Principles in a Pythagorean sense, as the gods are held to be in symbolic cosmology.

2) Another way of looking at the above relationship, from a slightly different perspective, is that Zeus is the Geometric Mean between Hermes and Apollo. This may be expressed mathematically as follows, which the reader is encouraged to verify:

$$\text{Zeus} = \sqrt{\text{Hermes x Apollo}}$$

or

$$612 = \sqrt{353 \text{ x } 1061}$$

Significantly, this arrangement relates to both the ancient Greek theories of Irrationals and Means, two subjects which were of particular interest to the Pythagoreans.[57]

While Stirling did not express these important observations, his work laid the foundation for modern gematria studies and went far toward verifying the statement of Plato that "geometrical equality prevails widely among both gods and men." Plato's complete passage, which is a reference to the nature of the canon, is as follows:

> And the wise men say that one community embraces heaven and earth and gods and men and friendship and order and temperance and righteousness, and for that reason they call this whole a *kosmos*, my friend, for it is not without order nor yet is there excess. It seems to me that you do not pay attention to these things, though you are wise in regard to them. But it has escaped your notice that geometrical equality prevails widely among both gods and men.[58]

A Little History of Divine Names

How it was that the names of the gods came to be correlated with specific, symbolic numbers will always remain something of a mystery. According to the *Excerpts of Theodotus*, an early Christian gnostic writing, "Pythagoras thought that he who gave things their names, ought to be regarded not only the most intelligent, but the oldest of the wise men."[59] Plato, writing about the Egyptian canon of music and proportion which maintained the stability of that civilization for thousands of years, concludes that the canon "must have been the doing of a god, or godlike being."[60]

The remarkable canon of Greek gematria presupposes that the names of the major divinities and mythological figures were *consciously codified* in relation to the natural ratios of geometry to equal specific numerical values. While this notion may initially strike the reader as unlikely, since we have nothing like it today, there is a good deal of historical evidence to support this contention. The name of the gnostic solar divinity Abraxas may ultimately be based upon a Hebrew word, but when "translated" into Greek it was certainly designed to equal 365, the number of days in a solar year.[61] Mithras, in its most common spelling equals 360, which was the value of a year in some places, but several old writers purposefully add an extra "e" to make it total 365, the more accurate reckoning of the solar year. Likewise, the name of every single one of the Hebrew planetary spirits and intelligences was consciously formulated, by someone, to bring out the precise number from the appropriate "magic square."

Like Plato's report on the Egyptian canon of proportion, according to the unanimous account of the ancients, the names of the divinities were revealed to humanity by some god, or godlike being. Iamblichus, the Neoplatonist, observes in his book *On the Mysteries* that in those names of the gods "which we can scientifically analyze, we possess a knowledge of the whole divine essence, power, and order comprehended in the name."[62] Moreover,

> we ought to think it necessary that our conference with the gods should be in a language allied with them. Because, likewise, such a mode of speech is the first and most ancient. And especially because those who first learned the names of the gods, having mingled them with their own proper tongue, delivered them to us, that we might always preserve immoveable the sacred law of tradition, in a language peculiar and adapted to them. For if any other thing pertains to the gods, it is evident that the eternal and immutable must be allied to them.[63]

Orpheus, the mythical founder of the Greek mysteries, the founder of initiations, is said to have invented the alphabet. According to Athenagoras, one of the first Christian writers, Orpheus "was the first to give the gods names."[64] There was an Orphic *Hymn to Number*, and the Pythagorean school was firmly rooted in the Orphic tradition.[65] Syrianus, in his commentary on Aristotle's *Metaphysics*, writes that "the Pythagoreans received from the theology of Orpheus, the principles of intelligible and intellectual numbers."[66] Moreover, a fragment from an ancient Orphic writing states that "Orpheus, the son of [the Muse] Calliope, having learned wisdom from his mother in the mountain Pangaeus, said that the eternal essence of Number is the most providential principle of the universe, of heaven and earth, and the intermediate nature; and further still, that it is the root of permanency of divine natures, of gods and divinities."[67] From this, Iamblichus concludes that Pythagoras "learned from the Orphic writers that the essence of the gods is defined by Number."[68]

If we look at this problem in its historical context, it is easy to see how the names of the Greek divinities were codified to reflect specific numbers. Everyone can agree that before the development of writing the names of the gods were surely employed. However, they were pronounced differently in different parts of the Greek world; even in classical times, the names of the divinities were spelled somewhat differently in the various Greek dialects. Most often, the differences are in the vowel sounds, which could be expressed in a variety of ways, thus altering the numerical value of the word. Since there were many different ways to potentially spell any word, *someone* had to decide the most appropriate form a divine name should take. Presumably, that important task was left to the learned; they had a stake in the matter at hand, being interested in matters of sacred concern. They were the priests, the poets, the followers of Orpheus. They may have even been Pythagoreans.

While the last statement may seem startling, it is important to remember that the Greek alphabet was in a state of flux until comparatively "late" times. The existence of the number canon is reflected in the codified spellings of Attic Greek, the Greek of classical Athens. But the Athenians did not officially adopt the Ionian alphabet until 403 B.C.E., during the time of Plato.[69] Given the historical facts, it is quite likely that the fully developed gematria we see, for example, in the name of Apollo was actually formulated under the influence of the Pythagorean league, whose main school was attacked by Cylon around 500 B.C.E. The Greek poet Simonides (556–467 B.C.E.), whose life overlaps that of Pythagoras, is said to have introduced the letters *Epsilon* (E), *Eta* (H), *Upsilon* (Υ), and *Omega* (Ω) into the Attic Greek alphabet.[70] If this widely repeated tradition is historically accurate, as it seems to be, the names *Apollo*, *Zeus*, and *Hermes* could not have previously offered up the cosmic numbers which they now do, for each divine name contains one or more of the "new vowels." Simonides, who also introduced the so-called "art of memory," was a devotee of Dionysus, suggesting an Orphic affiliation. While the matter is incapable of proof, Simonides himself, under the influence of the original Pythagorean school, may have had a hand in codifying the names of the ancient Greek divinities in terms of their official, canonical spellings.

The Recovery of the Canon

As we have observed, it was William Stirling in 1897 who first demonstrated in modern times that the names of the Greek divinities relate to one another through the primary ratios of geometry, thus confirming the statement of Plato that "geometrical equality prevails widely among both gods and men."

The next major contribution to the recovery of the Canon stems from the work of the architect Bligh Bond and Dr. Simcox Lea, a Christian divine. These two scholars possessed a mystical bent and were widely read in the esoteric writings of antiquity, including the available gnostic gospels and the early patristic literature. In 1917 they published a remarkable volume, with an equally remarkable subtitle. It was called:

GEMATRIA

A Preliminary Investigation of The Cabala
contained in the
Coptic Gnostic Books
and of a similar Gematria in the Greek
text of the New Testament

SHOWING THE PRESENCE OF A SYSTEM OF TEACHING BY MEANS OF THE DOCTRINAL SIGNIFICANCE OF NUMBERS, BY WHICH THE HOLY NAMES ARE CLEARLY SEEN TO REPRESENT AEONIAL RELATIONSHIPS WHICH CAN BE CONCEIVED IN A GEOMETRIC SENSE AND ARE CAPABLE OF A TYPICAL EXPRESSION OF THAT ORDER.

This volume is based partly on a study of two late gnostic gospels, *Pistis Sophia* and *The Books of Ieou*, which contain the post-resurrection teachings of Jesus, "the Living One," that is, the omnipresent Universal Logos. Their book, *Gematria*, represents a fundamental breakthrough, for Bligh Bond rediscovered a central key of the ancient number canon. As an architect and practicing geometer, Bond knew only too well that the primary Root Ratios such as √2 and √3 underlie the genesis of form in the natural world. In a Platonic sense, these primary "root *logoi*" are the sources of order in three-dimensional space yet, like the perfect Circle, do not have their existence in space or time. The early gnostics, in their elaborate cosmological myths, refered to such first principles as *Aeons* or "Eternities," which are contained in the *Plêrôma*, the "Fullness" or Treasury of Light. The material cosmos, which exists at a lower level of manifestation, is an emanation of the Aeons in the Pleroma. In his study of the esoteric gnostic books, Bligh Bond saw that they contained a numerical symbolism, based on the "aeonial" root ratios of geometry. From this relationship, Bligh Bond concluded that Greek gematria is an expression of the eternal, aeonial relationships of a higher, extra-spatial order. As he states succinctly, "The Formative principles expressed by the mathematical powers One, Root Two, and Root Three, are assumed as the Aeons whose operation has been invoked to bring into manifestation the visible Universe. These may be said to determine the form of the Regular [Platonic] Solids and are hence fundamental."[71] He then gives an example:

> Taking as a plastic unit the 600 of κοσμος [COSMOS], we discover in the Gematria of the Macrocosm and the Microcosm the following very perfect example of this mode of interpretation.

To illustrate his point, Bond gives the following example of related terms, linked together in the progression of 1, √2, √3:

1)	600 x 1 = 600	ΚΟΣΜΟΣ = COSMOS
2)	600 x √2 = 849	ΜΕΓΑΣ ΚΟΣΜΟΣ = MACROCOSM
3)	600 x √3 = 1040	ΜΙΚΡΟΣ ΚΟΣΜΟΣ = MICROCOSM

Both the *Pistis Sophia* and the *Books of Ieou* touch upon the so-called First and Last Mysteries, associated with the letters Α and Ω. According to *Pistis Sophia* and *Ieou*, Jesus has come to reveal these Mysteries to his disciples, and all the other Mysteries of the Treasury of Light as well. As Bond realized, these Mysteries are related to the nature of the "higher space" which is reflected in geometrical forming principles. For example, Bond and Lea point out that the FIRST MYSTERY to which Jesus refers has, in Greek, the gematria value of 1179 (Α ΜΥΣΤΗΡΙΟΝ) while the Last Mystery, OMEGA ('ΩΜΕΓΑ) is 849. These numbers are fractions of the primary root ratios, reciprocals of one another, and are related to the volumes of the Platonic solids as is shown on the next page in *figure 16*.

Unfortunately, Bond and Lee expressed their work in such a way that only a very small group of people would ever be able to grasp their most profound discoveries. They often give untranslated Greek and don't explain the significance of many formulas, leaving it for the reader to decipher the significance. There must have been a reason for this: they felt that their work was preliminary and that it was important for others to study these relationships, to experience the realities they had discovered

	 Tetrahedron	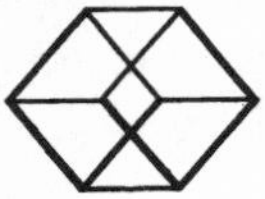 Cube
	A (α) **ALPHA**	Ω (ω) **OMEGA**
Side Length	1.00	1.00
Volume	.1179	1.00

At the same relative proportion:

Volume	1.00	8.49

By gematria

1 = A — 849 = OMEGA; MACROCOSM

1179 = FIRST MYSTERY

Figure 16. The First and Last Mysteries

By gematria, FIRST MYSTERY (A ΜΥΣΤΗΡΙΟΝ) is 1179, while OMEGA (ΏΜΕΓΑ), the Last Mystery, is 849. Together, the First and the Last represent the extreme poles of creation which are reconciled through the power of Logos.

Mathematically, these numbers are related to the primary root ratios, for FIRST MYSTERY, .1179, is 1/12 √2, and 8.49, OMEGA, is the reciprocal of this value.

In the Platonic tradition, the four elements of Greek cosmology—earth, water, air and fire—are correlated with the regular polyhedra, the so-called Platonic solids. The most elemental Platonic solid, the tetrahedron, is the first three-dimensional form and, appropriately enough, is associated with the element of fire or light. If a tetrahedron has a side length of 1.00, then it will have a volume of .1179 cubic units, equivalent to the First Mystery. A Cube, representing earth, with the same edge length will have a cubic volume of 1.00.

However, if the tetrahedron is made to have a volume of 1.00 at the same scale, then the cube will have a volume of 8.49, the value of OMEGA, the Last Mystery. In addition, these two polyhedra, representing the poles of the elemental continuum, also display the forms of the primitive Greek letters Alpha and Omega. (Adapted from Bond and Lea, *Gematria*.)

first-hand, through an investigation of Greek, the gnostic books, and the ratios of fundamental geometry. Given also the highly mystical orientation of their work, it was impossible that their important study would ever be accessible to a larger audience, and that is obviously what they wished. Perhaps they felt that not everyone is prepared for the realization that the early Christian writings were based in part upon a numerical code, inherited from earlier times.

Bligh Bond's most important realization is that certain gematria numbers themselves represent quantified values of the root ratios which exist at the timeless heart of creation. The interpretation of these ratios may be developed in a mystical direction or a scientific, cosmological direction, or in both directions. Both lines of interpretation were followed in antiquity, and Bligh Bond was more sympathetic to the mystical dimension. Whatever way one wishes to go, however, it will be found that certain gematria numbers are based upon the archetypal *logoi*, ratios, or "Aeons" which underlie the structure of the manifest universe. Bligh Bond was probably led to this momentous recognition because he was an architect and was familiar with the decimal expressions of the root ratios from his mathematical tables. Their book *Gematria* was followed by two other volumes, *Materials for the Study of the Apostolic Gnosis*, parts I and II, which also contain some valuable material.

The next great contribution to the study of the number canon was recorded by that modern doctor of Pythagorean studies, John Michell, in his remarkable study of Greek and gnostic gematria, *City of Revelation*, published in 1972. In particular, John Michell made a great breakthrough, in that he discovered how the miraculous story of the "153 fishes in the unbroken net" (John 21) is definitively based upon an underlying and unfolding geometrical diagram. Earlier writers had noted that the Greek words FISHES and THE NET, which appear in the New Testament tale, both amount to 1224, and that 153 is exactly 1/8 of this amount. In other words, the number of the 153 "Fishes" in "The Net" is in no way arbitrary, but is based on gematria. But John Michell was the first to show how this story was intentionally constructed upon an underlying geometry. His analysis of this is reproduced in Appendix 1, followed by my commentary which shows how the geometry and values relate to the earlier symbolism of Apollo at Delphi.

Drawing upon the findings of these earlier researchers, I have been enabled to make some extensive, additional inroads into the recovery of the ancient Greek canon of number, leading to the central realization that the key numbers of Greek gematria are not arbitrary, but represent the codified values of the primary ratios which underlie different classes of phenomena and the genesis of form. As such, the central gematria numbers represent the key aspects of the Universal Logos, envisioned as the source of ideal harmony and the principle of mediation between extremes.

While the early Christians saw the Logos personified in the figure of Jesus, the earlier Greeks personified the Logos in the figures of Apollo and Hermes. As we have seen, Apollo is the god of music, geometry, and harmony, all of which depend upon the ratios of *logos*. Apollo's shrine at Delphi was the center of the universe, the meeting place between heaven and earth, spirit and matter. As the personification of the "golden mean," Apollo's temple was inscribed with the gnomic utterance "Avoid extremes," while as the instrument of the god of music, Apollo's lyre symbolizes the *harmonia* or "fitting together" of the universe. As the Pythagoreans showed, this *harmonia* is achieved through the power of *logos* or proportion, the formal expression of which is the musical scale.

The other Greek personification of the Logos is Apollo's little brother, Hermes. Hermes was actually called "the Logos" by the Greeks and his identification with Thoth, the Egyptian personification of the Logos, is well known. Hermes was the inventor of the lyre, which he gave to Apollo.

According to the Pythagoreans, the polarities of existence are represented by the numbers One and Two, symbolizing Unity and Multiplicity respectively. Therefore, the ideal Logos of Mediation between these extremes is $\sqrt{2}$, the Geometric Mean, which unites the extremes together into one continuous proportion and represents the ideal harmony of the universe. That is why the names of Apollo and Hermes, the Logos personified, were derived from this central value, as is shown facing in *figure 17*. (See also "Apollo: The First 'Word' of Celestial Harmony.")

Not only is this symbolism fully in accord with the teachings of Pythagorean cosmology, but these numerical values possess many unique "magical powers," befitting the divinities in question. These are summarized in *figure 18*. For example, THE GOD APOLLO (1.415) and THE GOD

	Exact value	Greek Gematria
$\sqrt{2} \times \frac{1}{1} \times 1000 =$	1414.2136	1415 = THE GOD APOLLO
		1414 = THE GOD PYTIOS
$\sqrt{2} \times \frac{3}{4} \times 1000 =$	1060.6602	1061 = APOLLO
		1060 = PYTIOS
$\sqrt{2} \times \frac{1}{2} \times 1000 =$	707.1067	707 = THE GOD HERMES
$\sqrt{2} \times \frac{1}{4} \times 1000 =$	353.5533	354 = THE GOD
		353 = HERMES

Figure 17. Root Two and the Titles of the Pagan Logos

By dividing √2 into four parts, we arrive at a simple arithmetic progression which defines the following names and titles: HERMES, THE GOD HERMES, APOLLO, and THE GOD APOLLO. Where gematria values are based on mathematical ratios, the "decimal point" has been moved over three places; this is indicated above by multiplying √2 by 1000.

HERMES (.707) are reciprocals of one another (1.415 x .707 = 1), underscoring the fact that they are "brothers" of one another in Greek mythology. Interestingly, we can see from this material that we are not dealing with concrete "numbers" as much as we are dealing with *functions* or *powers*, which is how the nature of the gods was envisioned by the learned minds of old.

From these central values of Hermes and Apollo, which represent aspects of the ideal Logos, many of the other key gematria values are mathematically derived. Several of these are listed in *figure 19*. Other gematria values were derived from the ratios of music or other important

Some Unique Properties of $\sqrt{2}$

$\sqrt{2}$ is the one unique number in the universe where

$$A \times \frac{1}{2}A = 1$$

thus

1.414 x .707 = 1

The God Apollo x The God Hermes = 1

$\frac{1}{2}\sqrt{2}$ is the one unique number in the universe where

$$A^3 = \frac{1}{2}A$$

thus

$.707^3 = .353$

The God Hermes^3 = Hermes

$\sqrt{2}$ is also the one unique number with the following properties :

$$\sqrt{A}+1 \times \sqrt{A}-1 = 1$$

or: 2.414 x .414 = 1

$$\sqrt{A}+2 \times (\frac{1}{2}\sqrt{A} \times \sqrt{A}-1) = 1$$

or: 3.414 x (.707 x .414) = 1

In addition, all of these relationships may be represented geometrically.

Figure 18. Some Magical Properties of √2

Unity

1, 10, 100, 1000, etc. = THE MONAD, THE ONE, THE FIRST CAUSE

√2 Values

√2 = "The First Logos"

	Values	**Greek Gematria**
1 x √2 x 1000 =	1414.2	1415 = THE GOD APOLLO
1 x √2 x 1000 x .75 =	1060.6	1061 = APOLLO
1 x √2 x 1000 x .5 =	707.1	707 = THE GOD HERMES
1 x √2 x 1000 x . 25 =	353.5	353 = HERMES
		354 = THE GOD

√3 Values

A further differentiation of the original unity

1 x √2 x √3 x 1000 =	2449.4	2448 = FISHES + THE NET
1 x √2 x √3 x 1000 x .5 =	1224.7	1224 = FISHES, THE NET
1 x √2 x √3 x 1000 x .25 =	612.3	612 = ZEUS

π Values

1 x √2 x √3 x π x 100 =	769.5	769 = PYTHIOS, Apollo at Delphi
1000 ÷ π =	318.3	318 = HELIOS, the Sun

The Harmonic Ratios of Music

2/3 x 1000 =	666.6	666 = Prominent solar number
		(String ratio of perfect fifth)
8/9 x 1000 =	888.8	888 = JESUS, the Christian Logos
		888 = OLEN, founder of Apollo's oracle
		(String ratio of Pythagorean whole tone)

Figure 19. Natural Ratios at the Source of the Number Canon

Because the central values of the Greek number canon were derived from the most archetypal ratios, they possess many remarkable properties in relation to one another. While they were codified as whole numbers, none of these values symbolize regular numbers *per se*; rather, they represent *functions* or *logoi*, the ideal principles of universal relation. These values also symbolize a process of emanation whereby the Primal Unity passes through the "First Logos" and subsequent stages of harmonic differentiation.

geometrical forms. For example, HELIOS, 318, the Greek name of the Sun, is derived from the ratio of the circle, for the reciprocal of π is .318. In other words, a circle measuring 1000 units in circumference (representing Unity) will have a diameter of 318 units. In music, .666 is the string ratio of the perfect fifth, while .888 is the string ratio of the whole tone. The Greeks did not use the decimal point at all, and, in every instance where gematria values are based on mathematical ratios, the "decimal point" has been moved over exactly three places. In other words, while we define these ratios in relation to "1," we conclude that the Greeks defined these ratios in relation to "1000," which represents the same principle, the Monad or Unity, the ineffable First Cause.[72]

Since these mathematical principles are the fundamental *logoi* which underlie plane geometry, solid geometry (polyhedra), and musical tuning systems, the language of gematria makes perfect sense, both in terms of esoteric theology and scientific cosmology: the "gods" are the first principles which underlie the creation of the universe and multiple classes of phenomena. A sense of this can be gathered from the following examples, where these values relate to different classes of geometrical manifestation.

The Land of the Gods

• Earlier, we saw how in terms of plane geometry or *length*, Apollo, Zeus, and Hermes are linked together through the ratio of the *vesica piscis* ($\sqrt{3}$), and how Zeus was therefore the Geometric Mean between Apollo and Hermes. This can also be expressed in a different way, as shown facing. The ancient Greek philospher Thales proved in his famous theorem that a perpendicular raised in a semi-circle is the Geometric Mean between the base line segments on either side. As shown facing in *figure 20*, the perpendicular mediating between HERMES and APOLLO will measure 612, ZEUS, while the total measure of the base line is 1415, THE GOD APOLLO.

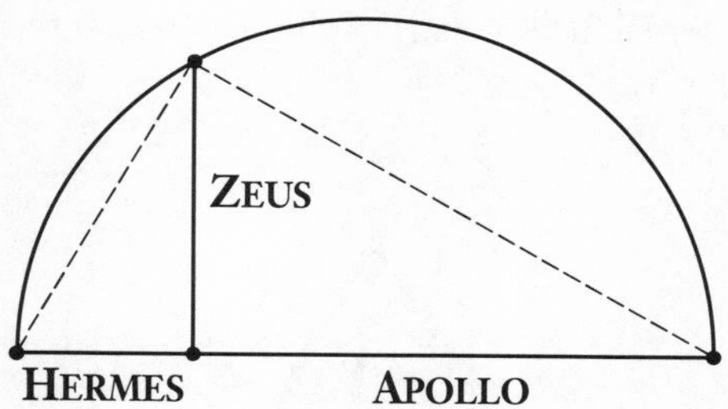

Figure 20. Greek Gematria and the Theorem of Thales

• In terms of *surface areas*, an octahedron built around three perfectly interpenetrating squares will have the following measures (*figure 21*):

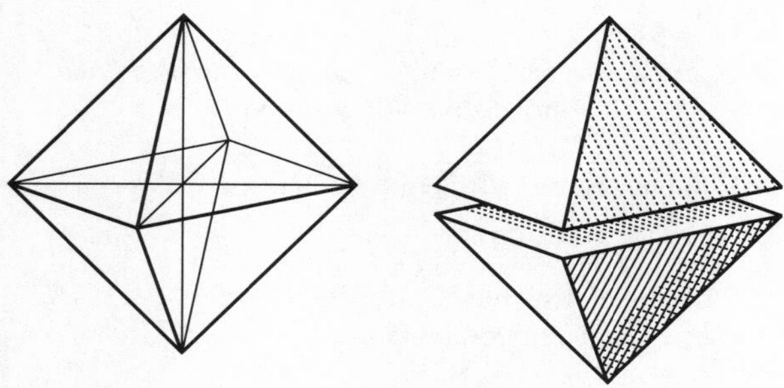

Figure 21. Greek Gematria: Surface Areas

Surface area of each internal square = 353, HERMES
Area of all three internal squares = 1061, APOLLO
Area of the four combined equilateral triangles, forming a pyramid over the square of 353 = 612, ZEUS
Total surface area of the octahedron = 1224, THE NET

• Finally, in terms of *lengths*, *surfaces* and *volumes*, a tetrahedron—the first three-dimensional form—with a volume of 612 cubic units will have the following measures (*figure 22*):

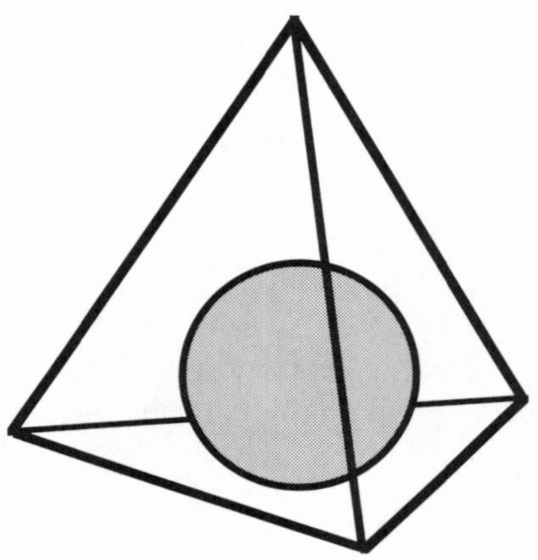

Figure 22. Greek Gematria: Length, Surface Area, and Volume Combined

Volume of tetrahedron in cubic units = 612, ZEUS

Insphere radius = 3.53, HERMES
Insphere diameter = 7.07, THE GOD HERMES
Volume of cube surrounding insphere = 353, HERMES

Intersphere radius = 6.12, ZEUS
Intersphere diameter = 12.24, FISHES; THE NET

Circumsphere radius =10.61, APOLLO
Circumsphere surface area = 1414/1415, THE GOD APOLLO

* The *insphere* is defined as a sphere which will fit within a polyhedron, perfectly touching the center of each face (shown above). The *circumsphere* is that sphere which will contain the entire polyhedron so that each vertex of the polyhedron precisely touches the boundary of the sphere. The *intersphere* exactly touches each mid-edge of the polyhedron.

Hence, the tetrahedron brings out the key canonical numbers in terms of cubic volume, surface area, and length *simultaneously*.[73] In Greek cosmology, it was appropriately associated with the element of fire or light and, as a natural design type, defined the structure of Apollo's mystical tripod at Delphi.

As we can see from the above examples, it is possible to express a law which applies to the ancient canon of number: as long as one employs the most archetypal forms of geometry, the specific form in which the gematria relationships are expressed is entirely "arbitrary." However, there is nothing arbitrary about the mathematics of Greek gematria, for it is based on the archetypal laws of geometry which underlie the genesis of form and harmonic manifestation.

The Harmony of Apollo: The Pythagorean Science of Harmonic Mediation

> [While] philosophers initiated in the mysteries of music . . . expounded some things in their writings, they reserved the more esoteric secrets for their discussions with one another. The reason lay in the enthusiastic affection of the men of those times for all that is finest. But now, when indifference to music (to put it politely) is so widespread, we cannot expect people with only a mild interest in the subject to tolerate being faced with a book in which not everything is explicitly spelled out.
>
> —Aristides Quintilianus, *On Music*

> The numbers to do with music are sacred and of perfect efficacy.
>
> —Aristides Quintilianus, *On Music*

In this concluding section we will see how the numbers of Greek gematria are related to the ratios of music in a very intimate way. In fact, the idea of a numerical canon is inherently related to the study of harmonics in Greek thought. While the Greek term *kanôn* means "a rule" or "standard" against which something else is measured, in Pythagorean thought it refers specifically to the monochord, or the template used to mark off the divisions of the harmonic intervals. That is why Euclid's work on harmonics is simply entitled *On the Division of the Canon* and why the study of tuning theory was also called "canonics."[74]

The goal of Pythagorean science was to explicate the universal principles of harmony which underlie the structure of the cosmos and formally mediate between ideal extremes.[75] While *harmonia* means a "fitting together," for the Pythagoreans it had a very specific meaning and referred, in particular, to the musical scale discovered by Pythagoras.[76] That is because the musical scale bridges the gap between the two extremes of the octave via Arithmetic, Harmonic, and Geometric Proportion.[77] The result is the diatonic scale, the basis of all musical expression in Western civilization. Interestingly, the ancient philosopher Proclus identified the three types of harmonic mediation with the three Horai, the daughters of Themis: the Arithmetic Mean is the image of *Eirênê* (Peace), the Harmonic Mean is the image of *Dikê* (Justice), the Geometric Mean is the image of *Eunomia* (Fair Order), and *Themis* (Law), their mother, comprehends them all.[78] In these attributions, we can see a clear relation between the underlying principles of music and those ideals which everyone longs for in a harmoniously-governed state, whether within an individual's soul or a larger social context.

The basis of the musical scale is the so-called 6:8::9:12 "musical proportion" whose discovery is attributed to Pythagoras. Iamblichus said that Pythagoras learnt of this from the Babylonians, bringing it back to Greece,[79] but whatever the situation actually was, everyone agrees that the Pythagoreans were the first to study scientifically the mathematics of harmonic mediation in the West. This they did theoretically and practically, expressing their insights on the monochord.

The miraculous thing about the 6:8::9:12 musical proportion lies in two related facts. First, it is the most simple, perfectly symmetrical whole number proportion in the universe with four terms. Second, it encompasses the perfect, harmonic ratios of music: the octave (6:12), the perfect fifth (6:9 and/or 8:12), and the perfect fourth (6:8 and/or 9:12). It even defines the ratio of the Pythagorean whole tone (8:9), which is the ratio between a perfect fifth and a perfect fourth.[80] (*Figure 23.*)

To fully appreciate the nature of these harmonic relations one needs to experience them on the monochord, but a piano can substitute should a monochord not be available. However, one thing that will only be noticed on a monochord is the perfect law of reciprocity between string length and the corresponding tone. For example, by dividing the string length in half (1/2), a tone is produced with double the frequency (2/1) of the

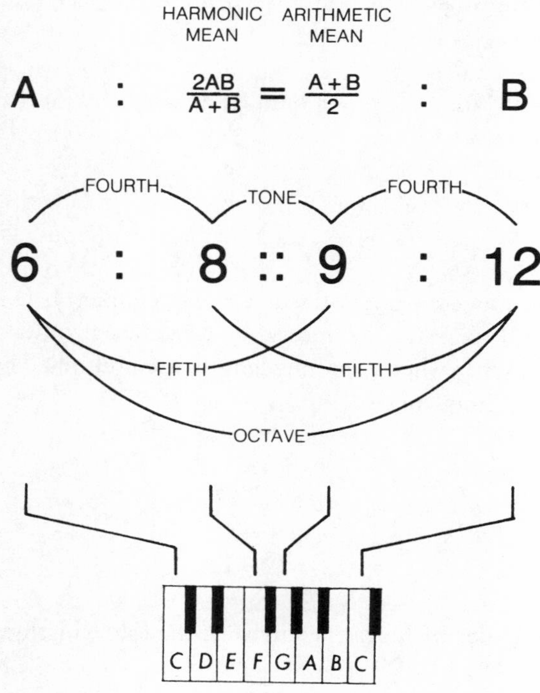

Figure 23. The Musical Proportion, 6:8::9:12

The Arithmetic and Harmonic Means define the perfect fifth, perfect fourth, and whole tone, all of the ratios needed to construct the musical scale.

undivided string. This principle of reciprocity is an underlying law of harmonic manifestation, whereby the relationship between string length and frequency is always resolved in Unity. In the case of the octave, the string length (1/2) times the produced frequency (2/1) equals 1 or Unity, and such is always the case.

In the example of the 6:8::9:12 musical proportion, its symmetry and reciprocity is further demonstrated by the fact that the tonal frequencies correspond with the string divisions in a symmetrical and reciprocal fashion. The monochord string is divided into twelve parts to bring out the appropriate tones, which are in themselves a mirror image of the string divisions:

String Division	Tonal frequency	Note
12 parts = *entire string*	6	Low C
9 parts	8	F
8 parts	9	G
6 parts	12	High C

In the table above we can see the underlying symmetry, while below we can see how these values reciprocally "cancel each other out" in the principle of unity,[81] when the string lengths are multiplied by the corresponding tonal frequencies:

$$12 \times 6 = 72$$
$$9 \times 8 = 72$$
$$8 \times 9 = 72$$
$$6 \times 12 = 72$$

Expressed in decimal form, we arrive at the following figures:

$$1 \times 1 = 1$$
$$.75 \times 1.333 = 1$$
$$.666 \times 1.5 = 1$$
$$.5 \times 2 = 1$$

The symmetry of these harmonic relations is most easily visualized if the musical scale is represented as a circle, where the beginning and the end are bent back upon themselves. This is appropriate, for in the scale the beginning and the end are "equivalent" (low C and high C), the only "difference" being the fact that they are separated by an octave, the principle of harmonic identity. (*Figure 24.*)

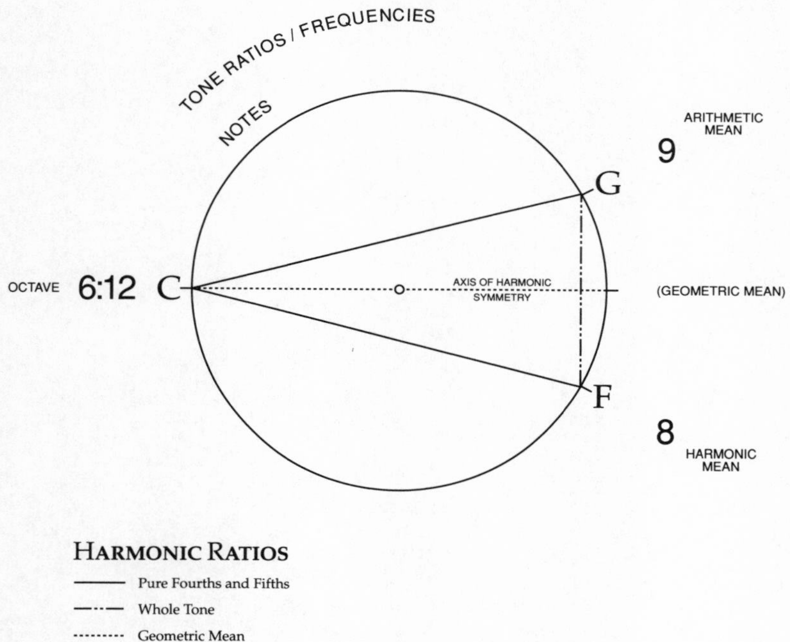

Figure 24. The Musical Proportion on the Circular Graph

The logarithmic representation of the octave on a circular graph or "tone mandala" allows one to visually discern any harmonic symmetries. Here the musical proportion is shown with the corresponding intervals.

According to the ancient Pythagoreans, the musical scale encapsulates the principles of Arithmetic, Harmonic, and Geometric mediation. This is indeed the case, and the formulas for the Arithmetic, Harmonic, and Geometric Means are shown facing, along with the corresponding notes. (*Figure 25.*)

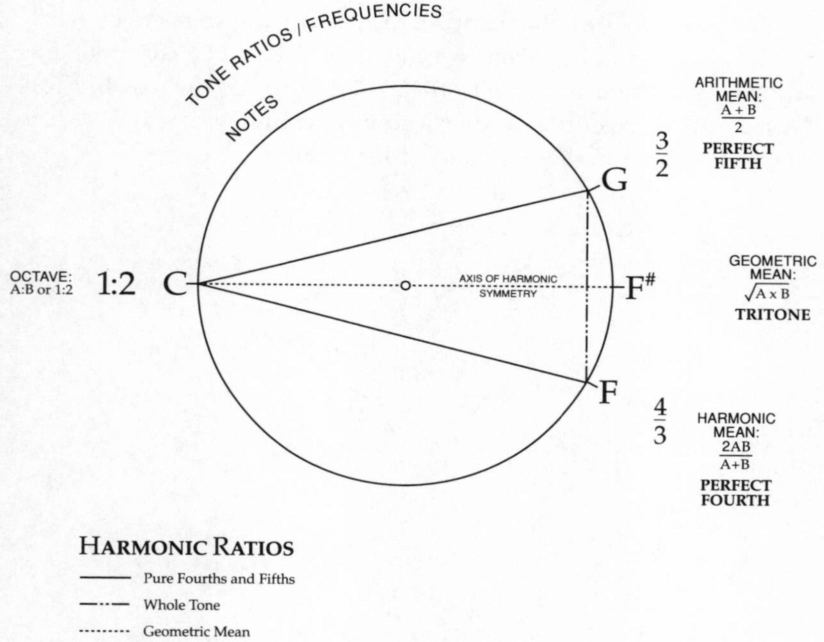

Figure 25. The Arithmetic, Geometric, and Harmonic Means

Shown here are the formulas for arriving at the values of the Arithmetic, Geometric, and Harmonic Means.

If we express the musical proportion in decimal form, with the Geometric Mean added, we arrive at the values depicted in *figure 26*.

This illustration shows that the esoteric ratio of √2 represents *the axis of harmonic symmetry* of the entire octave. Not only is √2 or THE GOD APOLLO the Geometric Mean between the extremes of the octave, but it is *also* the Geometric Mean between the perfect fifth and perfect fourth, the Arithmetic and Harmonic Means respectively. The corresponding string length which gives rise to 1415, THE GOD APOLLO, is 707, THE GOD HERMES, his little brother who invented the lyre and gave it to Apollo as a token of their harmonic friendship.

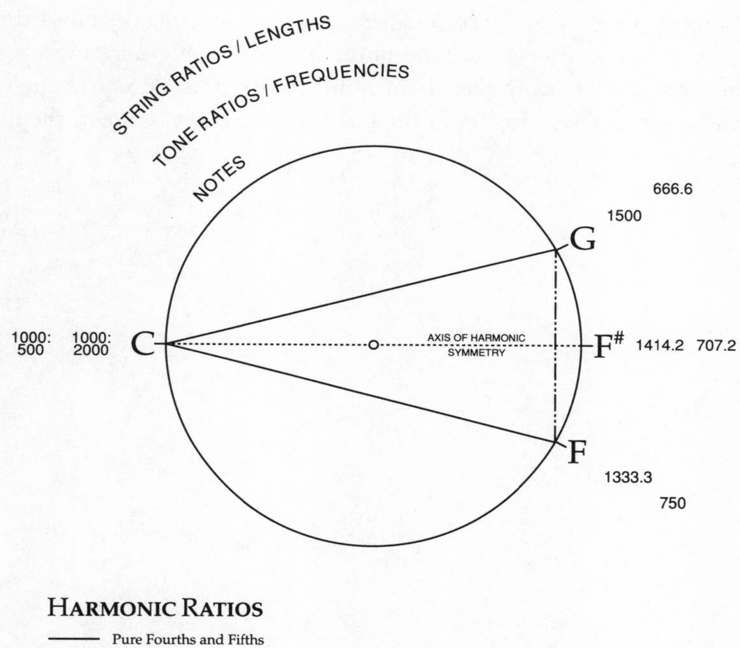

Figure 26. The Ratios of Harmony Expressed in Decimal Form

Shown above are the tone and string ratios of the Means expressed in decimal form if Unison is taken to be 1000. Each pair of ratios is also a set of reciprocals which if multiplied together will always equal 1000000.

In this illustration, *figure 27*, we insert the Geometric Mean between unison and the perfect fifth which brings out the tonal vibration of 1224, the number of FISHES and THE NET. We also insert its twin, the Geometric Mean between the octave and the perfect fourth. This brings out the string length of 612, the number of ZEUS. Because these new values are symmetrically placed, the numbers 707 and 1415 on the axis of harmonic symmetry also act as the Geometric Means between the new values.

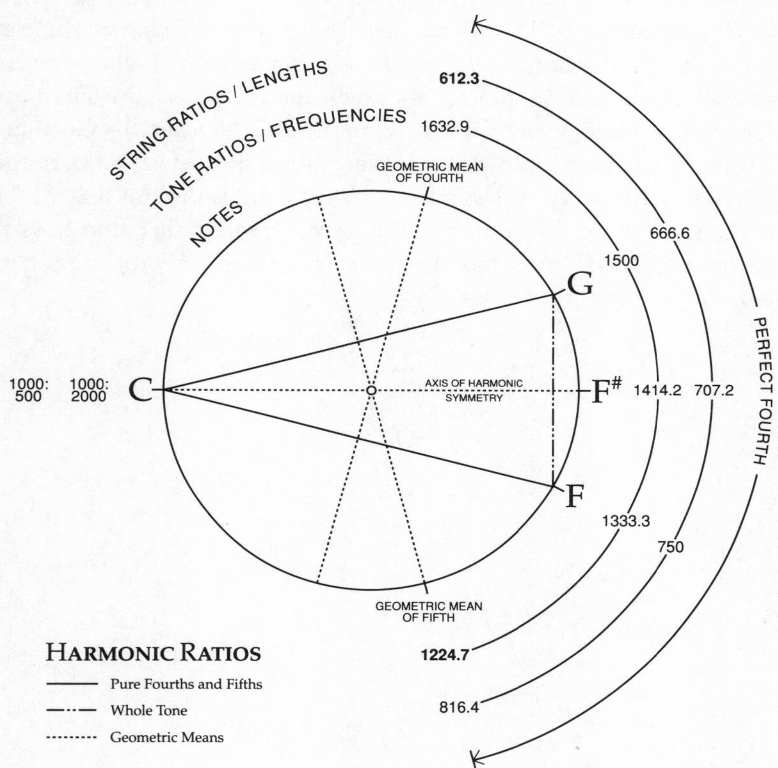

Figure 27. The "Super-Harmonic Proportion"

By inserting an additional pair of Geometric Means, the canonical numbers 612 and 1224 are brought out.

In this final illustration, *figure 28*, we see how the ratio of the whole tone also encompasses the canonical ratios. The string ratio of the whole tone is 888, the number of JESUS, the Christian Logos and Celestial Mediator, but it is also the number of OLEN, the founder of Apollo's oracle at Delphi. Additionally, the ratio between the Arithmetic Mean and the Geometric Mean, which is identical to the ratio between the Geometric Mean and the Harmonic Mean, is 1061, the number of APOLLO, the god of celestial harmony. Another way of stating this is that APOLLO, 1.061, is the ratio of the half-tone in Pythagorean tuning; this ratio links the Arithmetic, Geometric, and Harmonic Means perfectly together in one continuous proportion.

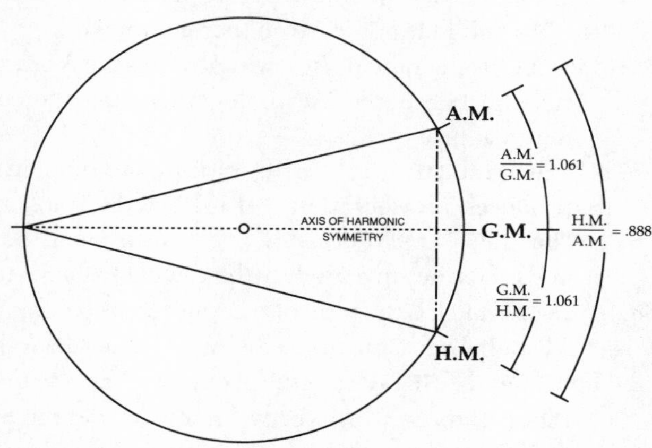

Harmonic Ratios

- Pure Fourths and Fifths
- Whole Tone
- Geometric Mean

Figure 28. The Ratios of the Tone

The Pythagorean whole tone, the ratio between the Arithmetic and Harmonic Means, encompasses the canonical numbers 888 and 1061.

To summarize this harmonic data, we have seen how the central numbers of the Greek number canon are brought out in the pure harmonic ratios of the musical scale, if the ratios of the octave are expressed in decimal form:

1415, THE GOD APOLLO, is the Geometric Mean between the extremes of the octave—and the extremes of the Arithmetic Mean (perfect fifth) and Harmonic Mean (perfect fourth).

1061, APOLLO, is the ratio or *logos* which unites the Arithmetic, Geometric, and Harmonic Means together into one continuous geometrical proportion.

707, THE GOD HERMES, is the string ratio of the Geometric Mean, which produces the vibration 1414–1415. Hermes and Apollo are "brothers," reciprocals of one another, and both are musical gods. Hermes invented the lyre which he gave to Apollo.

888, JESUS or OLEN, is the ratio of the tone, the relation of the Harmonic Mean (perfect fourth) to the Arithmetic Mean (perfect fifth).

1224, FISHES and THE NET, is the Geometric Mean between unison and the Arithmetic Mean, between unison and the perfect fifth.

612, ZEUS, is the string ratio of the Geometric Mean between the octave and the Harmonic Mean, between the octave and the perfect fourth.

It is clear from this why Clement of Alexandria, the early church father who fought to maintain a gnostic perspective within "developing orthodoxy," was well justified in referring to Christianity as the "New Song," a new expression of the eternal Logos. In a cosmological sense, Christianity was seen, at least among certain individuals, as a new synthesis, more appropriate for the times, of the earlier symbolism of the Logos, which had been personified in terms of Hermes and Apollo. From the ratios expressed in the laws of perfect harmony, it is obvious why Clement referred to the power of Jesus, the Logos, in musical terms: "Behold the might of the New Song!" says he. It has "composed the universe into melodious order, and tuned the discord of the elements to harmonious arrangement, so that the whole world might become harmony."[82] Elsewhere, after a discussion of "the mystical meanings in the proportions of numbers, geometrical ratios, and music" necessary for a complete understanding of scripture, he refers to the symbolism of the loaves and fishes, and how, in the ancient days, "the choir of mute fishes" rushed to the music of Apollo, or Orpheus.[83] Now, Clement writes, the first Christians have sought the healing balm of the New Song, a new expression of the universal harmony, whose timeless chords have just been heard again of late.[84]

CHAPTER FIVE

The Miraculous Feeding of the Five Thousand and Other Mysteries of the New Testament

> Yet among the initiates (*teleioi*) we do impart wisdom, although it is not a wisdom of this age or of the rulers of this age who are doomed to pass away. But we impart a secret and hidden wisdom of God, which God decreed before the ages for our glorification.
>
> —Paul, 1 Corinthians 2.6–7

THE EARLIEST New Testament writings are not the four gospels but the letters of Paul, who actively transmitted his version of the Christian message to Greek speaking people in Asia Minor and mainland Greece. Paul was a good writer and an eloquent speaker: so eloquent, in fact, that the people of Lystra thought that Hermes, the god of speech and language, had paid them a visit.[1] As the earliest New Testament writer—and the only one who claimed to know acquaintances of the historical Jesus in Jerusalem—Paul quite surprisingly has almost nothing to say about the historical Jesus, aside from a brief treatment of the last supper and several references to the crucifixion and resurrection. Paul doesn't seem to be interested in the historical Jesus at all, but rather finds meaning in the idea of "the Christ," which has manifested itself to "fulfill" the Mosaic Law by showing the latter's inadequacy. The question still remains, however, that if Paul actually knew people who were friends of the historical Jesus, why wasn't he more involved in disseminating the facts of Jesus' life and teachings? Why don't we find something more about the historical Jesus in Paul's writings? One answer to this question may be found in the fact that while the historical is limited, the spiritual is not; as he writes, "even though we regarded Christ from a human point of view, we regard him thus no longer."[2] Paul often speaks of the ever-present spirit of Christ, and alludes to the experience of "the spirit within." He speaks of the secret and primordial Wisdom of God, the Jewish equivalent of the Greek Logos, which has been revealed anew among the first Christians, resulting in their glorification. From this perspective, we can suggest that Paul saw the early Christian movement, which he had a major hand in spreading, as an important reflection of underlying spiritual realities. For this reason, he was understandably less interested in the mere fragments of history, which "are doomed to pass away," than in a larger reality: the manifestation of the Christ within, which was both closing the previous cosmic cycle and marking the beginning of a new one.

Paul's Letters were written roughly during the period of 40 to 60 C.E. As for the gospel accounts in the New Testament, they were written later by people who had no contact with the historical Jesus; we don't even know who wrote the gospels, for the attributions to Matthew, Mark, Luke, and John came later and did not appear in the earliest written copies.[3] While the gospels in the New Testament are among the earliest to survive, gospel writing was a widespread activity during the first centuries of the Common Era. While some of the "other gospels" survive, either in whole or in part, many others were condemned and destroyed because they contained details that were not in harmony with the opinions of developing orthodoxy.[4] To show why only the New Testament versions should be accepted, the church father Irenaeus pointed out that there can only be four authentic gospels because there are only "four principal winds"—and thus the organized church should only have "four pillars, breathing out immortality on every side, and vivifying man afresh."[5]

Over the last hundred and fifty years, important strides have been made in the study of the New Testament writings from a variety of perspectives including textual critcism, form criticism, and other types of scholarly detective work. In addition, the astonishing discovery of the gnostic gospels in Egypt in 1945 has thrown a remarkable light on the diverse nature of early Christianity and the early Christian communities.

The Origin and Sources of the Four Gospels

While we do not know where or by whom the four New Testament gospels were written, scholars realize that they are compilations assembled by what we would today call editors, who drew on various traditions, both oral and written, of the early Christian communities. Because of this, the written gospels originate from complex layers of earlier materials from a wide variety of sources. These include collections of "sayings of the Lord" (like the sayings *Gospel of Thomas*), collections of miracle stories used by early Christian missionaries, dialogues attributed to Jesus, a passion narrative, miscellaneous legends, and other special sources specific to individual gospels, to name the most obvious. From a historical standpoint, this diversity of sources makes it difficult to paint an accurate portrait of the historical Jesus. While there are undoubtedly some historically reliable teachings and accounts of Jesus in the New Testament, it's impossible to know which ones are and which ones aren't. This fact was recognized long ago by the early church father Origen, who pointed out that some incidents related in the gospels never took place in a "material" or "corporeal" sense, but are spiritual allegories meant to be studied as such; as he states quite clearly, "the careful student may observe countless other instances in the Gospels, and may thus be convinced that with the historical events, literally true, different ones are interwoven which never occurred."[6]

The shortest, simplest, and probably the earliest gospel is that of Mark, written around the year 70 C.E. The book starts with the introduction "Here begins the Gospel of Jesus Christ," which was intended as a title; the phrase "according to Mark" was appended later.[7] While we do not know who "Mark" was or where he lived, New Testament scholars realize that he did something very important. The author of Mark was the very first person, as far as we can tell, to take the various sources to which he had access and pull them together into a narrative framework of this extent. By imposing a narrative, biographical sequence on the various accounts and episodes, the first gospel—and an entire literary genre—was born.

The Gospel of Matthew, perhaps written around 80 C.E., for the most part builds upon the narrative of Mark by adding material to it. Matthew was writing for a Jewish-Christian audience, and tends to see Jesus as something of a "New Moses." Whereas Mark will present an episode in the life of Jesus by giving only the basic details, Matthew will often add an editorial comment to show how it relates to a specific Jewish scriptural passage.[8]

Another user of the Gospel of Mark is the author of Luke, who also wrote the Acts of the Apostles. "Luke" may have been raised and educated a Christian, wrote good Greek, and probably belonged to the third generation of Christians.[9] The Gospel of Luke is not likely to have been written before the year 90, and may have been written in the beginning of the second century.[10]

The writings attributed to Mark, Matthew, and Luke are called the Synoptic Gospels by scholars of early Christianity; they "look the same" (*syn-optic*) because they share the narrative structure established by Mark. They may thus profitably be studied side-by-side, which is easy to do in the available "parallel editions."[11] In addition to the material copied from Mark, the gospels of Matthew and Luke also drew upon another source of common material, known as either the Synoptic Sayings Source or "Q," from the German word *Quelle* (Source). This collection of sayings attributed to Jesus was probably very similar to the *Gospel of Thomas*, discovered in a complete copy at Nag Hammadi in Egypt. Many scholars believe that the *Gospel of Thomas* in its very earliest form was not only very similar to "Q" in form, but probably originated around the same time.[12]

The final New Testament account, the Gospel of John, the so-called "Spiritual Gospel,"[13] portrays the story and mission of Jesus in the most mystical light, identifying Jesus at the outset as the Logos, a cosmic power, and bears minimal relation to the Synoptic accounts. It was probably written around 95 C.E. or later.

The study of early Christian literature is a serious undertaking and may be infinitely pursued to ever deeper levels, if so desired. Any level of serious inquiry, however, reveals that the gospel accounts are essentially literary creations, inspired only in part by historical events. Unfortunately, from a strictly historical perspective, there are so many discrepancies between the various accounts, and so many mysterious background sources, that it is impossible to rely upon any specific detail from any particular gospel as a statement of historical fact about Jesus. We are left instead with various degrees of historical probability. Ultimately, the only thing one can maintain with certainty is that the early followers of Jesus saw him as a teacher of spiritual wisdom who was crucified, and that a belief developed in his resurrection, or the continuing presence of his spirit among his disciples.

Yet, despite the fact that the gospels cannot be read as straightforward historical records, few would deny that they contain teachings of great spiritual magnitude. Moreover, there is a profound mystery associated with the appearance of these writings, as with the appearance of early

Christianity in general. How was it, for example, that certain allegories found their way into the New Testament? Do they go back to Jesus, or to other sources? And who exactly were the people that compiled the gospels and the earlier documents on which they were based?

In attempting to approach these questions, it might be helpful to consider how certain "sayings of the Lord" made their way into the New Testament. The early Christian communities possessed and circulated collections of wise sayings (*logia*) attributed to Jesus. The *Gospel of Thomas* provides an excellent example of such a collection, and many of these sayings, or close variants, appear in the New Testament text. But how many of them actually go back to Jesus? Scholars assume that the earliest stratum of Christian teaching consisted of "oral tradition." In fact, until a fairly late date, the oral tradition was more highly prized by some than the written gospel accounts.[14] Under such conditions, many historical inaccuracies will occur. The original sayings may be remembered in some form, but later edited or modified. Other wisdom sayings or spiritual apothegms not made by Jesus might make their way into such a collection. And since Jesus was seen as the Logos, any spiritual insight seen as coming from the Logos could legitimately be added to the collection as "a saying of the Lord." Finally, around such simple sayings, dialogues and discourses would crystallize—perhaps even teaching stories and parables—as we find in some New Testament accounts.[15] Given this scenario, it is easy to see why the apostle Paul was more interested in the transcendent spirit of Christ than in trying to record the details of the historical Jesus.

Gematria as the Basis of Early Christian Allegories

Interestingly, there is another, mysterious dimension present in certain New Testament accounts which has been overlooked by most scholars, simply because they have been looking in other directions. This has to do with the ancient mathematical symbolism of the Logos and the fact that some New Testament miracle stories were consciously composed in relation to geometrical diagrams. The dimensions of these cosmological diagrams are defined by the values of the Greek number canon, explored in chapter 4, which were seen as reflecting the underlying harmony of the universe.

The first discovery of this sort was published by John Michell in his 1972 study of Greek gematria, *City of Revelation*, and involves the miraculous story of the 153 fish in the unbroken net (John 21). This analysis, which has not received the recognition it deserves, is reproduced in Appendix 1.

Significantly enough, the whole New Testament story of the "number of fish in the net" is thought by some scholars to go back to a story about Pythagoras.[16] According to an ancient account, he encountered some fishermen "who were drawing in their nets heavily laden with fishes from the deep."[17] The fishermen said that they would do anything Pythagoras might ask, if he could correctly predict the number of the fish in the net. This he did precisely, and the fishermen followed his subsequent command to return the still-living fish to the sea. While the number of fish in the net is not given in the story as it has come down to us, it seems likely that it was related in some fashion to the diagram of the 153 fishes rediscovered by Michell, and that this diagram originated in a pre-Christian, "Pythagorean" milieu. Additionally, as I point out in Appendix 1, the ratio of 153:265 was used as the measure of the *vesica piscis* or "fish" long before the emergence of Christianity. Therefore, anyone who knew a bit about mathematics would have immediately recognized the tale of the "153 fish in the net" for what it is: a "geometrical story problem," though one, in this case, with a cosmological dimension.

While John Michell has definitively shown that the story of the 153 fish was based on an underlying pattern of "sacred geometry," this does not prove that Greek gematria was used by the *earliest* Christians. That is because the Gospel of John is the latest gospel of the New Testament canon, written perhaps as late as the year 100 C.E., or even later. Moreover, the Gospel of John originally ended at chapter 20 with the words, "Now Jesus did many other signs in the presence of the disciples which are not written in this book; but these are written that you may believe that Jesus is the Christ, the Son of God, and that believing you may have life in his name." Chapter 21, in which the story appears, was added later as an epilogue or appendix, and no one knows precisely when this took place.

However, it is now possible to confirm that the earliest Christians did use gematria, for in 1984 this writer discovered the underlying geometrical basis of another New Testament allegory, the miraculous feeding of the five thousand through "the multiplication of the loaves and fishes." Like the 153 fish in the net, it is based on the pre-Christian canon of number, in which the Logos was personified in the earlier figures of Hermes and Apollo. But, unlike the story of John 21, the feeding of the five thousand appears in one of the first Christian documents. It occurs in the Gospel of Mark, which scholars have identified as the earliest written gospel in the New Testament; moreover, the feeding of the five thousand is the only miracle story to appear in all four canonical gospels.[18] Since, as we have seen, the Gospel of Mark is a compilation written around the year 70 C.E. which incorporates earlier materials of many Christian communities, the feeding of the five thousand clearly demonstrates that Greek gematria was consciously used by some of the earliest Christian authors.

Let us now look at this spiritual parable and the remarkable geometry on which it is based.

The Miraculous Feeding of the Five Thousand

The Feeding of the Five Thousand:
Mark 6.30–38

The apostles returned to Jesus, and told him all that they had done and taught.

And he said to them, "Come away by yourselves to a lonely place, and rest a while." For many were coming and going, and they had no leisure even to eat. And they went away in the boat to a lonely place by themselves. Now many saw them going, and knew them, and they ran there on foot from all the towns, and got there ahead of them.

As he went ashore he saw a great throng, and he had compassion on them, because they were like sheep without a shepherd; and he began to teach them many things.

And when it grew late, his disciples came to him and said, "This is a lonely place, and the hour is now late; send them away, to go into the country and villages round about and buy themselves something to eat."

But he answered them, "You give them something to eat." And they said to him, "Shall we go and buy two hundred dernarri worth of bread, and give it to them to eat?" And he said to them, "How many loaves have you? Go and see." And when they had found out, they said, "Five, and two fish."

Then he commanded them all to sit down by companies upon the green grass. So *they sat down in groups, by hundreds and by fifties*. And taking the *five loaves* and the *two fish* he looked up to heaven, and blessed, and broke the loaves, and gave them to the disciples to set before the people; and *he divided the two fish among them all*. And they all ate and were satisfied. *And they took up twelve baskets* full of broken pieces and of the fish. And *those who ate the loaves were five thousand men*.

Stage One

Jesus feeds 5000 men sitting in a "field," and this is the starting point for the development of the geometry. The 5000 sitting in a field is represented mathematically as a perfect square containing 5000 sq. units, one for each person.

A square containing 5000 sq. units has the side measure of 70.7 units in length, and 707 is the value of the Greek phrase THE GOD HERMES.

In Greece, the god Hermes was an earlier representation of the Logos, "the guide of souls," and Hermes was also the god of shepherds. The Logos is the Teacher, Guide, and Leader not only of matter, but also of "unawakened irrational nature." The power of Reason in the soul both organizes and leads the irrational passions in the same way that a shepherd guides his herd.[19] In the story under consideration, Jesus "saw a great throng, and he had compassion on them, because they were like sheep without a shepherd; and he began to teach them many things" (Mark 6.34).

" . . . those who ate the loaves were five thousand men."

—Mark 6.44

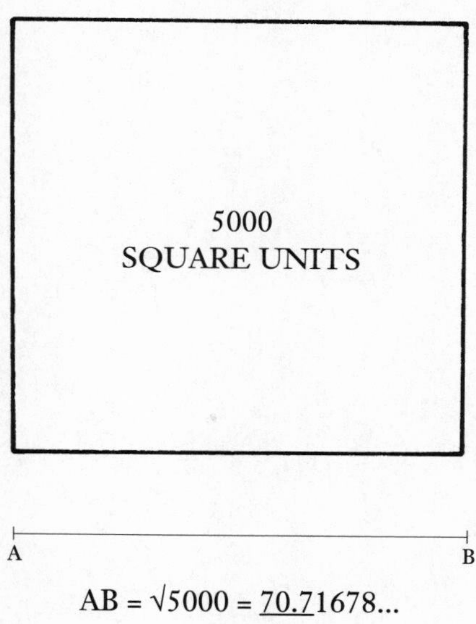

$AB = \sqrt{5000} = \underline{70.7}1678...$

Figure 29

Stage Two

The text states that the crowd sat in groups, "by hundred and fifties." This relates to the fact that the diagonal (AA) of the square containing 5000 sq. units is exactly 100 units long, while the half-diagonal (BB) measures 50 units in length.

"... they sat down in groups, by hundreds and by fifties."

—Mark 6.40

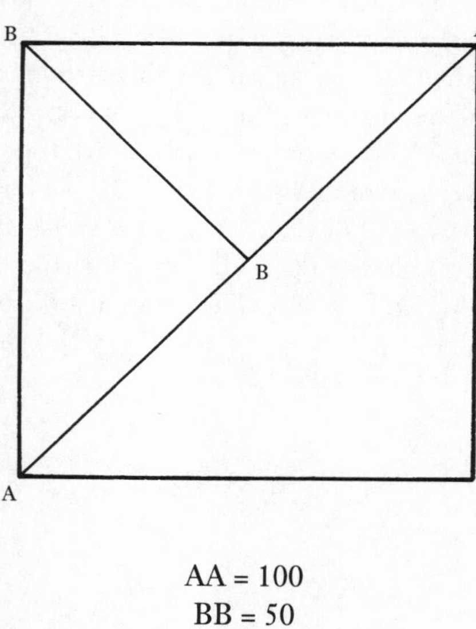

AA = 100
BB = 50

Figure 30

Stage Three

Jesus divides the two fish among the 5000, and this is represented by drawing three perfectly interpenetrating circles, thus forming "the three worlds diagram" of Hellenistic cosmology. This gives rise to two "fish" or *vesica piscis* forms in the square of the 5000. Each vesica has a horizonal axis which measures 61.2 units in length; together they measure 122.4 units, and 1224 is the gematria value of the Greek word FISHES.

Each one of the circles has a circumference of 222 units, and each vesica therefore has a perimeter of 148.0 units. 1480 is the value of CHRISTOS, and the "vessel of the fish" was an early emblem of his nature.

The perimeter of the square measures 282 units, and 282 is the value of the Greek word BIOS, Life, an important aspect of the Universal Logos.

In terms of the vertical dimensions, length AB is HERMES, AC is THE GOD HERMES, AD is APOLLO, and AE is THE GOD APOLLO. In other words, the diagram is based upon the pre-Christian canon of Greek theology. (See "The God Apollo: The First 'Word' of Celestial Harmony.")

"... he divided the two fish among them all."

—Mark 6.41

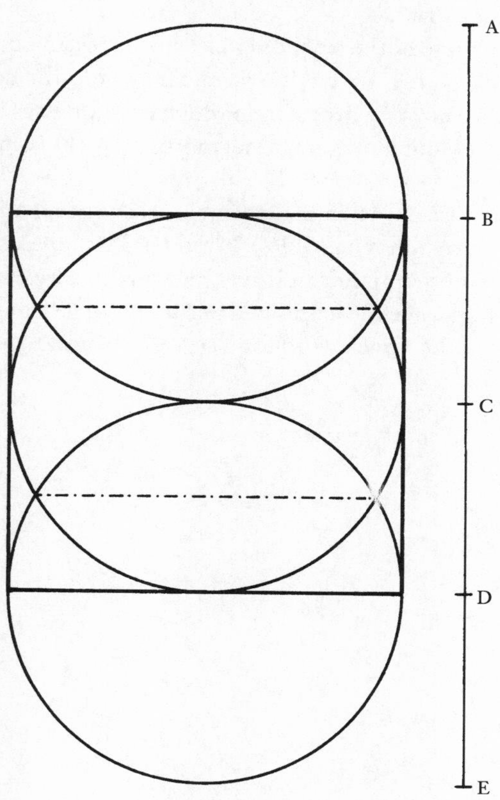

Figure 31

Stage Four

Having obtained the basic geometry, the square containing the 5000 is removed for clarity.

Since each one of the smaller circles measures 222 units in circumference, the combined tri-circle perimeter is 666, the sum of the magic square of the sun. The great circle which encompasses the entire pattern measures 444 units around, one more than the Greek phrase THE LOGOS.

If a hexagon is drawn in the lower circle, the hexagon will hold a circle which has a circumference of 192.3, and 1923 is the value of CHRIST, THE LOGOS. To represent the five loaves, five smaller circles are drawn herein. Together they have the combined perimeter of 481 units, and this is the value of *artoi*, the Greek word for LOAVES. Length XY is 122.4, and 1224 = FISHES.

"[There were] . . . five loaves . . ."
— Mark 6.41

Figure 32

Stage Five

The provisions of the "meal" having been supplied, one final aspect of the story needs to be represented: the twelve baskets used by the 12 disciples to collect what is left over.

This is represented by drawing the perfectly symmetrical 12-fold flower design in the upper circle: . This is accomplished by drawing 12 arcs with a compass, set at the original size of the three primary circles. Each arc has a measure of 74 units. Therefore, the total measure of the arcs making up the pattern in the circle is 74x12, or 888, and 888 is the number of JESUS, the early Christian representation of the extratemporal Celestial Word—the Logos personified as teacher, leader, shepherd, and provider of sustenance.

"And they took up twelve baskets . . ."
—Mark 6.43

Figure 33

Allegory, Initiation, and the Movement Toward Insight

What are we to make of this?

The feeding of the five thousand and the story of the 153 fish clearly show that certain New Testament stories were composed as initiatory, spiritual allegories. We may call them "initiatory" for the simple reason that they presuppose a movement from the outer world of manifest form to an inner perspective of genuine insight. They were intended both to entertain and edify at an outer level, designed to bring enjoyment even to children, yet they were also designed to possess within a deeper, hidden dimension reflecting the harmonic nature of the cosmic pattern. However, since the unknown scholars who composed these tales, based upon the ancient models, were intentionally crafting vehicles for the transmission of spiritual insight, it is unlikely that they desired their teaching stories ultimately to be read in literal or historical terms. This was recognized by the initiated church father Origen, who complains that "very many mistakes have been made, because the right method of examining the holy texts has not been discovered by the greater number of readers."[20] It is important to realize, Origen wrote, that

> wherever the Word found historical events capable of adaptation to these mystic truths, He made use of them, but concealed the deeper sense from the many; but where in setting forth the sequences of things spiritual there was no actual event related for the sake of the more mystic meaning, Scripture interweaves the imaginative with the historical, sometimes introducing what is utterly impossible, sometimes what is possible but never occurred . . . And not only did the Spirit thus deal with the Scriptures before the coming of Christ, but, inasmuch as He is the same Spirit, and proceedeth from the One God, He has done the same with the Gospels and the writings of the Apostles; for not even they are purely historical, incidents which never occurred being interwoven in the "corporeal" sense . . .[21]

Not everyone will benefit from the knowledge that some New Testament allegories are based on geometrical ratios, and that they were composed in this way to reflect the nature of the Logos, which was studied in mathematical terms and seen as underlying the harmony of the cosmos. Some individuals, at their present stage, are content to conduct their lives following "the letter of the law," with no regard for its inner spirit. As in the ancient times, others spend their lives in pursuit of money, prestige, or power, without ever investigating those qualities that make life truly worth living in the first place. Yet in every age there are individuals who, not content with outer appearances alone, wish to penetrate further, to the very heart of reality. Because of this eternal dichotomy in human behavior, the spiritual allegories of the ancient world were framed to possess both an outer and an inner dimension. Put in another way, since various individuals have different concerns in life, and since the universe can accomodate every perspective and level of insight, the ancient allegories were crafted to possess simultaneously different levels of meaning. On the outer level, the feeding of the five thousand was a delightful tale used by the early Christian missionaries to entertain their hearers and impress upon them the miraculous powers of the saving Word. On the inner level, however, the feeding of the five thousand provides nearly inexhaustible food for thought, for it is based on the Greek canon of number which was already old when Christianity was new. Despite the important questions for contemporary scholarship posed by these discoveries, one major theme of this New Testament allegory can be precisely articulated, even from our present vantage in time: in the same way that the story-book Jesus nourishes the crowd of five thousand in a strictly literal reading of the text, so too does the Celestial Logos—the gnostic, cosmological Jesus—eternally "sustain" the harmonic form of the created order.

Sacred Geometry and the Transfer of Spiritual Authority

Since nearly every spiritual teaching possessed an inner, esoteric dimension in antiquity, the use of gematria in the allegories of the fish in the net and the feeding of the five thousand should not come as too great a surprise, but it still remains difficult to determine exactly who constructed these beautiful parables. Like the symbolism of the Logos as a cosmological agent, the key numbers of these two allegories are pre-Christian and associated with the figures of Apollo and Hermes, the classical Greek personifications of the celestial harmony. Moreover, as I point out in my commentary on the 153 fishes in the net in Appendix 1, this particular geometry of "the three worlds" is symbolically associated with Apollo's shrine at Delphi. Like Jesus, Apollo had his sacred fishes, and Apollo's omphalos stone, which represented the center of the universe, was marked with the pattern of a net.[22] Simon Peter, who became "the omphalos of Christianity," was a fisherman. Significantly, in the story of the 153 fishes in the unbroken net, Simon Peter is the central character and the first inscribed circle representing him is "the foundation stone" which defines the dimensions of all the geometry that follows. After the allegory is completed and the entire figure is drawn out, the resurrected Jesus commands Peter to care for his flock: he is told three times to "feed my sheep." Simon Petros, "the Rock," hence is given the charge to realize his function as the foundation stone of Christianity. What we are seeing here, in an esoteric sense, is a transfer of spiritual authority from the old omphalos of Apollo at Delphi to the new omphalos of Christianity in Rome.

Whoever was responsible for incorporating this material into the New Testament canon was obviously aware of the significance of these symbolic relationships. But how did they gain the knowledge and the authority to do so, to set this process in motion? Given the central link between the symbolic figure of "Peter," the geometry, and the underlying intent of John 21, we conclude that the person who wrote the epilogue to the Fourth Gospel not only knew about this geometry, based on the earlier Delphic model, but may have even composed the allegory himself.

As for the feeding of the five thousand, since the Gospel of Mark appears to be a simple compilation with a less overriding purpose than John 21, Mark probably did not compose the allegory himself but merely incorporated it into his work along with other source material. If this is the case, it suggests that the allegory was circulated among the first Christian communities, thereby dating the use of sophisticated gematria back to the earliest days of Christianity. It also suggests that the identification of Jesus with the pre-Christian symbolism of the Logos goes back to the earliest days of the Christian movement, a date far earlier than either the Prologue to the Fourth Gospel or John 21.

The emerging Christian revelation must have been seen by its first scholars as a new synthesis of the ancient wisdom traditions, Jewish, Egyptian, and Greek. These learned individuals helped give the emerging synthesis form through the medium of the new allegories, based upon the established foundation of the numerical canon—itself an expression of the order behind the universe, which is a very firm foundation indeed. While we cannot know what drew these anonymous individuals to

Christianity, we can be certain that this process did take place, and that these allegories were composed in reference to the pre-existing geometry. Given the precise mathematical foundation of the stories, which express an eternal truth, these conclusions are based on much firmer ground than anything we may speculate about the teachings of the historical Jesus, which are beyond our power of verification.

CHAPTER SIX

The Gospel of John and the Gnostic Tradition

> The Logos said, "If you know the truth, the truth will make you free" (John 8.32). Ignorance is a slave. Knowledge is freedom. If we know the truth, we shall find the fruits of the truth within us. If we are joined to it, it will bring our fulfillment.
>
> —*The Gospel of Philip*

Gnosis and *Gnosticism*

THE GREEK word *gnôsis* means "knowledge" or "understanding" and, as such, refers to both spiritual and scientific insight. This word, *gnôsis*, however, usually comes up in discussions of the "gnostic" spiritual teachings which flowered during the early days of the Christian era. In this sense, the word refers to the saving spiritual knowledge, often of a secret or esoteric character, which reveals the true situation of the soul, reminding it of its origin, purpose and end. Hence, according to one early Christian source, *gnôsis* is "the knowledge of who we have been and what we have become; where we have been, where we have been cast; where we are hastening, where we were redeemed; what birth is, what rebirth."[1] The term *gnôsis* appears in the New Testament, and Paul, the earliest New Testament writer, describes *gnôsis* as one of the spiritual gifts.[2]

Gnosis in the ancient world comprises such a complex and varied tapestry of expressions, that by speaking of "Gnosticism" as a whole one is led to make generalizations that may later interfere with our ability to understand and appreciate a particular form of gnosis. While there were many individuals and groups in antiquity who sought the experience of gnosis, the saving knowledge of the divine realities, never once did any of these parties consider themselves part of a larger movement called "Gnosticism," a term which was only coined in the eighteenth century.[3] There were dozens and dozens of gnostic expressions, arising in pagan, Jewish, and Christian spheres. From a scholarly perspective, one must honor this diversity and approach each teaching on its own terms. In the same way that there is no such thing as "Gnosticism" *per se*, never has there existed an entirely unified phenomenon suggested by the monolithic term "Christianity"; from a scholarly perspective, we can only speak of the different types of early Christianity, of which there were many. Even today the forms and manifestations of Christianity are diverse and varied, and such has always been the case. Despite the diversity, however, it is possible to say something about the general features of Gnosis for, from a study of the different manifestations, certain patterns do emerge.

Forgetfulness, the Call, and Recollection

At the center of the human soul is a Divine Spark which has fallen into the world of fate, birth, generation, and decay. Putting on the rags of mortality, we have descended from the "Fullness" (*Plêrôma*) of Light, the timeless realm of perfection, and have forgotten our true nature, heritage, and birthright. Our existence on earth is a sleep, until some type of call, messenger, or revelation awakens us to the re-cognition of our origin and true nature. This recollection represents the birth of gnosis within. As the *Gospel of Truth* puts it,

> if one has knowledge, he is from above. If he is called, he hears, he answers, and he turns to him who is calling him, and ascends to him. And he knows in what manner he is called. . . . He who is to have knowledge in this manner knows where he comes from and where he is going. He knows as one who having become drunk has turned away from his drunkenness, (and) having returned to himself, has set right what are his own.[4]

Nowhere is the gnostic theme of the soul's sleep and forgetfulness more beautifully expressed than in the so-called "Hymn of the Pearl," which appears in the *Acts of Thomas* and is reproduced here as Appendix 2. In this beautiful allegory the themes of the soul's true home and forgetfulness are clearly articulated. A young Prince strips off his robe of glory, his body of light, and descends into the realm of matter, symbolized by Egypt; he is on a mission to recover a treasure. He is instructed by his parents, the King and Queen (Sophia) in the realm of Light, not to forget his mission, and they make a covenant with the Prince, written in his heart:

If you go down into Egypt
And bring back the One Pearl
Which is in the midst of the sea
In the abode of the loud-breathing serpent,
Then you shall once again put on your splendid robe
And your toga, which lies over it,
And with your brother, our next in rank,
You shall be heir in our kingdom.

Yet, during his sojourn in the terrestrial sphere, the Prince puts on a robe like those of the Egyptians, so as not to arouse suspicion. Eating the food of the Egyptians, he falls into slumber, forgetting his mission and his true, royal identity. This forgetfulness causes his parents to grieve, and they resolve to send him a message reminding him of his origin, nature, and destiny; this is the call of recollection:

Awake and arise from your sleep,
And hear the words of our letter!
Remember that you are a son of Kings.
See the slavery of your life!

This letter, bearing the exhortation to remember, takes the form of an eagle and, alighting beside the slumbering prince, it becomes speech, awaking him from his sleep. At this decisive point the bonds of sleep and forgetfulness are broken, allowing the Prince to complete his special task and begin his return to the royal kingdom, the Realm of Light, where he once again will put on his robe of glory and dwell with his true companions.

A Gnostic Cosmology: The Account of Valentinus

Gnostic teaching is characterized by a dualistic tendency which contrasts the world of Light to the darkness and oblivion of matter. Dualism conditions our experience of phenomenal existence, lying at the root of one of the eternal questions facing the human spirit: how can evil enter the world if God is truly good? Gnostic teachers attempted to answer this through the use of elaborate creation myths which describe the origin of the cosmos. Dazzling in their complexity, genius, and powerful dramatic elements, many of these accounts tell of how the universe came into being through the work of an ignorant Creator (Demiurge) who mistakenly thought himself to be "the only true God," not realizing that there existed higher levels of reality above him.

According to the creation account of Valentinus (*circa* 100–160 C.E.), one of the most important gnostic teachers, the Ineffable Father exists before the beginning and can only be described as Depth or Profundity (*Bythos*). He is surrounded by a female power called Silence (*Sigê*); together Depth and Silence give birth to the other Aeons or archetypal beings, through a process of emanation in which the Aeons emerge in male-female pairs known as syzygies. Each one of these Aeons is a divine principle unto itself, but is also an eternal aspect of the Ineffable Father, who is beyond all names. Together these aeonic pairs comprise the Fullness (*Plêrôma*) of the Godhead, the archetypal realm of spiritual perfection.

In this influential teaching, Depth-and-Silence gives birth to Mind-and-Truth, who gives birth to Word-and-Life, who gives birth to Man-and-Church. These first Aeons make up the Ogdoad.

Word-and-Life go on to make ten new Aeons, the Decad. These are: Deep/Mingling, Undecaying/Union, Self-Existent/Bliss, Immovable/Composition, and Only-Begotten/Happiness. Meanwhile, Man-and-Church gives birth to twelve Aeons, the Dodecad: Comforter/Faith, Paternal/Hope, Maternal/Love, Ever-Thinking/Understanding, Ecclesiastical/Happiness, and Longed-For/Wisdom, thus completing the Pleroma of the thirty Aeons. (*Figure 34.*)

All of the Aeons had a desire to know the Ineffable Father, but only Mind, because of his resemblance to him, was capable of realizing this. The desire to know the Father was strongest in the thirtieth Aeon, Sophia or Wisdom; this passion for knowledge overwhelmed her and she was thrown into total confusion, upsetting the balance of the Pleroma. Her anguish, which resembled a fog, was exiled outside of the Pleroma, and Mind produced a power called Cross to act as the boundary of the Pleroma, protecting the Aeons from Sophia's "abortion."

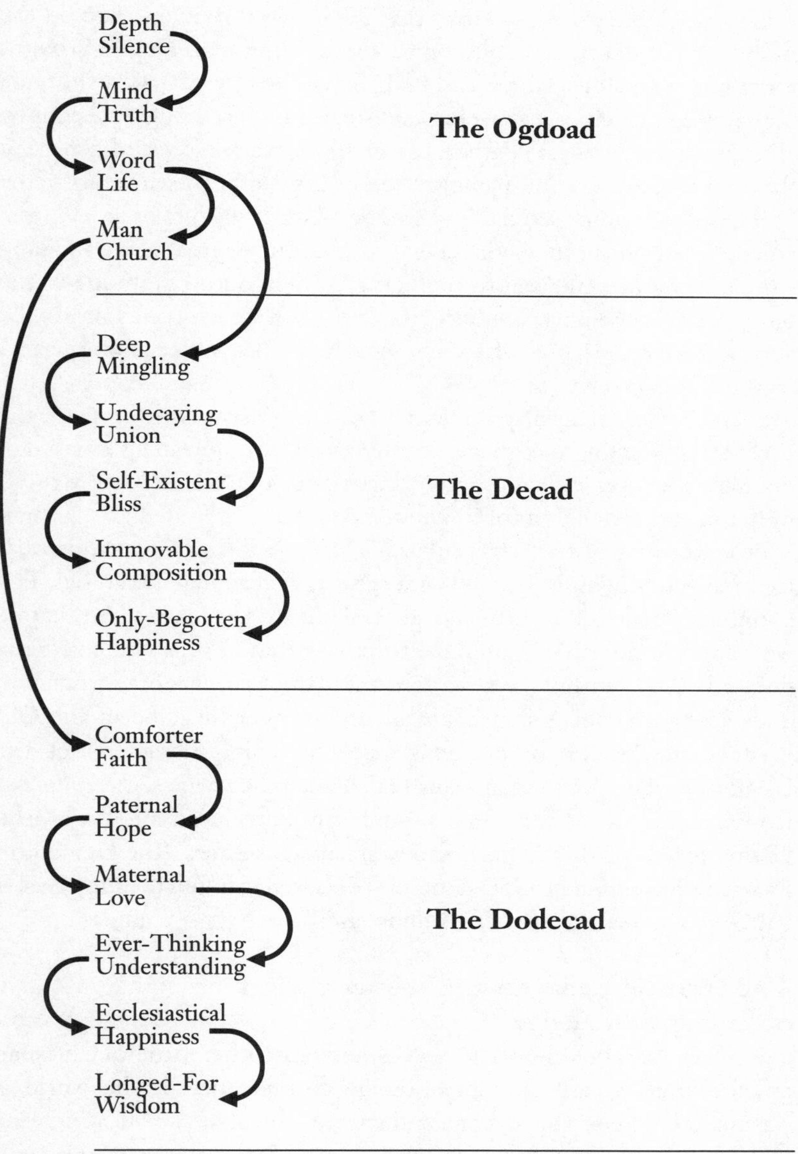

Figure 34. The Generation of the Pleroma

Because of the alarming effect that the passion of Sophia had on the Aeons which make up the Pleroma, Mind, acting with Depth, brought forth two new Aeons, Christ and Holy Spirit, in order to pacify the fears of the other Eternities. Christ reestablished concord among the Aeons by teaching them about the Father, revealing that they possessed a share in the eternal because of the incomprehensible and unbegotten nature of the Father to whom they owed their existence. Under the influence of Christ and the Holy Spirit, the Aeons coexisted in a state of great peace and sang a joyful song of exaltation to the Father. Then, out of gratitude to the Father, all the Aeons brought forth a new Aeon, each contributing the very best he or she had to offer. This new Aeon, "the very star and perfect fruit of the Pleroma," was Jesus.

Later, in the Valentinian account, Christ and Jesus venture outside the Pleroma, projecting themselves through the Cross, to come to the aid of Sophia's abortion, Achamoth, the Lower Wisdom, which was the result of her unsuccessful attempt to know the Father.

From the passions of Achamoth came forth the Demiurge, the fabricator of the physical universe, the father and king of all that is material. The Demiurge created the earth and the seven heavens and thought that he was alone responsible, ignorant of the fact that he was being secretly guided by Achamoth. Moreover, he created things in an ignorant fashion. This Demiurge the Valentinians identified with the God of the Old Testament. Because of his ignorance—his chief characteristic—the Demiurge was unaware that a spiritual element had been secretly deposited in him by Achamoth, and through him introduced into the world. "Being incapable of recognizing any spiritual essences, [the Demiurge] imagined himself to be God alone, and declared through the prophets, 'I am God, and beside me there is none else.'"[5]

The Gnostic Redeemer: The Incarnation of Saving Knowledge

As we can see, in Valentinian gnosis, and most other forms of Christian gnosis, Jesus is seen as a pre-existing cosmic power. The world is composed of material, psychic, and spiritual elements, from which the three types of humanity arise: *hylic* (material), *psychic*, and *pneumatic* (spiritual). It is the pneumatic race which contains within itself the Spark or Light Seed which arose when Achamoth gazed in ecstasy upon the angelic lights surrounding her savior, Jesus. Those who contain this Spark within also possess something of the nature of the Pleroma, namely the knowledge of the spiritual fullness and eternities.

The psychic race can either move toward the spiritual or the material. If they choose the former they will be saved; if the latter, they will become like the hylic type, who dwells in utter darkness, totally ignorant of the higher realities.

According to the Valentinians and other Christian gnostics, the Jesus of the gospels was a pre-existing spiritual entity who took on an "animal" or psychic form, but not a material form. He only appeared to be a physical being, taking on a visible nature for the sake of the psychic types:

> *he came by means of fleshy appearance* while nothing blocked his course because it was incorruptibility (and) irresistibility. Again, speaking new things, still speaking about what is in the heart of the Father, he brought forth the flawless word. Light spoke through his mouth, and his voice gave birth to life.[6]

In the Valentinian account, Christ imparted form to Achamoth, while Jesus gave her intelligence. The function of the "earthly" savior was likewise to impart the healing balm of saving gnosis, mirroring the act of salvation which had already taken place on the extraterrestrial level. Hence, according to the Valentinians, Jesus, who appears in the world but is not of the world, provides "a way for those who were gone astray and knowledge for those who were ignorant, a discovery for those who were searching, and a support for those who were wavering."[7] Another Valentinian account, the *Tripartite Tractate*, tells us that "the Son, who is the redemption . . . is the path toward the incomprehensible Father."[8] It is important for us to realize that, in the gnostic view, this path, the nature of Christ, is not a static form of salvation but *the very incarnation of saving gnosis itself.*

In Valentinian cosmology the world comes into existence because of ignorance, the lack of knowledge of the Father. Yet, through the savior—the revelation of gnosis—humanity is raised above the world of ignorant matter. Quite simply, "Since oblivion came into existence because the Father was not known, then if the Father comes to be known, oblivion will not exist from that moment on."[9] To "accept the savior" is to recognize within oneself the saving gnosis which results in a transformation of the human personality. The mission of the savior is to facilitate this process, to remind us of our nature and origin; the mission of the savior is to bring the Pneumatic Seeds or Light Sparks, originally from above, to complete fruition and perfection by directing those who are of a pneumatic and psychic nature to the knowledge of the Pleroma and the higher realities.

Gnosis Before Christ

The idea of Gnosis, and the corresponding figure of the Gnostic Revealer, is not unique to Christianity, but found a comfortable home within Christianity at a very early date. In the Nag Hammadi Library, for instance, we find documents of a Jewish gnosis with alternate redeemer figures, where Jesus is not mentioned at all. In *The Sophia of Jesus Christ*, also in the Nag Hammadi Library, we have a clear example of an earlier, pagan "religio-philosophical epistle," *Eugnostos the Blessed*, which has been heavily Christianized and adapted to a Christian framework.[10] In a similar vein, one particularly beautiful writing, the Naassene Psalm, is thought by some scholars to be a document of pagan gnosis, which was later Christianized by replacing the name of an earlier version of the Gnostic Revealer with the name of "Jesus":

> *The Naassene Psalm*
> Primal principle of all things was the first-born Mind;
> The second, poured forth from the first-born, was Chaos;
> The third, which received [being and form from both], is the soul.
> And it is like the timid deer
> Which is hunted upon the earth
> By death, which constantly
> Tries its power upon it.
> Is it today in the Kingdom of Light,
> Tomorrow it is flung into misery,
> Plunged deep in woe and tears.
> On joy follow tears,
> On tears follows the judge,
> On the judge follows death.
> And wandering in the labyrinth
> It seeks in vain for escape.
> Jesus said: Look, Father,

Upon this tormented being,
How far from thy breath
It wanders sorrowful upon earth.
It seeks to flee the bitter chaos,
but knows not how to win through.
For its sake send me, Father;
Bearing the seals I will descend,
Whole aeons I will travel through,
All mysteries will I open,
And the forms of gods will I display;
And the hidden things of the holy way
—Gnosis I call it—I will bestow.[11]

In the pagan Hermetic writings, the Gnostic Revealer is Nous or Logos, either standing alone as a cosmic power or personified in the figure of Hermes Trismegistos or Poimandres, "The Shepherd of Men." The Christian identification of the Logos with the Gnostic Revealer is made clear in the Fourth Gospel and in many other texts.[12] Other examples of the Revealer in gnostic texts include Wisdom (*Sophia*), the Spirit of Truth, Insight (*Epinoia*), the Power of Thought (*Ennoia*), the Light-Bearer (*Phôstêr*), the Angel of Gnosis, and so on.[13] Historical individuals who are figured as gnostic redeemers or "apostles of light" include Old Testament figures, Simon Magus, Zoroaster, Buddha, and Jesus. As Kurt Rudolph notes, "What is offered by Gnosis in this area is therefore very rich, and it shows that it quite shamelessly exploited the most varied traditions and ideas for its own purposes. Purely mythical beings stand along-side more or less historical figures. It is to be assumed that the former belong to the oldest constituent and that a 'historicising' of the redeemer figure set in only later, particularly in connection with the introduction of the figure of Christ into Gnosis."[14] If the major themes and patterns of Gnosis are pre-Christian, it becomes easy to see how gnostic interpretations of Jesus arose so forcefully and so early, immediately after his death.[15]

Divine Knowledge as Self-Knowledge

> Jesus said, "That which you have will save you if you bring it forth from yourselves. That which you do not have within you will kill you if you do not have it within you."
>
> —*Gospel of Thomas* 70

> For he who has not known himself has known nothing, but he who has known himself has at the same time already achieved knowledge about the Depth of the All.
>
> —Jesus in *The Book of Thomas the Contender*

The Gnostic Revealer comes unto his own to fan the slumbering Spark of Divinity in the heart of the soul. Correspondingly, when the gnostic awakens from his slumber and recognizes the Divine Spark within, he realizes his origin in the timeless Kingdom of Light, his kinship with the living Christ. In the words of the *Gospel of Philip*, whoever achieves gnosis is "no longer a Christian, but a Christ."[16] This recalls the words of Jesus in the *Gospel of Thomas*, "He who will drink from My mouth will become like Me. I myself shall become he, and the things that are hidden will be revealed to him."[17]

For the gnostic, the only hope of salvation lies in recognition of the Logos within, through which an individual is connected with the timeless heart of creation.[18] When this occurs, the Kingdom of Heaven is manifest in the soul and the gnostic realizes that he "will not experience death."[19] As Jesus says in the *Gospel of Thomas*, "the Kingdom is inside of you, and it is outside of you. When you come to know yourselves, then you will become known, and you will realize that it is you who are the sons of the living Father. But if you will not know yourselves, you dwell in poverty and it is you who are that poverty."[20]

What we have here in these gnostic writings is the idea of a "realized eschatology." *Eschatology* is the doctrine of "last things," the end of the world, the second coming, or the appearance of the Kingdom of God, for which many of the early Christians were waiting. Yet, when the disciples ask Jesus "When will the Kingdom come?" in the *Gospel of Thomas*, they receive the reply: "It will not come by waiting for it. It will not be a matter of saying 'here it is' or 'there it is.' Rather, the Kingdom of the Father is spread out upon the earth, and men do not see it."[21] In terms of Gnosis, the Kingdom of Heaven is eternally present, yet it only becomes perceptible upon awakening, upon a transformation of consciousness. Hence, when the disciples ask "When will the repose of the dead come about, and when will the new world come?", Jesus replies, "What you look forward to has already come, but you do not recognize it."[22] As Helmut Koester, professor of Christian origins at Harvard University, notes in this regard,

> the *Gospel of Thomas* proposes an interpretation of the sayings of Jesus which has no futuristic eschatological component, but instead proclaims the presence of divine wisdom as the true destiny of human existence. The message of the *Gospel of Thomas* is fundamentally esoteric and is directed to a limited group of elect people. . . . Eschatological change means nothing but insight into the divinity of the self.[23]

This type of perspective is characteristic of Gnosis in general, yet the notion of a *realized eschatology* is also characteristic of an important New Testament writing, the Gospel of John.

The Gospel of John and Gnosis

The Gospel of John presents the most spiritual view of Jesus' nature and mission, and has little in common with the three other gospels of the New Testament canon. Clement of Alexandria tells us that "John, the last of all, seeing that what was corporeal was set forth in the [other] Gospels, on the entreaty of his intimate friends, and inspired by the Spirit, composed a spiritual Gospel."[24] This beautiful work was popular among the gnostic Christians, but with its spiritualized message and gnostic appeal it found, especially in Rome, "only very hesitant acceptance."[25]

One of the most interesting problems offered by the Gospel of John are the long speeches and discourses by Jesus describing his nature, which have no parallels in the Synoptic gospels. Characteristic of these speeches are the "I am" sayings, where Jesus openly reveals his nature. The *Gospel of Thomas*—which in its earliest form most likely predates the Gospel of John—contains many sayings which are parallel to the "I am" sayings of John, and there is considerable evidence that, in the early Christian tradition, entire discourses and dialogues crystalized around such sayings.[26] Helmut Koester points out a number of parallels between the

Gospel of John and the *Gospel of Thomas* in his excellent *Introduction to the New Testament*:[27] For example, John 8.52, "Whoever keeps my word will not taste death," is a variant of *Thomas* 1, "Whoever finds the interpretation of these sayings will not experience death." *Thomas* 77, "I am the light that is above the All," "corresponds entirely" to the Johannine style, and to such passages as John 8.12, "I am the light of the *kosmos*; he who follows me will not walk in darkness, but will have the light of life." *Thomas* 108, "He who will drink from My mouth will become like Me" can be compared with John 7.37–38:

> If any one thirsts, let him come to me and drink. He who believes in me, as the scripture has said, "Out of his heart shall flow rivers of living water."

It can also be compared with John 14.12, where the believer takes on the work of Christ: "Truly, truly, I say to you, he who believes in me will also do the works that I do . . ." These parallels could easily be extended, and anyone who undertakes a careful reading of these two gospels will be struck by many underlying similarities.

In the Gospel of John, the "Spiritual Gospel," the figure of Jesus appears as the "Gnostic Revealer." The significance of Jesus lies in his words and teachings, which awaken a sleeping humanity to the world of the spirit. As Helmut Koester observes:

> Even the word of the earthly Jesus is nothing other than the voice of the heavenly revealer who calls human beings into a new existence determined by the spirit. Baptism is rebirth into this new heavenly stage by means of the spirit; an eschatological component of baptism is absent (John 3.2ff). If the words about the bread of life and the true vine (John 6.26ff; 15.1ff) are interpretations of the eucharist, bread and wine are understood as symbols for the participation in Jesus' heavenly message. Bread and wine are, therefore, not related to Jesus' coming in the future, or to his fate of suffering (as in the understanding of Paul and the Synoptic Gospels), but rather, they represent Jesus' words which give life.[28]

Given the fact that Jesus conforms to the figure of the Gnostic Revealer in the Gospel of John, and that the gospel itself is based upon a "realized eschatology" which is characteristic of gnostic positions, is it safe to assume that the Gospel of John is "a gnostic writing"? Helmut Koester argues that while John contains modified elements of Gnosticism, the gospel itself stresses the fact that the Logos became flesh, and thus rejects a truly gnostic position which would have involved "the radical rejection of the earthly and human sphere."[29] According to Koester, "The word of the revealer thus does not, as it would in Gnosticism, appeal to the ultimately divine knowledge of the hearer, but to the yearnings and expectations that arise from human experience."[30]

Gnosticism: Pessimist, Optimist, and Literalist

The difficulty with Dr. Koester's position is that it relies upon a very rigid definition of *Gnosticism*, giving it the narrow sense of always being world-rejecting and anti-cosmic in orientation. The problems with this view are that the whole definition of *Gnosticism* is a modern one, and that the actual manifestations of Gnosis in antiquity were considerably more varied than anything that can comfortably be accommodated by a textbook definition. Therefore, in his analysis of whether the Fourth Gospel is gnostic in orientation, Helmut Koester may have fallen into the trap of "mistaking the map for the territory."

Gnostic mythology, it is true, usually presents a dualistic picture of the universe, one in which the world of the Pleroma, the realm of light, is contrasted with the oblivion of terrestrial existence. In some teachings, the physical universe is even said to have been created in error by a Demiurge, who stupidly proclaimed himself to be the true God, ignorant of the higher realities. Such teachings, at least on the surface, represent a "pessimist" form of Gnosis which takes a negative view of the physical cosmos. On the other hand, there were also "optimist" forms of Gnosis in which the physical universe was seen—in the classical Platonic sense—as a theophany or a manifestation of the divine. One form of optimist Gnosis is most clearly seen in some of the Hermetic writings, where the divinely beautiful cosmos is seen as representing "a god" unto itself or is pictured as "the Son of God."[31]

One of the most influential books in shaping the modern view of "Gnosticism" was *The Gnostic Religion: The Message of the Alien God and the Beginnings of Christianity* by Hans Jonas, published in 1958. While Jonas offered a brilliant analysis of *Gnosticism* that became definitive for many scholars, it is important to realize that Jonas' own outlook was heavily colored by the nihilistic perspective of existentialism. He thus defined *Gnosticism* as a form of "ancient nihilism,"[32] a radical dualism in which man is alienated from the cosmos. Jonas even added an epilogue to his book entitled "Gnosticism, Existentialism, and Nihilism," in which he claimed that modern existentialism provides the most important key to understanding of the ancient gnostic attitude.

When certain gnostic myths speak of the world as having been created in error by an ignorant Demiurge, the existentialist theologians like Jonas were only too ready to read them in a superficial and literal fashion. However, since the gnostics claimed that their teachings were secret and esoteric, it seems quite mistaken to ignore their inner meaning. Gnostic mythology does indeed paint a radical and dramatic picture of existence, but it was a mythology with a *purpose*, and there is nothing to suggest that these esoteric teachings should be read literally, any more than the writings of the spiritual alchemists should be used as laboratory texts. In any event, if a myth possesses a purpose, it cannot be seen as nihilistic.

If we want to understand the gnostic myths, rather than simply taking them at face value we might investigate what *function* they perform. The initial, obvious function of gnostic mythology is to show in a startling fashion that the world is not as simple as it seems; there is another, hidden level to reality which is rarely acknowledged by society or by most religious institutions. Moreover, we do live in a world where ignorance prevails, and ignorance is the source of vast suffering. This was mythologically expressed by Valentinus when he taught that the world was created from the passions of Sophia—her grief, fear, bewilderment, and ignorance—which developed from her unfulfilled desire to know the ineffable Source. But the reference here, I believe, is not so much to the physical universe being cast out of ignorance as it is to *the world of humanity*. Nature itself is not ugly or evil; these qualities only enter the universe through humanity when individuals fall short of their intrinsic nature—when we forget what it truly means to be human. It is the purpose of the Gnostic Revealer to remind us. Perhaps the gnostic myths also emerged to serve a similar function, to shock us into a higher level of awareness by taking the familiar and turning it on its head. In this way we can look at the universe with new eyes: we are led to think anew about important things that we often take for granted.

While gnostic mythology may be investigated in terms of its function, it is also a reflection of human experience, and these two factors are intrinsically related. The gnostics were interested, above all, in spiritual experience, and from this experience grew the realization that the religious forms of their day were incapable of accommodating the profound realizations to which they were being led. Thus we can detect in their myths a sometimes radical critique of contemporary religious symbolism. The ignorant Demiurge who created the world in error is identified with the jealous God of the Old Testament, not necessarily out of the belief that the world really *was* created in error, but out of the recognition that the wrathful God-image of Jehovah was incapable of reflecting the highest realizations of the Spirit. Thus, in this instance, we have an inner spiritual realization coupled with an eye-opening "social critique," expressed in mythological form.

The dualistic tendencies present in Gnosis, as in most Hellenistic religions, have perhaps been over-emphasized by a literal reading of esoteric texts. As for the myth of the world being created in error, this theme did fulfill an important function by acknowledging the presence of ignorance and evil in the world, and by radically criticizing inadequate belief systems; but, as Jesus says in the gnostic *Gospel of Thomas*, "Whoever believes that the All itself is deficient is (himself) deficient." Similarly, the Greek gematria present in the New Testament is certainly "gnostic," but it represents a form of gnosis which falls outside our inadequate contemporary definition of what Gnosticism was all about. Modern scholars are aware that certain gnostics were interested in gematria and number symbolism, but, because they have not taken the subject seriously, have overlooked the fact that there existed a scientific language of gematria based on the study of first principles, the principles which the Pythagoreans saw as underlying the harmony of the universe. In this sense, both the geometry of the 153 fish in the net and the feeding of the five thousand are assuredly gnostic, yet they reflect a gnosis of cosmic harmony, and not a Gnosticism of a world created in error.

Given these facts, and seeing the inadequacy of the contemporary term *Gnosticism*, we are now in a better position to see whether or not the Gospel of John possesses any type of gnostic orientation.

Starting off with its description of the Logos, the writer of the Fourth Gospel places his entire account within a cosmological framework that goes hand-in-hand with a gnostic perspective: Jesus is identified as the

Logos, a cosmic power characteristic of gnostic speculation. The *kosmos* was made through the Logos, but the world knew him not, having forgotten its own celestial origin. Like other gnostic accounts, the Revealer is manifest in the world, but not all recognize him; those who do, however, become illuminated: having been touched by the energies of the Logos, they become sons of God.

We are next told that the Logos was made flesh and manifest among humanity, a statement which for some has shown that the Fourth Gospel is "not gnostic" because it is "not docetic." The problem with this position is that it wrongly *assumes* that all forms of Gnosis were inherently docetist, or claimed that Jesus "only *appeared*" to be human. This need not be so, however, and in any event we are dealing with the manifestation of a pre-existing cosmic power in the earthly sphere. Even if interpreted literally, we are dealing with a "pneuma Christology" of which docetism is only a variation. In both views "Christ is a heavenly being (whether as spirit or as angel) temporarily clothed with flesh, i.e. appearing in human form."[33] Moreover,

> it is not his earthly appearance which is decisive but his heavenly and otherworldly origin which only faith can perceive. That he has come "in the flesh" means only this, that he has entered into the earthly and human sphere, just as Gnosis also assumes with regard to the redeemer. But the "fleshy Christ" is not the true one, it is the non-fleshy, the Christ of glory, the Logos.[34]

It is against this backdrop of the Christ as a Celestial Power that the entire Fourth Gospel is set.

Unlike the other New Testament accounts, John presents Jesus primarily as a Revealer of saving knowledge. Though the word *gnosis* is never used, the idea is clearly expressed. Moreover, it is clear in many of the speeches and "I am" sayings that Jesus is not speaking as a mere human, but in his capacity as the Logos, the Gnostic Revealer. Whether Jesus says "It is I who am the light which is above them all" in the *Gospel of Thomas* or "I am the light of the world" in John, or many other similar sayings, it is highly unlikely that we are dealing with the words of the historical Jesus; instead, we are faced with statements which can *only* be made by the Celestial Logos, the primordial power of harmony which transcends time and space.

Like other gnostic accounts, the Gospel of John is characterized by many dualistic expressions. Light is contrasted with darkness; the world of the Father is contrasted with the state of this world. Those individuals who are "of God" are contrasted with those who are "not of God,"[35] while those who are "of the truth" hear the voice of Jesus, and those who are not of the truth do not.[36] Even more suggestive of a gnostic perspective is the fact that the emphasis of the entire gospel is on the saving words of Jesus; salvation is imparted by becoming aware of his words, not through the sacraments of an ecclesiastical body.[37] Consequently, there is no mention of the institution of the eucharist at the last supper, where a foot-washing scene appears instead.

Finally, as we have noted, we are dealing in John with a "realized eschatology" very similar to that expressed in the *Gospel of Thomas*. The Kingdom of Heaven, the day of judgment, and the reality of eternal life are not coming realities, but present now for those who have eyes to see: "Truly, truly, I say to you, he who hears my word and believes him who sent me, has eternal life; he does not come into judgment, but has passed from death to life."[38] The emphasis here is on the inner change of perspective which results from "the birth from above."[39] Those who realize the nature of the Logos experience the divinizing light of the Christ within; they become "sons of God," and through this transformation they are led to the experience of "eternal life," which in Greek is *zoê aionios*, the "life of the aeons."

Even though we are not dealing with a complex mythological Gnosis as we find in other sources, the Gospel of John is a clear example of a Christian Gnosis.[40] Jesus is the Logos, the cosmic plan of harmony on which the universe is based. He descends into the terrestrial sphere of mortality to remind those who are "of God" and "of the truth" of their essential nature. As the branches of "the true vine," these "sons of God" are the offspring of the Logos, and thus have something in common with its nature.[41] Those who are led to this realization recognize their intrinsic kinship and relation to the Logos; moreover, they realize their intrinsic immortality in the here-and-now, and thus manifest the Kingdom of Heaven on earth.

CHAPTER SEVEN

New Light on the Mithraic Mysteries

ONE of the most fascinating and widespread religious movements of the Hellenistic age is the worship of the solar divinity Mithras whose birthday was celebrated on December 25, the shortest day of the year, marking the return of *Sol Invictus*, the Unconquered Sun. Mithras was popular among the Roman soldiers who helped spread his worship to every corner of the Empire. Mithraic sanctuaries have been discovered as far north as Scotland; throughout France, Germany, and Italy; to the south in Africa and Egypt; and as far east as the Black Sea. In the area around Rome, over one hundred Mithraic temples have been discovered.[1] This widespread diffusion of the Mithraic mysteries led one scholar to suggest that "If Christianity had been stopped at its birth by some mortal illness, the world would have become Mithraic."[2]

In the same way that seemingly inert flint contains a hidden spark of fire, Mithras was born from a rock as a sturdy youth, symbolizing the heroic and alchemical release of spirit from matter.[3] (*Figure 35.*) Like Jesus, Mithras was born in a *grotto* or cave,[4] and the solar divinity was worshipped in underground cave temples known as *Mithraea* which were designed as models of the universe.[5] The roof of the cave, for example, represented the celestial vault; hence the ceilings of some Mithraea were decorated with stars.[6] The central cult image of the temple was known as the *tauroctony* or bull-slaying scene (*figure 36*), which showed Mithras sacrificing the cosmic bull to bestow everlasting life on his followers, similar in theory to the atoning sacrifice of Christ.[7] As the inscription from one Mithraic sanctuary reads, "Us too you have saved by shedding blood which grants eternity."[8] Initiation into the mysteries was perceived as a form of

Figure 35. Mithras Born from the Rock

The young Mithras born from the rock, holding a torch and trowel, has been likened by scholars to the spark released from flint. This representation, a bas relief, was found in the crypt of St. Clements at Rome.

rebirth[9]—a birth into the light—and Mithraic temples were often oriented to the heavens so that, on a special day, sunlight would enter an opening and bathe the head of the god in heavenly radiance.[10] According to St. Jerome, there were seven levels of initiation, each corresponding to one of the seven planets. Symbols of the seven grades are found in some Mithraic temples, and the initiates were given the following names as they made their ascent toward the higher degrees:[11]

Name of Degree	Meaning	Associated Planet
Pater	Father	Saturn
Heliodromus	Sun-Runner	Sun
Perses	Persian	Moon
Leo	Lion	Jupiter
Miles	Soldier	Mars
Nymphus	Bride	Venus
Corax	Raven	Mercury

Several early Christian fathers were troubled by the many resemblances between the myths and rituals of Mithras and those of the early church.

Figure 36. Mithraeum at Sofia

Mithraic sanctuaries were given the appearance of a cave. The image of Mithras slaying the bull formed the central focal point of the temple.

As noted, Mithras was born on December 25 in a cave and his birth was witnessed by shepherds.[12] Initiates into the mysteries were baptized,[13] and the initiates enacted a resurrection scene.[14] According to Justin, the Mithraic initiates partook of a eucharistic meal of bread and water,[15] though there is also some evidence for the use of wine.[16] The existence of these parallel sacraments in the mysteries of Mithras led one church father to conclude that "the devil," too, "has his Christians."[17]

Mithraism reached its peak in the third century C.E. and succumbed to Christianity in the fourth. After Christianity became the official state religion of the Roman Empire, many churches were constructed atop sanctuaries formerly sacred to Mithras, including St. Peter's in Rome.[18] In other instances, the Mithraic sanctuaries were destroyed or ritually polluted so that they were unfit for use.[19]

New Light on a Secret God

Couched in an aura of strict secrecy with its attendant grades of initiation, one scholar has described Mithraism as "the Freemasonry of the Roman world."[20] Despite the widespread diffusion of the mysteries—hundreds of Mithraea are known to have existed—the oath of secrecy taken by the devotees of Mithras was not taken lightly. Literary references to the Mithraic mysteries are not particularly helpful and so scarce that they only fill a small booklet.[21] Because of this situation, reconstructions of Mithraic myth and doctrine have always been somewhat speculative and have relied more on the surviving archaeological evidence than the scanty written records.

Until quite recently, the study of the Mithraic mysteries was dominated by the writings and ideas of the Belgian scholar Franz Cumont. In the late 1800s, Cumont compiled and published a massive two-volume collection of source material with commentary entitled *Texts et monuments figurés relatifs aux mystères de Mithra* (Texts and Monuments Relating to the Mysteries of Mithras). This was followed by a more popular work, *The Mysteries of Mithras*, published in 1903. Dr. Cumont believed that the worship of the Hellenistic divinity Mithras was imported from Persia, and that Mithras is identical with his Persian namesake Mithra who was also something of a solar divinity.

For more than seventy years Cumont's assumptions remained unchallenged, despite the fact that his theory doesn't adequately account for many aspects of the Roman mysteries. For example, in the Persian worship of Mithra there are no grades of initiation, no cave temples, and no version of the bull-slaying myth which is the central focus of the Mithraic mysteries in the West.

Cumont's theory of Persian origins received a couple of difficult blows at the First International Congress of Mithraic Studies held in 1971. A paper delivered by John Hinnells, an expert on Persian religion, concluded "that the portrayal of Mithras given by Cumont is not merely unsupported by Iranian texts but is actually in serious conflict with known Iranian theology."[22] Another paper by R. L. Gordon showed that Cumont severely distorted the available evidence by forcing the material to conform to his predetermined model of Zoroastrian origins. Gordon concluded that the theory of Persian origins was completely invalid and that the Mithraic mysteries in the West was an entirely new creation.[23]

Since that fateful year, the entire field of Mithraic studies has experienced a quiet yet profound revolution, a transformation best recorded in David Ulansey's book *The Origins of the Mithraic Mysteries: Cosmology and Salvation in the Ancient World* (1989).[24] In this groundbreaking work, Ulansey chronicles how recent scholarly investigation has focused on the symbolism of the tauroctony, the bull-slaying scene which forms the focus of the Mithraic temples. In the tauroctony, Mithras is shown poised over the bull, driving a knife into its shoulder. Oftentimes the sun and moon are represented above, along with the signs of the zodiac. Also common to representations of the tauroctony are the torchbearers Cautes and Cautopates who look like miniature versions of Mithras himself and usually flank the central scene; Cautes holds his torch upward, while the torch of Cautopates is inverted. Finally, there is the mystery of the accompanying animals and symbols: a dog laps up the blood released from the wound of the bull, while wheat grows from the tail of the bull, indicating fertility. Also present are a scorpion, snake, and raven—all symbols which the Cumont hypothesis never adequately explained.

After Cumont's hypothesis had been called into question, scholars took a fresh look at the theory of the German scholar K. B. Stark, published in 1869, which identified the tauroctony as representing a star map. Stark noted the main symbols of the tauroctony represent constellations located in a narrow band of the night sky, moving west:

Symbol	**Constellation**
Bull	Taurus the bull
Dog	Canis Minor the dog
Snake	Hydra the snake
Raven	Corvus the raven
Scorpion	Scorpius the scorpion

This astral theory was revived in 1973 by Roger Beck, who noted that all of these constellations are present in an area between Aldebaran in Taurus and Antares in Scorpio, along with the bright star "Spica, the wheat ear, whose counterpart in the tauroctony is the metamorphosed tail of the dying bull."[25] Then, in 1977, Iranologist Stanley Insler arrived independently at a similar interpretation, unaware of the earlier work of Stark and Beck. These interpretations, as David Ulansey points out, are fine as far as they go. But, if the tauroctony is actually a star map, what celestial phenomenon accounts for the figure of Mithras in the tauroctony?

Mithras, Perseus, and the Personification of Hidden Knowledge

Mithras is pictured as a young hero, dressed in a flowing cape with a Phrygian cap, poised over the sacrificial bull from which he is looking away. Since the tauroctony is a star map, we need only look above the constellation of Taurus to find the original representation of the Mithras figure, the constellation of Perseus, the young hero who slew the Gorgon with his sword. Mithras was known as "the Persian god" and the name *Perseus* was connected in ancient times with "Persia." *Perseus* was also a name of the sun among the Stoics,[26] and, in ancient astronomical representations, is shown wearing a Phrygian cap with his sword upraised above Taurus. Poised above Taurus the bull, Perseus is shown facing backwards on ancient star maps in the same way that Mithras looks toward the rear of the bull in the tauroctony. Like Mithras, the conquering hero Perseus was born in a cave.

David Ulansey further notes that all the figures in the tauroctony represent a narrow band of constellations located along the celestial equator where it dips below the ecliptic between the intersection points of Taurus and Scorpio, as they stood during the astrological Age of Taurus, roughly 4,000–2,000 B.C.E., when the spring sun rose in the constellation of Taurus. In some instances a cup and a lion appear in tandem in the tauroctony. While the cup alone may represent the constellation Crater in the local band of the star map, the cup-lion symbol clearly represents Leo and Aquarius, the summer and winter solstices during the Age of Taurus. David Ulansey's findings also explain the symbolism of Cautes and Cautopates, the two torchbearers who flank the tauroctony. As he points out, in Mithraic iconography Cautes with his raised torch is associated with a bull, while Cautopates with his lowered torch is associated with a scorpion. Taurus and Scorpio represent the two extremes of the star map, the exact points where the celestial equator intersects the ecliptic, the two equinoxes during the Age of Taurus. Cautes with his raised bull torch represents the point of the spring equinox in the constellation of Taurus, when the sun increases, while Cautopates with his lowered scorpion torch represents the point of the fall equinox in the constellation of Scorpio, when the sun declines. (*Figure 37.*)

While all of the symbolism fits perfectly, the question still remains as

Figure 37. Mithraic Tauroctony Found in London

This marble bas relief, found in London, shows Mithras slaying the cosmic bull, surrounded by the twelve signs of the zodiac. Outside the zodiac, in the lower corners are busts of the winds; in the upper corners are the chariot of the sun drawn by its four horses and the chariot of the moon drawn by a team of bulls.

Scholars now identify the Mithraic bull-slaying scene as a star map which depicts the beginning of the Age of Aries. Perseus-Mithras, a version of Aeon or Infinite Time, sacrifices the Bull of Taurus, in order to usher in the cosmic month of Aries. The dog is Canis Minor, the snake is Hydra, and the scorpion is Scorpio, all constellations draped along the celestial equator in the vicinity of Taurus. The two torchbearers, associated with Taurus and Scorpio, represent the spring and fall equinoxes respectively during the Age of Taurus, two important points in the annual journey of the sun.

to why Perseus is shown as "killing the bull," and why the Mithraic star map shows the cardinal points of the year as they existed during the Age of Taurus, when the spring sun rose in the constellation of the bull. The bull-slaying scene, as Ulansey explains, has to do with the astronomical phenomenon known as "the precession of the equinoxes." Due to the fact that the earth subtly wobbles on its axis, over the course of 2,160 years the spring point of the rising sun slowly slips into a new zodiacal sign. When Christianity was getting underway with its prevalent fish symbolism, the spring sun had slipped into the constellation of Pisces, thus inaugurating the astrological Age of the Fishes. At this writing, the spring equinox is slipping into the constellation of the Water-Bearer, which will inaugurate the so-called Age of Aquarius. In antiquity, as today, knowledge of the precession of the equinoxes constituted a form of specialized and hence esoteric knowledge. Moreover, this phenomenon was intimately connected with ancient concepts of the Great Year, composed of the vast astrological ages or "Cosmic Months," and with widespread ideas regarding the renewal or regeneration of time, topics which are discussed in the following chapter.

The precession of the equinoxes was discovered by the Greek astronomer Hipparchus around 128 B.C.E. and described in his work *On the Displacement of the Tropical and Equinoctial Points*. According to Ulansey, the impact of this discovery must not be underrated:

> Hipparchus discovered . . . the revolutionary fact that the entire cosmic structure was moving in a way no one had ever before known. It is not difficult to imagine the extraordinary impact which Hipparchus' discovery must have had on those who were able to understand its full significance, not least of all on Hipparchus himself.[27]

Hipparchus lived on the Greek island of Rhodes shortly before the time of the influential Stoic philosopher Posidonius, discussed in chapter 1, who also made his home there. Posidonius was thus familiar with the discovery of Hipparchus, as were other Stoic philosophers who possessed a keen interest in the doctrine of universal sympathy, cosmic cycles, the Great Year, and the allegorical interpretation of myth. For the Stoics, the Greek gods represent the ultimate causes behind natural and cosmic phenomena; therefore, a cosmic principle may also be symbolically personified as a divinity.

According to Ulansey, the monumental discovery of the precession accounts for the symbolism of the tauroctony and that of Perseus-Mithras. The discovery of a new, unexplainable force which could turn the very wheel of the fixed heavens over the course of millennia implied "the existence of a new divinity responsible for this new cosmic phenomenon, a divinity capable of moving the structure of the entire cosmos and thus a divinity of immense power."[28] Ulansey suggests convincingly that the mythological synthesis and expression of the precession took place in the university town of Tarsus, the birthplace of St. Paul and a center of Stoic philosophy. Perseus was said to have been the founder of Tarsus and is commonly represented on the city's coins; another symbol of Tarsus is the astronomical representation of a lion attacking a bull. Tarsus had a large Persian population and was the capital of the Cilician kings and Persian satraps. Moreover, in the first century B.C.E. Tarsus and Asia Minor came under the rule of Mithradates VI, whose name means "given by Mithra," providing further inspiration for the divinity's name. Interestingly, the coins of the Mithradatic rulers depict Perseus and represent the descent of the Mithradatic dynasty from the legendary "Persian" hero, the slayer of the Gorgon. Finally, Mithradates VI was intimately involved with the so-called Cilician pirates who are known to have been responsible for introducing and disseminating the worship of Mithras.[29]

Since the symbolism of the tauroctony was devised in the waning years of the Age of Aries, Ulansey suggests that the figure of Perseus-Mithra, hovering over the constellation of Taurus with his knife ready to strike, represents the incarnation of the precessional force which overcame the previous Age of Taurus, ushering in what was then the current world age. Perseus-Mithras is a personification of the mysterious force which underlies the precession of the equinoxes—the slow precessional movement of the seemingly fixed stars which leads, over millennia, to a shifting of the astrological ages. Hence, the Mithraic tauroctony encodes an esoteric knowledge of the precession of the equinoxes, an esoteric secret possessed by a small group of initiates: "This image signified the god's tremendous power, which enabled him to end the Age of the Bull by moving the entire universe, in such a way that the spring point moved out of the constellation of Taurus."[30] Thus, Ulansey concludes that "Mithraic iconography was a cosmological code created by a circle of religious-minded philosophers and scientists to symbolize their possession of secret knowledge: namely, the knowledge of a newly discovered god so powerful that the entire cosmos was completely under his control."[31]

Mithras, Aeon, and Pole-God

Another figure associated with the Mithraic mysteries is the Hellenistic god Aeon (*Aiôn*), the personification of Infinite or Boundless Time. As the god of infinitely long durations and the unmoving center of creation, Aeon was associated with both the precession of the equinoxes or cosmic ages, and the celestial axis of the earth and its corresponding point in the heavens: the "unmoved mover" of the pole star, around which the celestial sphere revolves. In earlier Greek symbolism, the god of the celestial pole is Apollo. Not only is the name *Apollo* linked with the celestial pole (*polos*) by Plato and other commentators,[32] but his sacred omphalos stone at Delphi, representative of the creative center, was known as "the axis," the symbolic pole of Greek sacred geography.[33] Put another way, in ancient cosmology the omphalos was symbolic of the celestial axis, while the pole star in the heavens is the omphalos of the celestial vault.

In the so-called Mithras Liturgy, preserved in an ancient magical papyrus, an initiate records a magical invocation "which the great god Helios Mithras ordered to be revealed to me by his archangel, so that I alone may ascend into heaven as an inquirer and behold the universe."[34] In this account, which describes the soul's upward ascent along the cosmic axis, the initiate "born mortal from mortal womb, but transformed by tremendous power" calls upon "the immortal Aeon and master of the fiery diadems," the lord of the pole, to assist him in the spiritual ascent.[35] In the course of his journey, the initiate passes through the door of the mystical "polar sun," after which he encounters the seven polar gods, and is rewarded with a vision of Helios, the Spiritual Sun, "a youthful god, beautiful in appearance, with fiery hair, and in a white tunic and a scarlet cloak, and wearing a fiery crown."[36] After being hailed by an appropriate fire greeting, Helios comes to the celestial pole, after which the initiate encounters the seven Pole Lords of heaven; he then sings a hymn to these "guardians of the pivot . . . who turn at one command the revolving axis of heaven."[37]

In this particular text, we can see the relationship between Aeon, the pole-god and lord of the quiet center, and Helios-Mithras, "the polar sun" who is the revealer of the vision and invocation. These figures, in fact, turn out to be idential: Mithras can be seen as equivalent to Aeon, the god of the celestial pivot, the pole star, which gives birth to the flow of time and the precession of the equinoxes. Aeon-Mithras is therefore the Spiritual

Figure 38. Aeon-Mithras Turning the Zodiac

This Gallic relief shows the child Mithras holding the cosmic sphere in one hand and turning the zodiac with the other. Mithras is here identified as both *kosmokratôr* and Aeon, the god who gives birth to the vast zodiacal ages and the precession of the equinoxes.

Sun, of which the physical sun is a lower reflection. This explains the common Mithraic representations which depict Mithras and Helios *together*, suggesting that the two gods are not equivalent. In some representations Helios even kneels before Mithras, the supreme *kosmokratôr* or "lord of the *kosmos*." A likely interpretation is that Aeon-Mithras, who turns the axis of the universe (*figure 38*),[38] is the unconquered sun, the *true* Spiritual Sun, while Helios, the visible sun who submits to him, is his lower image in time and space. This idea, that the physical sun is only an image of Mithras and not the actual god, is confirmed by the writings of a Mithraic initiate in the Emperor Julian's *Hymn to King Helios*.[39] Futhermore, Mithras in his highest aspect was closely identified with the Orphic divinity *Phanes* (Illuminator or Manifestor), another version of the great cosmic god Aeon.[40] As Joscelyn Godwin notes regarding the beautiful relief of Aeon-Phanes-Mithras reproduced on page 259 of the present volume, this particular image can be seen as "a theophany of the god who directs the universal order from beyond the Pole Star, holding the axis-staff, with the serpent round his body denoting the path of the stars—and of the initiate."[41] Further confirmation of the identity of Mithras with the Aeonic Sun atop the cosmic axis is found in an esoteric text preserved by the church father Hippolytus. Recalling that the original form of the aeonic bull-slayer and lord of the precession was Perseus, this text states that "Perseus is the winged axis which pierces both poles through the center of the earth and rotates the cosmos."[42]

In the end, we are left with the realization that Perseus-Mithras and Phanes are but aspects of the pole-god Aeon—and with a deep mystery, considering the fact that a wobble on the earth's axis precipitates the precession of the equinoxes in the first place. For if Mithras slaying the bull is, at its highest level, a symbol of the time god Aeon—the precession of the equinoxes—is it only coincidence that the action of the earth's axis, itself under the rulership of the pole-god Aeon, is the very cause of the cosmic precession?

Mithraic and Christian Mysteries

David Ulansey's findings, reviewed earlier in this chapter, beautifully account for the *origins* of Mithraic symbolism, but tell us nothing about the development of Mithraism as a mystery religion, a religion that ultimately appealed to the legions of the Roman Empire. Thus he writes:

> As the history of Christianity eloquently demonstrates, a religion can become a very different thing hundreds of years and thousands of miles from its time and place of birth. The Mithraic mysteries ended as a religion of soldiers, based on an ideology of power and hierarchy. But if my arguments are valid, then the Mithraic mysteries began as the response by a group of imaginative intellectuals to the unsettling discovery that the universe was not quite as simple as they had thought it to be.[43]

This useful analogy between the inception and decline of the Mithraic mysteries and a parallel movement in the early Christian mysteries may be developed further. Both Mithraic and Christian symbolism are based on esoteric cosmological insights which formed the inner core of the mystery. By gematria, the name MITHRAS amounts to 365, the number of days in a solar year, while the name of the Christian savior JESUS amounts to 888, symbolic of the Spiritual Sun, the Logos. In their inception, both Mithraic and Christian mysteries gave expression to esoteric insights regarding the nature of human life and the structure of the cosmos through the medium of art, symbolism, myth, and allegory. The Mithraic tauroctony, for example, encapsulates a mystery which is simultaneously spiritual, scientific, psychological, and social, thus unifying the levels of universal expression; this multi-dimensional symbol opened as a compass which helped orient the Mithraic initiate in the mystery of creation, linking his temporal existence with the transcendental experience of infinite time. True icons, by opening into the world of eternity, also work in reverse: they serve a theurgic or magical function by acting as gateways and manifesting, through human consciousness, the eternal principles of being in the temporal world of human affairs.

To continue our analogy, both Mithraic and Christian symbolism are connected with the figure of Aeon, the secret god of Infinite Time who turns the very axis of the cosmos: Mithras embodies the nature of Aeon by slaying the bull of Taurus and inaugurating the era of Aries, while Jesus is the sacrificial lamb of God who closes the Age of Aries, opens the Age of Pisces, and establishes the early Christian mysteries with their Piscean fish symbolism. Within the undulating cycles of infinite time, symbolic expressions rise and fall. Perhaps for this reason the Mithraic mysteries with their beautiful and profound inner symbolism were ultimately destined to pass away—and destined in part to become assimilated within the emerging fabric of the Christian synthesis.[44] That is because, in the ceaseless renewal of time, the moment was right for the manifestation of the emerging Christian revelation, a revelation keyed to the movement of the stars, which drew upon and transmuted the most ancient traditions.

CHAPTER EIGHT

The Birth of the Aeon: Christianity and the Renewal of Time

The Levels of Time

ONE of the most profound and mysterious human experiences is the experience of time. Plato maintained, in his cosmological dialogue the *Timaeus*, that "Time is a moving image of eternity."[1] Plato realized that there are different levels to the expression of time. On the one hand, there is the pole of eternity, the timeless world of archetypes, gods, and first principles; on the other hand, there is the ever-flowing world of time, nature, and manifestation. The realm of manifestation is the living image of the eternal realm, as is time in its cyclical aspect, where the same patterns and stages are eternally manifest, repeating, only now in the circular flow of time.

The different manifestations of time are neatly summarized in that wonderful sketchpad of nature, humanity, the microcosm. One of the useful things that depth psychology has shown is that the ego is merely a complex, a small island of consciousness floating within a much larger sea. When we are most closely identified with the ego, perhaps making a series of phone calls, running errands, or doing other things on our list, we experience time in its most superficial, linear aspect. However, at different moments in life, we have many opportunities to experience deeper levels of time. Since everyone at heart is connected with the timeless center of creation, by moving toward this center we experience the deeper levels of time. From this standpoint, humanity is seen to be a mediator between time and eternity, and both our lives and history itself can be seen as an ongoing dialectic between these different levels of being.

In her excellent book, *Time: Rhythm and Repose*, Marie-Louise von Franz summarizes the different levels of time with the following diagram (*figure 39*) and description:

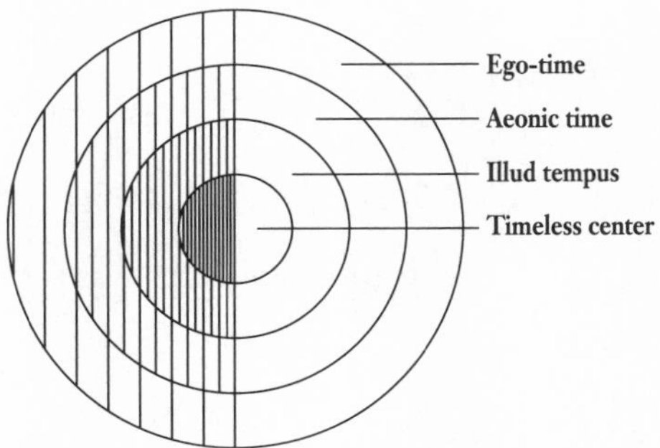

Figure 39. The Levels of Time

> One could compare time to a rotating wheel: our ordinary communal time, which we are aware of in our ego-consciousness, would be the outermost ring which moves more quickly than the others. The next inner ring would represent aeonic time, moving progressively more slowly as the centre is approached. This aeonic time is represented in the idea of the Platonic Year or the Aztec ages or Suns—a time which lasts infinitely longer than our ordinary time. The next and smallest would represent Eliade's *illud tempus*, which is right on the razor's edge between time and no-time, representing, as he says, an 'extratemporal moment of creation.' It is right between unutterable eternity and the beginnings of aeonic time, the latter being the slow-moving life of the archetypes. And finally there is the hole, the non-rotating empty center of the wheel, which remains permanently quiet, outside movement and time.[2]

While our culture encourages us to identify with the outermost ego level of time, which in many respects seems to be moving ever faster, earlier cultures were far more aware of the deeper, slower moving aspects of time. While we tend to view time as a movement of "progress" from point A to point B, earlier civilizations were more aware of the cyclical dimension of time, revealed in the repeating course of the seasons and the heavenly bodies. Events tend to repeat themselves cyclically, and even time itself, from this perspective, like the phenomena of nature, is capable of rebirth and renewal.[3]

The Rebirth of the Light

Many ancient religious festivals are connected with the idea of the renewal of time. In Christianity, the two most important are Christmas, when the sun is reborn from the wintery depths, and Easter, the spring festival.

The ancient winter solstice, December 25, signifies the rebirth of the Unconquered Sun (*Sol Invictus*). At this point in the year the days grow longer and light re-enters the world. As we noted in the last chapter, this festival of the Reborn Sun was initially associated with the solar divinity Mithras and, like so many other ancient religious customs and celebrations, was taken over by the early Christians to maintain a sense of continuity between the old and the new.[4] While these elements were adopted by the early church, we should realize that the process involved transcends that of a mere conscious adaptation. That is because festivals such as Christmas, the solstice celebration, are permanently rooted in both the fabric of the natural world and human nature.

January 1, the main festival of the Roman divinity Janus, also represents the rebirth of the cyclical year and the renewal of time. Before the adoption of December 25 as the birthday of Jesus the Spiritual Sun, the Nativity was celebrated on January 6, the day of "Epiphany" or "manifestation of the Lord." Within early Christianity, three significant events were celebrated on this date:

1) The birthday of Jesus

2) The baptism of Jesus and the descent of the dove (signifying his divinity), and

3) The "turning of the water into wine" at Cana, Jesus' first divine act in the Gospel of John.

Today, of course, Epiphany is celebrated as the date of the visit of the three Magi, the Persian astrologers who saw the birth of the Logos foretold in the stars.

Significantly, January 6 was a major pre-Christian holy day in the ancient world. In Alexandrian Egypt it was the birthday of "Aeon"—the personification of Infinite Time.[5] According to the church father Epiphanius, the birth was celebrated in Alexandria at the Korion, a pagan temple of the divine maiden or Virgin. After ritually processing with an effigy of the divine child, which bore the image of a golden cross, the celebrants exclaimed at dawn: "Today, at this hour, the Korê, that is to say the Virgin, has given birth to the Aeon."[6] Likewise, the birthday of Jesus was the *natalis mundi*, the birthday of the world; as one scholar observes, "In the New Testament, he already reveals the characteristics of the Aeon; he is the alpha and the omega, the beginning and the end, the first and the last, he who is, who was, and who is to come."[7]

January 6 was also the date of Dionysian wine miracles. Water drawn from the Nile on this day was said to turn to wine, and many similar instances are reported from antiquity as taking place on this date.[8] Jesus states in the Fourth Gospel that "I am the true vine," the true Dionysus. Since Dionysus was the resurrected savior of the Orphics in Greece, it is unlikely that the author of the Fourth Gospel was ignorant of the connections he was acknowledging with the January 6 wine miracle at Cana.

The Greek word Aeon (*Aiôn*) has several meanings. In classical Greek it means a "lifetime" or an "age," a great expanse of time. Aristotle, in his work *On the Heavens*, explains that the term is derived from *aei ôn*, "always being."[9] For the Christian gnostics, *Aeons* (literally, "eternities") are the eternal powers or archetypes behind creation, the emanations of the ineffable and transcendent God. The term *Aeon* appears in the New Testament where Paul refers to "the rulers of this age (*aiôn*)"[10] and in the Johannine phrase "life everlasting (*zoê aionios*)."[11] As noted in the last chapter, Aeon was also a cosmic divinity, the personification of Infinite or Boundless Time. In this regard, Aeon was variously identified with Apollo, Abraxas, Harpocrates, Mithras, Jesus, and so on.

The Great Year and the Platonic Months

Yet *Aeon* had another meaning in the ancient world which is frequently overlooked. It referred to the vast ages, the twelve Aeons or Platonic Months which make up the Great Year. Because of the precession of the equinoxes, the sun moves backward through the zodiac, one degree every seventy-two years. Every 2,160 years the spring point or vernal equinox slips into a new zodiacal sign. We are now entering the Age or Aeon of Aquarius; two thousand years ago, the Age of Pisces was getting underway. As we saw in the last chapter, David Ulansey has shown that the central symbol of the Mithraic mysteries conceals an astrological code, related to the precession of the equinoxes. The same sort of astrological symbolism is prevalent in early Christianity, with its pervasive fish symbolism, which corresponds with the movement of the spring point into the constellation of Pisces. In antiquity, the precession of the equinoxes was well known to the learned; the church father Origen even refers to it as "a well known theorem."[12] But was the precession known long before the beginning of the Christian era? David Ulansey follows the view of classical scholars that it was discovered by the astronomer Hipparchus around 128 B.C.E. While there are no surviving historical records to contradict this view, the careful observer, looking back over the ages, is struck by a curious relationship between the contemporary religious symbolism and the corresponding Platonic month. (*Figure 40.*) Moreover, professional astronomers have suggested that the effects of the precession were known long before Hipparchus.[13]

The earliest period of which we have historical record is the Platonic month of Taurus (♉), *circa* 4000–2000 B.C.E, when the cult of the bull flourished in Egypt. At this time, "The bull played a considerable role in the Old Kingdom, and in the Pyramid Texts the King is often called 'bull of the sky.'"[14] What is more, around 3200 B.C.E., the Mastaba of the Serpent King was constructed at Saqqara, surrounded by 346 bull-heads made of clay, but containing real horns.[15] As we saw in the previous chapter, the iconography of Mithras slaying the bull denotes the end of Taurus and ushers in the Aeon of Aries.

The Age of Aries the ram (♈), *circa* 2000–1 B.C.E., corresponds with the reign of fiery Jehovah, who became angered by the Israelites' worship of the golden calf, a throwback to the earlier Age of Taurus.[16] This same period corresponds with the rise of Amen-Ra, the ram-headed solar god in Egypt, who was later identified by the Greeks with Zeus.[17] Since Alexander the Great saw himself as a son of Zeus, and visited the oracle of Ammon at the oasis of Siwah in the Libyan desert, Alexander is frequently shown on coins with ram's horns to symbolize his link with Zeus Ammon. Another relic of traditional symbolism relating to the Platonic Month of Aries is the voyage of Orpheus and the other Argonauts in quest of the Golden Fleece.[18]

Finally, the Era of Pisces (♓), *circa* 1–2000 C.E., corresponds with the birth of Christianity and its prevalent fish symbolism. The apostles were known as "fishers of men,"[19] while the early Christians were known as "little fishes."[20] For the early Christians the Greek word 'ΙΧΘΥΣ, "Fish," was an acronymn, standing for "Jesus Christ, Son of God, Savior."[21] Jesus was both the "Lamb of God," whose sacrifice closed the Platonic month of Aries,[22] and the rising sun of the Piscean Era, the Celestial Fish of the new Aeon.[23] The Christian savior was born of a Virgin, and when the newly born spring sun slipped into and rose in the constellation of Pisces two thousand years ago, Virgo, the virgin, was standing on the Western horizon, for it is exactly opposite Pisces in the zodiac.

What is it that accounts for these remarkable fluctuations in religious symbolism? The answers have to do with what C. G. Jung called "changes in the constellation of psychic dominants"—a changing of the gods—and the cyclical nature of time. While there are underlying patterns in the unfolding nature of time, things do not stay the same, and certain times have their own specific qualities. The Egyptians, like many other ancient cultures, were keenly aware of this reality, picturing the flow of time as a procession of gods.[24] Each hour of the day and night is divine, yet each possesses its unique quality. Ultimate reality may remain unchanged, but our ways of perceiving, approaching, and representing it are intrinsically tied up with our cultural setting, which is itself determined by the gods and qualities of time. The same is true of music: while the laws of musical harmony are one and the same everywhere, musical expression is influenced by the qualities, colors, and gods of time and culture. One can see this merely by studying the music of Western civilization, but the idea is more firmly expressed, say, in the nature of the Indian *raga*. Each *raga* is associated with a specific time of day, a specific divinity and form of mental imagery, a particular scale and rhythmic pattern, and is meant to evoke a very specific mood.

Like civilizations, forms of religious expression rise and fall. There is a period of birth, development, maturity, and decline. The only certainty is that the process will continue in its cyclical fashion, given the fact that both civilization and spiritual realization are intrinsic requirements of the human spirit, itself sanctified by, and a reflection of, universal nature.

The Image of the Golden Age in Times of Cultural Renewal

The more closely one investigates the origins of Christianity, or any other profound cultural or spiritual manifestation, the more mysterious it becomes. Religious and cultural movements, like music, draw upon

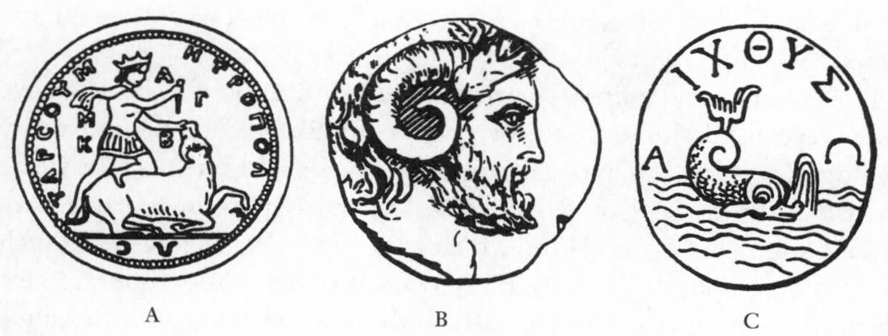

Figure 40. Precessional Symbolism in Religious Iconography

Many scholars have noticed a relationship between ancient religious symbolism and the passage of the great astrological ages brought about by the precession of the equinoxes.

A) As detailed in chapter 7, the iconography of Mithras slaying the bull symbolizes the cosmic precession and the end of the astrological age of Taurus, 4000–2000 B.C.E.

B) During the age of Aries, the ram became prevalent in ancient religious symbolism. An example is the depiction of Zeus Ammon with ram horns which arose during this period, 2000–1 B.C.E.

C) Jesus, the spiritual avatar of the age of Pisces, 1–2000 C.E., was known as the Fish to the early Christians. In the above depiction, Jesus is symbolized as a dolphin, flanked by the letters Alpha-Omega, and crowned with the inscription ΙΧΘΥΣ, "Fish," an acronym of the Greek phrase "Jesus Christ, Son of God, Savior." Before the coming of Christianity, the dolphin was the sacred animal of Apollo. For the Greeks, the dolphin was seen as a psychopomp or guide of souls because of its propensity to rescue sailors lost at sea, a symbolism which was assimilated by the early Christians.

preexisting elements and situate their expression within a temporal context, but cannot entirely be described as the outcome of specific historical events, one leading to another, like a chain of falling dominoes. That would be to ignore the eternal reality of inspiration, which is something that possesses individuals, at least as much as individuals are thought to "possess inspiration." Many writers have noticed that there are sensitive moments within the flow of time when certain ideas suddenly seem to be "in the air." Charles Fort, that rascal philosopher, pointed out that cherry trees have no difficulty figuring out when to bloom; and, when reviewing the fact that several people independently invented the steam engine at the same time, mused sagely that "perhaps it was steam engine time."

Every traditional culture maintains that civilization and its arts have been revealed by some type of god or godlike being. Behind every profound cultural and spiritual expression, such as the birth of Christianity, the birth of the Gothic cathedrals, or the Renaissance, there is an underlying vision or revelation which takes hold of a generation. In such periods of temporal, cultural, and spiritual renewal, it is as though a new spirit of promise is in the air, felt gently blowing from afar. Sensitive individuals, like poets, artists, musicians, and philosophers, realize that they are standing at the end of an era, yet at the beginning of a new cycle. The old forms of expression are seen to be degenerate, no longer what they once were, inadequate vessels for the transmission of living insight. People once again ask the eternal questions: What is humanity? Why are we here? What are those qualities and pursuits which make life worth living in the first place? How is it possible to invoke and manifest the highest principles of the universe and live our lives on the highest possible level?

During such periods of cultural renaissance and renewal, a spiritual impulse is released into the world of human affairs. Those visionaries who have long been watching the horizon detect the first rays of light; they are the first to detect the soothing breath of spring's first breeze, announcing the promise of a new season. By participating in this process, which can only unfold through the agency of humanity, individuals experience an expansion of their faculties and perceptions, and are led to a glimpse of the Golden Age, the light of which is shining in their midst.[25]

The Golden Age is referred to in myths around the world as the state of primordial perfection where the first men are said to have lived in a paradisical condition, having free communion with the eternal forces which bind and govern the cosmos, subsisting in perfect harmony with both the gods and their environment. In Jewish myth, it is the primeval paradise of Eden, the word *paradise* meaning a garden or grove.[26] The Greeks envisioned the Golden Age as the age of Kronos or Saturn; it was a time of human and natural perfection, when men lived without cares or labor, and where death was no more terrible than sleep.[27] The ancient Egyptians lived in a Golden Age under the rule of Osiris, who revealed the arts of civilization to his subjects.[28] The Golden Age is recapitulated in subsequent high cultural epochs, such as the time of Solomon and his Temple, the reign of King Arthur in Britain, or in the lovely image of Orpheus charming the beasts with his lyre, symbolizing the Peaceable Kingdom, the manifestation of divine harmony on earth.

In a metaphysical sense, the Golden Age is a representation of the eternal harmony which informs the fabric of creation. As such, it is an image of the Logos: not something which merely existed in the distant past, but an ever-present reality, if we are perceptive enough to see. The Golden Age is a symbol of the timeless, eternal realm, the realm of first principles, the realm of perfect harmony. At the end of a cultural cycle, and the beginning of a new one, people are drawn to a vision of the Golden Age for obvious reasons. This occurs not out of escapism, but out of the natural dialectic between time and eternity. When the temporal vehicles of culture break down and no longer suffice in leading to the realizations of the spirit, amidst the rubble of crumbling foundations people are led once more, out of necessity, to a perception of eternal realities. And while it is not possible to realize perfection on earth in a sense tangible for all, it surely is possible for every person and every society to realize perfection's best possible image, as Plato suggests, each according to their innate ability. In periods of cultural renewal, this process starts in the lives of a few individuals. Those first touched find themselves devoted to invoking the highest beauty and set out on an uncompromising quest for spiritual knowledge and personal realization; the enchantment then spreads outward, eventually touching the entire culture.

We can see this process at work at many points in Western civilization. It accounts for the ahistorical element of revelation in every significant period of cultural renewal. One of the clearest, most interesting examples is to be found in the lyrics of the Troubadours and the birth of courtly love in the Middle Ages. In the 1100s, there arose in the courts of Provence, in southern France, a new form of lyric poetry, accompanied by music, which sang of the poet's unobtainable love, to which he was willing to devote his entire life. Marriage in the Middle Ages was predominately an economic and civic affair, with little relation to personal passion, compatibility, or mutual attractiveness. It is astonishing to realize that the whole phenomenon of romantic love, which is accepted today as a deep-seated cultural ideal, was primarily introduced through the medium of the Troubadours. As one scholar succinctly notes, "with the coming of the

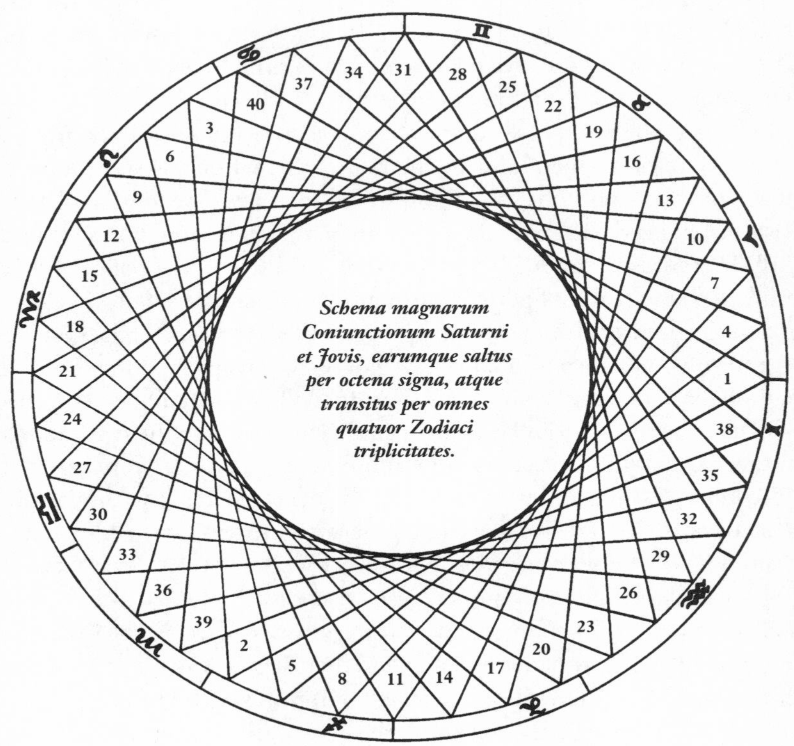

Schema magnarum
Coniunctionum Saturni
et Jovis, earumque saltus
per octena signa, atque
transitus per omnes
quatuor Zodiaci
triplicitates.

Figure 41. The Great Conjunctions of Saturn and Jupiter

This illustration by the astronomer Johannes Kepler (1571–1630) shows the sequence of great trigons sketched out in the heavens by conjunctions of Jupiter and Saturn, the two outmost planets of traditional astrology. Jupiter-Saturn conjunctions occur roughly once every 20 years. Triple conjunctions occur about every 139 years, while triple conjunctions in Pisces occur roughly once every 900 years. The triple conjunction of Jupiter and Saturn in the constellation of Pisces in 7 B.C.E. is thought by many scholars to be the celestial wonder which heralded the birth of Jesus.

Troubadours, love is taken seriously for the first time."[29] And while many have tried to trace the realizations and expressions of the Troubadours back to this particular source or that, the work of those inspired, noble poets can only be seen as a unique outpouring of the spirit, in a specific cultural framework, which was to have far-reaching effects. They were the first to realize that love ennobles both the lover and the beloved, a profound realization that cannot merely be explained in terms of cultural, economic, or historical forces.[30] Their enchanted vision, however, continued to flow outward for centuries, enlivening medieval culture, inspiring chivalry, the Grail legends, and the entire Western attitude regarding the possibility—and desirability—of romantic love.

We can see similar forces at work during the early days of the Christian movement, which arose at the end of a spiritual cycle and was characterized by an expectation for the renewal of time. This renewal, it was thought, would come about through the work of an enlightened and anointed monarch, a "Messiah," who would re-establish the Golden Age. There was a great expectation for the dawning of a new age at the beginning of the Christian era, correlated with the passage of the spring point into the Platonic month of Pisces, the sign of the fishes. For example, a pagan document from 9 B.C.E, commemorating the introduction of the Julian calendar, states the following:

> The Providence which rules over all has filled this man with such gifts for the salvation of the world as designate him as Savior for us and for the coming generations; of wars he will make an end, and establish all things worthily.
>
> By his appearing are the hopes of our forefathers fulfilled; not only has he surpassed the good deeds of earlier time, but it is impossible that one greater than he can ever appear.
>
> The birthday of God has brought to the world glad tidings that are bound up in him.
>
> From his birthday a new era begins.[31]

Likewise, the Latin poet Virgil, writing around the year 37 B.C.E, foretells the coming of a divine child, a solar king, who will re-establish the Golden Age:

Come are those last days that the Sybil sang:
The ages' mighty march begins anew.
Now comes the virgin, Saturn reigns again:
Now from high heaven descends a wondrous race.
Thou on the newborn babe—who first shall end
That age of iron, bid a golden dawn
Upon the broad world—chaste Lucina, smile:
Now thy Apollo reigns.[32]

As can be seen from these passages, the times were characterized by messianic longings, and not only amongst the Jews.[33] Greek state religion, which had always been mainly a civic affair, had grown sterile and was incapable of meeting the spiritual needs and expressions of the *individual*, that new creation brought about by the collapse of the city-state. A new synthesis, a new expression of the ancient wisdom was expected to reveal itself, and was correspondingly invoked by those who were waiting. As the story of the three Magi makes clear, the heavens were watched for the appropriate sign which might usher in the spiritual revelation of the new Aeon.

That sign came in the year 7 B.C.E. in an extremely rare triple conjunction of Saturn and Jupiter, the two portentous hands of the cosmic clock, which occurs only once every nine centuries in Pisces, where the event took place.[34] (*Figures 41 and 42.*) At one moment the two outermost planets looked as if they were nearly touching in the sky, separated by only 1 degree. It must have been a spectacular sight for anyone looking upward. It must have been an even more spectacular event for the learned astrologers. Since the triple conjunction occurred in the constellation of Pisces, it must have been seen as inaugurating the start of the Age of the Fishes. According to the gospel accounts, it was at about this time that Jesus, the avatar of the new age, was born in Bethlehem.

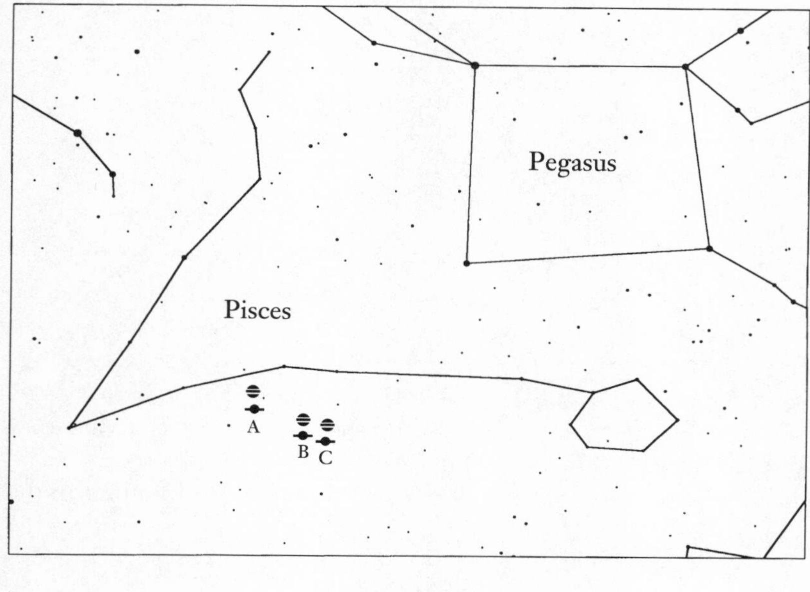

⊜ = Jupiter
-●- = Saturn

A) First conjunction, May 27, 7 B.C.E.: 0.98 degrees of separation.
B) Second conjunction, October 6, 7 B.C.E.: 0.98 degrees of separation.
C) Third conjunction, December 1, 7 B.C.E.: 1.05 degrees of separation.

Figure 42. The Triple Conjunction of 7 B.C.E.: "The Star of Bethlehem"

Shown above are the three conjunctions of Jupiter and Saturn in the constellation of Pisces in 7 B.C.E. In astrological symbolism, Pisces is the sign of the Jews and the "last days" because it is the final sign of the zodiac. Jupiter is the planet of kingship (the Messiah) and Saturn is the planet associated with Yahweh and Israel/Palestine. Because of these factors, the triple conjunction was seen as signalling the birth of the awaited Jewish Messiah. The triple conjunction was probably seen by some as the decisive event which opened the astrological age of Pisces.

CHAPTER NINE

The Orphic Christ and the "New Song" of Christianity

HOW was it that Christianity came into being and where did its teachings come from? The conventional view is that it developed from Jewish roots, the teachings of Jesus, a spiritual leader and exorcist, whose followers propagated a religion based upon his teachings, and upon a belief in his death and resurrection.

There is no doubt some truth to this assumption, but it tells less than half the story. While the teachings and practices of Christianity did focus around the central figure of Jesus, there is no evidence whatsoever that Jesus himself had any plans or desire to start a new religion. In fact, while the gospel accounts cannot be read as historical documents, the impression they give is that Jesus, like the gnostics, was not happy with the effects of organized religion in the first place. Many of Jesus' actions and teachings, as portrayed in the gospels, are strongly critical of contemporary Judaism. Jesus is pictured as preaching a message of spiritual love rather than one based in the Mosaic Law; he breaks the observance of the sabbath and criticizes religious officials for blind adherance to custom while ignoring the reality of the spirit; like a rebel reformer, he casts the money lenders out of the Temple; he accuses the Pharisees of taking the keys of knowledge and hiding them; and he teaches the mysteries of "the kingdom within," the mysteries of transformed consciousness, rather than expounding teachings to be upheld by a priestly class. This "libertarian" message did not, apparently, go over well with the authorities in charge. Moreover, while there was great hope for a Jewish Messiah or deliverer at the time, the Messiah was pictured as a liberating monarch, in regal and stately terms. The notion that the expected liberator might take the form of a carpenter and exorcist from Nazareth, who consorted with lowly tax collectors, fishermen, and prostitutes, cannot have have been an appealing notion to the messianic party.

Not surprisingly, the new faith did not find many converts among the Jews, but spread quickly amongst the Greeks. While there are a plethora of Jewish elements present in early Christianity, they have been overemphasized to the detriment of the Hellenistic contribution. Christianity is, after all, a Hellenistic religion and the New Testament is written entirely in Greek, the learned tongue of the Roman Empire. And while the figure of Jesus did not conform to the conventional Jewish image of what a Messiah would be like, there are other powerful reasons why Christianity, as a religious movement, was more enticing to the spirit of Greek culture. As Vittorio Macchioro notes in his study *From Orpheus to Paul*:

> The Greeks themselves had been working toward Christianity for many centuries. Christianity, apart from the person of Jesus, appears as the inevitable issue of the long process we have depicted. The Jewish revival, centering around the Messianic person of Jesus, can not be considered the real Christianity. What people call Christianity, and what Christianity turns out really to be, is the product of Greek thought, is the result of Greek belief in Jesus.[1]

Christianity Before Christ: The Orphic Impulse in Ancient Greece

Christianity arose at a time when Roman imperial religion had grown sterile.[2] The state cult consisted of ceremonies and sacrifices made in the temples. Perhaps wisely, it preached no dogma. It was largely a civic affair and held out no promise of personal salvation. The gods were represented in human form, a fact which philosophers had been complaining about since before the time of Plato. Yet, alongside the exoteric state religion, there existed the esoteric, underground stream of Orphism, named after the mythical poet and bard Orpheus. According to popular account, it was Orpheus, "the founder of initiations," who had established the religious mysteries and the spiritual teachings of the Greeks. Orphism possessed a theology and held out the promise of eternal life in the other world for the initiate. And, contrasted with the state religion, Orphism was intensely *personal*.

The Orphics taught that the god Dionysus, as a child, had been slain by the evil Titans. One day, while innocently playing with some toys—dice, a top, a ball, a mirror, apples, a bull-roarer, and a tuft of wool[3]—the Titans approached Dionysus from behind. They ripped him to shreds and devoured his fragments. Infuriated at the senseless attack, Zeus destroyed the Titans with his thunderbolt. From the ashes of the Titans humanity came into being. Because humanity arose from the ashes of the Titans, people possess a lawless and sometimes destructive "Titanic" nature. However, because the Titans had consumed Dionysus, humanity also contains a Divine Spark of Dionysus. This is the essential Self, a spark of the Godhead, which possesses eternal life.

The myths of the Greeks tell of the dismemberment of Dionysus, but also of his resurrection.[4] Origen refers to the dismemberment of the young god, after which "he was put together again and was, as at were, restored to life, and went up to heaven."[5] According to a variant of the Titan myth, Apollo took the pieces of Dionysus to Delphi, the center of the universe, and buried them by the omphalos.[6]

According to the Orphics, the soul pre-exists before descending into the realm of generation, the world of the manifest universe. Our birth is a forgetting of the spiritual realities we once knew. The world is pictured as a Wheel, the ever-spinning realm of generation, the cycle of incarnations. Through asceticism and spiritual practice, it is possible to help purify the soul of its Titanic nature and strengthen the Divine Spark within. Then, if we attain a sufficient level of spiritual realization, it is possible eventually to transcend the cycle of births and deaths and live eternally with the gods.

Most significantly, Orphism taught that it was possible to attain union with a divinity. Because of the divine spark in humanity, humanity is in part divine, participating in the nature of the gods, in the nature of the dismembered and resurrected divinity, Dionysus. The Orphics, in short, spiritually participated in the mystical nature of Dionysus in the same way that the early Christians participated in the "mystical body of Christ."

The concept of mystical identification with a divinity is a Hellenistic idea and quite alien to Jewish theology and religious aspiration. That is why the apostle Paul, in teaching mystical union with Christ, had little success in propagating his message to the Jews. Among the Greeks, however, Orphism had prepared the way, and Paul's mission met with great success. The personal identification with a slain and resurrected savior divinity was out of place in the Jewish world; amongst the Greeks it was commonplace and readily acceptable.[7]

The New Song

In the Gospel of Matthew, the author adds many exegetical interpretations not present in the other Synoptic gospels to show how Jesus fulfilled the prophecies of the Old Testament. Written for a Jewish-Christian audience, Matthew portrays Jesus as the New Moses.

Similarly, writing for a Hellenistic audience, the great church father and initiate Clement of Alexandria portrays Jesus as the New Orpheus, and Christianity as the "New Song" of the Eternal Logos. As Clement explains, Arion of Methymna and Amphion of Thebes are renowned amongst the Greeks for the power of their song. Arion is famous for "having allured the fishes" with his lyre; Amphion for having built the seven walls around Thebes by the power of his music alone. "Another Thracian," that is, Orpheus, "tamed the wild beasts by the mere might of song; and transplanted trees—oaks—by music."[8]

While the harmony of Orpheus possessed the power to tame the beasts and move stones and trees, Clement exhorts his readers to

> Behold the might of the new song! It has made men out of stones, men out of beasts. Those, moreover, that were as dead, not being partakers of the true life, have come to life again, simply by becoming listeners to this song. It also composed the universe into melodious order, and tuned the discord of the elements to harmonious arrangement, so that the whole world (*kosmos*) might become harmony (*harmonia*). . . . And this deathless strain—the support of the whole and the harmony of all—reaching from the center to the circumference, and from the extremities to the central part, has harmonized this universal frame of things, not according to the Thracian music [of Orpheus], which is like that invented by Jubal, but according to the paternal counsel of God . . .[9]

One is here reminded of the Orphic *Hymn to Apollo*, where it is stated that Apollo harmonizes the poles of the *kosmos* with his versatile lyre.[10]

Clement explains that through the agency of the Holy Spirit, the Logos of God has tuned the universe, and especially man, who, being composed of body and soul, is a universe in miniature. Through the agency of humanity, the Holy Spirit "makes melody to God on this instrument of many tones." Humanity, states Clement, is "a beautiful breathing instrument of music" made after God's Image, that of the Logos.[11] This Clement calls "the Extraterrestrial Wisdom, the Celestial Logos, the all-harmonious, holy instrument of God."[12] As we know from the teachings of Hellenistic cosmology, the Logos is eternal—it has always existed and always will. In the words of Clement, "inasmuch as the Word was from the first, He was and is the divine source of all things; but inasmuch as He has now assumed the name Christ, consecrated of old, and worthy of power, he has been called by me the New Song."[13]

Clement portrays Christianity as the New Song of the Logos, Jesus as the New Orpheus.[14] Based on his description above, however, Clement could have just as accurately described the Hellenistic Christ, the Celestial "Word," as the New Apollo.

Judaism provided Christianity with the notions that Jesus was the Messiah, that his coming was foretold by the prophets, and much else besides. But the primary appeal of the Christian faith was that it allowed the average believer a personal relationship to a slain and resurrected divinity, and, through this participation, the possibility of everlasting life. This idea, and the desire for such a relationship, was totally alien to Judaism, but something readily accessible to the Greeks. The way had been prepared by Orphism and the resurrected Dionysus, so that when Jesus says in the Fourth Gospel that "I am the true vine," it was no doubt read, and probably meant, that he was the true savior, "the true Dionysus."[15] Orphism promulgated the idea of eternal life, a concept of "original sin" and purification, the punishment of the wicked in the afterlife, and the allegorical interpretation of myth, which the early church fathers applied to the Christian scriptures. Orpheus was known as the Good Shepherd,[16] and Jesus was frequently represented as Orpheus, playing music and surrounded by animals, a symbol of the Peaceable Kingdom or Golden Age, representing the ever-present harmony of the Logos. (See "Orpheus the Theologian.") Like Orpheus, Jesus descended to Hell as a savior of souls.

Even the myth of the Gnostic Revealer is prefigured in the Orphic and Platonic idea of recollection. This explains that we who have descended to the terrestrial sphere have drunk from the stream of Forgetfulness and are asleep; we have forgotten our celestial origin. In Platonic thought, the path of philosophy—the activation of the *logos* in the soul—leads to the recollection of first principles, the knowledge of our celestial origin. In later gnostic mythology, the Logos is personified in the figure of the Gnostic Revealer who descends from above to remind sleeping humanity of their true origin in the transcendental light of the Pleroma, the timeless realm of spiritual perfection. The Orphics taught that slumbering humanity possesses a Divine Spark of Dionysus in the soul; the Gnostics spoke of a Divine Spark or Seed of Light in the soul, which the Gnostic Revealer fans until it blazes forth in re-cognition of its nature, origin, and end.

The Development of the Christian Mysteries

There can be little doubt that, among the initiates of the early church, Christianity was seen—*and consciously developed*—as a reformation of the earlier mysteries; Jesus was seen as a new manifestation of the pre-existing Logos. Behind the scenes of the early Christian movement, there existed an unknown number of enlightened scholars who were attempting to take the best elements of Jewish, Greek, and Egyptian spirituality and synthesize them into a new, universal expression. Exactly who these individuals were we do not know. The process, however, had already begun before the birth of Jesus. In Philo of Alexandria, writing around 25 C.E., we find a fully developed Logos doctrine, based on Greek sources, used to interpret the symbolism of the Jewish scriptures allegorically: a clear example of the conscious merging and synthesis of traditions.[17] Likewise, as we have seen in chapter 6, the idea of the Gnostic Revealer is pre-Christian, and gnostic mythologizing drew on a wide range of sources; we can even see examples in the Nag Hammadi Library of early gnostic texts which were later "Christianized" by inserting the name of Jesus.

Clement of Alexandria, the most learned of the Christian fathers, was privy to the mysteries of the early church and consciously attempting to synthesize the teachings of Christianity and Judaism with the highest insights of Greek learning. As one writer notes,

> Clement would have enriched Christianity with the deep spirituality of Platonism and enthroned Christ on the highest culture of the age if the *vox populi* and the masters of ecclesiastical organization had permitted. He

> acclaimed Greek philosophy as inspired of God while critically sifting its propositions, and he begged Christians not to be frightened of it as of ghosts. He protests against those who would attribute the rise of philosophy to the devil; "man has been born chiefly for the knowledge of God," and Clement discovers in Greek philosophy an aid to the attainment of that knowledge, just has he represents Christianity as "the faith of knowledge" (gnostic faith). . . . He advocated a Christianity resting not on credulity but on frank inquiry: "it is impossible to find without having sought, or to have sought without examining, or to have examined without analysing and raising questions with a view to lucidity," and "one indeed is the way of Truth, but into it, as into an ever-flowing river, streams from everywhere are confluent," and one of these main tributaries was the Greek wisdom which other apologists set in opposition to Christianity.[18]

Clement openly refers to the inner mysteries of the New Song, though he is careful not to reveal too much in writing.[19] For example, his discussion of the symbolism of the mystery of the loaves and fishes digresses to another topic at a key point, yet it is significantly presented in a chapter about the use of numerical ratios in the interpretation of scripture.[20] By presenting Christianity as the New Song of the eternal Logos, Clement sought to channel and transmit the highest realizations of the Greek spirit within the fabric of the new faith, as others had sought to do before him. While Clement was advocating the acceptance of classical learning, philosophy, and even ancient science within the fabric of Christianity, a growing number of Christians were suspicious of any type of learning; they felt that unquestioning belief was the surest road to salvation.

While some well-known scholars, such as the late Arthur Darby Nock, have vehemently rejected the notion that the early Christians consciously adopted elements from the "pagan mysteries,"[21] this view can no longer be supported, seeing that the stories of the 153 fish in the net and the feeding of the five thousand were consciously based on the geometry of the Greek number canon, associated with the mysteries of Apollo and Hermes. The only explanation for the presence of this material in the New Testament is that some individuals saw Christianity as a new synthesis of the ancient wisdom, and that they helped give form to this synthesis through the accepted means. From this perspective, certain elements of Christianity literally were a new manifestation of the eternal Logos, as Clement of Alexandria straightforwardly tells his readers.

The Decline of the Early Vision

The high vision of the early Christian initiates was that the Christian movement itself would represent a manifestation of the universal harmony in the spiritual and social spheres. By drawing upon the ancient Greek, Hebrew, and Egyptian wisdom traditions and inviting all to join the community of the Logos, the early Christian mystics sought to assemble a spiritual temple of living stones, through which every member of humanity would be uplifted by adding their voice to the chorus of the New Song. Within the earliest days of the Christian movement there was room for a rich diversity of voices, making for a truly universal song. There was room for spiritual knowledge in addition to spiritual faith, and there was even room for the sacred science of traditional cosmology. These early days, of which we really know so little, were obviously the Golden Age of Christianity, for, during this time, the Christian vision met with the greatest degree of success; it allowed for the greatest degree of diversity, all the while encircling and resounding with the Choirleader of the Logos.[22] This was the age of great scholars, visionaries, and mystics, most of whom remain unknown; at this time, the emerging mythology of Christianity was flowering, and those suitably qualified could add to the unfolding story. During this period the oral tradition was of primary importance, as were the written allegories and sayings that circulated amongst like-minded communities; these teachings were alive, flowing, and flowering, and had not yet congealed into dogmas to be enforced by an organized church.

As Christianity became a wider movement, however, an organizational structure began to crystallize. This involved the transfer and retention of funds, a job with which the first bishops were entrusted. With the bishops as the first treasurers, a clearly articulated power structure began to emerge. As the process continued, the early church modelled its organization on that of imperial Rome and became increasingly dogmatic. As it consolidated power, the church associated itself more with temporal concerns, and thereby emphasized the historical claims of the early Christian revelation. In the eyes of developing orthodoxy, the events that marked the beginning of Christianity were seen not so much as a new manifestation of eternal truth or of the perennial wisdom, but as a unique historical event in the linear flow of time.

The reason for this emphasis was clearly political, for it justified the existence of the ecclesiastical officials. Jesus, it was said, came and left at a particular point in time; however, before his departure, he had appointed the organized church to carry forth the sacred flame until the end of the age. In this fashion, the church justified its existence as a temporal authority, and as the spiritual mediator between heaven and earth. Like any temporal authority, the church desired to maintain the status quo and make sure that things ran smoothly, a task which was threatened by the gnostic views. The gnostics felt that the primary importance of the Christian revelation was the experience of the Christ within, which bypassed the need for a powerful ecclesiastical structure. The ahistorical perspective of the gnostic Christians hence undermined the church's political claims to temporal authority and also suggested that Christianity itself, rather than being based on something which happened in the past, potentially represented an ongoing revelation. Consequently, the church decided to eliminate the gnostic Christians from its ranks, and based its rules for redemption on belief and profession of a Creed, rather than on the inner realities of spiritual knowledge and lived experience.

At a certain point the organized church also proclaimed—unlike any other religious teaching of the ancient world, except Judaism—that it possessed the one and only truth, the *only* way to eternal salvation. In the Fourth Gospel Jesus states that "I am the way, and the truth, and the life; no one comes to the Father, but through me." However, like the saying in the *Gospel of Thomas*, "I am the light which is above. . . . Split a piece of wood and I am there," this is a statement of the Universal Logos and not the historical Jesus. While the spiritual Logos was indeed seen as the ideal mediator between the individual and the ineffable Source, the Logos can assume as many forms as there are individuals on this planet, and, in fact, has assumed forms other than Jesus in history. When the church proclaimed that it alone possessed the exclusive truth and that "no one comes to the Father but through me," it did this not for the betterment of humanity, but out of narrow self-interest.

Because of its emphasis on faith and unquestioning belief, the organized church developed an anti-scientific attitude and open hostility to the cultured spirit of classical civilization. People like Clement of Alexandria worked against this trend, but it was to no avail. Christians refused to send their children to pagan schools and, during the fourth century and most of the fifth, pagan literature and science were banned.[23] The underlying position of the church was later summed up by Augustine when he wrote "Nothing is to be accepted except on the authority of Scripture, since greater is that authority than all powers of the human mind," leading one scholar to note that, with this type of attitude, "ignorance was sure to become a matter of piety and inquiry, a sacrilege."[24] For those who value the freedom, autonomy, and cultivation of the soul, these events can only be viewed with a sense of sorrow (and perhaps horror), and with the question of what might have been, had not events taken the turn that they did. As one writer noted back in 1895, "The dying down of the fervid inspiration of the first Christians, and the formation of a hard skeleton of creed and a crust of mystery and ritual, cannot be a pleasant thing to observe."[25]

Christianity originated as a mystical movement, if not opposed, then at least indifferent, to the imperial might of Rome. But ironically, as it developed into a political body, the Church itself became a temporal authority and the official state religion of the Roman empire.[26] The openness to the ways of the spirit of the early Christian mystics, scholars, and gnostics, gave way to organized forms of spiritual repression and intolerance. As Elaine Pagels notes in her book *The Gnostic Gospels*, in the early days,

> Those who identified themselves as Christians entertained many—and radically differing—religious beliefs and practices. And the communities scattered throughout the known world organized themselves in ways that differed widely from one group to another.
>
> Yet by A.D. 200, the situtation had changed. Christianity had become an institution headed by a three-rank hierarchy of bishops, priests, and deacons, who understood themselves to be the guardians of the only "true faith." The majority of churches, among which the church of Rome took a leading role, rejected all other viewpoints as heresy. Deploring the diversity of the earlier movement, Bishop Irenaeus and his followers insisted that there could be only one church, and outside of that church he declared, "there is no salvation." Members of this church alone are orthodox (literally, "straight-thinking") Christians. And, he claimed, this church must be *catholic*—that is,

> universal. Whoever challenged that consensus, arguing instead for other forms of Christian teaching, was declared to be a heretic and expelled. When the orthodox gained military support, sometime after the Emperor Constantine became Christian in the fourth century, the penalty for heresy escalated.[27]

After the time of Constantine, or perhaps even before, the gnostic transmission of the early scholars, which had clothed the ancient relics of esoteric cosmology in the dress of the New Song, came to an end; most traces of the original gnosis had been eliminated, and the cosmological teachings of the Logos tradition survived only in small circles. Rather than encouraging people to directly experience the liberating nature of the Cosmic Christ, the ecclesiastical authorities prescribed intellectual obedience to preordained creeds. In some of its earliest expressions, Christianity emerged as a profound philosophical and mythic synthesis which sought to understand man's place and purpose in a hierarchy of universal principles. But the original Christian inheritance of the ancient wisdom—the Knowledge of the Logos and its scientific expression—was quickly suppressed by the political needs of the emerging church, which drew its strength from uncritical belief rather than the understanding of archetypal law. Despite a brief renaissance and outpouring of the spirit, rooted in the idea of the universal brotherhood of man, the original harmony of the New Song was all too quickly forgotten.

CHAPTER TEN

The Harmony that Was, Is, and Shall Ever Be

> As to the philosophy, by whose assistance these mysteries are developed, it is coeval with the universe itself; and however its continuity may be broken by opposing systems, it will make its appearance at different periods of time, as long as the sun himself shall continue to illuminate the world.
>
> —Thomas Taylor

Harmony, Strife, and the Growth of Consciousness

As long as time can remember, people's lives have been touched by the experience of strife and harmony. Like every pair of opposites, these two realities go together, hand in hand. People who are experiencing strife and conflict, either physically or spiritually, have a natural desire for harmony in their lives. Similarly, when things are going well, when we are feeling the most secure, some situation always seems to arise to introduce an element of strife or conflict. In one sense we can be thankful for this. In the Golden Age, people were very happy but not particularly conscious. Like little children, they didn't need to be, since their needs were provided for. It is only through experiencing the conflict and interaction of the opposites that knowledge and consciousness can arise. That is why the Greek philosopher Heraclitus aptly said that "In opposition there exists true friendship," for without the friction of the opposites the spark of awareness would never be kindled.

Earlier, in chapter 4, we looked at a geometrical diagram illustrating the states of Unity, Duality, and Harmony, and their mutual relations. This diagram is reproduced here in *figure 43*:

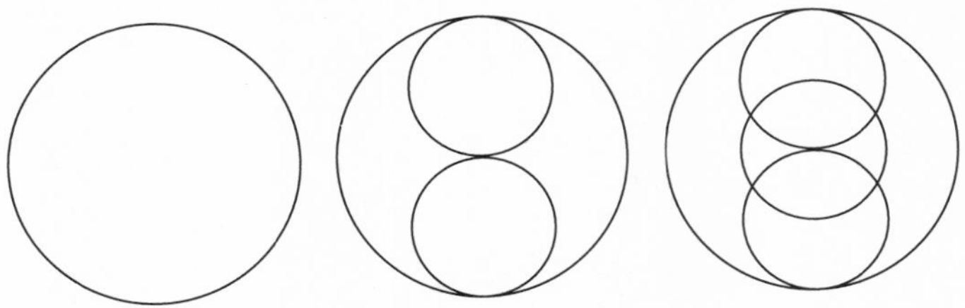

Figure 43. Unity, Duality, and Harmony Revisited

As we saw in chapter 4, this pattern underlies the various cosmologies of Greek philosophy. In the beginning, there is a primeval unity; out of this unity, two opposites emerge; these opposites harmonically combine, giving birth to life and to the universe. This pattern also relates to the mythology of time and the development of consciousness.

In the Christian mythology of time, the first circle of unity corresponds with the Golden Age, the primeval perfection of Adam and Eve in the Garden of Eden. When Adam and Eve partook of the fruit of knowledge, they were cast out from the sphere of eternity into the realm of time, history, and conflict, symbolized by duality. The pattern of harmony corresponds with the coming of Christ, the divine mediator, who ushers in the Age of the Spirit; and by unifying all the elements of creation, the spirit of Christ absolves the "original sin" of duality.

In terms of the development of consciousness, the first stage is that of primordial unconscious wholeness, experienced by everyone in childhood and before: this is the Golden Age experienced on a personal level, when each person was most closely identified with the timeless state. This state of consciousness corresponds to what psychologist Erich Neumann calls the uroboric period of psychological development, named after the tail-biting serpent, a symbol of the primordial wholeness.[1] Since there is no separation between the observer and the outside world, at this stage of consciousness the concept of linear time is an alien one.

Linear time is measured by the rational intellect which divides reality into segments, parts, and ratios for comparison and analysis. Hence the concept of linear time is associated with the function of the ego or the logical intellect which develops during the second stage of conscious development. This stage, naturally, corresponds with phase of duality, for the heroic solar ego arises from and opposes itself to the unconscious matrix from which it arose, mythologically envisioned as an evil dragon to be conquered. The ego thus differentiates itself against "the other," leading to a conflict of "us against them." The spiritual fallacy of this experience can be seen by the simple fact that, in the diagram, both "the ego" and "the other" are part of one underlying reality, encompassed within the sphere of consciousness itself.

Once this realization arises, we move toward the final stage, the realization of the true Self, the true personality, which is far greater than the ego, representing both the center and totality of consciousness. The spiritual Self is the mediator between conscious and unconscious, and all perceivable opposites. In the language of traditional symbolism, the emergence of the Self is represented by the discovery of the Philosophers' Stone, the "true foundation" of the soul;[2] it is also represented by the birth of "the philosophical son,"[3] the birth of "the Christ within,"[4] or the rising of the Spiritual Sun in the center of the soul.[5] In this stage, the individual is no longer identified exclusively with the ego, but realizes its true nature as a being capable of authentic knowledge and action. Through this realization of harmony in the soul, an individual becomes capable of unified action on all levels of being and manifestation.

Regarding these three phases of consciousness, Jill Purce makes the following observation in her book *The Mystic Spiral*:

> There are within each of us three stages of knowledge. This is the spiral process by which not only individual man but the cosmos itself becomes realized; for it represents the course of evolution. Thus in the early days of humanity, as in childhood, there was no separation between ourselves and the outside world, until we, individually or as a race, became self-conscious. As a result of successive windings, our individual and collective ego crystallized, and we could see ourselves as subject, and as distinct from the world, which became the object of our scrutiny. As we looked, the continuum differentiated into "things." Each branched into more things, which in turn branched into even more, until the continuum had developed into a hierarchy; language, which once flowed in verbs and processes, broke up into nouns and connectives.

> The third stage for the individual is that of intuitive knowledge or enlightenment, in which subject and object again become one. In collective terms, this return to a continuum implies not only the need for a new language, like that which physicists are trying to develop, but that the analytic and quantitative world is winding itself into a new simplicity.[6]

Through the manifestation of the archetypal self in the third stage, the individual is able to reconcile the temporal with the eternal in the living fabric of life, thus fulfilling an "alchemical marriage" of opposites on a cosmic scale. In this stage, through the medium of humanity and the individual, time is married with eternity, and the "philosophical sun" of consciousness is born: through the medium of humanity, the universe becomes conscious, the heavens delight and become self-aware.

In this sense, consciousness itself is seen to be an intrinsic cosmological phenomenon. First, the universe is one; second, it polarizes into subject and object; and third, consciousness, the mediating element, arises between subject and object. This process is mirrored in the psychological development of humanity and the individual. First, there is an unconscious psychic wholeness; second, the heroic ego arises to confront "the other"; and third, in those who realize their true humanity, the archetypal Self arises, mediating between the pairs of opposites and integrating the polarities of creation through the faculty of authentic knowledge. Consciousness is thereby seen as the ultimate redeemer of diversity, and is itself a harmonically differentiated image of the primordial unity.

Harmonic Science and the Philosophy of Whole Systems

As the Pythagoreans realized, the study of proportion and harmony constitutes an objective science and comprises the starting-point for a philosophy of whole systems. A philosophy of whole systems is based on the premise that there is an underlying unity behind the nature of things, and that the many parts of an organism are intrinsically related to one another within the context of a greater whole. This principle of relatedness is seen to exist inherently in the structure of the human body, the biosphere, and the structure of the solar system. A philosophy of whole systems recognizes this "fitting together" and trains the mind to see how the parts relate to the whole; it helps us to think in terms of whole systems, leading our minds and our conceptions to follow the path of Nature itself.

In order to achieve this type of "proportional thinking," the ancient Pythagoreans both studied and exposed their intellects to the pure principles of geometrical and musical harmony, which are the most primeval types of natural relationship (*logos*), and thus underlie the more complex organic relatedness of phenomena in the natural world.

A philosophy of whole systems starts with the realization that there is unity behind diversity, and that, in the manifest world, unity expresses itself through the differentiated image of multiplicity. This manifestation is controlled by the related principles of Number, Logos, and Harmony, as seen in the Pythagorean sense.

This reality of "unity in multiplicity" is made clear by the most elemental experiment on the monochord, the manifestation of the harmonic overtone series, which clearly shows how the One reveals itself as the Many.

A curious phenomenon occurs when a string is plucked. First of all, the string vibrates as a unit. Then, it vibrates in two parts, in three parts, in four parts, and so on, moving toward infinity. As it simultaneously vibrates in smaller and smaller portions, each part gives off a separate tone, which grows progressively less audible in the series. This overtone series may be demonstrated on the monochord by dividing the string geometrically at the naturally occuring harmonic nodal points. To manifest the individual overtones, pluck the string while gently touching the string at the one-half point, the one-third point, the one-quarter point, and so on. If you are "on the mark" of the harmonic nodal point, the proper overtone will ring out; if not, you will merely deaden the string. With attention, it is possible to hear the haunting chorus of the overtones without emphasizing them individually. (See *figure 44*, next page.)

The manifestion of the overtones on the monochord demonstrates several notions of Pythagorean concern. The Pythagoreans maintained, for example, that *One* is not a number at all, but the underlying continuum which innately contains and gives birth to all numbers. This idea, that all the numbers or "the gods" are an emanation of the One, is nicely illustrated by the natural emergence of the overtones from "the one string vibrating."[7] We can also see that the realm of tone is innately governed by the principle of Number, which is the natural limiting factor (*peras*) in the potentially infinite sea of tonal flux (*apeiron*).

The most important observation for the current discussion, however,

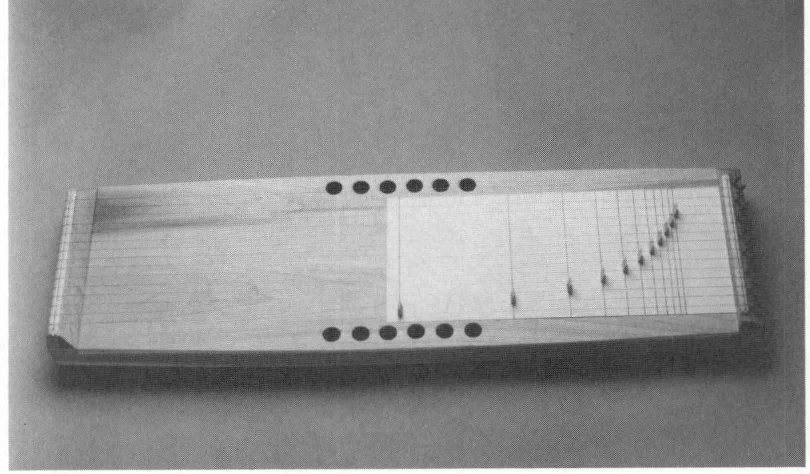

Figure 44. The Harmonic Overtone Series

Above: The naturally occuring harmonic nodal points are indicated on the monochord: (1) whole string; (2) one-half string; (3) one-third string; (4) one-quarter string; and so on. By gently touching the string at the nodal point and plucking it, the overtone can be emphasized and made to ring out.

Below: The overtone series can be demonstrated on a piano. Play the progression here as a sustained chord, starting with the fundamental tone (1) and adding the overtones in sequence. The notes are (1) C; (2) C; (3) G; (4) C; (5) E; (6) G; (7) B flat; (8) C; (9) D; (10) E. When a single string is plucked, all these overtones are produced. See how well you can hear them by just striking the fundamental tone and carefully listening to the sound decay. The octave, fifth, and fourth are perfect consonances.

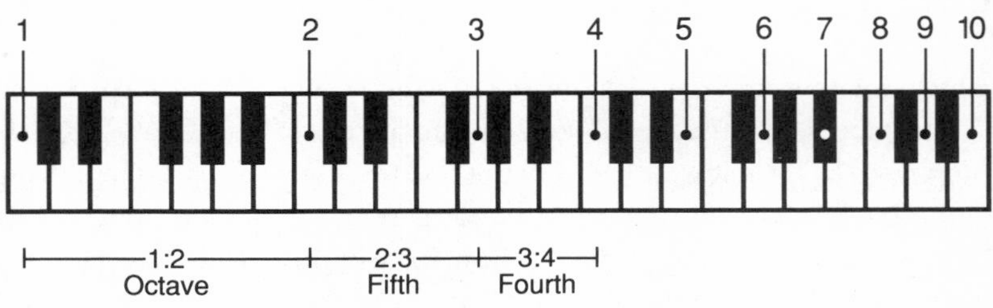

is the fact that, on the monochord, *the principles of perfect harmony are seen as innately existing in the natural order of things.* The harmonic overtone series, itself reflecting the simple primacy of Number, is the basis of all musical expression and contains the perfect consonances of unison (1:1), the octave (1:2), the perfect fifth (2:3), and the perfect fourth (3:4). When a single string is plucked, at first glance it seems as though you are producing a single note; but, if you listen more closely, you are led to the realization that you are really producing *a chord*, reflecting the principles of perfect harmony.

While this reality can only be fully appreciated at first hand on the monochord, it is possible to discuss its fascinating and inescapable implications. We are led to the primary realization that the laws of harmony are truly universal principles,[8] of the same order of magnitude as other universal phenomena, such as light, energy, or gravitation. When someone decides to create a tuning system, certain elements of that system may be based on a particular motive, but the underlying framework of every tuning system, and the key intervals encompassed therein, are dictated by the inescapable, universal laws of harmony: the perfect consonances. This is confirmed by the research of musicologists, who have discovered that music from around the world is based on these same perfect consonances, which provide the framework for all harmonic expression. Different cultures have different musical syntaxes, and, as in ancient Greek music, certain intervals are movable for flavor, but the same perfect intervals are found everywhere. Since the laws of harmony are truly universal, it also follows that the perfect consonances would be reflected in the music of other civilizations, on other worlds. The music of an extraterrestrial civilization might well have a syntax unlike anything we are used to, but the underlying harmonic intervals would, of necessity, be the same. In this sense, perhaps music really is the universal language that people have always imagined it to be.

From this observation we are led to the central insight which underlies the ancient canon of number. Stated in its most simple terms, we can say that the laws of harmony are not invented, they are discovered. Like the perfect consonances of music (with which they are related), the numbers and geometry of ancient cosmology were never arbitrarily devised; rather, they were discovered and reflect the underlying nature of Reality itself. These values—numbers like 318, 666, 888, 707, 1415, 612 and 1224—are codifications of the primary ratios which underlie the genesis of form and harmonic expression. Because they are universal, they will eternally be discovered by anyone—on this planet or any other planet—who makes a serious study of geometrical and harmonic forming principles.

These central numbers—their nature, properties, and place in the universal scheme—were studied long before the appearance of Christianity and were seen as encapsulating the primary functions of the Logos, the pattern of harmony and order behind creation. When Christianity arose, the central divinity of the new faith was identified with the nature of the Logos, as Hermes and Apollo had been identified with the Logos before, in ancient Greece. In the same way that the old Greek myths reflected higher truths for those who had eyes to see, some of the early Christian allegories were built upon the ancient canon of number which originated from a profound and scientific study of the laws which underlie creation. Thus, at least some of the earliest Christians were in the possession of a precious inheritance from an earlier age, that science of harmony which is coeval with the origin of the universe itself and is always awaiting discovery by minds looking in the right direction.

The Eclipse of the Universal and the Emergence of Relativism

While the organized church was fairly effective in suppressing the Pythagorean science inherited by the Christian initiates, the Logos itself is eternal. As we have noted above, like the laws of harmony, the numbers of ancient cosmology were never arbitrarily invented; rather, they were discovered and reflect the underlying principles of the universal fabric. As the early Christian theologians recognized, the Logos is not only eternal, it is present everywhere; the natural order depends upon it, whether we are consciously aware of it or not. Like the laws of physics which underlie the structure of the universe, the laws of harmony are themselves immaterial. They can be studied, recognized, and utilized, but they cannot be touched, tasted, or bottled up, to be placed on a laboratory shelf. Nonetheless, their reality is incontestable, and while we cannot physically touch the laws of the universe, we can certainly know of their existence through their effects and manifestation in the ever-shifting world of change.

If we put these insights into the language of ancient philosophy, we would say that the laws of harmony are "ontological," or reflect the nature of Being, which is eternal and not subject to change. Being (in Greek, *to on* or *ôn*) simply means "*that which is.*" In ancient philosophy, particularly the Platonic stream, these ontological principles of Being are seen not as mere abstractions or definitions arising from the study of the physical world, but as eternal, underlying realities that condition it. These principles have a universal reality in themselves, even though they do not exist as "tangible things." However, because they do not exist in time and space, they are not limited by time and space, and can thus always be present everywhere.

According to the great thinkers of antiquity, there exists a very special affinity between the principle of Mind—the principle of consciousness—and the ontological level of Being. Based on the notion that only "like can know like," insofar as consciousness can actually know the principles of being which transcend time and space, consciousness itself is revealed as participating in the eternal and transcendental nature of being. Consciousness, or Mind (*Nous*), is therefore recognized in ancient philosophy as representing an ontological principle itself. Insofar as consciousness can partake of universal knowledge, consciousness itself is shown to exist on a universal level of being. If consciousness can grasp certain principles which are not limited by time and space, the realizations of consciousness are likewise universal, not limited by time and space. When we reach this level of realization and resonance, we become truly human and recognize the universal nature of humanity, which is a living manifestation of consciousness. In this realization, we are led to recognize the divine essence and function of humanity, the true "community of the Logos."

Needless to say, this type of thinking goes against the grain of modern materialism and relativism, which arose as a reaction against centuries of ecclesiastical repression in Europe. As the foundations of classical civilization crumbled, in the Latin West the path of philosophical inquiry was replaced with theological dogmatism. It was inevitable that a reaction would follow. Unfortunately, the reaction did not consist of an attempt to create, or recreate, the ancient system of education which would carefully prepare the individual for the experience of higher cognitive states. Instead, the reaction consisted of trying to abolish the possibility of metaphysical knowledge itself.

Three of the key figures in this movement were David Hume, John Locke, and Immanuel Kant. David Hume tried to do away with the principle of causality, which has a place in both classical physics and metaphysics. He said that just because you hit one billiard ball with another and expect it to fly off in the opposite direction doesn't mean that a law of cause and effect *really* exists: that's an "assumption," merely based on your past experience. John Locke taught that all knowledge arises from external, sensible perceptions. And Immanuel Kant, through volumes of excruciating prose, argued that it is impossible to have true knowledge of universal principles—it is only possible, he said, to have knowledge of the mental categories though which we perceive the world, and it is not possible to know what really lies behind these categories. The effect of Kantian theory was to demolish classical metaphysics, and to put philosophy on a new relativistic footing.

Remarkably, little was done to question these ideas, and modern "philosophy" was born. At least the dogmatic stranglehold of "theological certainty" was demolished, but one evil was replaced with another. Freed at last of ecclesiastical constraint, science and technology broke loose, fueled by centuries of pent up, unrealized potential. But, because the "new philosophy" was largely relativistic and inimical to the principle of value, there was little left to guide the progress of science and technology. In the popular mind, and in the minds of most scientists, science had become a new faith, based upon the creed of materialism.

True science, however, is by nature always allied with the higher cognitive modes; it is ultimately a spiritual pursuit. Technology has always been, and always will be, subservient to economic interests, but true science will always be based upon the quest for Reality. Kant believed in *a priori* categories within the human mind, but he did not hold that we could grasp the *a priori* realities behind them. However, if it is not possible to have direct knowledge of reality, it is unlikely that physicists could produce atomic fusion. Scientific inquiry, itself liberated by Kant, has shown his relativistic cosmology to be inadequate.

There are two fundamental pathways to knowledge. On the one hand, there is the empirical method: we conduct a series of experiments, gather data, or take in some information from the external world, and extrapolate an observation or theory from the *sensibilia*. On the other hand, knowledge may directly proceed from the *a priori* principles contained within the field of Mind. There are countless examples of mathematical and scientific insights arrived at through the faculty of the intellect alone, without physical experimentation, which were later discovered to be physically verifiable. The curvature of space was anticipated by Plato in the *Timaeus*, and necessitated by Einstein's Theory of Relativity; it was subsequently verified by astronomical observations which demonstrated that the path of light from a distant star was subtly warped by the mass of the sun. The existence of black holes was posited by theoretical necessity; subsequent observations indicate that they probably exist. As noted above, it is unlikely that anyone would have been able to "invent" the atomic bomb based upon mere observations from the physical world, especially given the fact that we can neither see nor touch atomic particles in the first place. Only the Promethean power of Mind, which can see directly into the heart of creation and resonate with the very principles of Being, could ever steal the Fire of the Gods.

Science, Spirituality, and the Discovery of Value

If, as the Pythagoreans saw, the study of natural harmony constitutes the starting point for a philosophy of whole systems, this approach may be of some value to the modern world, which is characterized by political, economic, intellectual, philosophical, and cultural fragmentation. If the universe is ultimately One, then, it seems, there must be some type of perspective which is capable of recognizing the underlying unity and reflecting it in every realm of manifestation, while simultaneously honoring the diversity of human insight and expression.

Nowhere does our approach to reality appear to be more disparate than in the apparently competing spheres of science and religion. However, if we look behind the dogmatic and doctrinal tendencies to which both science and religion are prone, they actually have a great deal in common, in terms of their underlying premises. As a starting point, we may note that both science and religion are rooted in the realization that the universe is a *kosmos*. This word, meaning "order," "ornament," or "arrangement," affirms the realization that the physical, spiritual, and intellectual dimensions of existence are shaped by—and hence reflect—the principles of beauty and organization.

That the physical universe possesses an order is obvious to all. From the seed to a tree to a spiral galaxy—all represent organized systems existing within larger systems, all of which are shaped by universal laws and principles. All scientific and scholarly inquiry is implicitly based upon the justified premise that there *is* an order to things, and that persistent study and contemplation will bring certain elements of this order to light. Likewise, it seems reasonable to assume that there exists an underlying order to the psychological and spiritual realms of existence as well. The principle of Mind itself reflects the principles of organization and obviously has something in common with the order which underlies the physical universe. If there were no connection at all, how could we ever hope to gain knowledge of the order behind natural phenomena? Yet, the fact that we can gain insight into the order of the cosmos has been proven time and again by countless scientific discoveries.

Another aspect of the universe highlighted by the word *kosmos* is its *beauty*, a beauty which defies purely rational analysis. There are many rational things one may say about beauty, but the discursive rational intellect, at its highest, establishes only *facts*. Conversely, the cognitive power through which we experience beauty establishes value and meaning. Beauty ultimately transcends reductive analysis—at its fullest it may only be experienced, and through the experience of beauty we become truly human. To experience beauty is to know that we are vitally and authentically connected with the heart of the cosmic pattern.

Like authentic spiritual insight, true scientific insight originates from a higher level of cognition that is in harmony with the principles which comprise the universe. Scientific theory seeks to know the order behind the universe, as does religion. And both are ultimately concerned with beauty, meaning and value. The problem is that proponents of religious traditions are usually unwilling to analyze their creeds objectively and scientifically in an attempt to separate the genuine spark of spiritual insight from the inherited dogmatic chaff. Likewise, many scientists are ignorant of philosophical issues, having been educated primarily as technologists, and have no inkling of the underlying epistemological and teleological foundations of the scientific endeavor. In terms of epistemology, or the theory of knowledge, scientific enquiry is based on the underlying premise that it is possible to attain a state of authentic insight into universal principles which is itself true and universal. In terms of teleology, or the end toward which it is drawn, the scientific endeavor is intrinsically involved with value, for when we experience any type of universal insight there is a corresponding sense of beauty, completion, and the experience of Being.

Given the fact that scientific inquiry and the spiritual aspirations of humanity have so much in common, it is unfortunate that there has not been a more concerted attempt to overcome the fragmentation of knowledge which characterizes the modern era. Science, religion, and our political and educational institutions are all guilty parties in this regard. The excesses of organized religion created the split in the first place. Scientism rebelled and set itself up as a secular, materialistic faith. Once the battle lines were drawn, people were left to choose between two one-sided alternatives: the metaphysical dogmatists on the one hand, the materialists on the other. But life, and reality, are more subtle than that.

The way out of the impasse is to realize that both the scientific quest and the spiritual quest are based upon a common, underlying recognition: first, that there is an order to the universe—the universe is a *kosmos*; second, that the principle of Mind is related to the nature of this order, insofar as it can fathom its secrets; third, that by realizing the nature of this order and our relation to it, humanity experiences a sense of beauty, a sense of completion. The spiritual and scientific quests are both a search for meaning and value, the knowledge and experience of Being. Moreover, both spiritual and scientific insights originate from higher levels of cognition; but since these insights can only be approximated in words, as Plato understood, both science and religion fall into grave danger when their ensuing and provisional models are taken literally to represent the actual territory.

Unfortunately, when Kant and modern scientism justifiably reacted against centuries of intellectual repression, they unjustifiably tossed out the baby with the proverbial bathwater. The human imperative of free inquiry had so long been shackled by the chains of dogmatic theology—which did speak of a "higher order," but one mainly shaped by political expediency—that, ever since, science, philosophy, and our academic communities have nervously tried to side-step any questions dealing with the nature of value and meaning. Because of this, however, science, philosophy, and our academic communities have failed to realize their own intrinsic potential. Sadly, they have for the most part betrayed the human spirit.

The Invocation of Harmony and the Unification of Culture

One of the most fascinating aspects of classical Greek civilization, when contrasted with the contemporary world, is the astonishing level of cultural unity and integration, something that is clearly alien to the present era. This remarkable level of integration of every level and aspect of society was achieved not with force, theocratic rule, or allegiance to a particular dogma. Rather, it was an inspired artistic vision, reaching back into the deepest strata of prehistory, which sustained and spontaneously gave form to the rich beauty and harmony of Greek civilization.

Every successful civilization is guided by a living mythological vision which imparts unity to the varied forms of cultural expression. Through mythology and a common symbolic vision, a living culture is transmitted across the generations. Without such a mythic vision there is no common language; a confusion of tongues results and every individual is adrift and alone. Without the symbolic language offered by a living mythology, poets grow silent, alienated from the springs of inspiration, or resort merely to describing aspects of the physical world or their own neuroses. The artist, who in a healthy civilization presents us with ways of seeing the world, without a living vision resorts to mere technique, "photorealism," or interior decoration.

From this perspective, Shelley was right when he wrote that "Poets are the true legislators of the world," at least insofar as poets are inspired by a living vision. In antiquity, culture was transmitted through the stories of the bards, who, accompanied by music, sang the ways of the ancient gods and heroes. These stories were associated with particular locales, festivals, and times of the year. The stories of the gods were handed on from generation to generation, and certain places boasted of having been the sites of mythological scenes and heroic deeds in the ancient days.[9] These events were reflected in the local folklore, sacred geography, and temple architecture—even in the symbolic designs pressed on the local coinage.[10] In this way a level of enchantment was maintained. The ancients realized that they inhabited a sacred landscape, sanctified by the gods and the spirits of their ancestors.

This process of enchantment was enacted on many levels, accomplished through music, architecture, and the arts. The more carefully we study this process, however, the more mysterious it becomes, eluding the grasp of our rational intellects. As one moves closer to the central mystery, we are led to the realization that this enchantment was an act of magical invocation, carried out, in part, through the agency of the temple. The first law of magic is that if one wishes to attract something, one needs to create an appropriate vessel in order to receive it. In traditional societies, the central vessel of invocation was the temple, which was designed to attract a particular god or spirit, and to make that spirit both accessible and active within human society.

Everyone practices magic, whether they realize it or not, for magic is the art of attracting particular influences, events, and situations within human life. Magic is a natural phenomenon because the universe is reflexive, responding to human thoughts, aspirations, and desires; students of cosmology, for example, realize that the universe will correspondingly provide evidence for any theory projected upon it. Because of the magical, reflexive nature of reality, a certain amount of awareness is required, for people attract to themselves what they really desire. People who don't know what they want usually attract what they need. This may be a seemingly random series of situations and perhaps unhappy events, destined to jolt them to a higher level of awareness in the long run. Since the universe does respond to our innermost desires, true philosophers have always held that one should be idealistic in spirit and perpetually aim to invoke the highest. People who have a low-minded view of things will discover this reflected in the events of their lives, thus confirming their perspective, while others who are high-minded and invoke the spirit of excellence find themselves capable of attracting it.

The careful observer will realize that there is, however, far more than "mere psychology" to the process of magical invocation, as was recognized by the best minds of antiquity and reflected within the institution of the temple. The temple, in its highest manifestation, was seen as constituting a microcosm, an image of the entire universe, and was laid out accordingly. The temple was seen as an organism, possessing a body and a living spirit. This spirit was attracted through the temple's underlying geometry and proportions, and gematria, thus reflecting the harmony of the universe and those principles which underlie the genesis of life. Based on the idea of "like attracts like," the temples of antiquity, like the Gothic cathedrals of medieval times, were designed to reflect, and hence enshrine, the living spirit of harmony which underlies the universe.

That this act of invocation was not merely theoretical, but a living reality, is one of the most difficult things for the modern mind, hypnotized by the dogmas of materialism, to understand. The spirit of harmony is not just a pretty notion, or an ideal formulation of the ultimate nature of things, but is capable of expressing itself in quite tangible ways, if carefully and properly invoked. While our experience of the Logos is shaped by cultural factors, the currents of time, and personal disposition, the harmony of the universe will always be present, if invoked, by preparing an appropriate receptacle in which to receive it. Since, when this spirit manifests itself, we can only recognize its presence through the power of consciousness, consciouness is itself revealed, in the human sphere, as the primary medium and receptacle of universal harmony. Therefore, the spirit of harmony can only spill over and become active in the world of human affairs by first manifesting itself within the individual.

High cultural epochs are marked by a welling over of this harmony, resulting in a process of sanctification and cultural renewal. While the vision of the Golden Age—the primordial harmony—can always reflect itself within the life of the individual, there are times when it becomes manifest, to varying degrees, in the social fabric. We can see this in the high Classical period of ancient Greece; in the outpouring of spirit among the first Christians; in the flowering of the Troubadour lyrics and the Grail romances; in the rebirth of classical learning in Renaissance Florence, inspired by Marsilio Ficino's translations of the Hermetic and Platonic writings. Such periods are characterized by a realization of harmony which inspires, fertilizes, and unifies every aspect of human culture. During such periods the sources of inspiration are invoked, and the Muses obligingly reveal themselves. A poetic, spiritual vision then takes hold of a generation; the long-dry channels of inspiration once again flow with living water, and the enchantment spreads outward. Such periods are also historically marked with the discovery, or rediscovery, of the canon—the natural laws of proportion—which provides a scientific basis for the understanding and expression of universal harmony. We can see this in the case of Classical Greece, in the allegories of the early Christian gnosis, and in the Pythagorean renaissance associated with the cathedral school of Chartres in medieval France, where Chrétien de Troyes wrote the first Grail romance.[11] Later, too, in the Florentine Renaissance there was a keen study of natural proportion: Palladio, for example, designed his famous villas based on the ratios of musical harmony.[12] The astonishing unification of vision which can arise in such periods is perhaps best reflected in the structure of the Greek myths and Christian allegories, where we see the union of the ancient number canon—a legacy of scientific insight—married with poetic tales, in very simple language, designed to delight and inspire both children and adults.

Such periods of renewal arise spontaneously and are beyond human control, but the principles of harmony, because they are eternal, can always be invoked and, to varying degrees, made manifest. The ancient philosophers and cosmologists sought not only to understand the principles of harmony, but also to put them to use wherever possible—whether it involved tuning a musical instrument, harmonizing the different parts of the soul, or, as Plato suggested, framing the constitution of a peaceful and flourishing community where each person receives what he or she is justly due. In this sense, the priests of Apollo, the Orphic bards, the Pythagoreans, the members of the Hermetic fraternities, the sacred geometers and temple architects, the Platonists, gnostics, and Christian mystics—those before and after, known and unknown—were all motivated by a common ideal, the dream of living in true harmony with both the laws of Nature and human society, to the greatest extent possible, on the highest possible level.

Because this dream is rooted in the nature of the universe, it is not limited by the dictates of space or time, and can manifest itself in any period, in any milieu. Wherever it has been felt—whether in the life of a lone individual or a larger culture—there is harmony, unification, vision, insight, and enchantment, and also the understanding that the realization of love, in all its forms, is the only authentic end of human existence. Love takes many forms, yet true love is a tangible manifestation of the harmony behind the universe, and inevitably leads to the timeless experience of Being and ever-greater levels of awareness.

Love, harmony, and brotherhood are always topical subjects, but they seem especially topical at this point in time, in the realization of our human, cultural, and planetary welfare. Man is the only creature who has the power to understand consciously the universal harmonies of nature—yet, ironically, he is the only one capable of destroying the earth. While it is true, in a historical sense, that the organized church ultimately derived its power from uncritical belief rather than the gnostic recognition of the Logos, no organization or political structure could ever succeed in destroying the harmonic order of the natural world and the imaginative, life-giving forms of consciousness from which the great myths of humanity emerge. Consciousness, like all other phenomena, is based upon certain natural patterns which underlie the fabric of the phenomenal world. Even if warring nation-states should destroy our planet in atomic hubris—or, in another scenario, the earth should suffer a slow death through poisoning and asphyxiation—consciousness will survive in quite similar forms elsewhere on other worlds, perhaps dreaming the same dreams and witnessing the same phenomena. That is because the same basic patterns—or, as the Platonists would say, Divine Ideas—shape not only the world of man, but also the world of the stars. If we should fail at our divinely appointed task of living in harmony with both nature and our fellow humans, perhaps some other civilization, elsewhere, will succeed where we have fallen short.

Documentary Illustrations

Orpheus the Theologian

"ALL THEOLOGY among the Greeks is sprung from the mystical doctrine of Orpheus" wrote Proclus the Platonic Successor, and hence it is with the name of this mythical culture hero that all inquiry into Western spirituality must begin. Everyone has heard the story of how Orpheus attempted to rescue his wife Eurydice from the Underworld. His music had not only the power to stay the gates of death, but the celestial harmonies which sprang from his magical lyre charmed all of nature. When he played, the animals and beasts gathered round, the fishes jumped out of the sea to greet him, even the rocks and trees moved closer, unable to resist the power of his song. According to Apollonius, his music could stop a stream in its course. Herodotus refers to "Orphic and Bacchic" as meaning actually "Egyptian and Pythagorean," and the Orphics in Greece were the first to teach the immortality of the soul, the doctrine of transmigration or "reincarnation," and the means through which an individual might transcend the cycle of births altogether.

According to traditional account, Orpheus traveled to Egypt, invented the alphabet, taught Greece the mysteries of initiation, was a priest of both Dionysus and Apollo, and, as the Christian apologist Athenagoras noted, "He was the first to give the gods names." Orphism not only taught the allegorical interpretation of traditional mythology, but according to the testimony of the ancients, Orpheus taught that "the eternal essence of number is the most providential principle of the universe," and that there is a distinct relation between the nature of the gods and certain "intelligible numbers." The Platonist Syrianus observed that "the Pythagoreans received from the theology of Orpheus the principles of intelligible and intellectual numbers," and the Platonists themselves were a continuing link in the golden chain of the Orphic-Pythagorean tradition.

Among the early Christians the educated took over much of the ancient theology, and in the same way that the Jewish-oriented Gospel of Matthew portrays Jesus as the New Moses, Hellenistic-oriented Clement of Alexandria portrays Christ as the New Orpheus, and Christianity as the New Song of the eternal Logos. Orphism, by teaching the primacy of divine harmony (an aspect of the Logos), the presence of a divine spark in man, and the mystical resurrection of Dionysus, did much to anticipate the mysteries of the Christian gnosis.

Christ as Orpheus

This illustration from the Roman catacombs represents Christ as Orpheus. The illustrations around the periphery are scenes from the Old Testament.

ABOVE LEFT: Orphic-Christian signet ring, fifth century. The inscription reads "The Seal of John, the Preeminent Saint."

ABOVE RIGHT: Cylinder seal, circa 300 C.E. The inscription reads "Orpheus Bakkikos" and represents Orpheus, the "True God," crucified.

The Pythagorean Traditon

EVERY GENERATION attempts to understand the nature of the universe according to its own particular models and modes of thought, but the discriminating spectator in the on-going flow of time cannot help but notice certain recurring motifs in the history of ideas. Modern physicists in their unending quest to fathom the mysteries of the microcosm have discovered that all forms of matter may be reduced to certain numerically arranged patterns of energy, causing some scientists to describe their outlook as "Pythagorean."

The legendary Pythagoras was the first philosopher to use the word *kosmos* as a description of the universe. He is the father of geometry and was the first Westerner to study the science of harmonics: the mediating ratios (*logoi*) at work in the musical scale. Hence, we owe to him not only the Pythagorean theorem in geometry, but also Pythagorean tuning, the diatonic scale on which our music is based.

While Pythagoras was both a scientist and a mathematician, he was also a religious reformer. Since little is historically certain about him, it is sometimes difficult to separate the man from his mythic image, as is also true of the historical Jesus. It is generally agreed, however, that Pythagoras travelled widely, assimilating the wisdom and sciences of the Egyptian priests and perhaps the Babylonians as well, before starting his own philosophical school at Croton. He is perhaps most famous for teaching that the proper study of numerical relationships and harmonies may lead to a form of philosophical gnosis, for the mathematical patterns in the natural world reflect the pure archetypal laws on which all phenomena are based. In terms of his theology, Pythagoras learnt from the Orphic writers that the nature of the gods is defined by Number, and the name Pythagoras itself is related to that of Pythios, the name of Apollo at Delphi. As Aristippus of Cyrene points out, Pythagoras derived his name from the fact of his speaking (*agoreuein*) truth no less than the god at Delphi (*Pythios*).

In terms of popular usage the epithet "Pythagorean" is applied to all systems of thought oriented toward understanding the unique and basic relationships which exist between man, number, and cosmos. However, for a comprehensive overview and analysis of classical Pythagorean philosophy, the reader is directed to the introductory essay by the present writer in *The Pythagorean Sourcebook and Library: An Anthology of Ancient Writings Which Relate to Pythagoras and Pythagorean Philosophy*.

PYTHAGORAS.

Gematria: The Sacred Language

GREEK is by no means the only sacred language where numbers are represented by letters. The same holds true for Hebrew, Arabic, and Sanskrit. From this foundation is developed the science of *gematria*, whereby words, names or phrases may be created to embody or reflect a certain numerical value. It is a known fact that many magical names and formulas were composed in antiquity to bring out symbolic numbers.

The evidence from antiquity suggests that the same holds true for the names of the Greek divinities. According to ancient authorities it is recorded time and again that the alphabet was revealed to humanity by a god or a god-like being. Orpheus is said to have given names to the divinities, and he is also said to have taught that the nature of the gods is related to Number. The Pythagorean movement may in fact only represent a further development of the Orphic tradition, especially considering that there once existed an Orphic *Hymn to Number*.

To the ancient philosophers and cosmologists, the universe physically reflects the "Word" or Logos of creation: an ordered matrix of harmoniously arranged principles which, when viewed as a unity, is the living manifestation of the Absolute. As the study of Greek gematria demonstrates, the names of the gods were designed to resonate on many levels, mirroring the mathematical principles behind creation. In short, they were composed to relate to one another through a hierarchy of natural relationships based upon the primacy of the first geometrical principles and ratios.

To determine the numerical value of any Greek or Hebrew word by gematria, one simply adds together the standard numerical equivalents of the individual letters to produce a final sum for the value of the entire word. One unit, known as a *colel*, may be added or subtracted from the obtained value without affecting the symbolic meaning of a word or phrase. Since the decimal point was unused in ancient mathematics, HERMES, 353, may also be expressed as .353, 3.53, 35.3, or 3530; Unity or the First Cause may be expressed as 1, 10, 100, or 1,000.

Ἑ΄ΡΜΗΣ

HERMES = 353

5 + 100 + 40 + 8 + 200 = 353

1	2	3	4	5	6	7	8
Aleph	ࠀ	א	1	Α α	*	Alpha	A
Beth	ࠁ	ב	2	Β β	*	Beta	B
Gimel	ࠂ	ג	3	Γ γ	*	Gamma	G
Daleth	ࠃ	ד	4	Δ δ	*	Delta	D
He	ࠄ	ה	5	Ε ε	*	Epsilon	E
Vau	ࠅ	ו	6	Ϝ	*	Digamma	Fv
Zain	ࠆ	ז	7	Ζ ζ		Zeta	
Heth	ࠇ	ח	8	Η η		Eta	
Teth	ࠈ	ט	9	Θ ϑ θ		Theta	
Jod	ࠉ	י	10	Ι ι	*	Iota	I
Caph	ࠊ	כ	20	Κ κ	*	Kappa	C
Lamed	ࠋ	ל	30	Λ λ	*	Lambda	L
Mem	ࠌ	מ	40	Μ μ	*	Mu	M
Nun	ࠍ	נ	50	Ν ν	*	Nu	N
Samech	ࠎ	ס	60	Ξ ξ		Xi	
Oin	ࠏ	ע	70	Ο ο	*	Omicron	O
Pe	ࠐ	פ	80	Π π	*	Pi	P
Tzadi	ࠑ	צ	90	ϛ		Episemon bau	
Koph	ࠒ	ק	100			επισημον ϐαυ	
			100	Ρ ρ	*	Rho	R
Resh	ࠓ	ר	200				
			200	Σ σ	*	Sigma	S
Shin	ࠔ	ש	300				
			300	Τ τ	*	Tau	T
Tau	ࠕ	ת	400				
			400	Υ υ	*	Upsilon	U
			500	Φ φ		Phi	
			600	Χ χ		Chi	
			700	Ψ ψ		Psi	
			800	Ω ω		Omega	
			900	ϡ		Sanpi	

The Numerical Values of the Greek and Hebrew Alphabets

The One and the Many

NATURAL PHILOSOPHY is based on the insight that the principle of Unity expresses itself through Diversity in an ordered and harmonic fashion. Conversely, when viewed from the proper vantage point, the dance of Multiplicity dynamically reveals the underlying principle of Unity and the Many appear as aspects of the Whole. That is why in Hellenistic theology divinity was held to be both One and Many: there is the transcendent High God, the One, yet there also exist lesser divinities, aspects of the One, who embody the multifarious aspects of being. Likewise, in the solar system, each planet is independent and unique, while on another equally valid plane, each is but an aspect of the central Sun.

One meaning of the world *logos* denotes the principle of *relation*, and hence the Celestial Logos in one of its guises is associated with the function of mediation, for it is the principle by which the One is related to the Many, and the principle by which the Many are related to the One. To become aware of this relation is therefore to become aware of the Logos, and to become aware of the Logos or "Christ-principle" in its fullness is to become aware of this relation. Through this conscious realization, Unity "fallen" into diversity is "re-membered," the mystical body of God restored. According to the gnostics, man is a fallen creature but through the sin of ignorance, the forgetfulness of God and one's own divine nature. The true gnostic, on awakening from his slumber, realizes who he is, where he has been, and where he is going.

The Tree

Natural archetype of Unity in Diversity

Diversity in Unity

Qualitative Number

The above illustration makes clear one qualitative manifestation of Number, the principle of Number as an increasing differentiation of Unity, where each qualitative state is a different aspect of the One. Each expression is a whole system unto itself, contained in the greater whole system of Number, and each of these expressions reflects a unique *logos* of relation between the multiplicity of the circumference and the transcendental unity of the center. The One, or that which is, must become two—knower and known—for the third factor of knowledge or consciousness to arise. But, by the same token, absolute reality still is One.

Kosmos: The Ordered World

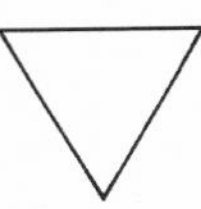

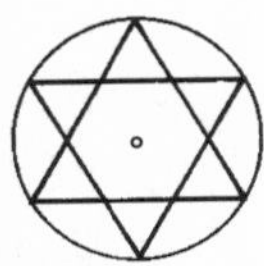

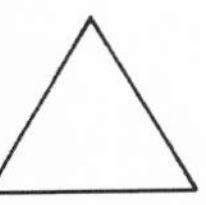

WATER
INSTINCT
LUNA
INVOLUTION
PASSIVE

RECONCILIATION
OF OPPOSITES

ΚΟΣΜΟΣ
COSMOS = 600

FIRE
INTELLECT
SOL
EVOLUTION
ACTIVE

IN THE emblematic, alchemical language of traditional cosmology, the six-pointed star symbolizes the marriage of opposites through a third and higher medium, representing the creative union of the analytical intellect with the mythopoeic matrix of imagination. The upright triangle, as a symbol of the solar ego, when balanced with the inverted triangle of the lunar unconscious, produces the birth of the philosophical son: the heart and higher self.

The Pythagorean philosopher Nicomachus called the hexad "The form of forms, the only number adapted to the soul . . . and the producing cause of the vital habit. Hence also, it is harmony, the perfection of parts, and more properly Venus herself."

The archetypal geometry of the hexad, as an underlying design type of both natural phenomena and the three-dimensional coordinate system itself, holds a special place in the systems of traditional cosmology. It is the geometrical basis of the Pythagorean Tetraktys, the kabbalistic Tree of Life, and the "fish net" symbolism of the early Christian gnostics. As a prime archetype underlying three-dimensional space and the worlds of inner and outer phenomena, there is every reason to believe that this matrix of creation will eternally influence the fabric of nature.

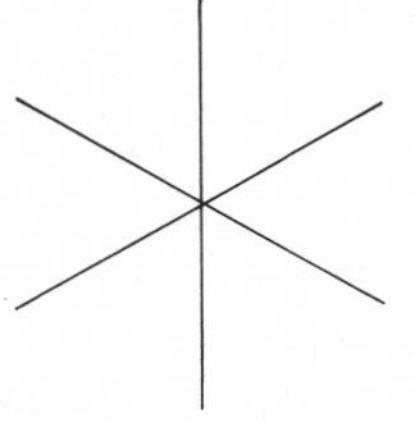

SIX DIRECTIONS IN SPACE:
UP, DOWN, N, S, E AND W

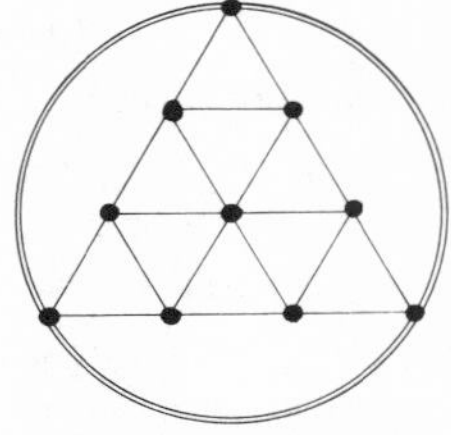

THE PYTHAGOREAN
TETRAKTYS

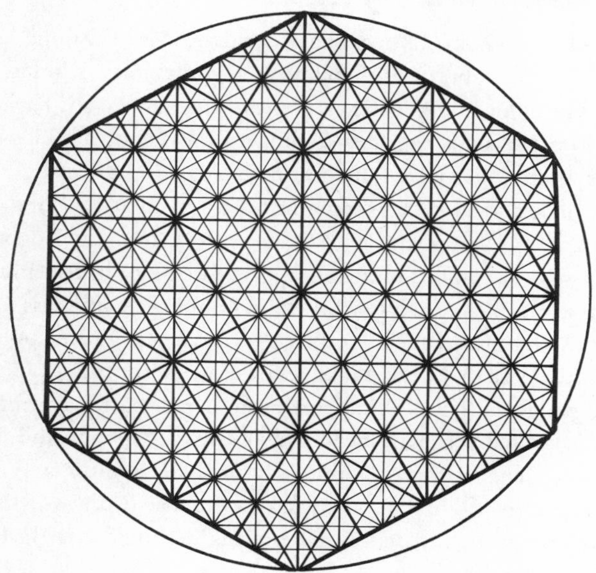

The Cosmic "Fish Net"

In Greek mythology the so-called robe or veil woven by HARMONIA was probably in reference to the above geometrical design-type. It is a "fish net" for the entire pattern is governed by $\sqrt{3}$ which, in the realm of geometry, springs from the *vesica piscis*, the "vessel of the fish." To the early Christian gnostics the net was an important cosmological symbol, but this natural symbolism predates Christianity and represents the woven web of nature or the vivifying power of harmony which enforms the pattern of creation. The Orphics possessed books entitled *The Net* and *The Veil*, and the omphalos stone in the temple of Apollo at Delphi was covered with a netting pattern. In the language of ancient mysticism, to unravel the veil is to discover the weaver.

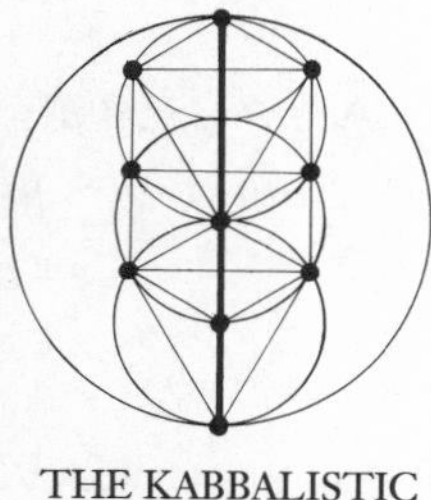

THE KABBALISTIC TREE

THE TREE EXPANDED: THE GEOMETRY OF A SNOWFLAKE

The Celestial Man of Light

"GOD MADE MAN in His own image," and the idea of Cosmic Anthropos, Celestial Man of Light, or ideal archetype of humanity is found in a wide variety of Hermetic and gnostic teachings, whether Pagan, Jewish, Christian, or Islamic. Nor is the idea limited to the West. The Cosmic Man represents both the source and ultimate goal of humanity, serving as exemplar, guide and *telos*, and is sometimes portrayed as the "First Man," the inventor of all arts and sciences, or Gnostic Revealer—the Logos personified. In Orphic thought the figure is represented by Phanes (Illuminator), hatched from the Cosmic Egg, who "shines out in the darkness," and is the seed of gods and men. In the Hermetic writings the figure appears as the Light-Word, emanated from Mind, who is called "the Son of God." In the Christian gnosis, Christ is the divine exemplar of perfected humanity, of humanity perfected in the mystical body of Christ. Not only did "the Word become flesh," but the Logos, in its mediational role, is intimately connected with the function of Humanity. In Jewish Kabbalah, the Cosmic Man is called Adam Kadmon, and his Cosmic Body is identified with the kabbalistic Tree of Life (see right).

In all these teachings the same basic idea is expressed, for the idea is one eternally rooted in human imagination, at least insofar as particular humans are rooted in the universal principle of Man. Zosimos of Panopolis, the Christian Hermeticist and alchemist, observed that the name of the primal man is *Phôs*, which, depending merely on how it is accented in Greek, means either Man or Light. Light is invariably associated with the figure of Cosmic Man, for Anthropos is a manifestation of Mind, and "Light" or illumination is the hallmark of consciousness. In the traditional philosophy alluded to here, it is through the principle of Anthropos that the universe is perfected, for it is through the agency of humanity that the universe becomes self-conscious, that the eternal principle of Understanding (Nous) is realized in actuality.

According to the Hermetic writings, Eternity (Aeon) is an image of God; Cosmos is an image of Eternity; the Sun is an image of Cosmos; and Man is an image of the Sun.

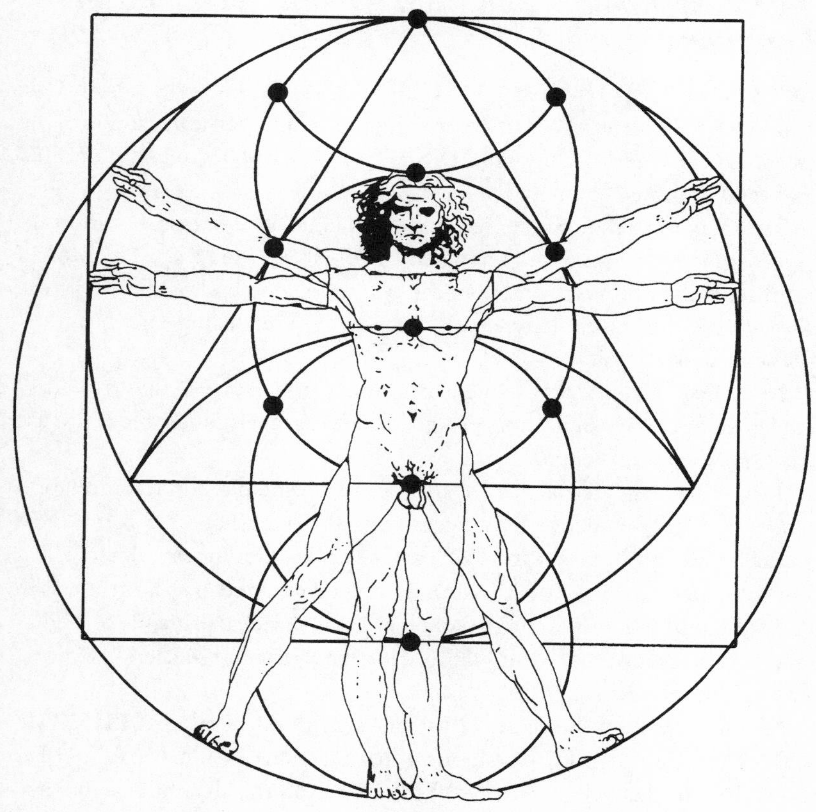

Man, the Microcosm

"Man is the measure of all things" only insofar as he reflects the principles inherent in the Celestial Man of Light, who, in turn, is a reflection of God. The proportions of the human body reflect these principles in an admirable fashion, and in the above illustration the kabbalistic sephira are shown in their correct position, while the four circles correspond to the elemental continuum of Greek cosmology. The upper three circles relate to the Pythagorean and Platonic division of the soul, the three worlds in man. As Plato observes in the *Republic*, true self-mastery is obtained by "bringing into tune those three parts, like the terms in the proportion of a musical scale, the highest and lowest notes and the mean between them, with all the intermediate intervals." In traditional cosmology, humanity actualizes this function of mediation on a universal level, binding together intelligible and sensible, eternal and temporal, Mind and matter.

The God Apollo: The First "Word" of Celestial Harmony

ACCORDING TO THE PYTHAGOREANS, the universe is both One and Many. The beautiful *kosmos* represents a dynamic, harmonic union of the two ideal extremes of Unity and Diversity, Form and Matter, the Limited and the Unlimited elements.

In Pythagorean thought, these two fundamental poles of manifestation are represented by the numbers 1 and 2, the Monad and the Dyad. The Monad represents the Source of creation, the beginning and end of all things; the Dyad represents multiplicity, manifestation, division, duality, and the movement away from unity.

Not only is the universe a living harmony of the interplay of these two ideal extremes, but this cosmic *harmonia* or "joining together" is capable of precise mathematical representation.

Two "opposing" terms need a third term, a principle of *ratio* or relation (*logos*) to bind them together. According to the Pythagoreans, the most perfect mediator between any two extremes is the Geometric Mean, which binds the two extremes together in a continued geometric proportion, as in A:B:C. Therefore, represented mathematically, the ideal principle of mediation between Unity and Multiplicity, between Spirit and Matter, between 1 and 2, is $\sqrt{2}$, for $1:\sqrt{2}:2$.

As can be seen on the right, $\sqrt{2}$ provides the number value of 1415, THE GOD APOLLO. 3/4 of this value is 1061, APOLLO, while 1/4 of 1415 is HERMES, another representation of the Logos. In this diagram can be seen the actual source and primary symbolism of the key numbers of Greek gematria.

The God Apollo is a representation of the ideal Logos (*ratio*) which links together Unity and Multiplicity, 1 and 2. The Logos is the harmonic blueprint behind creation, the mediator between extremes, and the differentiated "image" of the transcendental Unity, the One. Through the function of the Logos, unity may pass into multiplicity and multiplicity may return to unity. As the first and foremost manifestation of divine relation, THE GOD APOLLO, 1415, is, by definition, the First "Word" of Celestial Harmony.

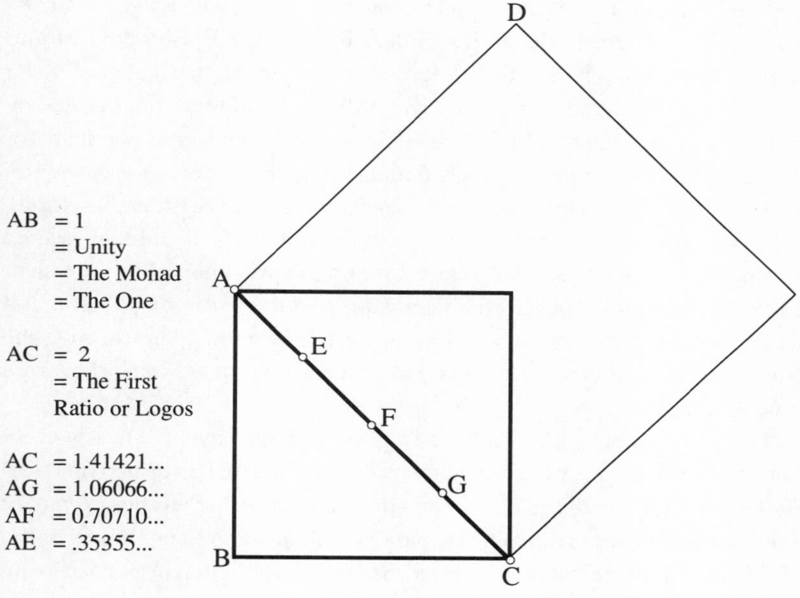

Apollo, the Mediator between Unity and Multiplicity

The square with the side AB contains 1 square unit. The square with the side AC contains 2 square units. Length AC is $\sqrt{2}$, the ideal geometric mean between unity and multiplicity, between 1 and 2. From this value are derived the numbers of Apollo and Hermes, the two Greek personifications of the Logos.

Length	**Actual Value**	**Gematria Value**	**Greek**	**English**
AC x 1000 =	1414.2	1415	ʽΟ ΘΕΟΣ ʼΑΠΟΛΛΩΝ	THE GOD APOLLO
AG x 1000 =	1060.6	1061	ʼΑΠΟΛΛΩΝ	APOLLO
AF x 1000 =	707.1	707	ʽΟ ΘΕΟΣ ʽΕΡΜΗΣ	THE GOD HERMES
AE x 1000 =	353.5	353	ʽΕΡΜΗΣ	HERMES
		354	ʽΟ ΘΕΟΣ	THE GOD

The Cosmic Temple I

A BABYLONIAN clay tablet indicates that, around 700 B.C.E., Sargon II ordered that the wall of Khorsabad be constructed to have a length of 16,283 cubits, the numerical value of his name. Likewise, the Washington Monument was built to a height of 555 feet, also for symbolic purposes.

A temple is a sacred edifice built to fulfill a magical function, situated on a site of pre-existing sanctity. In the same way that the Logos is a mediator between unity and multiplicity, the temple is a mediator between heaven and earth, the timeless and the temporal. Therefore, ever since the earliest times, religious architecture has been rooted in the timeless principles of "sacred geometry." By basing sacred architecture on the principles of transcendent form and harmony, temple architects expressed the harmony of heaven on earth. Not only do ancient temples express this harmony, but, through the use of gematria, they were designed to attract the spirit to which they were consecrated.

The present writer has conducted computerized analyses of nearly every ancient Greek temple where the dimensions are known. If measured in terms of the ancient Greek foot, the Parthenon and many other temples bring out the key numbers of the Orphic theological canon—and the numbers of the divinity to which they are consecrated. Shown on the right is just one of many fascinating examples. It is the temple of Apollo at Didyma, the most important Apollo temple after that of Delphi, and one of the largest Greek temples ever constructed. The topmost platform, the stylobate, has a length of 353.8 Greek feet. Therefore, the hexagon has a measure of 1061.4 Greek feet, and 1061 is the value of APOLLO. The square has a measure of 1415.2 Greek feet and 1415 is the value of the phrase THE GOD APOLLO.

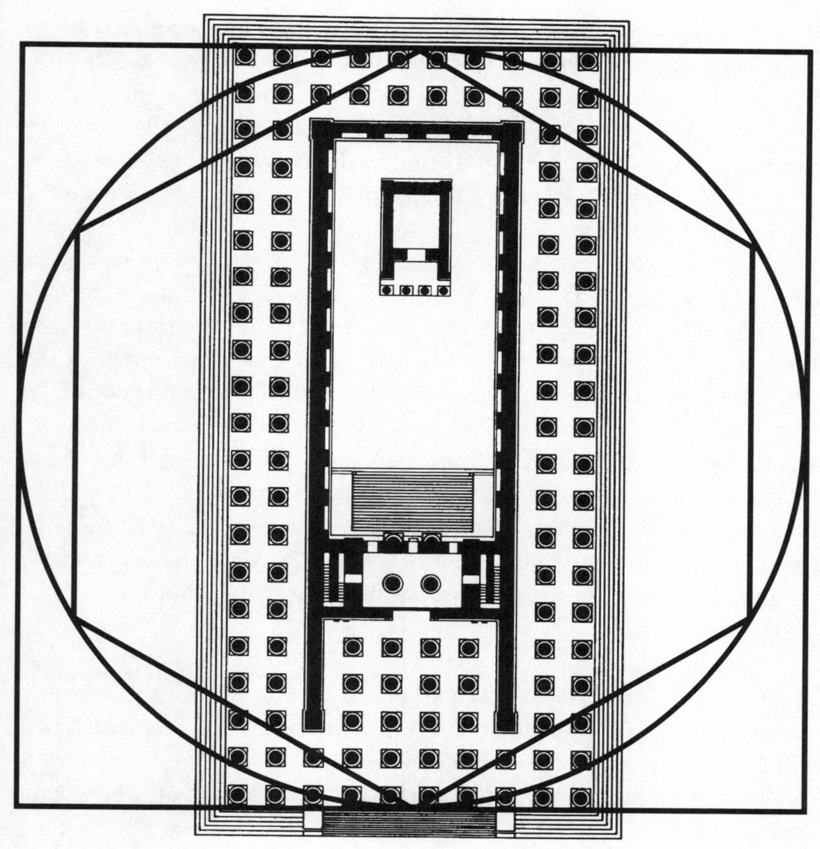

The Didymaion or Temple of Apollo at Didyma, near Miletos

Length of stylobate = 353.8 Greek feet
Perimeter of hexagon = 1061.4 Greek feet • 1061 = APOLLO
Perimeter of square = 1415.2 Greek feet • 1415 = THE GOD APOLLO

The Cosmic Temple II

THE PARTHENON is the temple of the virgin (*parthenos*) goddess Athena, the patron divinity of Athens, who was the personification of both terrestrial and cosmic Wisdom. Not only was Athena a virgin, but she also experienced a unique, virgin-birth from the skull of Zeus, in her most famous myth. Zeus swallowed his lover Metis (Thought), who was already pregnant with Athena, out of fear that she would bring forth a son who would surpass the power of his thunderbolt. Later, Athena sprang out fully armored from the head of her father Zeus.

Athena's temple, located on the uppermost point of the *acropolis* (highest city), is an embodiment of the highest art and celestial wisdom. Designed by the architects Ictinus and Callicrates, under the direction of the sculptor Phidias in 447 B.C.E., the Parthenon is governed on many levels by the controlling proportion 4:9 and represents the most perfect expression of the Doric order. The stylobate, or uppermost platform of the temple, measures exactly 100 by 225 Greek feet, thus bringing out the values of the Greek number canon shown in the facing illustration. Brought out are the numbers of APOLLO (illumination), ZEUS (wisdom), and HERMES (crafty intelligence); Athena is the embodiment of all these qualities, and the whole arrangement simultaneously depicts the "head of Zeus" from which she is born.

A circle drawn touching the four corners of the stylobate (not shown) has the circumference of 515 Greek cubits (one cubit = 1.5 Greek feet), which is the gematria value of *parthenos* or VIRGIN (ΠΑΡΘΕΝΟΣ). A square drawn within this circle has the measure of 464 cubits, the value of THE MOTHER (Ἡ ΜΗΤΗΡ). Both of these titles are classical appellations of Athena and, appropriately enough, in Christian times the Parthenon retained its name, for it was converted into a church dedicated to the Virgin Mary, the virgin mother of Jesus.

A complete analysis of this outstanding structure can be found in this writer's article, "The Gematria of the Parthenon and Some Other Greek Temples."

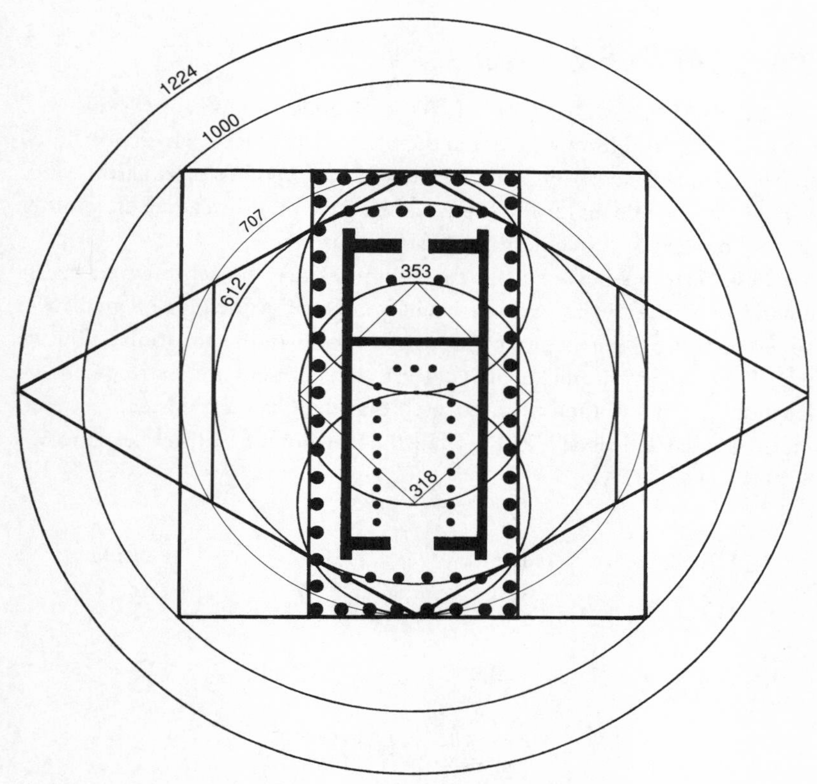

The Parthenon or Temple of Athena Parthenos in Athens

Inner circle = 353 = HERMES
Square contained within inner circle = 318 = HELIOS
Tri-circle pattern = 1061 = APOLLO
Circle contained within rhombus-hexagon = 612 = ZEUS
Circle with diameter of stylobate = 707 = THE GOD HERMES
1000 = THE ONE or THE MONAD
1224 = THE NET

The greatest expression of the Doric order, the Parthenon also encapsulates the central values of the Greek number canon. The diagonal of the square which contains the stylobate measures 318 Greek feet, the number of HELIOS, which is the diameter of a circle with a circumferance of 1000 units, symbolizing the Monad, the source of the *kosmos*. The dimensions of the inner geometry, held within the circle of the Monad, may be likened to the *logoi* or creative principles held within the germ of a seed. All dimensions are in Greek feet. The width of the stylobate, 100 Greek feet, is precisely one second of arc in the circumference of the terrestrial sphere.

The Music of the Sun I

HERMES AND APOLLO, the two Greek gods of music, are "brothers," the sons of Zeus. Hermes invented the tortoise-shell lyre, which he offered to Apollo in reconciliation, after stealing fifty of Apollo's prize cattle. Since wily Hermes made up for the theft, Apollo gave him the caduceus, another symbol of harmony, in a gesture of friendship.

These relations between the two divinities may be represented mathematically through the harmonic and geometric principles of mediation which underlie the structure of the musical scale. In the equation below we take HERMES, 353, and APOLLO, 1061, to represent the extremes to be harmonized. It will then be discovered that the Geometric Mean between Hermes and Apollo is 612, ZEUS, while the Harmonic Mean between the two is 531, LYRE (ΛΥΡΑ).

HERMES	LYRE	ZEUS	APOLLO
353	531	612	1061
A	$\frac{2AB}{A+B}$	$\sqrt{A \times B}$	B
	HARMONIC MEAN	GEOMETRIC MEAN	

Musical *harmonia* is manifest in the physical and aural realms when a single string is plucked, for that gives rise to the harmonic overtone series. First the string vibrates as a unit, then in halves, thirds, quarters, fifths, and so on, simultaneously, and continues toward infinity until the string comes to a rest. This gives rise to the overtones which, with practice, can be heard, and are easily brought out on the monochord. Each musical instrument has a unique timbre or tonal characteristic because it emphasizes certain overtones; for example, the clarinet possesses its characteristic sound because the instrument naturally highlights the odd numbered overtones.

On the facing page is shown the overtone series and its correlation with notes on a keyboard. If the eighth harmonic is given the value of 1415 vibrations, then all the other values shown will follow. Not only are Apollo and Hermes brothers, but they are musical gods, and both are associated with the lyre.

Vibrational Frequency	Note	Exact Value	Greek Gematria Value	
10	e^2	1768.75	1768	= THE GOD APOLLO + HERMES = APOLLO + THE GOD HERMES
9	d^2	1591.875	1592	= APOLLO + LYRE
8	c^2	1415	1415	= THE GOD APOLLO
7	b $flat^1$	1238.125	1238	= THE GOD HERMES + LYRE
6	g^1	1061.25	1061	= APOLLO
5	e^1	884.375	884	= HERMES + LYRE
4	c^1	707.5	707	= THE GOD HERMES
3	g	530.625	531	= LYRE
2	c	353.75	353	= HERMES
1	C	176.875	Unity; The Fundamental Tone; The Unplucked String	

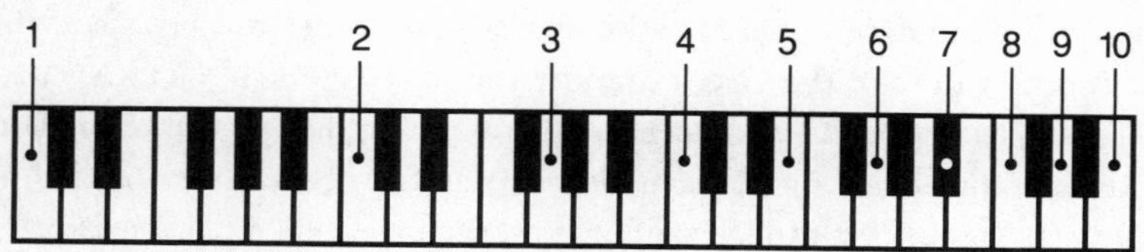

The Overtone Series and its Relation to Greek Gematria

The Music of the Sun II

ASK ANY MUSICIAN and he will tell you that the pillars of musical harmony are the perfect fifth and the perfect fourth. These fundamental ratios represent the foundation of the musical scale and harmony and are intimately related to one another: that is because moving down a perfect fifth (C to F) is the "same" as moving up a perfect fourth (C to F), while moving down a perfect fourth (C to G) is the "same" as moving up a perfect fifth (C to G). Moreover, the ratio of the perfect fourth to the perfect fifth defines the interval of the whole tone.

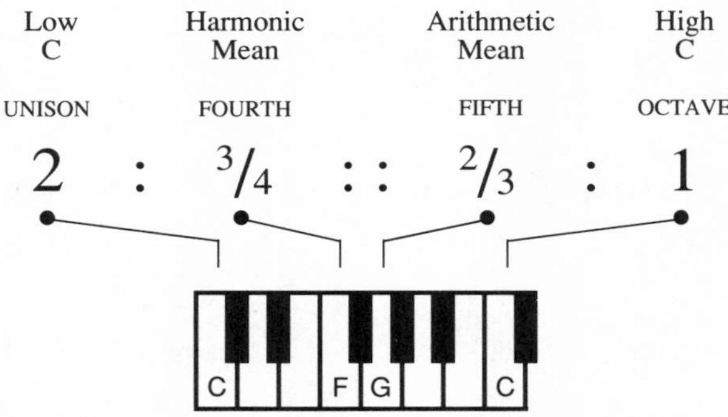

The Perfect Consonances: Unison, Octave, Fifth and Fourth

Pythagorean philosophy is primarily concerned with the problem of mediation between extremes via the principle of ratio, *logos*, or proportion; the result is *harmonia*, a "fitting together." In the case of the musical scale, the two extremes which must be united are the octave, 1 and 2, the interval from low C to high C. The Arithmetic Mean between the two extremes is the perfect fifth, while the Harmonic Mean between 1 and 2 is the perfect fourth. These ratios and relations are shown above in terms of relative string lengths.

As can be seen on the facing page, the harmonic ratios of the fourth and the fifth are intimately related to the "Music of the Sun," for they also define the central values of the Greek number canon: 1415, THE GOD APOLLO; 1061, APOLLO; 707, THE GOD HERMES; and 888, JESUS, another personification of the Solar Logos. 888 is also the number of the Greek bard OLEN ('ΩΛΗΝ), Apollo's first speaker of oracles, the inventor of hexameter verse, and founder of Apollo's shrine at Delphi. He wrote and sang many hymns to the gods and is said to have lived before the time of Orpheus.

$$\frac{1}{\sqrt{3/4 \times 2/3}} \times 1000 = 1415$$

$$\sqrt{3/4 \div 2/3} \times 1000 = 1061$$

$$\sqrt{3/4 \times 2/3} \times 1000 = 707$$

$$\frac{1}{3/4 \div 2/3} \times 1000 = 888$$

"The Harmony of the Sun"

1415 = THE GOD APOLLO
1061 = APOLLO
707 = THE GOD HERMES
888 = JESUS; OLEN

The perfect fourth and the perfect fifth represent the Harmonic and Arithmetic forms of mediation between the two extremes of the octave in musical tuning theory. They are the most powerful musical intervals and form the underlying basis of harmonic progression in all forms of music. The various relations shown above between the primary harmonic ratios bring out the numbers of Apollo, the Greek god of music; Hermes, the inventor of Apollo's lyre; Jesus, the Christian personification of the Solar Logos; and Olen, Apollo's first "prophet" and the founder of the oracle at Delphi. The above relationships show that the numbers 1415, 1061, 707, and 888 are intimately related—they are, in fact, mathematical variations upon a single harmonic theme: the so-called "musical proportion" discovered by Pythagoras, the underlying foundation of the musical scale.

Helios, the Image of the One

HISTORY BOOKS are silent on the ultimate origin of the astrological symbol of the sun, a circle with a dot in the middle: ⊙. As the preeminent celestial body and leader of the cosmic dance, the figure is elegantly appropriate, a symbol of cosmic wholeness and unity. In the words of a famous Hermetic saying, "God is a sphere whose circumference is nowhere but whose center is everywhere."

In ancient Egypt, ⊙ was a symbol of the sun god Ra. Each of the 28 divisions of the Egyptian Royal Cubit was consecrated to a particular divinity, and, appropriately enough, the first division of the cubit, the number 1, bears the symbol of ⊙.

The symbol of the sun also appears on a Greek coin minted at Delphi. On one side of the coin appears a representation of Apollo's Tripod; the other side, representing the omphalos, simply displays the abstract symbol ⊙.

The earliest form of the Greek letter Theta (Θ) was simply ⊙. According to ancient sources, the letters of the alphabet were revealed to humanity by a god or godlike being and, by gematria, the value of the Greek word THETA (ΘΗΤΑ) is 318, also the number of HELIOS (῾ΗΛΙΟΣ), the sun.

According to the Neoplatonists, the ultimate source of the cosmos is a transcendental unity, simply called the One, and the physical sun is its natural emblem in the created order. More precisely, the sun is a living image of the One on a lower level of being, and the gematria of HELIOS, 318, indicates the sun's relation to this higher principle of unity. That is because a circle with a circumference of Unity possesses a diameter of 318.

῾ΗΛΙΟΣ

HELIOS = 318

The first 15 divisions of the Egyptian Royal Cubit. Each division of the cubit was dedicated to a divinity, and the first division, on the right, shows the hieroglyph of the sun god Ra (⊙), symbol of divine unity.

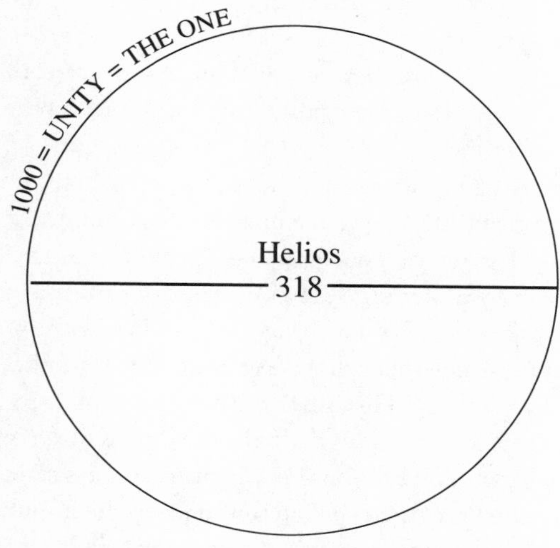

Helios, the Offspring of the One

CIRCUMFERENCE = 1000 = UNITY = "THE ONE"
DIAMETER = 318 = HELIOS

The Neoplatonists maintained that Helios the sun is the lower image of the Transcendental Absolute or the One. The One, or principle of Unity, may be represented by the numbers 1, 10, 100, etc. If it is represented by the number 1000, then a circle with that circumference is discovered to have a value of 318, HELIOS, the Greek name of the sun.

Plutarch, a priest of Apollo at Delphi, wrote that Apollo represented the One, for *a-pollôn* in ancient Greek means literally "not many." Likewise, Plutrach maintained that Helios, the Sun, was merely Apollo's offspring. As he notes in one of his Delphic essays, "Many among earlier generations [mistakenly] regarded Apollo and the Sun as one and the same god; but those who [correctly] understood and respected fair and wise analogy conjectured that as body is to soul, vision to intellect, and light to truth, so is the power of the sun to the nature of Apollo; and they would make it appear that the sun is his offspring and progeny, being for ever born of him that is for ever."

Hermes, the Logos

THE GREEKS referred to Hermes as the Logos, as he was the god of language and speech.

As a personification of natural harmony, Hermes invented the Greek lyre which he gave to his older brother Apollo; Apollo, in turn, gave the caduceus, another symbol of harmony, to Hermes. Hermes is the god of pathways and roads, travel, writing, and commerce—hence the name of his Latin counterpart, Mercurius, means literally "pertaining to merchandise."

For the Greeks Hermes was *psychopompos*, "the guide of souls." He was also the Logos seen in a cosmological sense. According to the gnostic sect of the Naassenes, "Hermes is the Word who has expressed and fashioned the things that have been, that are and that will be." According to Manetho, an Egyptian priest of Ra from Heliopolis, Hermes was the author of 36,525 books. Since the solar year is 365.25 days in length, if Hermes had written one book each day he would have completed the task in a century. One is reminded here of the conclusion of the Fourth Gospel, in reference to the innumerable deeds of another Logos: "But there are also many other things which Jesus did; were every one of them to be written, I suppose that the *kosmos* itself could not contain the books that would be written."

Hermes was identified with the Egyptian deity Thoth, the "scribe of the gods." As the Egyptologist E. A. Wallis Budge points out, Thoth was "the heart and tongue" of the sun god Ra, "the reason (*logos*) and mental powers of the god, and also the means by which their will was translated into speech." Thoth "spoke the words which resulted in the creation of the heavens and the earth" and "it was his great skill in celestial mathematics which made proper use of the laws (*maat*) upon which the foundation and maintenance of the universe rested; it was he who directed the motions of the heavenly bodies and their times and seasons; and without his words the gods, whose existence depended on them, could not have kept their place among the followers of Ra."

According to the analogical reasoning of traditional cosmology, in the same way that light exists in relation to the sun, Thoth exists in relation to Ra, and the Logos exists in relation to the transcendent God.

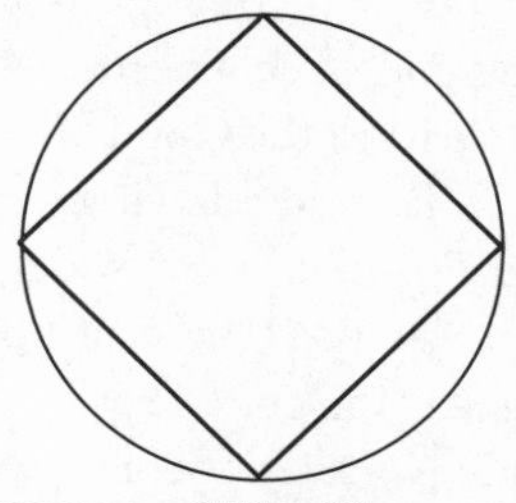

CIRCLE = 353 = HERMES
SQUARE = 318 = HELIOS

The "Word" of the Sun

According to the teachings of Egyptian theology, Thoth the Logos is the offspring of the sun god Ra. Similarly, in *Corpus Hermeticum* 1, the "Light-Word" emanated from divinity is called the "Son of God." The above illustration shows the relationship between Hermes, the Greek Logos, and Helios, the Greek name of the sun. If the circle has the circumference of 353 units, the value of HERMES, then the perimeter of the box contained within measures 318, the numerical value of HELIOS.

With the birth of Christianity, the Logos took on a new personification in the figure of Jesus. This is alluded to in the later infancy gospel of pseudo-Matthew. According to this account, when Joseph, Mary and Jesus entered an Egyptian temple in the vicinity of Hermopolis, the City of Hermes, the 365 idols which stood in the temple came crashing down. The story symbolizes the fact that the new-born Jesus was then superseding the earlier personifications of the Solar Logos in popularity.

Some Epithets of Thoth, the Logos of the Sun God Ra

, "Lord of Speech"

, "Tongue of Ra"

, "Who Comes Forth from Ra"

Hermes, the Good Shepherd

HERMES was depicted in Greek mythology as *psychopompos*, "the guide of souls," and he was also the god of shepherds, who lead their flocks. The artistic representation of Christ as the Good Shepherd was derived from a famous statue of Hermes at Tanagra carrying a goat, and the name of the Hermetic tractate entitled *Poimandrês* was widely interpreted as meaning "Man-Shepherd" in Greek. As the Guide of both material and spiritual nature, Hermes the Logos was the god of roads, pathways and boundaries, including the byways and boundaries of consciousness. Sacred to him was THE PATH or THE WAY (Ἡ ὉΔΟΣ), which, by gematria, is 352, one unit less than his own name, which amounts to 353. This term was not only an epithet of Christ, as when he says "I am the Way" in John 14.6, but was also a name of the early Christian movement. That is because the knowledge of the Logos represents "the path between opposites," for it is through the agency of *logos* that the polarities of creation are reconciled and transcended in a higher unity.

In the same way that the Logos, in a cosmological sense, is the Leader of Matter, the "word" or call of the shepherd guides his flock, as the musical harmony of Orpheus unified and led the irrational beasts of the field. Likewise, the *logos* within is the comforting voice of the holy spirit which exists at the center of the self, guiding and harmonizing all the parts of the soul. Because man is a microcosm, a reflection of the entire universe, we are not cut off from the order of the universe, but embody it on every level. Therefore, one way to experience the harmony of the *logos* is to turn quietly within, and attentively listen to the silent voice from the center.

ABOVE LEFT: Hermes animating and releasing lifeless shades.
ABOVE RIGHT: Hermes guiding a soul upward, releasing it from the Underworld.

Hermes, the Messenger of the Gods

In the language of traditional symbolism, Hermes is the reflective and mercurial spirit of consciousness: the "Good Shepherd" of the mind, or the comforting voice of the Holy Spirit. Long before the birth of Christianity, Hermes was regarded as a redeemer and guide who released souls from the realm of Hades, conducting them to the realm of eternal life. The symbol of the caduceus, a gift from the sun god Apollo, is called in the Orphic hymns "the blameless tool of peace." As a symbol of natural harmony, it may refer to the process of psychological evolution which occurs when the pairs of opposites are allowed to interact with one another around the quiet center of the Self.

Thrice-Greatest Hermes: The Triple Logos

THE NAME Hermes Trismegistos, "Thrice-Great Hermes," is connected with those valuable writings of pagan gnosis known as the *Corpus Hermeticum*. Like the introduction to the Gospel of John, the Hermetic writings orbit around the Hellenistic idea of the Solar Logos; hence, according to one of the Hermetic tractates, the Light-Word which emanated from Mind is the Son of God.

Having taken over the attributes of the ancient Egyptian divinity Thoth, Hermes Trismegistos was imagined as an ancient sage, the revealer of all arts and sciences, the inventor of the alphabet, mathematics, writing, theology, geometry, and so on. The Hermetic writings were naturally attributed to him because, as Iamblichus notes, "Hermes, the god who presides over language, was formerly very properly considered as common to all priests; and the power who presides over the true science concerning the gods is one and the same in the whole of things. Hence our ancestors dedicated the inventions of their wisdom to this deity, inscribing all their own writings with the name of Hermes."

The Hermetic "sermons" (*logoi*) are written in dialogue form between Hermes, the informing Word, and a student. Trismegistos is in reality the Egyptian personification of the universal order ("cosmic logos") as Gnostic Revealer: as one scholar notes, he was "the source of all knowledge previously known only to the gods." For the Christians, Christ the Logos was the Gnostic Revealer—the bestower of liberating knowledge and heavenly wisdom.

The "word" manifests itself as a mediator between the eternal, heavenly principles and their temporal, earthly reflections. A similar function is performed by the dialogues of Hermes Trismegistos and the teachings and miracles of Christ, both of which reflect a common system of cosmological and geometrical symbolism.

The Greek god Hermes, while an aspect of the Logos, does not in his stories and myths represent as exalted a figure as Hermes the Thrice-Great, who possesses, by far, a greater measure of cosmic wisdom. Evidently, the "Triple Hermes" should be identified with the fullness of the Apollonic Logos for, by gematria, one-third of APOLLO (1061) is equivalent to HERMES (353) and a small fraction.

Hermes Trismegistos

Hermes Trismegistos is the Greco-Egyptian personification of the Logos as Gnostic Revealer. He was held to be the revealer of all arts and sciences, a teacher of heavenly wisdom, and the author of the tractates which comprise the Greek Hermetic corpus.

The Emerald Tablet of Hermes Trismegistos

HERMES TRISMEGISTOS is not only connected with the important writings of *Corpus Hermeticum*, but, as the inventor of all arts and sciences, he is also associated with the ancient art of alchemy. One of the oldest and most profound of all alchemical documents is the so-called Emerald Tablet of Hermes Trismegistos, and this is reproduced on the right.

As C. G. Jung and other scholars have recognized, alchemy was heavily influenced by gnostic ideas. Gnosis teaches that Spirit has fallen into Matter. It is the task of the alchemist to assist in the liberation of spirit hidden in matter. Since all metals are naturally evolving toward gold, the apex of the mineral kingdom, the alchemist merely acts as a midwife, speeding along the process of what is ultimately a form of spiritual evolution. In the same way that Christ came to redeem all of humanity, the task of alchemy is the "redemption" of all matter.

Everyone who becomes aware of the Logos becomes, in some sense, a spiritual alchemist, involved in the redemption of matter. Through the power of the Logos creation becomes possible—the first unified principles are harmonically differentiated and expressed in the phenomenal multiplicity of the natural world. In the words of the Emerald Tablet, "Its power is perfect if it is converted into earth." Yet, through the individual's conscious recognition of the first principles "hidden" or reflected in matter, the ultimately spiritual nature of matter is revealed—matter is thereby redeemed and reunited to its source, multiplicity is reconciled in unity. Through the faculty of authentic knowledge, the individual realizes his nature as an aspect of the Universal Logos, a mediator between heaven and earth, between the One and the Many. Through the gift of gnosis one becomes not only a true Christian—one also becomes a Christ. As Jesus "the living one" says in *The Books of Ieou*, "Blessed is the man who knoweth this, and has brought the heaven down, and carried the earth and sent it to heaven" for such a person, says he, has become "the Midst."

The Emerald Tablet

1. In truth certainly and without doubt, whatever is below is like that which is above, and whatever is above is like that which is below, to accomplish the miracles of one thing.

2. Just as all things proceed from One alone by meditation on One alone, so also they are born from this one thing by adaptation.

3. Its father is the sun and its mother is the moon. The wind has borne it in its body. Its nurse is the earth.

4. It is the father of every miraculous work in the whole world.

5. Its power is perfect if it is converted into earth.

6. Separate the earth from the fire and the subtle from the gross, softly and with great prudence.

7. It rises from earth to heaven and comes down again from heaven to earth, and thus acquires the power of the realities above and the realities below. In this way you will acquire the glory of the whole world, and all darkness will leave you.

8. This is the power of all powers, for it conquers everything subtle and penetrates everything solid.

9. Thus the little world (microcosm) is created according to the prototype of the great world (macrocosm).

10. From this and in this way, marvellous applications are made.

11. For this reason I am called Hermes Trismegistos, for I possess the three parts of wisdom of the whole world.

12. Perfect is what I have said of the work of the sun.

THE ELEMENTAL CONTINUUM

1

GEOMETRICAL STAGE	PLATONIC SOLID	STATE OF MATTER	PSYCHOLOGICAL FUNCTION
THE POINT • **OR MONAD** NONDIMENSIONALITY	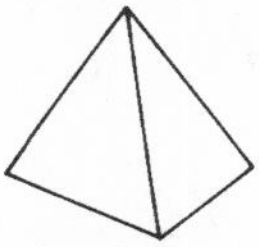 **TETRAHEDRON**	Fire PLASMA	**INTUITION** The Soul's Relationship with the World of Divine Ideas

2

GEOMETRICAL STAGE	PLATONIC SOLID	STATE OF MATTER	PSYCHOLOGICAL FUNCTION
THE LINE  ONE DIMENSION	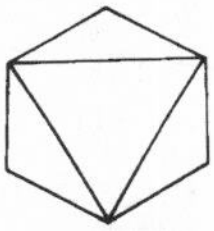 **OCTAHEDRON**	Air GAS	**THINKING** The Soul's Relationship with the Intellectual World

3

GEOMETRICAL STAGE	PLATONIC SOLID	STATE OF MATTER	PSYCHOLOGICAL FUNCTION
THE SURFACE 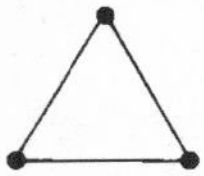 TWO DIMENSIONS	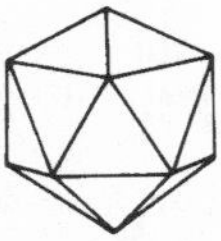 **ICOSAHEDRON**	Water LIQUID	**FEELING** The Soul's Relationship with the Emotional World

4

GEOMETRICAL STAGE	PLATONIC SOLID	STATE OF MATTER	PSYCHOLOGICAL FUNCTION
THE SOLID 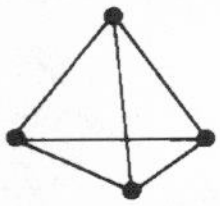 THREE DIMENSIONS	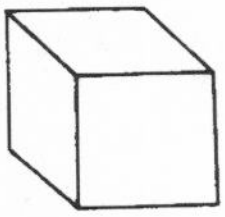 **CUBE**	Earth SOLID	**SENSATION** The Soul's Relationship with the Physical World

OF HELLENISTIC COSMOLOGY

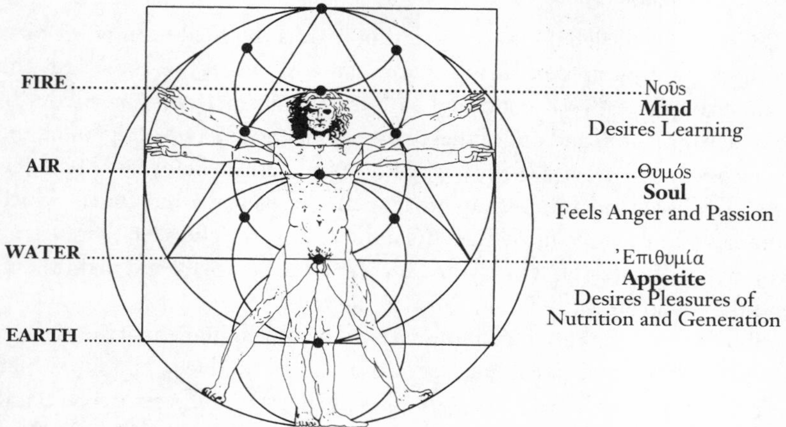

The Pythagorean and Platonic Division of the Soul: The Three Worlds in Man

"The soul is divided into reasoning power, anger, and desire. Reasoning power rules knowledge, anger deals with impulse, and desire bravely rules the soul's affections. When these three parts unite into one action, exhibiting a composite energy, then in the soul results concord and virtue. When sedition divides them, then discord and vice appear."

—Theages the Pythagorean, *On the Virtues*

The Tetraktys: A Symbol of Cosmic Wholeness

In Pythagorean thought, the so-called *Tetraktys* (Fourness) represents the four levels of reality, the four elements, the four states of matter, the four stages of geometrical existence, and so on. Symbolizing the Pythagorean philosophy of whole systems, the Tetraktys also expresses the perfect harmonies of music: 1:2 (the octave), 2:3 (the perfect fifth), and 3:4 (the perfect fourth).

The Tetraktys of Pythagoras

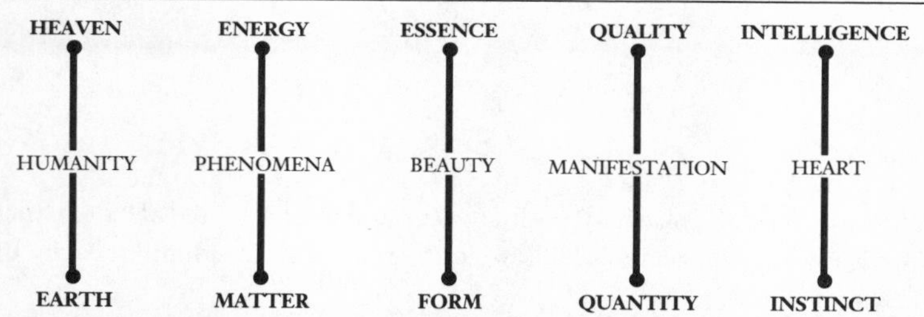

The Symbolic Continuum: Including the Harmonic Offspring of Ideal Opposites

The Astral Spheres

IT IS an ancient belief that the world of man is the final focal point for a variety of cosmic forces. In the traditional cosmologies of the West, the planetary spheres were associated with the various patterns and modes of human expression, and out of these correspondence systems originated the sciences of alchemy and Hermetic philosophy. Both alchemy and Hermeticism are based on the premise that man encapsulates the forces which comprise the cosmos, an idea nicely summed up by the church father Origen who wrote "Understand that you are a second little world, and that the sun and the moon are within you, and also the stars."

Shown on the right is the traditional Chaldean arrangement of the planets, from which the traditional number of the planet is derived. The sun, which orchestrates the celestial dance, occupies the heart of the cosmic tree. Some other traditional attributes of the planetary symbols are provided in the chart of correspondences for convenient reference.

According to the pessimist school of gnosis, humanity is unconscious, ruled by astrological Fate, and is trapped in a material world which was created in ignorance and error. Only the saving knowledge imparted by the Gnostic Revealer will awaken slumbering humanity to its true nature and celestial origin.

In contrast, according to the optimist school of gnosis, the *kosmos* is a beautiful theophany, a manifestation of the divine. Rather than accepting the alienated cosmology of pessimist gnosis, optimist gnosis realizes that "the world is full of gods" and that humanity, rather than being imprisoned in lifeless earth, treads, in fact, upon the bottom of the sky.

ABOVE RIGHT: The planetary positions set out upon the "Tree of Life," from the Jewish kabbalistic tradition, following the traditonal Chaldean hierarchy of the celestial spheres.

BELOW RIGHT: Some of the traditional planetary correspondences.

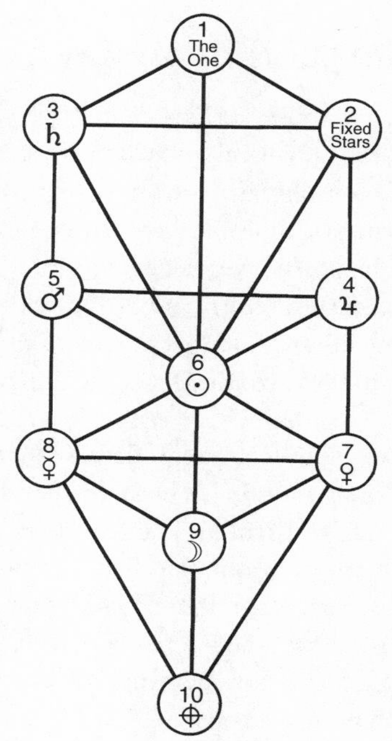

Sign	Position on Tree	Name of Planet	Greek Deity	Alchemical Metal	Symbolic Quality
♄	3	Saturn	Kronos	Lead	Time and Form
♃	4	Jupiter	Zeus	Tin	Paternal Wisdom
♂	5	Mars	Ares	Iron	Active Energy
☉	6	Sun	Helios	Gold	Harmony and Beauty
♀	7	Venus	Aphrodite	Copper	Emotional Relation
☿	8	Mercury	Hermes	Quicksilver	Reflective Intelligence
☽	9	Moon	Selene	Silver	Patterns of Instinct
⊕	10	Earth	Gaia	All of the Above	All of the Above

Celestial Archetypes I: Planetary Squares

MAGIC SQUARES are those curious numerical patterns of traditional cosmology which offer the identical sum when any line of numbers is added horizontally, vertically, or diagonally, from corner to corner. The smallest square, 3x3, contains the first nine numbers; the 4x4 square contains the first sixteen numbers; and hence the pattern continues.

Each one of the magic squares is associated with a planetary divinity, following the traditional Babylonian arrangement of the heavenly spheres. The closer one comes to the earth the larger the square becomes. According to the "doctrine of signatures," these magic squares represent archetypal patterns of energy and are mathematical reflections of the underlying natural order. Thus, as Jim Moran notes in his book on the subject, "Magic squares brilliantly reveal the intrinsic harmony and symmetry of numbers; with their curious and mystic charm they appear to betray some hidden intelligence that governs the cosmic order that dominates all existence. They have been compared to a mirror reflecting the symmetry of the universe, the harmonies of nature, the divine norm. It is not surprising that they have always exercised a great influence on thinking people."

Traditionally, the numbers of the planetary squares have been used in formulating the names of planetary spirits and intelligences, in constructing planetary talismans, in determining the measurements of temples, and so on. Based on the principle that "like attracts like," in all such instances the purpose is to invoke the presence, the knowledge, and the nature of a universal symbolic principle: the beauty of Venus, the fiery energy of Mars, the intelligence of Mercury, the harmonizing energy of the Sun, and so on. To those initiated into the mysteries of the old cosmologies, the divinities or archetypes of nature were recognized as autonomous patterns of energy which leave their imprint on many levels of human experience.

♄

4	9	2
3	5	7
8	1	6

♃

4	14	15	1
9	7	6	12
5	11	10	8
16	2	3	13

♂

11	24	7	20	3
4	12	25	8	16
17	5	13	21	9
10	18	1	14	22
23	6	19	2	15

☉

6	32	3	34	35	1
7	11	27	28	8	30
19	14	16	15	23	24
18	20	22	21	17	13
25	29	10	9	26	12
36	5	33	4	2	31

♀

22	47	16	41	10	35	4
5	23	48	17	42	11	29
30	6	24	49	18	36	12
13	31	7	25	43	19	37
38	14	32	1	26	44	20
21	39	8	33	2	27	45
46	15	40	9	34	3	28

☿

8	58	59	5	4	62	63	1
49	15	14	52	53	11	10	56
41	23	22	44	45	19	18	48
32	34	35	29	28	38	39	25
40	26	27	37	36	30	31	33
17	47	46	20	21	43	42	24
9	55	54	12	13	51	50	16
64	2	3	61	60	6	7	57

☾

37	78	29	70	21	62	13	54	5
6	38	79	30	71	22	63	14	46
47	7	39	80	31	72	23	55	15
16	48	8	40	81	32	64	24	56
57	17	49	9	41	73	33	65	25
26	58	18	50	1	42	74	34	66
67	27	59	10	51	2	43	75	35
36	68	19	60	11	52	3	44	76
77	28	69	20	61	12	53	4	45

Celestial Archetypes II: Planetary Numbers

WITHIN THE framework of traditional cosmology each planet has its own unique numerical signature, obtained from the numbers of the associated magic square.

One may obtain the most characteristic number of any given magic square by adding together any symmetrical group of four numbers. It will then be discovered that the sum of any symmetrical pattern of numbers is a perfect multiple of the obtained value, as is the total sum of the even-numbered squares. Therefore, the total of the Zeus (Jupiter) square is 136, or 4x34; Helios (Sun) is 666, or 9x74; and Hermes (Mercury) is 2080, or 16x130.

The illustration on the facing page summarizes the planetary numbers following the format:

A - B - C
D - E - F

A = Number of planet
B = Number of boxes in square, or AxA
C = Sum of any symmetrical group of four numbers
D = Sum of any line: horizontal, vertical, or diagonal
E = Sum of perimeter values (always a multiple of C)
F = Sum of entire square (always a multiple of C if A is even)

It will be noted that the sum of all lines in the magic square of the Sun amounts to 666, a number of particular significance to the early Christian mystics, being associated with the lower, physical aspect of the Sun as demiurge or world fabricator. As one aspect of the celestial song, there is nothing to be feared about this natural force unless manifested in its unbalanced extreme as the nuclear fire of authoritarian rule. For unless the harsh light of the fiery sun is balanced by the complementary and regenerating waters of the lunar faculty, human experience becomes a desert and the forests of meaning wither away.

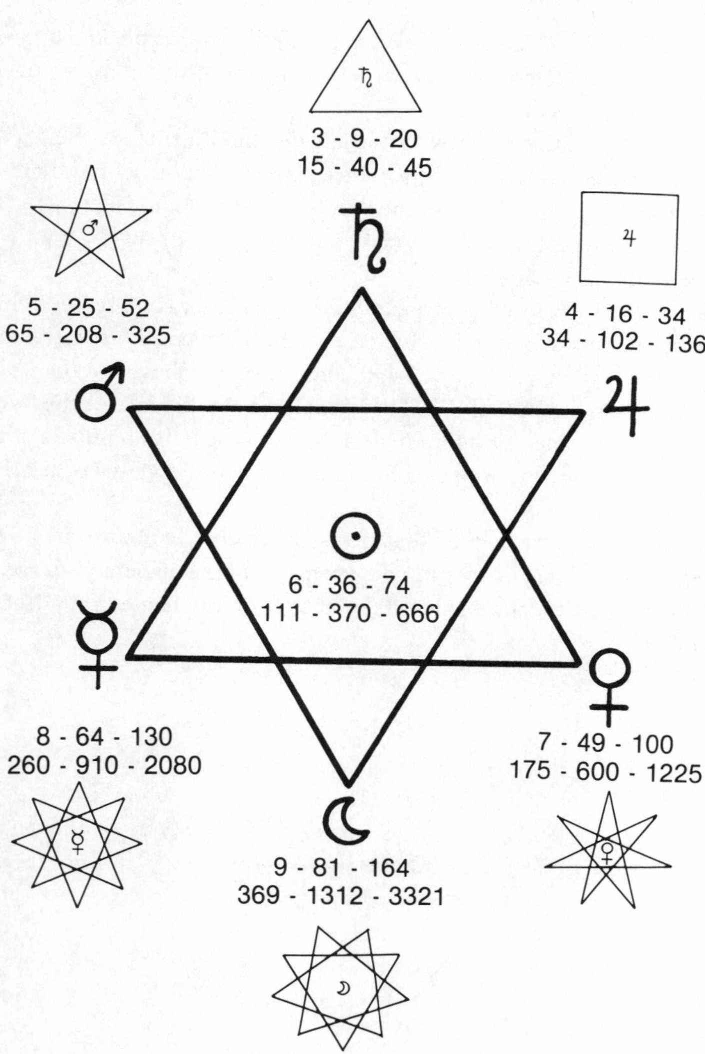

3 - 9 - 20
15 - 40 - 45
5 - 25 - 52
65 - 208 - 325
4 - 16 - 34
34 - 102 - 136
6 - 36 - 74
111 - 370 - 666
8 - 64 - 130
260 - 910 - 2080
7 - 49 - 100
175 - 600 - 1225
9 - 81 - 164
369 - 1312 - 3321

Celestial Archetypes III: Planetary Signatures

THE HEBREW names of the planetary Intelligences and Spirits were intentionally formulated so that they would relate to the numbers of the appropriate magic square.

For example, in the Hebrew Kabbalah the Intelligence of the Sun is NAKIEL (נכיאל), and this name, by gematria, is equivalent to 111, the sum of any line from the magic square of the Sun. The Spirit of the Sun is SORATH (סורת), whose numerical value is 666, the sum total of all the numbers comprising the magic square.

Additionally, each Intelligence and Spirit of a planet is represented by a curious figure known as a sigil, which is used in the magical invocation of a planetary force. The technique of sigil construction is shown on the facing page, using as an example the sigil of Nakiel, the Intelligence of the Sun.

Quite simply, planetary sigils are derived from the letter numbers of the name of the Intelligence or Spirit, connected in their sequential order. The zeros may be removed.

A sigil may therefore be seen as a total synthesis of the nature and power of a planetary force, incorporating the geometry of the planetary square, its numerical properties, and the letters used to form the name of the Intelligence or Spirit.

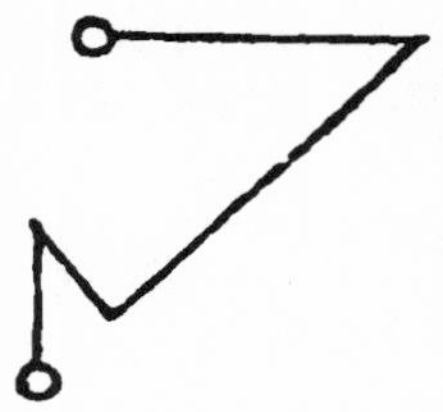

Sigil of Nakiel from Agrippa's *De occulta philosophia*

6	32	3	34	35	1
7	11	27	28	8	30
19	14	16	15	23	24
18	20	22	21	17	13
25	29	10	9	26	12
36	5	33	4	2	31

		3			1
	20				
		10			
	5				

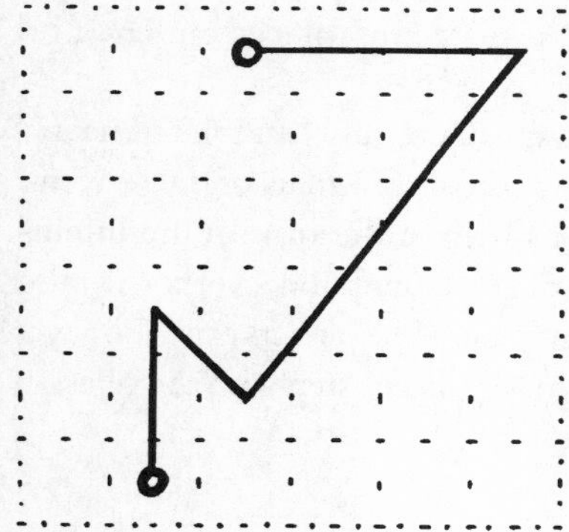

נכיאל = 111

NAKIEL = 111

N = 50 — Reduces to 5
K = 20
I = 10
A = 1
L = 30 — Reduces to 3
111

The Technique of Sigil Construction

Since Nakiel is the Intelligence of the Sun, its number was determined by adding together the values in any line of the magic square of the sun. Any line amounts to 111, and the name Nakiel was arrived at to equal this value. To construct the sigil, the number values of Nakiel's letters were plotted out on the magic square and then connected.

Celestial Archetypes IV: Cosmic Cycles

NOT ONLY were the seven planets associated with the seven strings of the Greek lyre, the seven vowels of the Greek alphabet, and the seven metals of alchemy, but each day of the week is dedicated to one of the planetary gods. This, moreover, was not haphazardly arrived at, as the illustration on the facing page clearly shows. Here the planets are arranged in their traditional order around the perimeter of a heptagon. However, if the planets are linked together on the inside as though one were drawing a heptagram or seven-pointed star, the correct order of the days is revealed.

Presumably, the names of the days reminded ancient people of their patron divinities. Yahweh was identified with Saturn, and Saturday is his day, the Jewish Sabbath. Sunday was taken over by the Christians as the day of their Lord, the "True Sun" and "Light of the World," who also rose from the dead on a Sunday. Friday is the day of sea-born Aphrodite or Venus; fishes were sacred to her and a Friday fish supper is still a popular custom amongst Roman Catholics.

Plato taught that "time is a moving image of eternity" and the measurement of time has eternally been linked with the phenomena of the heavens. By ordering the weekly circuit after the order of the planets, traditional cosmology not only stressed the existence of temporal cycles but also affirmed humanity's proximity to divine realities. The planets exist above yet also within. Our day-to-day life, in its own way, keeps step with the celestial dance and the changing currents of time.

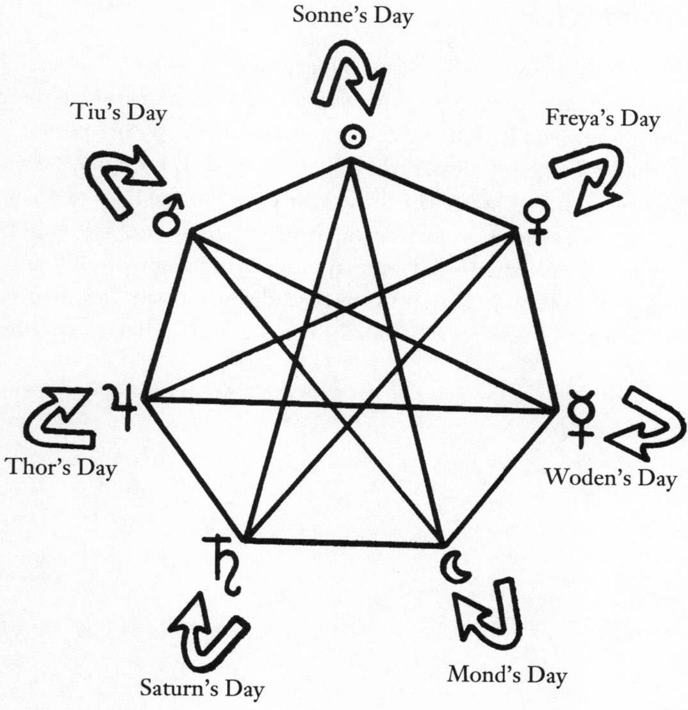

The Relation Between the Planets and the Days of the Week

ABOVE: The order of the planets around the outside of the heptagon follows their traditional order from the earth. By connecting the points inside to form a heptagram or seven-pointed star, the planetary cycle of the week is revealed.

BELOW: The names of the planets and their relation to the names of the days of the week.

Greek	English	Saxon	Day
Kronos	Saturn	Saturn	Saturday
Helios	Sun	Sonne	Sunday
Selene	Moon	Mond	Monday
Ares	Mars	Tiu	Tuesday
Hermes	Mercury	Woden	Wednesday
Zeus	Jupiter	Thor	Thursday
Aphrodite	Venus	Freya	Friday

The Solar Heart

IN THE ILLUSTRATIONS of the Hermetic philosopher Robert Fludd the Sun appears as the mediating principle between the two ideal poles of spirit and matter, situated at the creative midpoint between "heaven" and "earth." Fludd always identified the solar disc with the human heart, the center of the soul, and hence the arbitrator between the fires of analytical intellect and the waters of biological instinct. In so doing, Fludd was following the precedents set by the natural symbolism of alchemy and kabbalistic philosophy, and other forms of traditional cosmology, where the heart, as the seat of life, is regarded as the microcosmic reflection of the life-giving Sun.

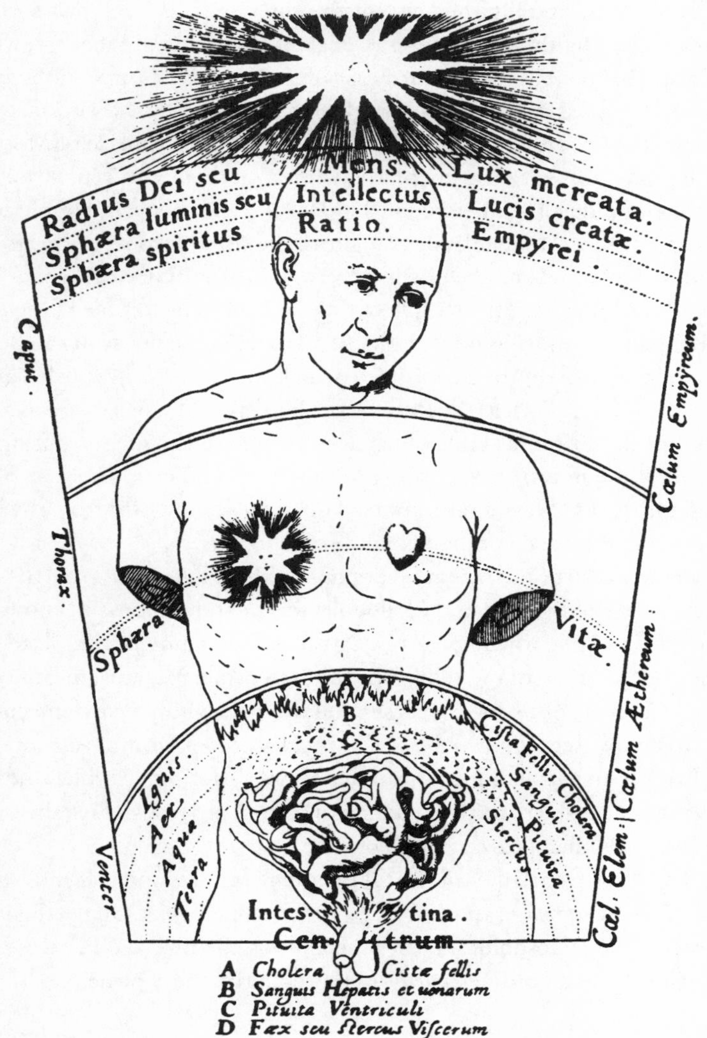
Mens.
Radius Dei seu
Intellectus
Lux increata.
Sphæra luminis seu
Lucis creatæ.
Ratio.
Sphæra spiritus
Empyrei.
Caput.
Cœlum Empyreum.
Thorax.
Sphæra
Vitæ.
Cœlum Æthereum:
A
B
C
D
Cista Fellis Cholera
Sanguis
Pituita
Stercus
Ignis
Aer
Aqua
Terra
Venter
Cœl. Elem:
Intes- tina.
Cen- trum.
A Cholera Cistæ fellis
B Sanguis Hepatis et venarum
C Pituita Ventriculi
D Fæx seu stercus Viscerum

Heliopolis: The City of the Sun

HELIOPOLIS, literally the "city of the sun," is the Greek name of the Egyptian city On, the great center of ancient learning and theology, which was located about five miles northeast of modern day Cairo. Pythagoras, Plato and Eudoxus are said to have studied there, imbibing the wisdom of the Egyptian priests, and it is also said to have been the birthplace of Moses.

Heliopolis, On, or Anu in hieroglyphics, became the center for the priesthood of Ra sometime around 3350 B.C.E., and the main temple of Ra was located there. Heliopolis was the site of the *ben-ben* stone, the prototype of both the pyramid and the obelisk. As E. A. Wallis Budge observes, "The Spirit of the Sun visted the temple of the sun from time to time in the form of a Bennu bird, and alighted 'on the Ben-stone, in the house of the Bennu in Anu'; in later times the Bennu-bird, which the Egyptians regarded as the 'soul of Ra,' was known as the Phoinix or Phoenix." The ben-ben was also a symbol of the Primeval Hill, which arose from the cosmic sea during the creation of the universe. According to the Pyramid Texts, "Atum-Khepri, you culminate as hill, you raise yourself up as the Bennu Bird from the ben-ben stone in the abode of the phoenix at Heliopolis."

There was an artificial lake at Heliopolis in which the sun was said to bathe each morning at dawn. Also at Heliopolis was a natural fountain, known for its excellent water, which gave rise to the Arabic name of the place, Ain Shems, or "fountain of the sun." The modern name, Matarea, means "cool water," and it is at this site that Jesus and the holy family rested during the flight to Egypt. According to the Arabic infancy gospel, from a sycamore tree "the Lord Jesus made to gush forth in Matarea a spring, in which the lady Mary washed his shirt. And from the sweat of the Lord Jesus which she wrang out there, balsam appeared in that place."

In the Greek translation of the Old Testament, Heliopolis is referred to as On ('ΩΝ)—a transliteration of the Egyptian name. Interestingly, this word in Greek is the philosophical term which means "Being," and Plato uses the symbol of the Sun, in the *Republic*, to represent this very principle.

Obelisk of Usurtasen I at Heliopolis

The ancient city Heliopolis, where the Priests of Ra constructed their temple, was the most renowned center of learning in the ancient world. The scholars of the temple were noted for their interest in mathematics and astronomy.

LEFT: The Bennu Bird or Phoenix. "I am this Phoenix which is at Heliopolis! . . . What is this? . . . It is eternity and perpetuity." (Papyrus of Ani, chapter 17). The Phoenix or Bennu Bird was said to occasionally alight on the ben-ben or omphalos of Ra at Heliopolis. The ben-ben was symbolic of the Primeval Hill, the Pillar of the Universe, which arose when the seed of Atum fell into the primordial sea.

Nile: The Celestial Stream

"EGYPT is the image of the skies," writes Lucie Lamie, "where the divine beings sail 'the waters on high'; and so the Nile has a heavenly as well as an earthly source. . . . Its periodic rise and fall are associated with the myth of Osiris, divine principle of perpetual return, death and rebirth, as symbolized by the annual cycle of vegetation."

The Nile provides life to all of Egypt and, like a celestial clock, its annual, life-giving flood was predictable to the day. Seneca wrote that "Egypt owes to the Nile not only the fertility of the land but the very land itself," for the annual flood of the Nile both irrigated the land and deposited fertile silt on the surrounding fields. Heliodorus, the ancient novelist, points out in his *Ethiopian Romance* that *Neilos* is called "Horus," "the giver of life," "the savior of all Egypt," "the father of Egypt," "the creator of Egypt," and "he who brings mud each year." Libanius, a father of the early church, said that the Christians in Egypt would like to abolish the food offerings made to the Nile; as of that date, however, they had not yet dared to, owing to their fear that the usual harvest would not take place.

In Roman times the Nile was itself called "the year." As one scholar notes, "This conception not only reflects the rather precise annual recurrence of the flood, but also apparently sought to relate it to the magical power of Time." Seeing that the Egyptians saw the Nile as "the exact counterpart of heaven" and "the year incarnate," it is only appropriate that the word Nile, spelled as it was in ancient Greek, totals 365, the number of days in the year—a fact noted by several ancient writers.

ΝΕΙΛΟΣ
NILE = 365

Hapi, the Nile God

This illustration, taken from the Denderah Zodiac, shows Hapi, the Egyptian god of the Nile, portrayed as the astrological sign for Aquarius, the Water Bearer.

The Nile, near Cairo, in the time of Napoleon

Syene: The Place of Heavenly Alignment

EVERYONE HAS HEARD the story of how Eratosthenes, the great mathematician and keeper of the library at Alexandria, measured the dimensions of the earth. The Egyptian town of Syene is located on the Tropic of Cancer. Therefore, on the day of the summer solstice, the sun is directly overhead at noon: well bottoms are illuminated and buildings cast no shadow. However, because Alexandria is to the north, buildings do cast a shadow there. By taking into account the distance between Syene and Alexandria, and the angle of the sun at Alexandria on the summer solstice, Eratosthenes was easily able to calculate the circumference of the earth.

Ancient Syene, or Suanu, corresponds to modern day Aswan, the site of the Aswan dam. Long before Eratosthenes, Syene was recognized as a place of celestial alignment—a harmonic nodal point where the laws of heaven are reflected on the earth. In Egyptian hieroglyphs Syene is also called Khekh: , , or simply . The symbol here depicted is an amalgamation of a plumb bob with a carpenters' square—an ancient Egyptian "level" used in construction to make sure that everything is properly "lined up." The symbol itself speaks more powerfully than do words, and the ancient glyph of Syene, Khekh, accurately reflects its place in the cosmic scheme.

The ninth book of Heliodorus' *Ethiopian Romance* is set in Syene at the time of the summer solstice, the time of the Neiloa, the festival of the Nile. After one character in the novel is shown the sundials which cast no shadow and this phenomenon is discussed, Heliodorus immediately states how the Nile "is actually the year incarnate" and points out that this is reflected in the number of Neilos, which amounts to 365. What Heliodorus fails to explicitly reveal, however, is the fact that the name Syene itself (ΣΥΗΝΗ) amounts to 666, the total value of all the numbers comprising the magic square of the sun.

ΣΥΗΝΗ
SYENE = 666

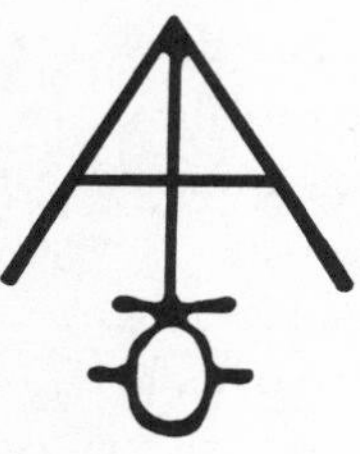

Khekh

Egyptian hieroglyph denoting the city of Syene on the Tropic of Cancer, where the sun is directly overhead on June 21, the summer solstice, the longest day of the year. The plumb bob here is based on the hieroglyphic representation of the human heart which, like a swinging pendulum, divides the flow of time with a constant pulse.

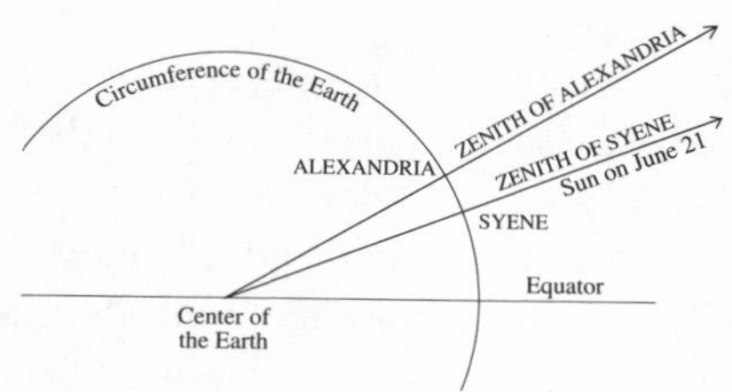

Syene and Alexandria

By taking into account the distance from Syene to Alexandria, and by measuring the angle of the shadow cast by the sun at Alexandria on the summer solstice, Eratosthenes was able to calculate the circumference of the earth. As the keeper of the fabled library at Alexandria, he may also have had access to earlier computations.

Syene

Osiris: The Cosmic Seed

JESUS SAID "The Kingdom of Heaven is like a grain of a mustard seed." And in reference to the parable of the sower he simply states "The seed is the *logos* of God." Likewise, St. Paul refers to the mystery of the seed when he says that "Christ has been raised from the dead, the first fruits of those who have fallen asleep," and also when he goes on to discuss the nature of the resurrected, spiritual body: "What you sow does not come to life unless it dies. And what you sow is not the body which is to be, but a bare kernel, perhaps of wheat or of some other grain. . . . What is sown is perishable, what is raised is imperishable."

According to the Stoic philosophers, at the heart of everything exists a fiery breath, a *spermatikos logos* or "seed pattern." The seed contains within itself the innate, future pattern (*logos*) of the manifest plant; it encapsulates, on a microcosmic level, the fiery life power of the sun. As modern physics has demonstrated, for better or worse, the seed of the atom contains within itself the Promethean fire of the gods, the fire of atomic fusion; likewise, the principle of the seed in the vegetable and animal realms mysteriously encapsulates and reflects the transcendental laws on which all of creation is based.

Dionysus and Osiris are both "dismembered" and "resurrected" gods, gods associated with the mystery of the seed and the vegetation cycle. A plant starts from the seed of unity, comes forth into manifestation, and dies through "dismemberment" in the course of the seasons. But the inner spark of life remains hidden in the transcendental, resurrecting power of the seed.

The gnostics taught that at the center of every human being there exists a divine spark or spiritual seed, our immortal essence. By properly cultivating this inner seed it is possible to realize our true identity. That is why the Greek word "initiation" (*teleô*) means, among other things, completion, realization, bearing fruit in due season, and ripening to perfection. As we recognize our inner, spiritual spark, we cannot avoid becoming who we truly are.

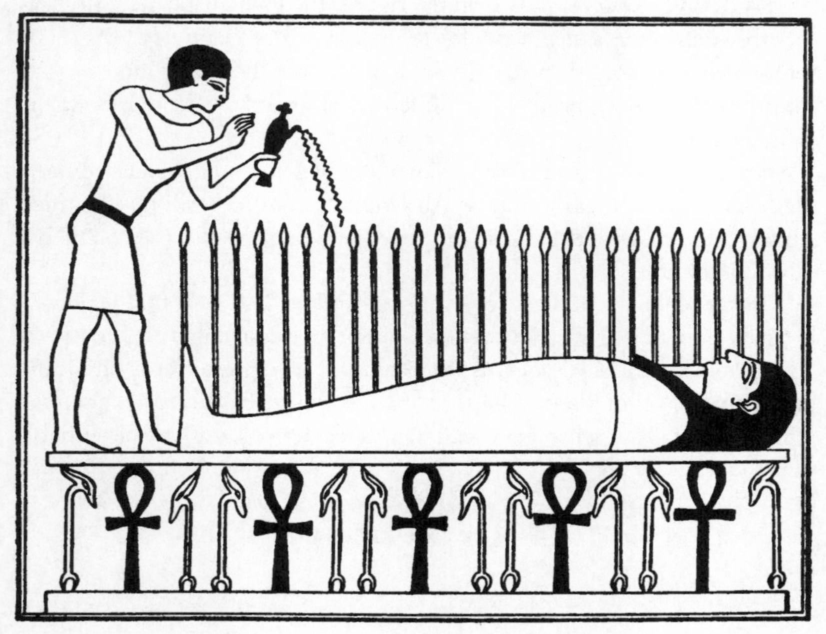

Osiris-Nepra, the Egyptian God of Grain

As E. A. Wallis Budge notes in his work *Osiris and the Egyptian Resurrection*, "The identification of Osiris as a corn-god is proved by the relief at Philae, in which corn is seen growing out of his mummified body, and by the custom of making a figure of the god in grain on a mat which was placed in the tomb. The germination of the grain typified the germination of the spirit-body of the deceased." In the above illustration, the hieroglyph of the ankh cross ☥ denotes Life, while the scepter denotes Power; hence the meaning is Life-Power, of which Osiris is the symbolic manifestation.

According to the early Christian gnostics, those people who possess a spiritual nature contain within themselves a slumbering Spark or Seed of Light. The Gnostic Revealer, descending from above, fans the slumbering spark within, causing it to blaze forth into recognition and fruition. Each one of these spiritual seeds is a spark of the Celestial Man of Light. When the restoration of all things occurs, all these sparks will be united and "re-membered" in the celestial realm of light.

Abraxas: The Demiurgic Sun

THE GREAT cockerel shown on the right is the Hellenistic deity Abraxas (or Abrasax), often associated with the name of the Demiurge, IAO. His symbolism is obviously one of a solar character, for the cock announces the return of the sun each morning while the whip and shield represent the sometimes fierce power of the disc at noon.

Abraxas is frequently represented on magical gems and amulets from the Hellenistic period, and the great Alexandrian gnostic Basilides identified Abraxas, the "Great Ruler" of the "365 heavens," as the creator of the physical universe.

Abraxas belongs to the general type of solar deity known as the *Anguipede*, or Snake-footed god, which occasionally appears in a strongly phallic aspect. Thus, Abraxas, the solar cock, as world fabricator, represents the physically generative power of the solar pattern, the Demiurge (Fabricator), but unlike Christos, he fails to represent the higher aspect of the creative Solar Logos.

'ΑΒΡΑΞΑΣ

ABRAXAS = 365

Abraxas

Mithras: "The Invincible Sun"

MITHRAS IS represented in many forms, the most common of which shows him compassionately sacrificing the cosmic bull to bestow everlasting life on his followers. Another representation shows Mithras in his aeonic aspect as Boundless Time, the silent and timeless point between opposites. Mithras is shown as a winged, invincible soul burst forth from the cosmic egg. As the spirit which has conquered the rock from which he sprang, Aeon hovers poised between the boundaries of time and space and the other archetypal forces.

As Dr. Cumont remarks in his study of the Mithraic mysteries, "He is, to speak in the philosophical language of the times, the Logos that emanated from God and shared His omnipotence; who, after having fashioned the world as demiurge, continued to watch faithfully over it."

The rising spiral of the serpent represents the organic flow of time, experience, and analysis which form the core of psychological evolution and lead to the blessing of divine gnosis or illumination. Alternately, in a cosmological sense, the serpent represents the coils of manifestation which surround the timeless center. The fiery profile of the lion's head is symbolic of the Solar Logos which burns eternally in the balanced nexus of his heart.

The name Mithras—like those of Abraxas and *Iêsous Christos*—has an "occult" or hidden significance which is easily obtained by summing the numerical letter-values of his cosmic name.

ΜΕΙΘΡΑΣ
MITHRAS = 365

Ancient cameo stone showing the name Mithras

The Aeonic Mithras

Janus: The Roman God of the Year

TWO-FACED JANUS was the oldest god of Italy and ruled over the beginning of all things. A god of light and the sun, Janus opened the gates of heaven at dawn and closed them at dusk. He was hence the god of gates (*januae*), and was known under the names "shutter" and "opener." His emblem was the key, and many of his attributes were absorbed by the figure of St. Peter, represented as holding the keys to heaven's gate.

Janus was also a god of time. He was worshipped at the beginning of days, months, and at the beginning of each year. He had twelve altars, one for each month, and his chief festival was January 1, that month being named after him. In later times he was identified as the father of Aeon, or as Aeon's very self.

His two faces are explained in a number of ways. According to one interpretation, they represent the sky at night and during the day. According to another, they allowed him to look both east and west without turning. Marsilio Ficino, the Renaissance Neoplatonist, explained that he was emblematic of the soul, facing, at the same time, both the worlds of spirit and matter. More rarely he was represented with four heads as god of the year, symbolizing the four seasons.

The Romans did not instinctively take to cosmological speculation as did the Greeks, and there is no compelling evidence to suggest that they possessed a system of theological symbolism akin to that of Greek gematria. Nonetheless, several ancient authorities report that, on the statue of Janus in Rome, the fingers were arranged so as to represent the number 365, the number of days in a solar year.

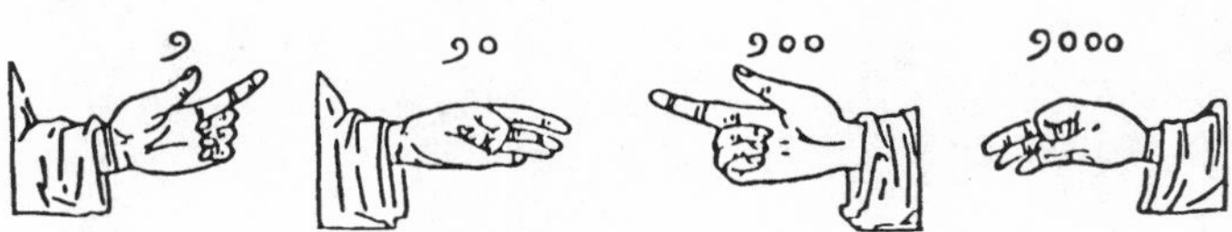

Numerical hand signs from a Renaissance text on mathematics

Janus

According to the pagan writer Macrobius, "Many people regard Janus as the god of the Sun; thus he is often shown in statues as forming the number 300 with his right hand and the number 65 with his left. This symbolizes the days of the year, which is the Sun's chief creation."

In Rome, the doors of Janus' main temple were only closed when there was not a war in progress. Since the Romans were not a very peaceful lot, this only occurred once between the reign of Numa and that of Augustus.

Harpocrates: The Infant Sun

HARPOCRATES, a form of the Egyptian solar divinity Horus, represents the new-born sun as an infant. His mother was the goddess Isis, and he is often represented seated upon her lap. This iconography of the goddess with her divine, solar child is thought by many scholars to have prepared the way for the Christian iconography of the "Madonna and child." Harpocrates is also shown seated upon a lotus flower and was frequently depicted in this form on magical gems and amulets. Early Christians in Egypt took over this symbolism and depicted Jesus, the Spiritual Sun, as Harpocrates seated on the lotus.

Several ancient solar amulets which contain representations of Harpocrates or Abraxas also contain a mysterious formula:

XABPAX
ΦΝΕΣΧΗΡ
ΦΙ ΧΡΟ
ΦΝΥΡΩ
ΦΩΧΩ
ΒΩΧ

These words have no meaning in any ancient language, but they are not without meaning. That is because, when added together, the values of the letters are equivalent to the number 9999. In a Paris papyrus the name of Agathos Daimon ("Good Spirit") is given as ΦΡΗ ΑΝΩΙ ΦΩΡΧΩ ΦΥΥΥΥ ΡΟΡΨΙΣ ΟΡΟΧΩΩΙ, another "nonsense formula" equivalent to 9999. Finally, the Berlin magical papyrus contains the following line in an address to Apollo: "I am the one who met you, and you gave me a gift of the greatest value; the name of you is knowledge (*gnosis*), the number 9999."

Since this number appears on solar amulets and in an address to Apollo, it seems likely that 9999 was deemed—like 888 (the number of Jesus) and 666 (sum of the magic square of the sun)—to have a solar significance. This is further confirmed by the observation that a circle with a circumference of 999.9 has a diameter of 318 units, for 318 is the value of HELIOS (῾ΗΛΙΟΣ), the Greek name of the Sun.

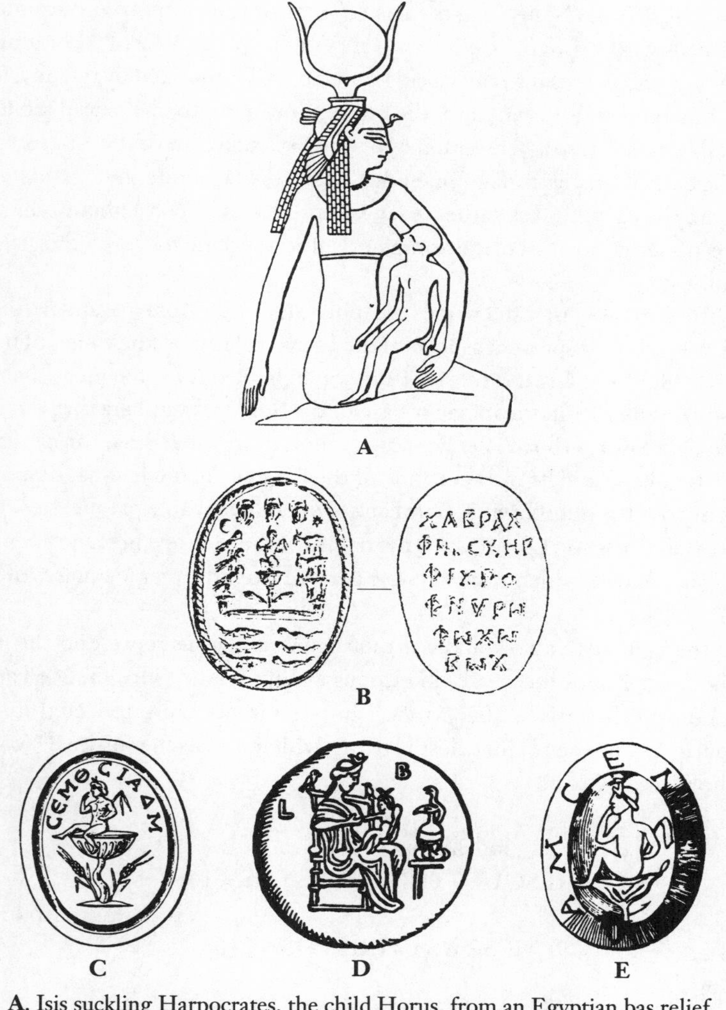

A. Isis suckling Harpocrates, the child Horus, from an Egyptian bas relief.

B. Harpocrates gem with the formula amounting to 9999.

C. Typical representation of Harpocrates seated on lotus from a "gnostic gem."

D. Isis and Harpocrates on an Alexandrian coin of the Caesers.

E. Harpocrates gem with the Hebrew phrase "Sun of the Universe" transliterated into Greek.

Jesus Christ: The Solar Logos

"IN THE BEGINNING was the Logos" reports the Gospel of John and, in the words of the Logos itself, "I am the Light of the World." Naturally, everyone who comes into the world is outwardly illuminated by the physical sun, but only those who turn their attention back to the world of first principles are inwardly enlightened by the Spiritual Sun of the Logos.

The early Christians maintained that *Iêsous* was "a name above all names." Origen, the early church father, even went so far as to boast about how the name of Jesus possessed more magical efficacy than those of the pagan divinities.

In the same way that the names of Apollo, Hermes, Abraxas, and Mithras were designed to represent aspects of the Universal Logos, the values of both IÊSOUS (888) and CHRISTOS (1480) are obtained from 74, the most characteristic number from the magic square of the Sun. It is unlikely that this is a coincidence, for, as Dr. Eisler has pointed out, the name *Iêsous* is "an artificial and irregular Greek transliteration" of the Aramaic name Joshua, designed to bring out the number 888. One can see an unmistakable parallel between the names *Iêsous* and *Christos*, and the names of the Hebrew planetary Spirits and Intelligences which were likewise derived from the magic squares of the planets.

As the Spiritual Sun of what was then a new age, Jesus represents the idea of the Solar Logos incarnate, the Logos as Illuminator, Healer, Mediator, and Gnostic Revealer. This symbolism was intentionally reflected in the numerical frequency of his celestial name, which reveals the spiritual "word" of the Piscean Aeon.

'ΙΗΣΟΥΣ ΧΡΙΣΤΟΣ
IÊSOUS = 888 / CHRISTOS = 1480

IÊSOUS CHRISTOS = 2368

⊙ The Solar Hierarchy or the Multiples of 74

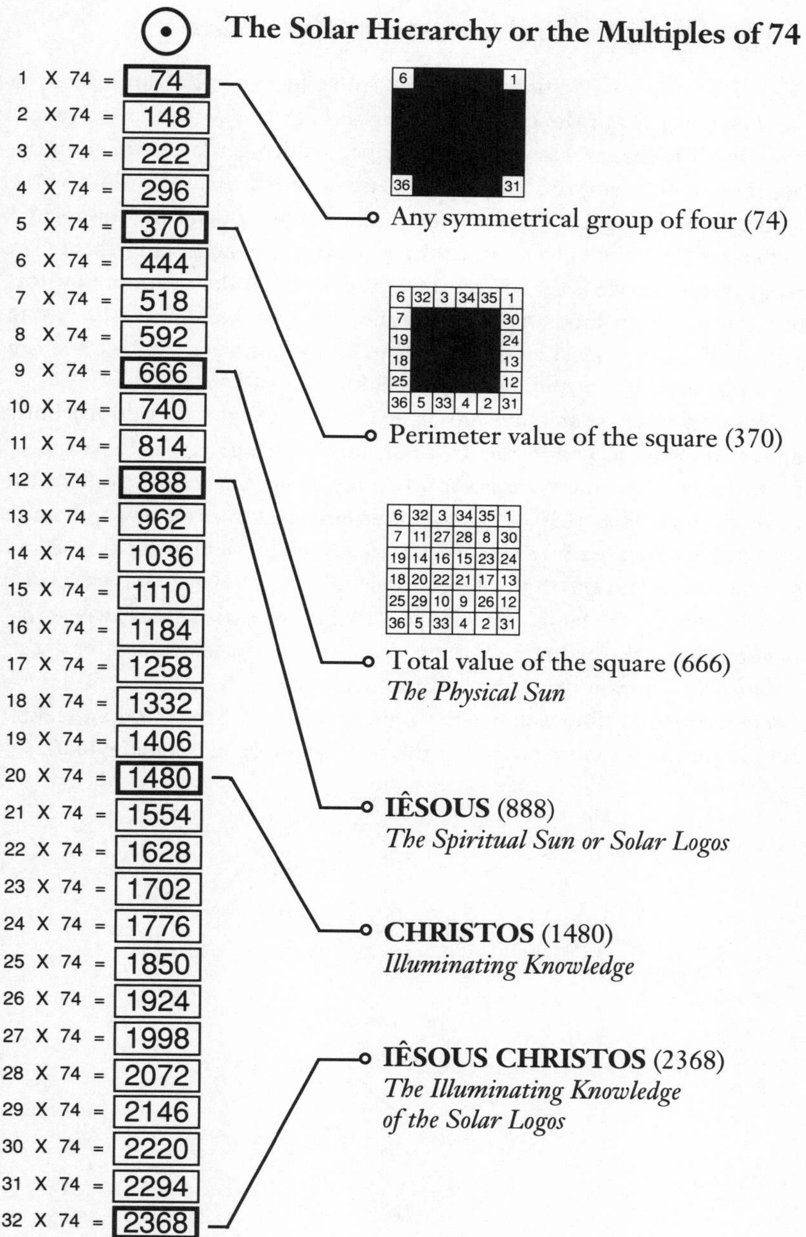

1 X 74 = 74
2 X 74 = 148
3 X 74 = 222
4 X 74 = 296
5 X 74 = 370
6 X 74 = 444
7 X 74 = 518
8 X 74 = 592
9 X 74 = 666
10 X 74 = 740
11 X 74 = 814
12 X 74 = 888
13 X 74 = 962
14 X 74 = 1036
15 X 74 = 1110
16 X 74 = 1184
17 X 74 = 1258
18 X 74 = 1332
19 X 74 = 1406
20 X 74 = 1480
21 X 74 = 1554
22 X 74 = 1628
23 X 74 = 1702
24 X 74 = 1776
25 X 74 = 1850
26 X 74 = 1924
27 X 74 = 1998
28 X 74 = 2072
29 X 74 = 2146
30 X 74 = 2220
31 X 74 = 2294
32 X 74 = 2368
6
1
36
31
Any symmetrical group of four (74)
6 32 3 34 35 1
7 30
19 24
18 13
25 12
36 5 33 4 2 31
Perimeter value of the square (370)
6 32 3 34 35 1
7 11 27 28 8 30
19 14 16 15 23 24
18 20 22 21 17 13
25 29 10 9 26 12
36 5 33 4 2 31
Total value of the square (666)
The Physical Sun
IÊSOUS (888)
The Spiritual Sun or Solar Logos
CHRISTOS (1480)
Illuminating Knowledge
IÊSOUS CHRISTOS (2368)
The Illuminating Knowledge of the Solar Logos

Jesus Christ: The Harmony of the Sun

AS WE HAVE SEEN, both Jesus (888) and Christos (1480) are related to the magic square of the sun. Both are multiples of 74, the square's most characteristic number, as is the number 666, which is the sum of all of the numbers which comprise the magic square of the sun.

Interestingly, both 666 and 888 are musical numbers, and are thus related to the principle of *harmonia*, an aspect of the Logos, whether represented as Jesus or Apollo. 666 is the string ratio of the perfect fifth, the most powerful harmonic relationship of the musical scale, the interval of C to G. 888 is the string ratio of the tone, the interval of C to D. The ratio 666 : 888 is therefore the harmonic relationship of the perfect fourth.

Not only do these relationships appear in the study of musical harmony and form the underlying structure of the musical scale, but they also appear in the realm of geometry, as is shown on the right. There, if the outermost circle measures 888, JESUS, then the innermost circle measures 666, the sum of the magic square of the sun. The circle poised between those of 888 and 666 measures 769, and this is the gematria value of PYTHIOS (ΠΥΘΙΟΣ), the name of Apollo at Delphi, the Greek god of music and the earlier personification of the "Solar Logos."

In the illustration below, the geometrical relation between the numbers 6660, 8880, and 1480 are shown through the medium of the *vesica piscis*. 8880 is brought out by adding together the two circles which measure 4440.

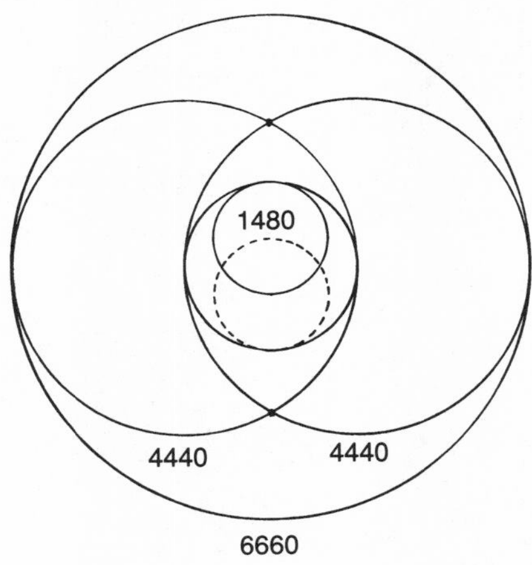

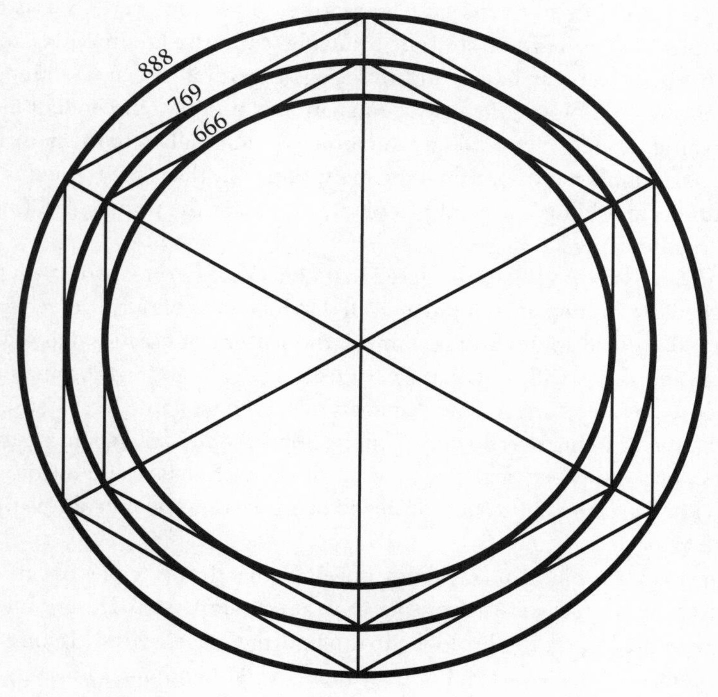

OUTER CIRCLE = 888 = JESUS
MIDDLE CIRCLE = 769 = PYTHIOS
INNER CIRCLE = 666 = SUM OF SOLAR SQUARE

The Harmony of the Sun

Not only do the solar numbers 666 and 888 define the ratios of the musical scale, but they are related to one another geometrically as is shown in the above diagram. The middle circle which measures 769 in circumference is the Geometric Mean between the numbers 888 and 666. 769 is the value of the Greek word PYTHIOS, the name of Apollo at Delphi, the Greek god of music and harmony.

Jesus Christ: The "Word" of Life and Light

CREATION does not proceed haphazardly, but follows certain laws and principles. Together these laws and principles comprise the Intelligence on which the universe is based, and this Logos or Intelligence was seen, in Hellenistic cosmology, as the first emanation from the transcendent God. According to ancient cosmology, the principles most allied to the nature of Logos are number and harmony, and in the same way that a seed contains the harmonic, unfolding blueprint of a plant, so too was the principle of Logos seen as informing all of creation.

Ancient cosmology never declared that God *decided* to create the universe and then drew up a plan; nor did it teach that humanity blindly evolved from the random collision of atoms. Rather, the pattern of creation has always existed and always will. This pattern of creation, the Logos, may be imagined as a differentiated "image" and "emanation" of the ineffable First Cause—a procession of Being overflowing from its Source—but the ancient philosophers never supposed that the creation of the universe resulted from the conscious act of an anthropomorphized divinity, as in the creation story of Genesis.

The Logos teaching did maintain, however, that the principles of Life and Light (consciousness) are integral parts of the cosmic pattern. Describing the nature of the Logos, the Prologue to the Fourth Gospel states, "In him was Life, and the Life was the Light of men." If life and consciousness are intrinsic principles of the Universal Logos which exists nowhere but is present everywhere, then it would be foolish to assume that the earth is the only inhabited planet in the universe, which is unimaginably vast. From a temporal perspective one may speak of a process whereby Life comes into manifestation in different corners of the universe; but, from the timeless perspective of first principles, it is incorrect to speak of the "evolution" of Life.

The Cosmic "Word" of Life and Light

From a cosmological perspective, the physical sun is the source of all life and light on the earth—but from a metaphysical perspective the Spiritual Sun of the Logos is the source of Life and Light as universal principles.

Like Apollo, Jesus Christ was intended to represent the celestial harmony and universal ordering power of the Solar Logos; but, like Dionysus, Jesus also represents the resurrecting power of the Cosmic Seed, the transcendental stream of Life.

As can be seen below, by gematria both JESUS (888) and CHRIST (1480) are related to the two Greek words for Life, *zoê* and *bios*. Each diagram also brings out the cosmological number 1332 (666 x 2) which is, like 888 and 1480, obtained from the magic square of the sun. The whole arrangement is one of Logos, ratio, and harmony, symbolizing Jesus the Christ as the Cosmic "Word" of Life and Light.

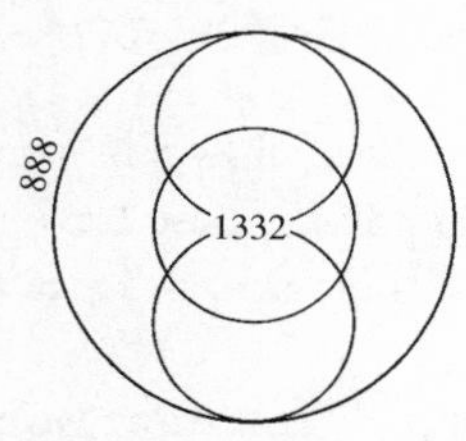

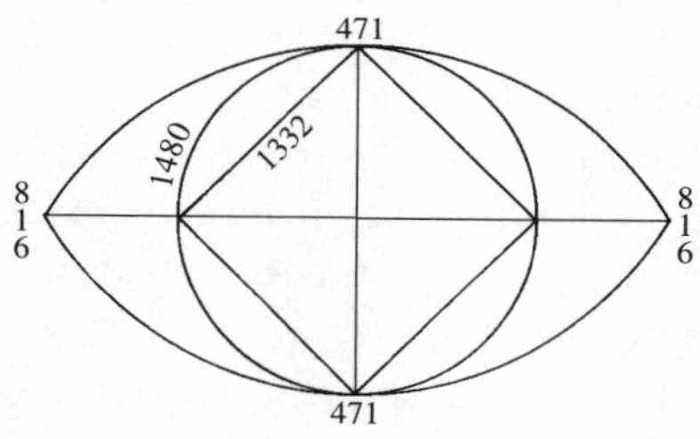

IÊSOUS = 888	CHRISTOS = 1480
CIRCUMFERENCE OF CIRCLE = 888	CIRCUMFERENCE OF CIRCLE = 1480
DIAMETER OF CIRCLE = 282	DIAMETER OF CIRCLE = 471
TRI-CIRCLE PERIMETER = 1332	PERIMETER OF SQUARE = 1332
	LENGTH OF VESICA = 816
888 = ΊΗΣΟΥΣ, JESUS = 74 X 12	1480 = ΧΡΙΣΤΟΣ, CHRIST = 74 X 20
282 = ΒΙΟΣ, BIOS or LIFE	470 = Ὁ ΚΟΚΚΟΣ, THE SEED
	471 = ΚΑΡΠΟΣ, FRUIT, "The Fruit of the Vine"
1332 = 666 X 2	
	815 = ΖΩΗ, ZOÊ or LIFE

1332 = 'ΑΛΦΑ • Ω, ALPHA • OMEGA= 74 X 18 = 666 x 2

Jesus: The Sun Behind the Sun

THE NUMBER of the physical world is six, the number of the spiritual world is eight. 600 is the number of KOSMOS (ΚΟΣΜΟΣ), while 800 is the number of the LORD (ΚΥΡΙΟΣ) of the cosmos. Similarly, the number of JESUS, 888, the Spiritual Sun, is contrasted with the number 666, that of the physical sun.

In geometry, it is the figure of the Cube which unites the numbers six and eight. That is because a cube has six sides and eight corners.

God created the world in six days and rested on the seventh, which was a Saturday. Jesus rose from the dead on a Sunday which, for the early Christians, became the eighth day, symbolizing the new, spiritual creation and the regeneration of time. The number 8, the Ogdoad, symbolizes the new order of Christianity, and JESUS, 888, was known as the Ogdoad to the early Christian gnostics.

In the lower illustration on the right, a cube is shown in isometric projection. Six rays emanate from a seventh inner point. These "seven stars" are the planets of traditional cosmology, led in their choral dance by the central point of the sun.

Viewed from another perspective, as in the upper illustration, we can see that there is more to the lower arrangement than meets the eye. Here, a seventh hidden ray is revealed, as is an eighth point, the hidden Spiritual Sun from which all things flow.

According to the gnostics, most people are asleep and do not realize that there exists a higher, spiritual reality; it is as though they see the lower illustration, take it at face value, and assume that there is nothing more. Through the faculty of gnosis, however, it is possible for the higher reason (*logos*) to discern the existence of a more inclusive reality. Jesus, the Ogdoad, the Sun behind the sun, is both a symbol and expression of this higher knowledge.

The literal-minded, like the proponents of materialism, see the world as through the lower diagram and see no further: literalism reads the letter of the law but does not grasp its spirit; materialism holds matter to be the only reality, but does not see that it is merely the effect of a higher cause. Those with the spark of gnosis, however, catch an occasional glimpse of the higher pattern—the Universal Logos, the intelligent pattern of order and harmony which informs all of existence.

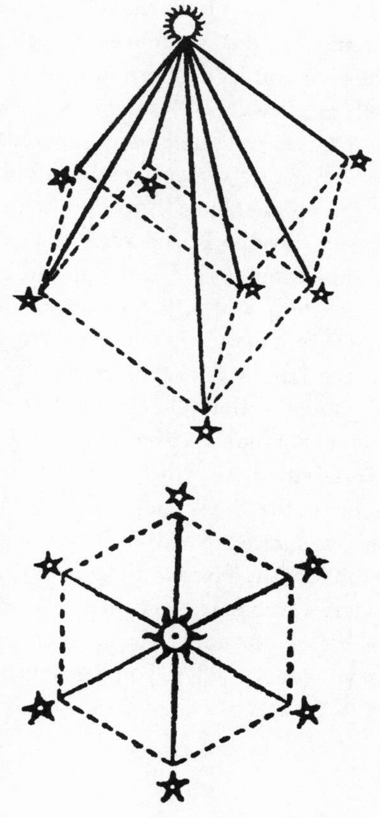

The Relation of the Spiritual Sun to the Physical Sun

According to the Jewish philosopher Philo of Alexandria, God is the "Intelligible Sun"—the "Sun behind the sun." The early Christian symbolism of Jesus as the Ogdoad, the Spiritual Sun, is both in keeping with this notion and with the geometrical figure shown above. Likewise, there is evidence to suggest that similar views were held concerning the solar divinity Mithras. As the Roman emperor Julian the Apostate points out, Mithras is not to be identified with the physical sun—and in his fifth *Oration* Julian refers to Mithras as "the seven-rayed god."

Alpha and Omega: The First and Last Mysteries

THE SYMBOLISM of Alpha and Omega, the First and the Last, is assuredly pre-Christian. The letters A and Ω symbolize the beginning (*archê*) and end (*telos*) of creation, the seed and its manifestation. As a symbol of the First Cause, the word ALPHA ('ΑΛΦΑ), 532, is numerically equivalent to ATLAS ('ΑΤΛΑΣ), the figure in Greek mythology who "upholds the entire cosmos." In Hellenistic times, Alpha and Omega were symbols of Aeon, Eternity personified as a mythological being. Appropriately, Alpha and Omega appear below on the gem showing Harpocrates, the new born sun, another symbol of Aeon, the timeless point between opposites.

In the gnostic gospel *Pistis Sophia*, Jesus instructs his disciples at some length concerning the nature of the First and Last Mysteries. He states that the First Mystery is the Last Mystery "from within outwards"; in other words, Alpha is contained within Omega, and the two are intimately connected. This statement of the Logos has a most elegant solution or proof, rediscovered by the present writer, which is shown on the facing page.

Before the emergence of the "New Song" of Christianity, it would appear that Apollo at Delphi was associated with the first and last mysteries. He was the god of geometry and music, a personification of the Logos, and the first and last strings of his lyre were associated with the vowels A and Ω. According to the Orphic *Hymn to Apollo*, he holds "the beginning (*archê*) and end (*telos*) to come" and, "with your versatile lyre you harmonize the poles."

Harpocrates the sun god on a magical gem, flanked by the letters Alpha (A) and Omega (ω).

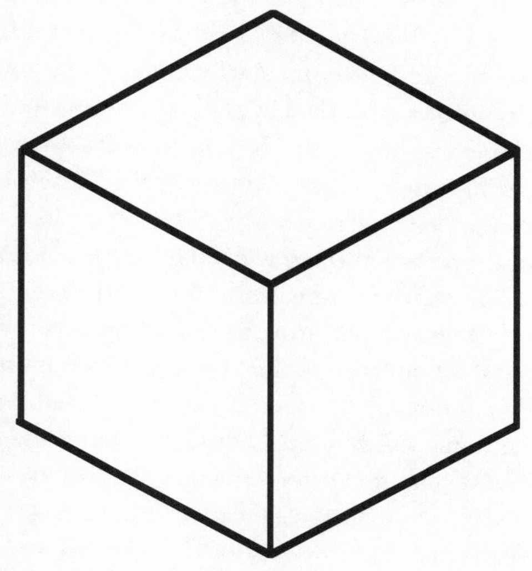

The First and Last Mysteries: Alpha and Omega

Volume of cube = <u>532</u>00 cubic units
Surface area of cube = <u>849</u>0 square units
Surface area of each side = <u>1415</u> square units

532 = ALPHA (ʼΑΛΦΑ)
849 = OMEGA (ʼΩΜΕΓΑ)
1415 = THE GOD APOLLO (ʽΟ ΘΕΟΣ ʼΑΠΟΛΛΩΝ)

The above relationship fully confirms the statement of the gnostic Christ that "the First Mystery is the 24th mystery from within outwards." Omega, the Last Mystery, is the 24th letter of the Greek alphabet.

Jesus also makes the following promise in *Pistis Sophia*: "He who shall have received the complete mystery of the First Mystery of the Ineffable . . . shall have the power of exploring all the orders of the Inheritance of Light." In this context, the "Inheritance of Light" is a reference to the pre-Christian, Orphic canon of number, which underlies the stories of several miraculous events in the Christian New Testament. Equipped with the proper key, it is within the power of anyone to explore this ancient inheritance.

Omphalos: The Philosophical Stone in Antiquity

ACCORDING TO MYTH, Zeus let fly two eagles from the opposite ends of the earth. The eagles flew toward each other at equal speed and met at the Greek town of Delphi, and the point at which they met was the center of the entire earth. This point was marked by the omphalos stone in the temple of Apollo. *Omphalos* means "navel" and the omphalos marks not only the center of the earth—it is the center of the universe as well. Therefore, the omphalos represents the center of sacred space. It is the meeting point between heaven and earth, the mid-point on the *axis mundi*, the world axis. According to the Greek author Nonnos, the omphalos is the "mid-navel axis," and when Harmonia wove the veil representing the entire universe she started with a representation of the omphalos at the center and worked outward.

The omphalos was not only the sacred seat of Apollo at Delphi but also the tomb of the slain and resurrected Dionysus. There was a model of the omphalos stone on display for visitors which may still be viewed in the Delphi museum, but the real omphalos was located within the temple of Apollo. It is frequently represented in Greek art and is often shown as being covered with an unusual netting pattern. The omphalos was also held to be the tomb of Python, the dragon that Apollo slew at Delphi. Thus a serpent, often coiled about the stone, is a frequent component of omphalos iconography. For the Pythagoreans, the omphalos at Delphi was an emblem of the Monad, the seed or first cause of the universe.

Every sacred culture possesses an omphalos in one form or another. The oldest known omphalos was the *ben-ben* at Heliopolis, the theological center in Egypt, and was established around 3350 B.C.E. The *ben-ben* was the prototype of both the pyramid and the obelisk. It was sacred to the sun, and the soul of the sun god Ra, in the form of the Phoenix (*Bennu*), would occasionally alight on it. The Temple of Solomon at Jerusalem was built upon the Rock of Foundation which holds down the waters of the flood and has been identified with the Moslem Dome of the Rock. There was also an omphalos in Ireland at Tara, the Lia Fal, associated with the function of sacred kingship. According to the Latin text of Giraldus Cambrensis: "Ireland was divided into five equal parts the heads of which met at a certain stone in Media, which stone was called the navel (*umbilicus*) of Ireland, being set almost at the middle of the earth."

Some representations of the omphalos stone from Greek art

Simon Petros: The Omphalos of Christianity I

THE ESOTERIC cosmological symbolism of the early Christian gnosis was based upon the inherited teachings of the earlier Greek theological science. In the same way that Apollo possessed his omphalos stone at Delphi, it was imperative that the New Song of the Solar Logos be built upon an appropriate foundation. Thus in the words of Jesus, "I say to thee, thou art Peter, and upon this rock (*petra*) I will build my Church." The Greek word Peter is literally *petros*, rock, and elsewhere Jesus gives Simon the name of "Cephas" (ΚΗΦΑΣ), based on the Aramaic word for rock: "Thou are Simon, the son of John; thou shall be called Cephas (which is interpreted Peter)."

The name Cephas was not chosen at random for, by gematria, it amounts to 729, and represents the cubic foundation stone shown facing. This number was most important to Plato and the Pythagoreans; not only is it a cube (9 x 9 x 9), but it is also a square (27 x 27), and is associated with the nature of the solar year (see next section).

Most appropriately, in the important yet little-known *Clementine Homilies*, Simon Petros teaches the following doctrine: God possesses "shape," for beauty cannot exist without shape. This shape may be perceived by the pure of heart, although God's shape does not exist in three-dimensional space. Rather, the form of God *underlies* the structure of three-dimensional space. God exists at the center and heart of the universe and his form is that of the "Cube" or three-dimensional coordinate system: from his form radiates the six directions of space while he contains within the seventh point of rest: "He is, as it were, in the center of the infinite, being the limit of the universe. . . . For in Him the six infinites end, and from Him they receive their extension to infinity."

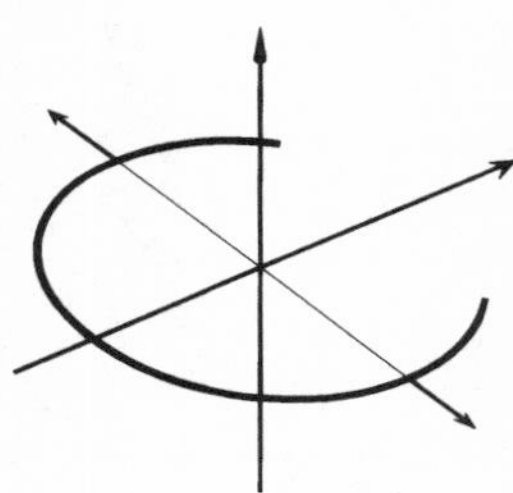

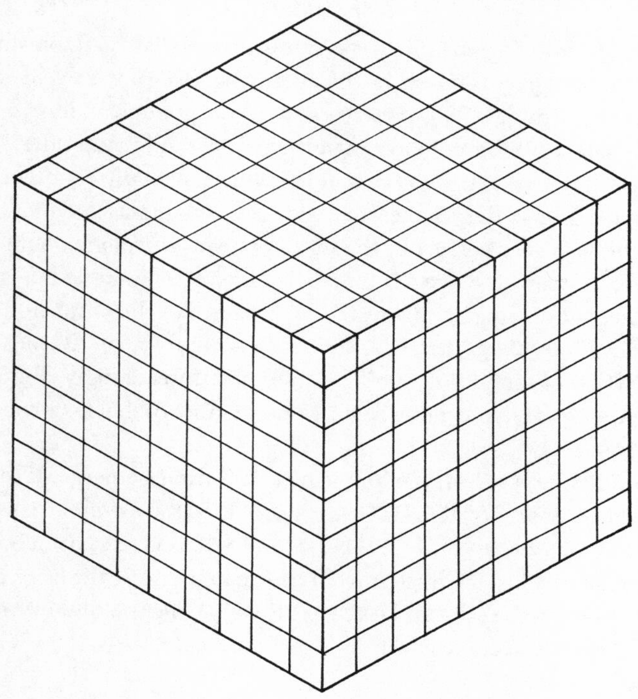

The Cube of Cephas, the Foundation Stone
CEPHAS (ΚΗΦΑΣ) = 729
9 x 9 x 9 = 729

Jesus gave the name of "Cephas" to Simon Petros, the Foundation Stone of the Christian assembly (*ekklêsia*). The above illustration shows the cube of Cephas, comprised of 729 smaller cubes within. This figure possesses a total surface area of 486 divisions, and 486 is the numerical value of the Greek word *petra* (ΠΕΤΡΑ) or "stone."

The cubic stone is associated with the notions of symmetry, balance and permanence, all of which are aspects of truth, beauty and harmony. Peter himself is associated with the teaching in the *Clementine Homilies* that God is the foundation stone at the center of the cosmos, possessing the form of a Cube, which gives rise to the dimensions of height, width and breadth. The gematria and symbolism of Peter are associated with the symbolism of the omphalos stone at Delphi, which was also covered with a pattern of network.

Simon Petros: The Omphalos of Christianity II

THE NUMBER of Cephas, 729, was significant to Plato and, presumably, to other Pythagorean thinkers in the ancient world. In the *Republic* Plato states that the Tyrant is 729 times worse than the good man, implying that the good man is 729 times better than the tyrant. Concerning the number 729, Socrates remarks that it is "a number which is closely concerned with human life, if human life is concerned with days and nights and months and years." This is proven correct by the remarkable magic square on the facing page which contains the first 729 numbers. There the number 365 appears in the centermost cell, alluding to the solar nature of the omphalos stone.

In earlier Greek gematria, 729 is the number of DELPHINION (ΔΕΛΦΙΝΙΟΝ), a temple of Apollo Delphinios. Interestingly, Plutarch, a priest of Apollo at Delphi, notes that 729 is a number of the Sun in one of his Pythagorean essays.

In the illustration below, the following relationships emerge. If the large circle has the measure of 486, PETRA or stone, then the tri-circle pattern has the measure of 729, both DELPHINION and CEPHAS, the name given to Petros, the omphalos of Christianity. The square framing the large circle is equivalent to 619, the value of DELPHI (ΔΕΛΦΟΙ), the site of the omphalos, the solar foundation stone at the center of the world.

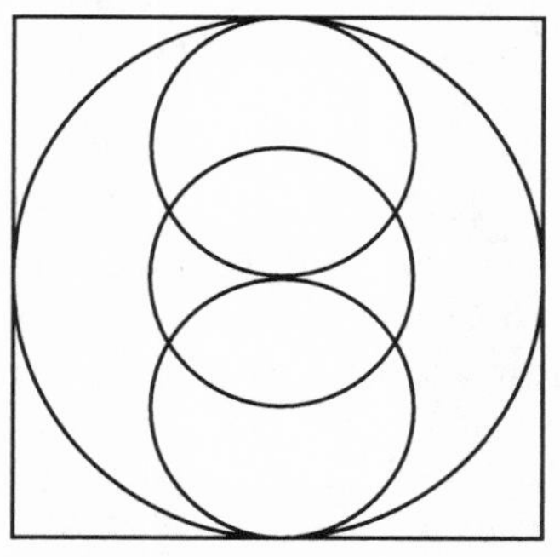

CIRCLE = 486 = PETRA
TRI-CIRCLE = 729 = CEPHAS
SQUARE = 619 = DELPHI

352	381	326	439	468	413	274	303	248	613	642	587	700	729	674	535	564	509	118	147	92	205	234	179	40	69	14
327	353	379	414	440	466	249	275	301	588	614	640	675	701	727	510	536	562	93	119	145	180	206	232	15	41	67
380	325	354	467	412	441	302	247	276	641	586	615	728	673	702	563	508	537	146	91	120	233	178	207	68	13	42
277	306	251	355	384	329	433	462	407	538	567	512	616	645	590	694	723	668	43	72	17	121	150	95	199	228	173
252	278	304	330	356	382	408	434	460	513	539	565	591	617	643	669	695	721	18	44	70	96	122	148	174	200	226
305	250	279	383	328	357	461	406	435	566	511	540	644	589	618	722	667	696	71	16	45	149	94	123	227	172	201
436	465	410	271	300	245	358	387	332	697	726	671	532	561	506	619	648	593	202	231	176	37	66	11	124	153	98
411	437	463	246	272	298	333	359	385	672	698	724	507	533	559	594	620	646	177	203	229	12	38	64	99	125	151
464	409	438	299	244	273	386	331	360	725	670	699	560	505	534	647	592	621	230	175	204	65	10	39	152	97	126
127	156	101	214	243	188	49	78	23	361	390	335	448	477	422	283	312	257	595	624	569	682	711	656	517	546	491
102	128	154	189	215	241	24	50	76	336	362	388	423	449	475	258	284	310	570	596	622	657	683	709	492	518	544
155	100	129	242	187	216	77	22	51	389	334	363	476	421	450	311	256	285	623	568	597	710	655	684	545	490	519
52	81	26	130	159	104	208	237	182	286	315	260	364	393	338	442	471	416	520	549	494	598	627	572	676	705	650
27	53	79	105	131	157	183	209	235	261	287	313	339	365	391	417	443	469	495	521	547	573	599	625	651	677	703
80	25	54	158	103	132	236	181	210	314	259	288	392	337	366	470	415	444	548	493	522	626	571	600	704	649	678
211	240	185	46	75	20	133	162	107	445	474	419	280	309	254	367	396	341	679	708	653	514	543	488	601	630	575
186	212	238	21	47	73	108	134	160	420	446	472	255	281	307	342	368	394	654	680	706	489	515	541	576	602	628
239	184	213	74	19	48	161	106	135	473	418	447	308	253	282	395	340	369	707	652	681	542	487	516	629	574	603
604	633	578	691	720	665	526	555	500	109	138	83	196	225	170	31	60	5	370	399	344	457	486	431	292	321	266
579	605	631	666	692	718	501	527	553	84	110	136	171	197	223	6	32	58	345	371	397	432	458	484	267	293	319
632	577	606	719	664	693	554	499	528	137	82	111	224	169	198	59	4	33	398	343	372	485	430	459	320	265	294
529	558	503	607	636	581	685	714	659	34	63	8	112	141	86	190	219	164	295	324	269	373	402	347	451	480	425
504	530	556	582	608	634	660	686	712	9	35	61	87	113	139	165	191	217	270	296	322	348	374	400	426	452	478
557	502	531	635	580	609	713	658	687	62	7	36	140	85	114	218	163	192	323	268	297	401	346	375	479	424	453
688	717	662	523	552	497	610	639	584	193	222	167	28	57	2	115	144	89	454	483	428	289	318	263	376	405	350
663	689	715	498	524	550	585	611	637	168	194	220	3	29	55	90	116	142	429	455	481	264	290	316	351	377	403
716	661	690	551	496	525	638	583	612	221	166	195	56	1	30	143	88	117	482	427	456	317	262	291	404	349	378

The Magic Square of 729

This remarkable 27x27 square contains the first 729 numbers and will offer up the same value if any line is added horizontally, vertically or diagonally from corner to corner. As Socrates states, 729 is a number concerned with "days and nights and months and years." The solar number 365 appears in the centermost cell of this magic square and the number 729 is the total number of days and nights comprising a year (365+364).

The Symbolism of the Cross

THE CROSS of Christ is a Christian manifestation of a universal archetype. The cross is a symbol of the sacred center of creation. The vertical axis is the spine or pole of the universe, the vertical pathway which unites the worlds: heavens, earth, and hells. The horizontal plane represents the realm of particular manifestation: the meeting point between eternity and the temporal, the infinite and the particular. As the most simple yet elegant symbol of cosmic unity, the cross naturally represents a state of atonement, being "at one" with the source of creation.

For the earliest Christians, the cross symbolized the center of the universe, prefigured by the tree of Paradise which was surrounded by four rivers before the beginning of time. As Hippolytus, a third century Bishop of Rome remarks in an Easter sermon, "This tree, wide as the heavens itself, has grown up into heaven from the earth. It is the fulcrum of all things and the place where they are at rest. It is the foundation of the round world, the center of the cosmos. In it all the diversities in our human nature are formed into a unity. It is held together by the invisible nails of the Spirit so that it may not break loose from the divine. It touches the highest summits of heaven and makes the earth firm beneath its foot, and it grasps the middle regions between them with immeasurable arms."

Similarly, as the gnostic *Acts of John* relates, the true cross—the Cross of Light—is a celestial principle, the "firmly fixed" power of *logos* and *harmonia*: "This Cross of Light is sometimes called Logos, sometimes Mind, sometimes Jesus, sometimes Christ." The Cross distinguishes and fixes all things, for it is "the harmony of wisdom" and the "wisdom in harmony." This Cross "has separated off what is transitory and inferior" yet, by the same token, it "has united all things by *logos*."

Early representations of the cross from the catacombs

Jerusalem: The Spiritual Center

IF SAINT PETER'S in Rome became the political center of Christianity, the holy city of Jerusalem still remains the spiritual center of the Christian faith. Sacred to Judaism, Islam, and Christianity, Jerusalem is the site of the Abrahamic omphalos, the Rock of Foundation, from which the waters of the flood both proceeded and receded. Above this omphalos was built the Temple of Solomon, and upon the Rock of Foundation rested the holy of holies: the Ark of the Covenant, which had acted as a "portable omphalos" during the nomadic days of the Jews in the wilderness.

As the site of the crucifixion, Jerusalem is the spiritual axis of the Christian faith, the point where the spiritual and material worlds most closely touch, the pivot of the universe. Because the atoning sacrifice of Christ ushered in a new phase of humanity, medieval representations of the crucifixion depict the tradition that the cross of Jesus stood exactly atop the skull of Adam, symbolic of fallen humanity.

In the Islamic period, Jerusalem was the first *qibla* or direction of prayer and Muhammad is said to have made a visionary ascent into the celestial spheres from the Rock of Foundation on Temple Mount. In 687, it became the site of the magnificent Dome of the Rock, later occupied by the Knights Templar during the crusades.

Contemporary archaeological research indicates that Solomon's Temple was not centered on the Dome of the Rock, but over the Dome of the Tablets, a nearby rock covered by a Moorish canopy. As John Michell and Christine Rhone show in a recent study, if this is the case, then the sacred sites of Jerusalem are united together in one vast scheme of Solomonic geometry. Remarkably, the axis of this geometry connects, in a perfectly straight line, the rock of Golgatha (the omphalos of Christianity), the Rock of Foundation (the resting place of the Ark in Solomon's Temple), and the Golden Gate on Jerusalem's east wall. According to Jewish and Christian traditions, it is through the Golden Gate that the Messiah will enter the Holy City.

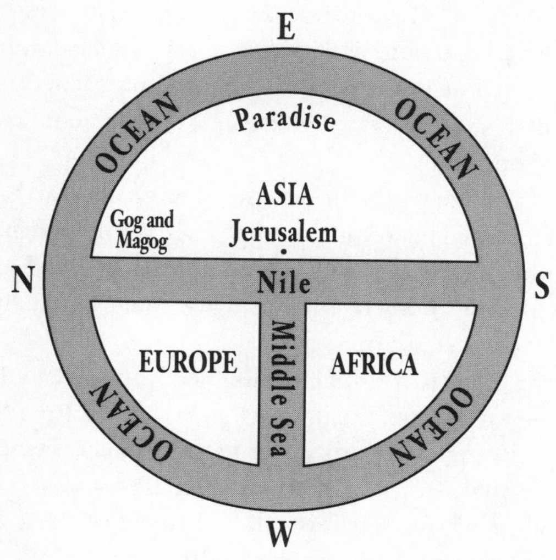

Jerusalem, the Christian Omphalos

ABOVE: A medieval map showing Jerusalem at the very center of the earth.

BELOW: A medieval representation of the omphalos in Jerusalem—the sacred center of the Christian world—depicted as a stone in a vessel.

Jesus the Fish

THE CURIOUS FIGURE known as the *vesica piscis*, or "vessel of the fish," plays a significant role in both early Christian symbolism and the language of sacred geometry. The vesica is formed by two interpenetrating circles of the same diameter, and as a symbolic glyph it represents the fusion and reconciliation of opposites.

Christ is said to be the mediator between heaven and earth, and it is well known in art history that he frequently appears in the mediatrix of the vesica. Further, since the temple is a gateway linking heaven and earth, and the church is known as the "body of Christ," a good many cathedrals are based on the geometry of this Piscean symbol.

The underlying pattern of "the circle doubled" gives rise to the unique and harmonious geometry of the hexad, which may ultimately be reduced to the mathematical ratio (or *logos*) expressed by the vesica, being $1{:}\sqrt{3}$ or the proportion 1:1.73205... By using this fundamental proportion, which underlies the fabric of the phenomenal world, traditional cosmology expressed a hierarchy of transcendental relationships in the world of symbolic ideas.

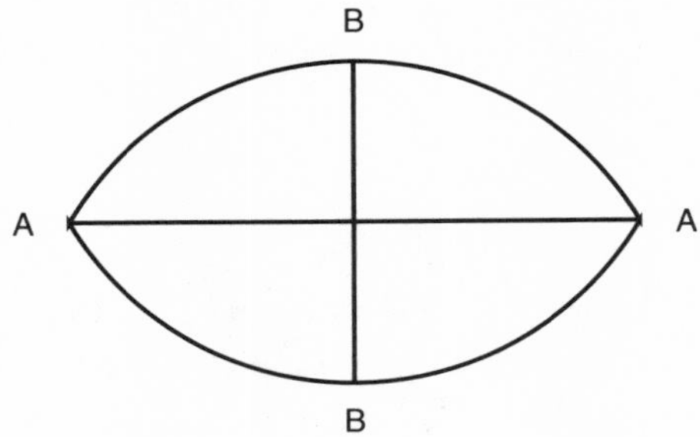

If axis AA is 1061 units in length, then BB = 612
and
If AA is 612 units in length, then BB = 353

1061 = APOLLO • 612 = ZEUS • 353 = HERMES

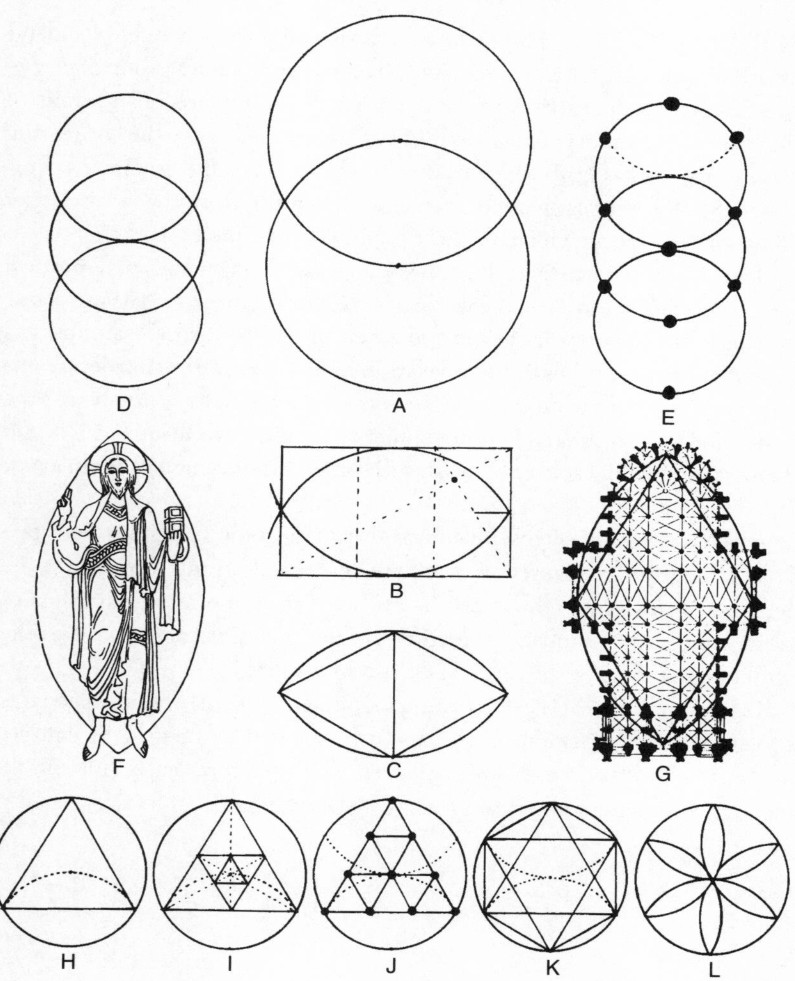

Some Faces of the Vesica Piscis and √3

A) Vesica as mediator; B) "Fish" in √3 rectangle; C) Vesica and rhombus; D) "Three worlds diagram"; E) Geometry of Kabbalistic Tree; F) Figure of Christ from the east window, Poitiers; G) Cathedral of Beauvais; H) Equilateral triangle; I) Expanding equilateral triangles and rhombuses; J) Pythagorean Tetraktys; K) Hexagon and star hexagram; L) Vesica-based "flower pattern"

Glastonbury Abbey

ACCORDING TO ancient tradition, Christianity was carried to England shortly after the crucifixion by St. Joseph of Arimathea and a group of twelve apostles. There the carriers of the Christian revelation erected a primitive church at Glastonbury, the ancient Isle of Avalon, said to be the last resting place of the Holy Grail, which once held the blood of the crucified savior. When St. Joseph planted his staff into the ground, it turned into the Glastonbury Thorn, which, to this day, flowers at Christmas.

Glastonbury is an ancient site of pre-Christian sanctity, the most mystical spot in all of England. Like the world of early Christianity, with its messianic longings for the renewal of time and a new order on earth, Glastonbury is intimately connected with the revelation of an ideal spiritual order: it was here, in 1190, that the monks of Glastonbury are said to have discovered the bones of King Arthur and his wife, Guinevere. As everyone knows, it is said that Arthur, like the spirit of Christ, will someday return and usher in a new era.

While the legend of Joseph's mission to Glastonbury cannot be interpreted literally, there is every reason to believe that this tradition refers to the actual transmission of the apostolic gnosis. This the present-day ruins of Glastonbury Abbey testify, reflecting in their geometry and measures the symbolic numbers of the original Christian revelation.

Reproduced on the right is the groundplan of Glastonbury Abbey as surveyed by Bligh Bond. The structure is based on a grid of squares measuring 74 feet on each side. Each square, therefore, has a side of 888 inches (74x12), the numerical value of JESUS, the Spiritual Sun.

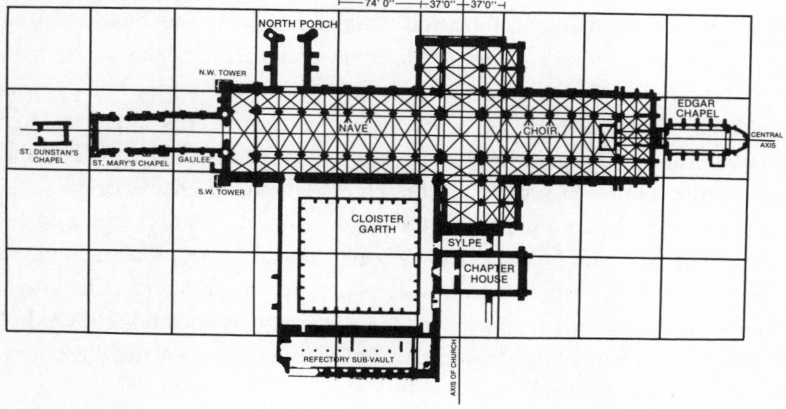

ABOVE: Glastonbury Abbey in England with its 74 foot grid.
BELOW: Detail of Saint Mary's Chapel at Glastonbury, built on the foundation of Saint Joseph's original church.

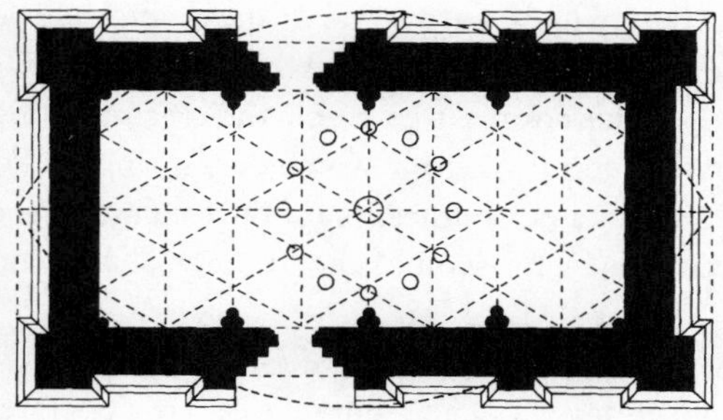

The Cosmic Tree: Reading a Symbol of Nature's Book

OF CENTRAL IMPORTANCE to the old Pythagorean cosmology is the observation that all phenomena of the natural world revolve around one point and sensitive center. The tree begins as a seed suspended in space. It becomes rooted as a process by assimilating and transforming the essence of the four elemental levels. The seedling is rooted in earth, the physical matrix of relationship, in which it grounds itself and draws nutrients. The process is fueled by the transformation of water through the patterns of the capillary system. Atmospheric gases are absorbed and changed in the leaves, and the entire process of photosynthesis is driven by the radiant energy of the solar plasma. All four levels are interrelated and transformed, and the Idea of the Tree is the embodiment of Earth, Water, Air, and Fire. The alchemical symbol of the cosmic tree is a universal archetype, and, as Mircea Eliade and C. G. Jung have shown, it appears in the most primitive societies as a symbol of cosmic unity and, in the dreams of modern individuals, relates directly to the central process of self-realization.

The tree is a bridge linking heaven and earth, energy and matter. It is rooted in the evolutionary spiral of realization by aspiring to the light of the higher realities, while the process itself is mirrored in the lunar matrix of relationship or *eros*, which provides the necessary foundation for three-dimensional, physical existence. The tree begins as a point in space representing the potential of creation, and the organic spiral of realization implies its complement, the involutionary spiral of incarnation. From the central seed growth occurs in two directions, and the "world axis" is created.

The branches of the cosmic tree reach their greatest diversity at the farthest limits of the central axis from which they spring, and the idea of the tree, when perceived as a personification of the totality of its environment, perfectly reflects as a living symbol the archetypal laws of the creative process.

The ancient view, that the cosmos is a celestial song, implies the existence of harmonics and resonance. The same musical laws operate on all levels, giving life to both the baroque composition of a majestic oak and the orchestrated beauty of the soul. This is because the Cosmic Tree, like the symmetry of the human form, reflects the eminently central organizing tendency in nature which insures that electrical particles orbit the atomic center, planetary bodies the solar heart, and thousands of stars their respective galactic centers.

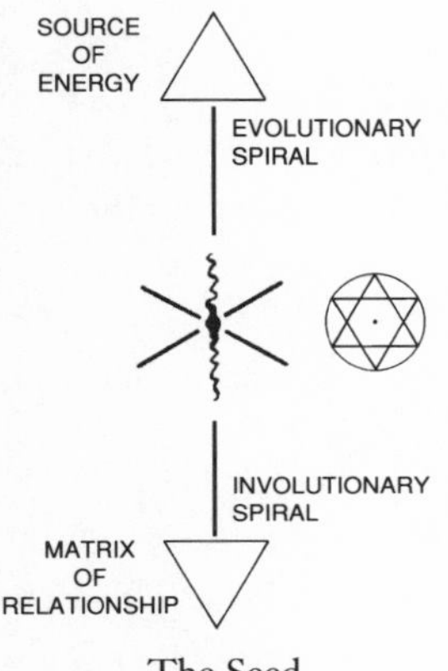

The Seed
suspended in space.

The Sacred Tree, archetype
of the *axis mundi*, above
which hovers the winged solar disc.

Maria Prophetissa. The seedling atop the Cosmic Mountain symbolizes the fusion of earth and sky. In the alchemical tradition Maria is said to shriek out in ecstasy: "One becomes two, two becomes three, and out of the third comes the One as the fourth." As a formula of the alchemical process, her saying also describes the germination of the seedling into the Cosmic Tree.

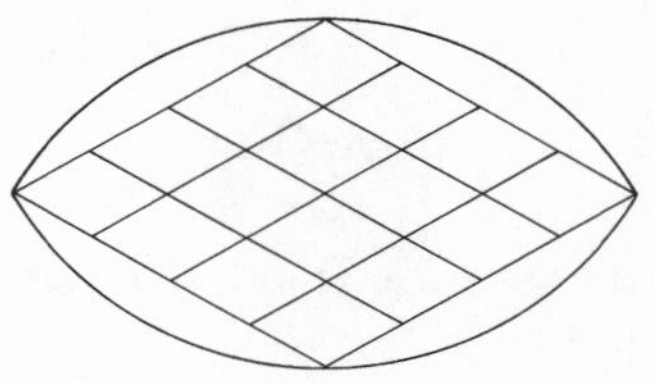

Appendix 1

The Miraculous Catch of 153 Fishes in the Unbroken Net

IN HIS book on Greek gematria and the ancient canon of number published in 1972, *City of Revelation*, John Michell shows how the early Christian story of the 153 fishes in the unbroken net is based upon an underlying geometrical design. Earlier scholars had noted that the Greek words FISHES and THE NET were both equivalent to 1224, and that 153 is 1/8 of this amount. Through a careful study of the Greek text, however, Michell was able to uncover the underlying geometry which had previously escaped the notice of modern scholars. His analysis is reproduced here with kind permission.

As John Michell points out in a more recent volume, "It is a traditional practice among teachers of esoteric philosophy to set forth their doctrines in the guise of simple parables which amuse children, enrich popular mythology and, for those who understand the science of interpreting them, illustrate various cosmological processes. The themes which are adopted by hagiographers and composers of sacred legends are those which occur spontaneously in different times and cultures and can therefore be called archetypal. Thus the founders of Christianity took certain episodes in universal folklore and made Jesus their central figure. In the tale of the 153 fishes he plays the part of the shamanic man of miracles whose traditional function includes bringing good luck to hunters or fishermen. By interpolation of names and numbers this story was made to reflect the construction of a geometrical diagram with cosmological significance, by reference to which the gnostic masters were able to demonstrate to initiates the basic truth behind the Christian legend."[1]

Stage One

Seven disciples are on the shore of Tiberias. Simon Peter enters a boat to go fishing; the others follow.

The number of ΣΙΜΩΝ 'Ο ΠΕΤΡΟΣ, SIMON PETER, is 1925. A circle is therefore drawn with circumference 1925 to represent Peter, and six more circles are placed so that the circumference of each passes through the center of the first circle and also through the centers of the two on either side. A larger circle contains them all. In this most economical fashion the seven disciples are packed into the circular boat, like the coracle of the Celtic saints, which, since the circumference of the lesser circles is 1925, will be found to have a diameter of 1224 [FISHES and THE NET].

Simon Peter said to them, "I am going fishing." They said to him, "We will go with you." They went out and got into the boat; but that night they caught nothing.
—John 21.3

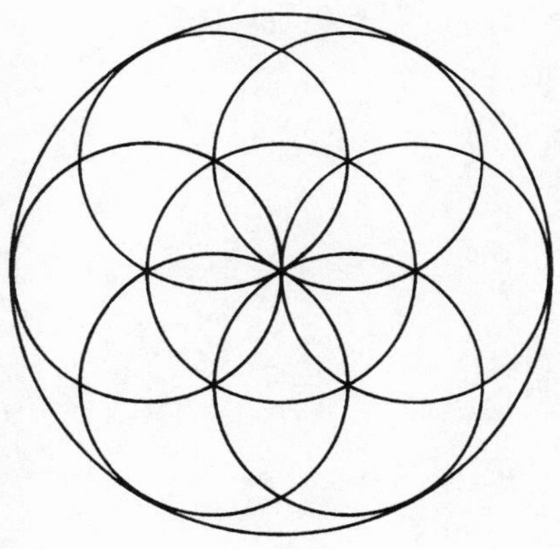

Figure 45.

Stage Two

That night they caught nothing. In the morning they saw the resurrected Jesus on the shore, but failed to recognize him. He said to them, "Cast the net on the right side of the ship and ye shall find." They did so and made a great catch.

The act of casting a net from the side of a boat is described by placing the compass point on the circumference of the circle of the boat and drawing the arc of another circle which contains the vesica piscis, the "fish." The diameter of this circle is also 1224, the number of TO ΔIKTYON, THE NET, and 'IXΘYEΣ, FISHES.

Just as day was breaking, Jesus stood on the beach; yet the disciples did not know that it was Jesus. Jesus said to them, "Children, have you any fish?" They answered him, "No." He said to them, "Cast the net on the right side of the boat, and you will find some." So they cast it, and now they were not able to haul it in, for the quantity of fish.

—John 21.4–6.

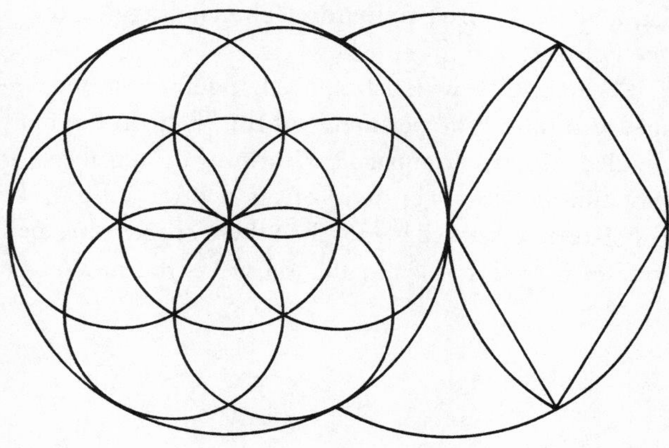

Figure 46.

Stage Three

"Now when Simon Peter heard that it was the Lord, he girt his fisher's coat unto him (for he was naked), and did cast himself into the sea."

The arc of a third circle is drawn to the left of the boat, and Simon Peter is moved from the center of the boat into the sea between the boat and the shore. The vesica that contains him represents THE FISHER'S COAT, for the Greek word is Ἡ ἘΠΕΝΔΥΤΗΣ, 1060, and since the width of this vesica is 612, its height is 1060.

"And the other disciples came in a little ship; (for they were not far from land, but as it were two hundred cubits) dragging the net with fishes." In the net were 153 great fishes.

The net, 1224, with fishes, 1224, together number 2448 and 2448 is the measure round the perimeter of the "fish" in the net. This great fish is divided into sixteen equal parts, forming the tetraktys of the Pythagoreans. The number 153 is brought out in two ways. First, the width of each of the sixteen lesser fish is 153; then there are sixteen smaller making up one greater fish, seventeen in all, and 153 is the sum of the numbers 1–17.

That disciple whom Jesus loved said to Peter, "It is the Lord!" Now when Simon Peter heard that it was the Lord, he put on his fisher's coat, for he was naked, and sprang into the sea. But the other disciples came in the boat, dragging the net full of fish, for they were not far from the land, about 200 cubits off.

When they got out on land, they saw a charcoal fire there, with fish lying on it, and bread. Jesus said to them, "Bring some of the fish that you have just caught. So Simon Peter went aboard and hauled the net ashore, full of large fish, a hundred and fifty-three of them; and although there were so many, the net was not torn.

—John 21.7–11

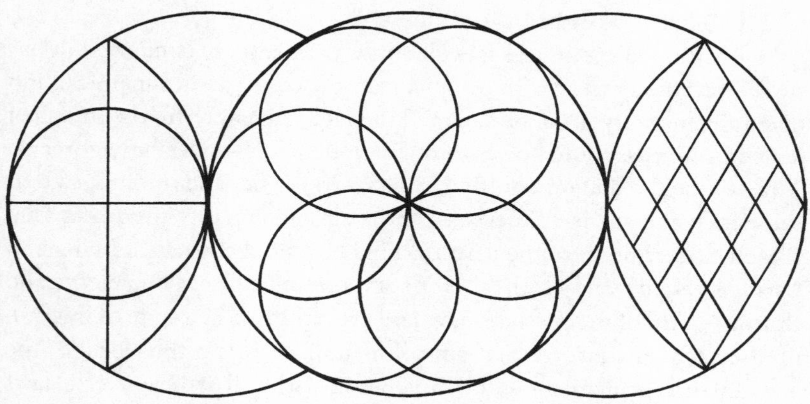

Figure 47.

A Commentary on the Symbolism and Pythagorean Origins of the Diagram of the 153 Fishes in the Unbroken Net by David Fideler

This commentary on the diagram of the 153 fishes in the net is for readers who wish to explore the origins and symbolism of the Greek number canon in further depth. It shows how the diagram relates to the Hellenistic concept of "the three worlds," the various levels of being in Greek cosmology, and the earlier mathematical symbolism of Apollo at Delphi, from which it originated. Also demonstrated is the mathematical origin and symbolism of the central gematria values of ancient cosmology.

1. The Three Worlds

Hellenistic cosmological speculation was essentially trinitarian in nature. The Pythagoreans, for instance, saw the cosmos as a dynamic union of complementary principles, joined through a mean term: the power of *logos* and *harmonia*, the power of mediation.

If we take the diagram of the 153 fishes in the net and orient it so that the net in the sea is at the base, the diagram suggests the traditional Platonic description of the relationship between the levels of Being and Change. (*Figure 48.*) The net in the sea represents the ever-changing and shifting world of manifestation, where everything is in a state of flux and nothing remains forever the same. The upper world—the world of the gods and first principles—is the Intelligible world: all of the universal laws on which manifestation is based. This world of the Forms does not exist in time or space, and because it is not limited by time or space it can be eternally present everywhere. The middle world, the world of Humanity, partakes of both spirit and matter, the eternal and the temporal. In the words of the Orphic gold plates, humanity is "a child of earth and starry heaven."

This type of trinitarian symbolism is used by Plato in his cosmological dialogue, the *Timaeus*. There he describes the cosmos as being the offspring of a father and a mother. The father is the world of Forms, all the laws of creation; the mother is "the Receptacle of Becoming,"[2] which resembles the ever-shifting sea.[3] The Forms manifest in the Sea of the Flux, and thus father and mother give birth to the cosmos, the middle world, which partakes of both Being and Change. Because of the inevitable distortions which occur in the world of Change—like the shifting

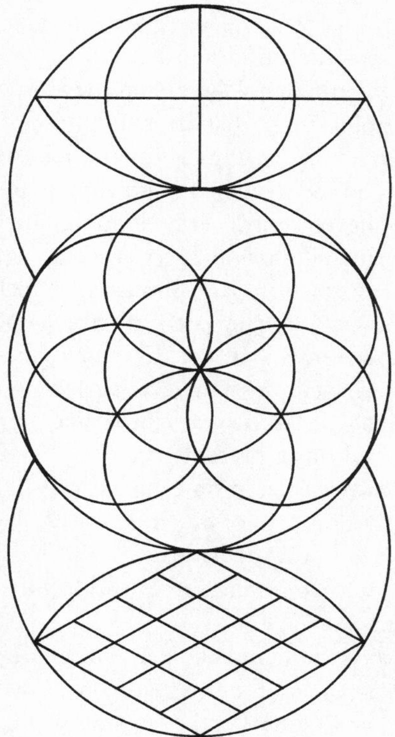

Figure 48. The Three Worlds of Hellenistic Cosmology

The net in the sea represents the sensible world of Change and Becoming, while the uppermost sphere represents the intelligible world of eternal Being. The central sphere which mediates between the two ideal extremes is the world of Humanity, which binds together the intelligible and sensible spheres, the worlds of spirit and matter.

In Christian terms, the central sphere is the Logos, the celestial mediator, which binds together heaven and earth, transcendent God and incarnate humanity.

currents of the sea—imperfections occur in the manifest world. Nonetheless, while the archetypal Forms are never perfectly manifest, the physical world remains the most beautiful and faithful reproduction—the best possible image—of the Intelligible world on the level of time and space.

One way of describing this situation is offered by the discoveries of physics and astronomy. Modern physics, for example, describes the fabric of space as a net, warped and stretched by gravitational force. In the ideal, Intelligible world, light travels in a perfectly straight line; however, in the physical world, the path of light is always warped by the presence of mass which results in the curvature of space. Similarly, in the Intelligible world, we can imagine planets as following perfectly circular orbits. In the world of manifestation, however, due to the distorting currents of the sea of Change, planets describe ellipses and never perfect circles. Nonetheless, the motion of a planet in an orbital ellipse is determined by precise mathematical laws, and this represents "the best possible image" of the perfect circular orbit described in time and space.

In the Christian development of the three worlds diagram, the central world is that of the Logos, the mediator between God and man, between heaven and earth. Alternately, the three worlds correspond to Father, Son, and Holy Spirit.

The diameter of the sphere in the upper world is 612, ZEUS, while the length of the vesica is a fraction more than 1060. One unit less, 1059, is the gematria value of PLEROMA, the gnostic source of creation and Treasury of Light; 1061 is APOLLO, the god of light and celestial harmony.

2. Plotinus on "the Net" as a Symbol of the World Soul

In the Neoplatonic cosmology of Plotinus, the four levels of reality are called the One, Mind, World Soul, and Nature. These levels of reality have analogues in earlier Hellenistic cosmology going back to the Pythagoreans and Plato, but for the sake of simplicity we here employ the descriptions and terminology of Plotinus.

The One is the ultimate, transcendental source of manifestation about which nothing can be said. It is unlimited, and therefore infinite, and because the One is indeterminate, it is "beyond Being."

Mind (*Nous*) is said to be the differentiated "image" of the One, insofar as the One can be reflected at all. Mind is a perfect, living unity-in-multiplicity of all the universal Forms and individual minds. It is the first level of Being because it is something distinct—it is also eternal and identical with "the Logos" in its most comprehensive form.

Soul is a further differentiated image of Mind, the living dispenser of individual forms and lives, the shaper of organic nature and incarnate form.

Nature, then, is the living image of Soul.

In a beautiful passage, Plotinus describes the World Soul as resembling a net, ever extended in the sea of manifestation:

> The Cosmos is like a net which takes all its life, as far as it ever stretches, from being wet in the water; it is at the mercy of the sea which spreads out, taking the net (*to diktuon*) with it just so far as it will go, for no mesh of it can strain beyond its set place: the Soul is of so far-reaching a nature—a thing unbounded—as to embrace the entire body of the All in one extension; so far as the universe extends, there soul is; and if the universe had no existence, the extent of soul would be the same; it is eternally what it is.[4]

In Christian terms, the *Father* corresponds to the One or the Unknowable Source. The *Logos*, or the "Son of God," is Nous or Universal Intellect. The animating breath of the *Holy Spirit* is the ever-extended net of the World Soul, which animates all living things in the shifting sea of manifestation. *Nature* is animated by this spirit and is the direct, living image of the preceding levels; it is a theophany, the very manifestation of the divine in the world of time and space.

3. The Symbolism of Apollo at Delphi

This diagram of the 153 fishes in the net is earlier than Christianity and is associated with the symbolism of Apollo at Delphi. As we have noted, Apollo is the earlier Greek personification of the Logos, the universal mediator, and it is ultimately from the mathematical symbolism of Apollo, the god of harmony, that both the diagrams of the 153 fish in the net and the feeding of the five thousand originate. Both of these diagrams are ultimately based on the numerical value of $\sqrt{2}$ (1.415), the mathematical symbol of the ideal mean between unity and multiplicity, which is reflected in the title THE GOD APOLLO, 1415.

In the Christian version of John 21, the "foundation stone" of the geometry is the central circle of SIMON PETROS, 1925, the omphalos of Christianity, whose number determines the dimensions of the entire diagram. In this Christian adaptation, we start with "the omphalos" to arrive at the symbol of "the net." Likewise, in the earlier symbolism of Apollo, his omphalos at Delphi was covered with a net, symbolizing the veil of manifestation, woven from the central source of harmony. In the earlier version, the central circle symbolizes the omphalos at Delphi, the meeting point of heaven and earth, "the golden mean" of Apollo. The number 153 also figures in Delphic symbolism, for 1530 is the sum of DELPHI, 619, and OMPHALOS, 911.

Finally, if we draw a circle around the three worlds diagram, the all-encompassing sphere has the measure of 7690, and 769 is the value of PYTHIOS, Apollo at Delphi. (*Figure 49.*)

Figure 49. The Symbolism of Apollo at Delphi

The centermost circle (dotted) is the starting point of the geometry. In the Christian version, it represents Simon Petros as the omphalos, the "foundation stone" of Christianity. In earlier Greek cosmology, it represents Apollo's net-covered omphalos stone at Delphi, the central point on the world axis and the meeting place of the three worlds. The length of the vesica enclosing the net is 1061, APOLLO, while the great circle encompassing the diagram has the circumference of 7690, and 769 is the gematria value of PYTHIOS, the name of Apollo at Delphi.

4. Greek Gematria and the Levels of Being

The central values of the Greek number canon which underlie the symbolism of Apollo and the early Christian diagrams reproduced in this book are not arbitrary, but embody a precise cosmological symbolism expressed via the Pythagorean language of Number. This mathematical symbolism is related to the process of emanation through which the universe comes into manifestation and represents the corresponding levels of being. Since each level of being depends on the preceding level, in the corresponding mathematical progression all the preceding levels are reflected and present in the final term. Similarly, the One, the Logos, and the World Soul are reflected and present in the final term of manifestation: the beautiful veil of living Nature.

The One. The starting point of the process is Unity, the One of Plotinus, which is the transcendental source of manifestation. This is represented by the value 1, 10, 100, 1000, etc., the decimal point not being used in Greek mathematics.

- Let the One be symbolized by 1.

The Logos. The One gives birth to the principle of the Nous-Logos which is represented by $\sqrt{2}$, the ideal principle of mediation and harmony between Unity and Multiplicity.

- Let the Logos be symbolized by $1\text{x}\sqrt{2} = 1.415$ = THE GOD APOLLO.

The World Soul. The World Soul is the differentiated image of the Logos, which is the image of the One.

- Let the World Soul be symbolized by $1\text{x}\sqrt{2}\text{x}\sqrt{3} = 2.448$ = THE NET+FISHES = 1.224x2.

If we represent this progression geometrically, we arrive at the dimensions the diagrams of the 153 fish in the net and the feeding of the five thousand, both of which are variations on the same underlying mathematical symbolism. (*See figures 50 and 51.*)

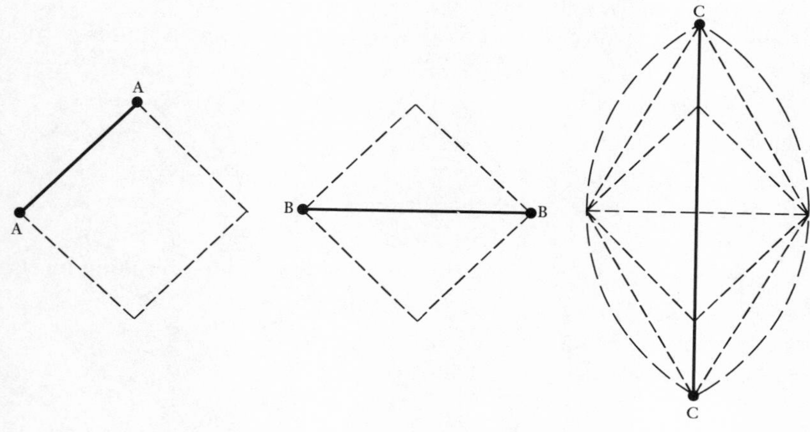

AA = 1 = The One
BB = 1x√2 = 1.415 = The Logos
CC = 1x√2x√3 = 2.448 = The World Soul

Figure 50. The Mathematical Origin of the Central Gematria Values

The mathematical progression 1x√2x√3 symbolizes the emanation of the levels of being and defines the gematria values of THE GOD APOLLO (1x√2 = 1.415) and FISHES+THE NET (1x√2x√3 = 2.448 = 1.224x2). This mathematical progression is naturally expressed by the simple geometrical sequence shown above, which represents the three levels of being outlined below.

Mathematical Stage	Level of Being	Greek Symbolism	Christian Form
1	The One	The Source; the Seed	The Father
1x√2=1.415	Nous-Logos	The God Apollo	The Son (Logos)
1x√2x√3=2.448	The World Soul	The Net; the Sea	The Holy Spirit

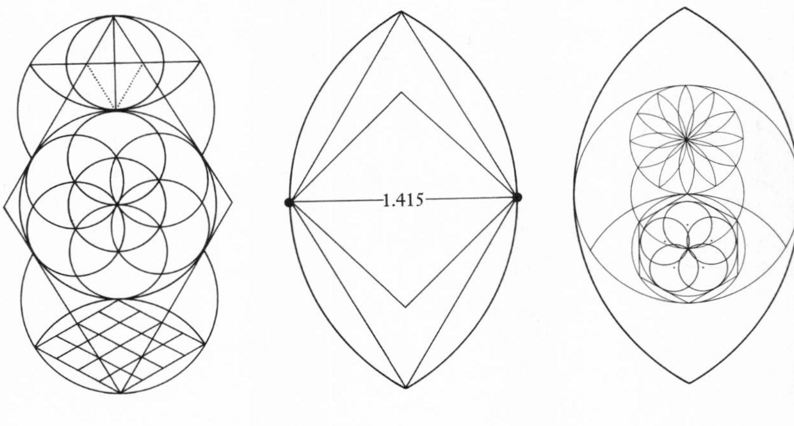

Figure 51. The Relationship between the 153 Fish in the Net and the Feeding of the Five Thousand

This illustration shows how the mathematical progression illustrated in the previous diagram underlies the dimensions of the fish in the net geometry and the feeding of the five thousand. Both diagrams are thereby shown to be differing expressions of the same, underlying cosmological code.

The central figure is a vesica with a width of 1x√2 (1.415 = THE GOD APOLLO), which defines the diameter of the feeding of the five thousand geometry on the right.

The height of the central vesica measures 1x√2x√3 (2.448 = FISHES+THE NET), which defines the height of the 153 fishes in the net geometry on the left.

In the diagram on the left, the rhombus intersects the length of the vesica in the upper world, dividing it into three equal segments of 353 units, the value of HERMES. This represents "Thrice-Great Hermes" or Hermes Trimegistos, a personification of the Logos.

5. 153 as the Measure of "the Fish" in Archimedes

Archimedes (*c.* 287–212 B.C.E.), in his treatise *On the Measurement of the Circle*, uses the whole number ratio 153:265 to accurately approximate the irrational ratio √3, "the measure of the fish" or the *vesica piscis*. Moreover, Archimedes uses this value in such a manner as to suggest that this approximation was well known to his contemporaries: it required no word of explanation at all.[5]

This ratio, 153:265, precisely relates to the dimensions of the 153 "fish" in the unbroken net, for it defines the height and width of each rhombus in "the net." (*Figure 52.*) Since 153 was known in the time of Archimedes as "the measure of the fish" or the vesica, ancient readers skilled in mathematics would have immediately recognized the allegory of the 153 fish in the net for what it is: a geometrical "story problem."

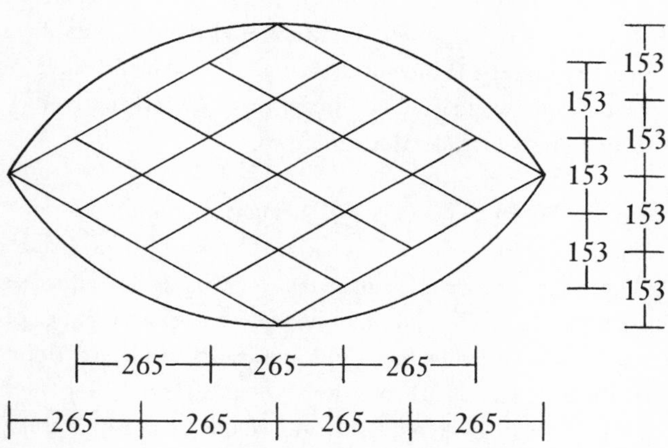

Figure 52. 153 as the Measure of "the Fish" in Archimedes

The whole number ratio 153:265, which Archimedes uses for √3 in his treatise *On the Measurement of the Circle*, corresponds to the height and length of each rhombus in the diagram of the 153 fishes in the net. Since 153:265 was known as the "measure of the fish" or *vesica piscis* in pre-Christian times, those skilled in mathematics would have immediately recognized the story of the 153 fish in the net as a geometrical "story problem." In terms of accuracy, the ratio 153:265 differs from the real value of √3 by about one part in 10,000.

6. Pythagoras' Prediction of the Number of Fish in the Net

Ultimately, the Christian story of the 153 fish in the net originated in the earlier Greek mathematical symbolism of Apollo and was most likely developed by the Pythagorean school. An earlier version of the tale was circulated among the Pythagoreans and tells how Pythagoras (570–496 B.C.E.) predicted the exact number of "fish in the net." While no number of fish is given in the story as it has come down to us, it is likely that the story was based on the Pythagorean, cosmological geometry discussed in this appendix, which underlies the later Christian version.[6] The accounts of Porphyry and Iamblichus are reproduced below.

From Porphyry, *The Life of Pythagoras* 27:

> Meeting with some fishermen who were drawing in their nets heavily laden with fishes from the deep, he predicted the exact number of fish they had caught. The fishermen said that if his estimate was accurate they would do whatever he commanded. They counted them accurately, and found the number correct. He then bade them to return the fish alive into the sea; and what is more wonderful, not one of them died, although they had been out of the water a considerable time.[7]

From Iamblichus, *The Life of Pythagoras*, chapter 8:

> One day, during a trip from Sybaris to Croton, by the sea-shore, he happened to meet some fishermen engaged in drawing up from the deep their heavily laden fish-nets. He told them he knew the exact number of fish they had caught. The surprised fishermen declared that if he was right they would do anything he said. He then ordered them, after counting the fish accurately, to return them alive to the sea, and what is more wonderful, while he stood on the shore, not one of them died, though they had remained out of their natural element quite a little while. Pythagoras then paid the fishermen the price of their fish, and departed for Croton. The fishermen divulged the occurrence, and on discovering his name from some children, spread it abroad publicly. Everybody wanted to see the stranger, which was easy enough to do. They were deeply impressed on beholding his countenance, which indeed betrayed his real nature.[8]

Appendix 2

The Hymn of the Pearl

THE HYMN OF THE PEARL, perhaps more so than any other ancient writing, beautifully expresses the gnostic themes of the soul's origin, forgetfulness, and subsequent recollection of its true nature. The hymn appears in the gnostic *Acts of Thomas* which was composed in Syriac. The version presented here is based on the translation in G. R. S. Mead's *Fragments of a Faith Forgotten*, which has been checked against the translations in Hennecke-Schneemelcher, *New Testament Apocrypha*, II; Cartlidge and Dungan, *Documents for the Study of the Gospels*; and Willis Barnstone, *The Other Bible*.

The Hymn of the Pearl

When I was a little child
And dwelling in my kingdom, in my Father's house,
In the wealth and glories of my parents
I had my pleasure.
From our home in the East,
My parents equipped me
And sent me forth.
And from the wealth of our treasury
They tied up for me a load.
Great it was, yet light,
That I might carry it alone:
Gold from Beth 'Ellay
And silver from Gazzak the great,
And rubies of India
And opals from the land of Kushan.
And they girded me with adamant
Which can crush iron.
And they took off from me the robe of glory,
Which in their love they had wrought for me,
And my purple toga,

Which was woven to the measure of my stature.
And they made a covenant with me
And wrote it in my heart, that I should not forget:
"If you go down into Egypt
And bring back the One Pearl
Which is in the midst of the sea
In the abode of the loud-breathing serpent,
Then you shall once again put on your splendid robe
And your toga, which lies over it,
And with your brother, our next in rank,
You shall be heir in our kingdom."
I left the East and went down,
Led by two messengers,
For the way was dangerous and difficult,
And I was young to travel it.
I passed over the borders of Maishān,
The meeting place of the merchants of the East,
And I reached the land of Babel,
And entered the walls of Sarbûg.
I went down into Egypt,
And my companions parted from me.
I went straight to the serpent
And stayed by his dwelling,
Waiting until he should slumber and sleep,
That I might take the pearl from him.
And when I was single and alone,
A stranger in this distant land,
I beheld there one of my own race,
A son of kings from the East,
A youth fair and well-favored,
An annointed one.
He came and joined me
And I made him my intimate friend,
A companion with whom I shared my business.
I warned him about the Egyptians
And against consorting with the unclean ones.
Yet I clothed myself like in their garments

Lest they suspect I had come from afar
To take the Pearl;
Lest they should arouse the serpent against me.
But in some way or another
They perceived that I was not their countryman.
So they dealt with me treacherously,
And I ate their food.
I forgot that I was the son of kings,
And served their king.
And I forgot the pearl,
For which my parents had sent me.
And from the heaviness of their food
I fell into a deep sleep.
But all the things that befell me,
My parents saw and grieved for me.
And a proclamation was made in our kingdom
That all should come to our gate—
Kings and princes of Parthia
And all the great ones of the East.
Thus they wove a plan on my behalf,
That I should not be left in Egypt.
And they wrote to me a letter,
And every noble signed his name to it:
"From your Father, the King of Kings,
And your Mother, the Mistress of the East,
And from your brother, our next in rank,
To you, our son in Egypt, greeting!
Awake and arise from your sleep,
And hear the words of our letter!
Remember that you are a son of Kings.
See the slavery of your life!
Remember the Pearl
For which you journeyed to Egypt.
Remember your bright robe,
And think of your glorious mantle,
Which you shall put on as your adornment
When your name is read in the book of heroes,

When you and your brother, our crown prince,
Shall be heir in our kingdom."
And the letter was a letter
Sealed by the King with his right hand
To keep it from the wicked ones, the children of Babel
And the savage demons of Sarbûg.
It took the form of an eagle,
The king of all winged fowl;
It flew and alighted beside me,
And became wholly speech.
At its voice and the sound of its rustling
I awoke and arose from my sleep.
I took it up and kissed it,
I broke its seal and read.
And according to what was traced on my heart,
So was the letter written.
I remembered that I was a son of Kings
And my soul yearned for its noble state.
I remembered the Pearl,
For which I was sent down into Egypt,
And I began to charm him,
The terrible loud-breathing serpent.
I hushed him to sleep and lulled him to slumber;
For my Father's name I spoke over him,
And the name of our next in rank,
And of my Mother, the Queen of the East.
And I seized away the Pearl,
And turned around to go back to my Father's house.
I stripped off their filthy robe
And left it in their land.
And I made straight my course
To the light of my homeland, the East.
And my letter, my awakener,
I found before me on the path;
While it had awakened me with its voice,
It now led me with its light:
Written on Chinese tissue with red ochre,

Shining before me in its form,
And with its voice and its guidance
It encouraged me to hasten,
Drawing me on with its love.
I went forth, passed by Sarbûg,
Left Babel on my left hand,
And reached the great city of Maishān,
The haven of merchants,
Which lies on the shore of the sea.
And my bright robe, which I had taken off,
And the toga in which it was wrapped about,
From the heights of Hyrcania
My parents sent thither
By the hand of their treasurers
Who, by their faith, could be trusted therewith.
I did not remember its splendor, its dignity,
For as a child I had left it in my Father's house.
Suddenly as I faced it,
The robe seemed like a mirror of myself:
I saw in it my whole self,
And I saw my whole self in facing it,
So that we were two, divided apart,
Yet one in a single form.
And the treasurers too
Who brought me the garment, I saw in like manner,
That they were two of a single form.
For the one sign of the King was engraved on them both,
The sign of him who had restored to me
My treasure and my wealth by means of them:
My bright embroidered robe adorned
Resplendent with glorious colors,
With gold and with beryls,
And rubies and opals
And sardonyxes of various color.
And made ready in its grandeur,
With stones of adamant,
Were all its seams fastened.

The image of the Kings of Kings
Shone in full over it,
And like the sapphire stone
Were its resplendant hues.
And again I saw that throughout it
The motions of *gnosis* were stirring.
And I saw too
That it was preparing for speech.
I heard the sound of its song
Whispered in its descent:
"I belong to him, the most valiant of men,
For whom they reared me before my Father;
And I perceived in myself his stature,
Growing according to his labors."
With kingly motions
It was spreading itself out towards me,
And from the hands of its bringers
It hastened that I might embrace it;
And my love, too, urged me on,
To run, to meet, and to receive it.
And I stretched forth and I received it.
With the beauty of its colors I adorned myself
And my toga of brilliant colors
I cast over my entire self.
I clothed myself therewith and ascended
To the gate of greeting and adoration.
I bowed my head and adored
To the splendor of the Father who had sent it to me.
His commands I had accomplished,
And he too had fulfilled his promise.
And at the gate of his princes
I mingled among the nobles.
For he rejoiced in me and received me,
And I was with him in his kingdom.
And with the sound of many voices joined as one
His servants praised him in song.
And he promised me that to the gate

Of the King of Kings I should speed with him,
And bringing my gift and my Pearl
I should appear with him before our King.

Notes

Chapter One

In the Beginning: Philosophy and Initiation in the Ancient World

1. Estimates range from 400,000 to 700,000 scrolls, representing some 30,000 works. At this writing, the Egyptian goverment in cooperation with UNESCO is rebuilding the Library at Alexandria. For more on the ancient library, see Parsons, *The Alexandrian Library: Glory of the Hellenic World*. For the new library, see the UNESCO document "Bibliotheca Alexandria: The Revival of the First Universal Library" in *Alexandria* 2.

2. For an excellent sketch of life in ancient Alexandria, see G. R. S. Mead, *Fragments of a Faith Forgotten*, 95ff.

3. As Ugo Bianchi points out, at the core of the Greek mysteries dwelt an authentic *mysteriosophy*: "By this term we mean a special manner of seeing the cosmos, man and the history of the gods: a manner which implies a *sophia* or general mystic conception of life and of the cosmos, of its divine origins, of the perpetual and recurring cycle of changes which govern it and also in particular a doctrine of the soul as subject to an alternation of decay in this world subject to destiny (or to matter) and of final re-integration, or at least of final integration into the divine world—under the image of the concept of soma-sema, the *body-tomb*" (Bianchi, *The Greek Mysteries*, 6).

4. For the path of philosophy likened to the path of initiation, see Plato, *Symposium* 210A and Plutarch, *On the Mysteries of Isis and Osiris* 382D, to cite merely two examples of this ancient, widespread analogy.

5. The great scholar of Greek philosophy, W. K. C. Guthrie, has suggested that Plato took the symbol of the Cave from the Orphic mysteries. See his *A History of Greek Philosophy*, vol. 4, 517–18. Later, the Neoplatonists used the symbolism of Hades, the underworld, to refer to the *current* state of humanity and not some post-mortem existence. For the Neoplatonic view of the underworld, see Thomas Taylor's *The Eleusinian and Bacchic Mysteries: A Dissertation*.

6. Plato, *Republic* 516ff. (Cornford translation, 229–30).

7. For an account of the philosophical ascent in later Platonic thought, see my introduction to *Porphyry's Letter to His Wife Marcella: Concerning the Life*

of Philosophy and the Ascent to the Gods.

8. See my introductory essay in the first issue of the annual review *Alexandria: The Journal of the Western Cosmological Traditions.*

9. Plato, *Timaeus* 37D.

10. Philip Wheelwright, *Heraclitus*, 29.

11. This is a common formula found inscribed upon thin gold foil sheets which were buried with the bodies of Orphic initiates. The inscriptions on the "gold plates" vary slightly from one to another, but are all very similar. They tell of two springs which the initiate will face in the portal of the afterlife, the springs of Memory and Forgetfulness. The latter must be avoided, but drinking from the former will confer immortality. The complete text of one plate is:

> To the left of the house of Hades
> under a graceful white cypress
> a well offers spring water.
> Don't drink there.
>
> Find the well by the lake of memory.
> Guardians protect the cold water.
> Tell them:
>
> I am a child of earth
> and of starry heaven,
> but my race is of heaven.
>
> This you know.
> I am parched
> and perishing.
>
> Give me cold water
> from the lake of memory.
>
> They will give you water
> from the sacred spring
> and you shall live
> a lord among heroes.

("Soul Ladder" in R. C. Hogart, *The Hymns of Orpheus*, 32.)

Plato himself drew upon the Orphic myths, especially in his idea of learning as "recollection." Mind, because it reflects the nature of universal principles, contains within a vast amount of innate knowledge which may be realized and demonstrated through the study of nature and mathematics. Thus Plato said that learning was "recollection," a remembering of something the soul previously knew in the world of first principles before entering the realm of generation, for "our race is of heaven." According to the Orphic mysteries, before the soul's incarnation, it drinks from the stream of *Lêthê* or Forgetfulness, and loses sight of its celestial origin. The Greek word for truth is *alêtheia* which means, literally, "not forgetting." Plato took the teachings of Orphism and clothed them in philosophical dress through the idea of "recollection" and the idea that philosophy represents a return to first principles.

12. Eduard Zeller, *Outlines of the History of Greek Philosophy*, 249.

13. Frederick Copleston, *A History of Philosophy: Greece and Rome*, vol. 1, part 2, 167.

14. Regarding this idea of microcosmus, Rudolf Allers writes that man, "Although inferior to the pure spirits . . . occupies at the same time an absolutely unique position by containing the whole world on a minor scale. Thus, he is placed in the 'middle' of the universe. His nature is the dividing line and, accordingly, also the bond between the material and the spiritual world" (Allers, "Microcosmus," 322).

15. Zeller, *Outlines*, 250.

16. *Corpus Hermeticum* 16.12 (Mead translation, *Thrice-Greatest Hermes*, II, 174).

17. For the Platonic theory of education, see *The Republic* 521C–531C. As Plato states, "It is quite hard to realize that every soul possesses an organ better worth saving than a thousand eyes, because it is our only means of seeing the truth; and that when its light is dimmed or extinguished by other interests, these studies will purify the hearth and rekindle the sacred fire" (Cornford translation, 245).

18. For some entertaining and edifying examples, see Michell, *Simulacra: Faces and Figures in Nature*.

19. For an interesting discussion, see the introduction to part 8, "The Mystery of Language," in Needleman and Appelbaum, *Real Philosophy: An Anthology of the Universal Search for Meaning*.

20. *Seventh Letter* 341D. In *Plato: The Collected Dialogues, Including the*

Letters, edited by Edith Hamilton and Huntington Cairns, 1589.

21. "I believe it because it is absurd," wrote the church father Tertullian. Augustine likewise stated, "I would not believe the Gospel if the authority of the Catholic Church did not compel me." See Angus, *Religious Quests of the Graeco-Roman World*, 116.

22. Angus, *Religious Quests*, 143 and 167.

23. As he writes in 1 Corinthians 15, "There are celestial bodies and there are terrestrial bodies; but the glory of the celestial is one, and the glory of the terrestrial is another. . . . I can tell you this, brethren: flesh and blood cannot inherit the kingdom of God, nor does the perishable inherit the imperishable."

24. Plato, *Republic* 527B.

25. The opinion of the church fathers was that the so-called "gnostics" based their teachings on the tenets of Pythagorean and Platonic philosophy. See, for example, chapter 2, p. 28, citing the conclusions of Hippolytus.

26. On the use of mystery terminology in early Christianity, see Wiens, "Mystery Concepts in Primitive Christianity and its Environment" and Hamilton, "The Church and the Language of the Mystery: The First Four Centuries."

27. Like the Platonists, the gnostics maintained that the true God is an ineffable, transcendental principle which exists above the level of Being itself. Being is the first manifestation of this transcendent Source, but the Source never consciously decided to create the universe, because the Source exists above and is superior to the nature of discursive thought and decision making. Rather, the Source eternally gives forth the universe without premeditation and without suffering diminution in any way. For the Neoplatonic view, see Michael Hornum's introduction to Porphyry, *Launching-Points to the Realm of Mind: An Introduction to the Neoplatonic Philosophy of Plotinus*, and his article "A Plotinian Solution to a Vedantic Problem" in *Alexandria* 1. For a look at a gnostic creation myth, see chapter 6 of the present work and also Fideler, "The Passion of Sophia: An Early Gnostic Creation Myth."

28. *Gospel of Thomas* 39 (in Robinson, *The Nag Hammadi Library*, 130–131). Compare with Luke 11.52 and Matthew 23.13.

29. *Gospel of Thomas* 94 (in Robinson, *The Nag Hammadi Library*, 136). See also Luke 11.9–10 and *Gospel of Thomas* 92.

30. Matthew 13.31–32 and parallels in Mark 4.30–32 and Luke 13.18–19.

31. Luke 8.11 and parallels in Mark 4.13–30 and Matthew 13.18–23.

32. Mark 4.33–34.

33. Luke 8:9–10.

34. Specifically the source "Q," which was a common source used by the authors of Matthew and Luke. As Helmut Koester, professor of New Testament Studies at Harvard points out, like the *Gospel of Thomas*, "The Synoptic Sayings Source (Q), used by Matthew and Luke, also does not consider Jesus' death a part of the Christian message. And it likewise is not interested in stories and reports about the resurrection and subsequent appearances of the risen Lord. The *Gospel of Thomas* and Q challenge the assumption that the early church was unanimous in making Jesus' death and resurrection the fulcrum of Christian faith. Both documents presuppose that Jesus' significance lay in his words, and in his words alone" (Helmut Koester, *Ancient Christian Gospels: Their History and Development*, 86). Moreover, Q and the parallel sayings in the *Gospel of Thomas* were probably written within ten or twenty years of Jesus' death, which makes them among the earliest sources for the teachings of Jesus—the gospels themselves are much later.

Interestingly, if the tradition preserved in a Christian infancy gospel is accurate, the historical Jesus may have also been acquainted with the gnostic science of gematria: here he instructs, at an early age, the scholars of the Temple in the mystical and cosmological dimensions of the Greek alphabet! (See Hennecke-Schneemelcher, *New Testament Apocrypha*, II, 392–393). *If* Jesus knew gematria, it might help account for the nature of his parables, and perhaps even the selection of his name, which amounts to 888.

35. Luke 8.17.

36. Matthew 13.35.

37. 1 Corinthians 2.6–7.

38. He continues: "This book is written in the mathematical language, and the symbols are triangles, circles, and other geometrical figures, without whose help it is impossible to comprehend a single word of it; without which one wanders in vain through a dark labyrinth" (Quoted in John Robinson, *An Introduction to Early Greek Philosophy*, 69).

39. Proclus, "On the Sacred Art," 146.

40. "If, then, anyone asks, 'What has this to do with Apollo?', we shall say that it concerns not only him, but also Dionysus, whose share in Delphi is no less than that of Apollo" (Plutarch, *The E at Delphi* 388E).

41. As the Neoplatonist Proclus observes, "To divide and produce wholes into parts, and to preside over the distribution of forms, is Dionysiacal; but to perfect all things harmonically, is Apolloniacal" (Proclus, *Commentaries on the Timaeus of Plato*, II, p. 77; Taylor translation).

42. Damascius, from L. G. Westerink, *The Greek Commentaries on Plato's Phaedo*, II, 80. For more on the symbolism of Apollo and Dionysus at Delphi, see Fideler, "The Voice from the Center: The Oracle of Apollo and the Oracle of the Heart."

43. Martin P. Nilsson, "The High God and the Mediator," 101.

44. Maximus of Tyre 39.5; quoted by Henry Chadwick in his edition of Origen's *Contra Celsum*, xvii. This idea is further elaborated in a fragment of the Neopythagorean writer Onatas, translated in Goodenough, *By Light, Light: The Mystic Gospel of Hellenistic Judaism*, 20–21.

45. See especially James Hillman, *Re-Visioning Psychology*.

46. As Heliodorus notes, "There is, I imagine, a school of natural philosophers and theologians who do not disclose the meanings embedded in these stories to laymen but simply give them preliminary instruction in the form of a myth. But those who have reached the higher grades of the mysteries they initiate into clear knowledge in the privacy of the holy shrine, in the light cast by the blazing torch of truth" (Heliodorus, *An Ethiopian Story* 9.9).

47. Sallustius, *Concerning the Gods and the Universe*, edited and translated by A. D. Nock, 5.

48. Sallustius, *Gods and the Universe*, 5.

49. Sallustius, *Gods and the Universe*, 5.

Chapter Two
Gematria: The Secret Language of the Christian Mysteries

1. For a discussion of the Pythagorean view of Number, see my introduction to Guthrie, *The Pythagorean Sourcebook and Library: An Anthology of Writings which Relate to Pythagoras and Pythagorean Philosophy*.

2. Pythagoras' *Sacred Discourse*, quoted in Iamblichus' *Life of Pythagoras*, in Guthrie, *Pythagorean Sourcebook*, 93.

3. Guthrie, *Pythagorean Sourcebook*, 94.

4. Farbridge, *Studies in Biblical and Semitic Symbolism*, 142.

5. Farbridge, *Studies in Biblical and Semitic Symbolism*, 94.

6. The Jews did not adopt numeral letters until Hellenistic times, under Greek influence; see Ifrah, *From One to Zero: A Universal History of Numbers*, 270, 277.

7. The study of gematria was not limited to the ancient world. For example, twelve days were devoted to the study of gematria in the curriculum at Oxford in the fourteenth century. See Peck, "Number as a Cosmic Language," 22, 63.

8. The gnostic masters who employed number symbolism in their teach-

ings include Basilides, Valentinus, Marcus, Colarbasus, and Monoimus. It's impossible, however, to imagine that this symbolism was limited to just these individuals, who were singled out as well-known "examples" by the heresiologists. The fact that mathematical symbolism underlies the New Testament allegories of the feeding of the five thousand and the 153 fish in the net shows that the practice goes back to the earliest days of the Christian movement.

9. Valentinus: Hippolytus, *Refutation of All Heresies* 6.25 (*Ante-Nicene Fathers*, V, 85); Marcus: *Refutation* 6.47 (*Ante-Nicene Fathers*, V, 97–98).

10. Hippolytus, *Refutation of All Heresies* 8.5–8. (*Ante-Nicene Fathers*, V, 120–122).

11. Hippolytus, *Refutation of All Heresies* 8.8 (*Ante-Nicene Fathers*, V, 122).

12. Hippolytus, *Refutation of All Heresies* 4.13 (*Ante-Nicene Fathers*, V, 30).

13. Some references to Abraxas and his number amongst the church fathers include: Irenaeus, *Against Heresies* 24.7 (*Ante-Nicene Fathers*, I, 350); Hippolytus, *Refutation of All Heresies* 7.14 (*Ante-Nicene Fathers*, V, 107); Jerome, *On Amos* 1.3 (quoted in Leisegang, "The Mystery of the Serpent," 222); Epiphanius, *Panarion* 24.7.1–6 (Amidon translation, 70–71). See also Campbell Bonner's *Studies in Magical Amulets, Chiefly Graeco-Egyptian* and Martin Nilsson, "The Anguipede of the Magical Amulets."

14. Jerome, *On Amos* 1.3; quoted in Leisegang, "The Mystery of the Serpent," 222.

15. Revelation 13.18. See Michell, *City of Revelation*, chapter 13, for a definitive analysis of this passage.

16. See Campbell Bonner's article, "The Numerical Value of a Magical Formula."

17. Hans Dieter Betz, editor, *The Greek Magical Papyri in Translation*, 17. One of the more central numbers of Greek gematria is 1110 or 1111. 1110 is equivalent by gematria to THE MICROCOSM—humanity seen as a reflection of the universe or the Divine Sun—while IOTA, the Greek vowel of the sun, has the value of 1111. A circle with this circumference has the diameter of HERMES; a hexagon inscribed therein measures APOLLO; and a square containing the circle measures THE GOD APOLLO. See the documentary illustration "The Cosmic Temple," on page 217, to see how this scheme was applied in the dimensions of the temple of Apollo at Didyma. For Iota as a symbol of the Aeon and the Monad, see Reitzenstein, *Hellenistic Mystery Religions*, 100, note 71. The gematria of Iota helps explain why the gnostic Monoimus–who based his teaching on geometry and number symbolism–

identified Iota as the Monad and Primal Man, the source of the universe; see Hippolytus, *Refutation of All Heresies* 8.5–8 (*Ante-Nicene Fathers*, V, 120–122) and 10.13 (*Ante-Nicene Fathers*, V, 146).

18. Irenaeus, *Against Heresies* 24.1 (*Ante-Nicene Fathers*, I, 393).

19. Irenaeus, *Against Heresies* 14.4 (*Ante-Nicene Fathers*, I, 337).

20. Irenaeus, *Against Heresies* 14.6 (*Ante-Nicene Fathers*, I, 338).

21. That is, if you don't count the three signs which were only used to represent numbers.

22. Origen, *Contra Celsum* 1.44. Origen's term "word of wisdom," pertaining to the science of gematria, is a reference to St. Paul's listing of the "spiritual gifts" in 1 Corinthians 12.8. Among the "spiritual gifts" here mentioned are "the word of wisdom" and "the word (*logos*) of knowledge (*gnôsis*)." These two phrases are more accurately translated as "the science of wisdom" and "the science of knowledge," a possible reference to Greek gematria.

23. Philippians 2.9.

24. Rahner, "The Christian Mystery and the Pagan Mysteries," 391.

25. *Christian Sibyllines* 323A–E; in Hennecke-Schneemelcher, *New Testament Apocrypha*, II, 709–710.

26. Origen, *Contra Celsum* 1.7.

27. Clement of Alexandria, *Stromata* 1.12 (*Ante-Nicene Fathers*, II, 313).

28. Clement of Alexandria, *Stromata* 5.9 (*Ante-Nicene Fathers*, II, 458).

29. Clement of Alexandria, *On the Salvation of the Rich Man* 5 (*Ante-Nicene Fathers*, II, 592).

30. Clement of Alexandria, *Stromata* 6.11 (*Ante-Nicene Fathers*, II, 501).

31. Clement of Alexandria, *Stromata* 6.10 (*Ante-Nicene Fathers*, II, 499).

32. On the relation between musical, arithmetic, and geometric harmony, and the harmony of "the whole universe," see Clement of Alexandria, *Stromata* 1.14 (*Ante-Nicene Fathers*, II, 313).

33. See Ifrah, *From One to Zero*, 304; see also Menninger, *Number Words and Number Symbols: A Cultural History of Numbers*, 266.

34. See the excellent discussion in Michell, *City of Revelation*, chapter 13.

35. *The Epistle of Barnabas* 9 (*Ante-Nicene Fathers*, I, 143).

36. "Light of the world" was also a title of Helios; see *Orphic Hymns* 8.18 (Athanassakis translation, 15) and our discussion on p. 371.

37. *Pistis Sophia* 1 (MacDermot translation, 3).

38. Bond and Lee, *Gematria: A Preliminary Investigation of the Cabala Contained in the Coptic Gnostic Books and of a similar Gematria in the Greek Text*

of the New Testament.

Chapter Three

The Solar Logos: The "Word of the Sun" in Hellenistic Mysticism and Cosmology

1. Goodenough, *An Introduction to Philo Judaeus*, 103. Goodenough's discussion of the true meanings of *Logos* here is excellent, and he properly notes that "Word" is an "utterly misleading translation."

2. *Analogia* in Greek refers to continued geometrical proportion.

3. As Plato notes in *Laws* 898E, "The sun's body can be seen by any man, but his soul by no man," at least through the physical eye. Yet, as Plotinus writes in an unforgettable passage, "No eye ever saw the sun without becoming sun-like, nor can a soul see beauty without becoming beautiful. You must become first all godlike and all beautiful if you intend to see God and beauty" (Plotinus, "On Beauty," *Enneads* 1.6.9.30; Armstrong translation).

4. For a good exposition of the idea of Helios as the Mediator (Μεσότης = "mean") and link between the two worlds, see Emperor Julian, *Hymn to King Helios* 138Dff.

5. Cumont, *Astrology and Religion Among the Greeks and Romans*, 73–74.

6. Emperor Julian presents the idea of the Threefold Sun: the first Sun is the transcendental Source, the Good, which dispenses the principles of beauty, existence, perfection, and oneness; the second Sun is Helios-Mithras, the ruler of the intellectual gods; the visible disc of the physical sun is third (Julian, *Hymn to King Helios* 132B–C). Put another way, the first Sun is the transcendental One, beyond Being; the second Sun, Helios, is the principle and fountain of Being, "the Sun of suns"; the third level is the realm of all suns, both our local sun and all the other stars in the cosmos.

7. *Asclepius* 29.3 (Mead translation, *Thrice-Greatest Hermes*, II, 229).

8. For light of life (ζωῆς φῶς) as an epithet of Helios, see *Orphic Hymns* 8.18 (Athanassakis translation, 15).

9. "God is the archetypal paradigm of all laws: He is the Sun of the sun, the intelligible object behind the object comprehensible by sense, and from invisible fountains he supplies the visible beams which our eyes behold" (Philo, *The Special Laws* 1.279). For an excellent discussion of the Hellenistic Logos doctrine as expressed in Philo, see Goodenough, *An Introduction to Philo Judaeus*, chapter 5; as Goodenough clearly shows, in the Logos teaching, as God is to the intelligible and undiminished sun, the Logos-Stream is to its rays. See also Angus, *Religious Quests of the Graeco-Roman World*, 286–287.

10. For the Logos as "Son of God" in Philo, see *On Husbandry* 13.51 and *The Confusion of Tongues* 14.63; these passages are discussed in Mead, *Thrice-Greatest Hermes*, I, 157–156. Philo had many other titles for the Logos, including "Angel," "First-born," "First-born Son," "Image of God," "Instrument," "Mediator," "Name of God," "Ray," "Seal," "Second God," and so forth. For a complete summary of these titles with sources, see Guthrie, *The Message of Philo Judaeus of Alexandria*, 28–29. Some other common Hellenistic symbols of the Logos include the Shepherd, the Teacher, Orpheus, the Seed, the Lyre, the Pilot of a Ship, Harmony, the Foundation Stone, the Choir Leader (Coryphaeus), and the Celestial or Heavenly City.

11. Clement of Alexandria, *Stromata* 1.15 (*Ante-Nicene Fathers*, II, 316).

12. Goodenough, *An Introduction to Philo Judaeus*, 95. See also Knox, *Some Hellenistic Elements in Primitive Christianity*, 34.

13. Plato, *Republic* 509B. The Good, symbolized by the Sun, "is not the same thing as being, but even *beyond being*, surpassing it in dignity and power" (Cornford translation, 220). This Platonic notion of the Source, the One, transcending even the nature of Being, was to be extremely influential in the thought of Plotinus and the later Neoplatonists.

14. As Clement of Alexandria succinctly notes, "The First Cause is not then in space, but above both space, and time, and name, and conception" (Clement of Alexandria, *Stromata* 5.11; in *Ante-Nicene Fathers*, II, 461).

15. As Origen notes, "The Word can also be 'the Son' because he announces the secrets of the Father, who is 'Mind' (Nous) analogous to the Son who is called 'Word' (Logos). For as the word (*logos* = reason) in us is the messenger of what the mind perceives, so the Word of God, since he has known the Father, reveals the Father whom he has known, because no creature can come into contact with him without a guide" (*Commentary on John* 1.278). When reading these Hellenistic texts, it is important to remember that Nous or Mind *on a cosmological level* represents the principle of pure Intelligence itself and is superior to the activity of discursive reasoning, mental analysis, etc. Therefore, God can be pure Mind without engaging in inferior activities such as thinking, planning, and decision making; nonetheless, it is through the cultivation of divine *logos* in the human soul that we are led upward toward the recognition of the Highest.

16. Clement of Alexandria, *Exhortation to the Greeks* 10 (*Ante-Nicene Fathers*, II, 199).

17. *Corpus Hermeticum* 11 ("Mind Unto Hermes"), 15 (in Mead, *Thrice-Greatest Hermes*, II, 117).

18. Plotinus, *Enneads* 4.4.35 (MacKenna translation, 364).

19. Maximus of Tyre 19.3 (Witt translation, "Plotinus and Posidonius," 201).

20. Clement of Alexandria, *Exhortation to the Greeks* 9 (Witt translation, "Plotinus and Posidonius," 201).

21. This concept is discussed by Origen. When "we read of the building of the tower, a building composed of many stones, but seeming to be one solid block, what can the meaning of the Scripture be except the harmony and unity of the many?" (Origen, *Philocalia* 8.2).

22. I have also translated *dwelt among us* as "manifest among us." See the discussion in the comments following the translation.

23. Some scholars suggest that John grew up at Qumran.

24. Luke 1.78.

25. As Julian notes, "The Phoenicians, who were wise and learned in sacred lore, declared that the rays of light everywhere diffused are the undefiled incarnation of pure Mind (Νοῦς)" (*Hymn to King Helios* 134). The tendency toward solar monotheism is particularly well-attested in Macrobius, who notes that *Sol mundi mens est*: "The Sun is the Mind of the universe" (*Saturnalia* 1.19.9).

26. Thus Justin Martyr writes: "When we say, as before, that he [Jesus] was begotten by God as the Word of God in a unique manner beyond ordinary birth, this should be no strange thing for you who speak of Hermes as the announcing word (*Logos*) from God" (Justin Martyr, *First Apology* 22; in Richardson, *Early Christian Fathers*, 256).

27. Hippolytus, *Refutation of All Heresies* 5.2 (*Ante-Nicene Fathers*, V, 50); translation by Doresse, *Secret Books of the Egyptian Gnostics*, 84.

28. Budge, *Gods of the Egyptians*, I, 407–408.

29. Iamblichus, *On the Mysteries* 7.1 (Taylor translation, 300).

30. Budge, *Gods of the Egyptians*, I, 407–408.

31. Budge, *Gods of the Egyptians*, I, 407.

32. Iamblichus, *On the Mysteries* 1.1 (Taylor translation, 17–18).

33. On the Hermetic communities of Egypt, see Stephan Hoeller, introduction to Mead, *The Hymns of Hermes*. With the discovery of the Hermetic tractate "The Eighth Reveals the Ninth"—written in Coptic and recording an actual initiation—the views of such scholars as Festugière, Nock, and Van Moorsel, that the Hermetica represent a non-Egyptian "reading mystery," are seriously called into question. See Keizer, *The Eighth Reveals the Ninth: A New Hermetic Initiation Discourse (Tractate 6, Nag Hammadi Codex VI)*,

especially 5, 45, 54–55, 72–73, 78–79. The recent study by Garth Fowden suggests that displaced Egyptian priests may have had a hand in the composition of the Hermetica; see Fowden, *The Egyptian Hermes: A Historical Approach to the Late Pagan Mind*, 166–168. Finally, ancient letters discovered in Egypt indicate that followers of "Hermes Trismegistos" referred to him in their correspondence and suggest the presence of a Hermetic brotherhood in Hermopolis; see Rees, *Papyri from Hermopolis and other Documents of the Byzantine Period*, 2–7.

34. C. K. Barrett, *The Gospel of John*, 31. See also the comments in C. K. Barrett, *The New Testament Background: Selected Documents*, 93ff. For a detailed study of the remarkable parallels between the surviving Hermetic hymns and a recently discovered document of Christian gnosis, see this writer's study, "A Comparison of the Prayer of the Apostle Paul with the Hymns of Corpus Hermeticum and Some Greek Magical Papyri."

35. Clement of Alexandria, *Exhortation to the Greeks* 11 (*Ante-Nicene Fathers*, II, 203).

36. *Corpus Hermeticum* 4 ("The Cup or Monad"), 3 (Mead translation, *Thrice-Greatest Hermes*, II, 56).

37. *Corpus Hermeticum* 4.4 (Mead translation, *Thrice-Greatest Hermes*, II, 57).

38. *Corpus Hermeticum* 13 ("The Secret Discourse Concerning Rebirth"), 1 (Scott translation, *Hermetica*, I, 239).

39. Scott, *Hermetica*, II, 372. One scholar notes that Hermetic "initiation may have been considered to produce the divine or 'resurrection' state, so that the Hermetic devotee had already 'died' and would not suffer death and reincarnation at the dissolution of his physical body" (Keizer, *The Eight Reveals the Ninth*, 32). Is there a relationship between this idea and the "realized eschatology" of Christian gnosis discussed in the present work, chapter 6? For more on the concept of rebirth and gnostic divinization in the Hermetic writings, see Fowden, *The Egyptian Hermes*, 104–112.

40. *Gospel of Thomas* 108 (in Robinson, *The Nag Hammadi Library*, 137).

41. John 3.3.

42. Origen, *Contra Celsum* 6.79.

43. Clement of Alexandria, *Exhortation to the Greeks* 6 (Loeb Classical Library translation, 155). Compare this passage with the Hermetic writing *The Virgin of the World*: "But when the Sun did rise for me, and with all-seeing eyes I gazed upon the hidden [mysteries] of that New Dawn . . ." (*Virgin of the World* 4; in Mead, *Thrice-Greatest Hermes*, III, 60).

44. In the epilogue to his work *Paganism in the Roman Empire*, Ramsay MacMullen discusses various reasons for the triumph of Christianity, including "the destructive political and economic forces at work upon the more prominent parts of paganism after 250." He notes that "[by the time of Arcadius there] existed, thanks to his Christian predecessors, many, many laws aimed against the prominent sort of pagans. They could not legally pass on their estates, they could not enter on profitable careers, their sanctuaries had been stripped of land and wealth. As added penalty, in the good gold solidus dispensed by Constantine and his successors to the Church, pagans could recognize the metal confiscated from the treasuries of their gods. They were financing their own destruction" (MacMullen, *Paganism in the Roman Empire*, 135–136).

45. *Gospel of Thomas* 77 (in Robinson, *The Nag Hammadi Library*, 135).

Chapter Four

The Harmony of Apollo: The Origins of Gematria in Ancient Greece

1. Neugebauer, *The Exact Sciences in Antiquity*, 35. The earliest Pythagorean school also possessed an interesting method using "Side- and Diameter-numbers" for calculating ever more accurate approximations of this primary value. See Thomas, *Greek Mathematical Works I: Thales to Euclid*, 133–137. For a clear exposition of this technique see Lawlor, *Sacred Geometry: Philosophy and Practice*, 39–41.

2. See van der Waerden, *Geometry and Algebra in Ancient Civilizations*. See also his work *Science Awakening I: Egyptian, Babylonian, and Greek Mathematics*.

3. While the Egyptian mathematical writings which survive are mostly simple problems for young scribes, a study of Egyptian bas reliefs conclusively demonstrates a profound understanding and application of geometrical forming principles. From this we can conclude that more sophisticated writings, if they existed, have not come down to us. Given the evidence, it is likely that the Egyptians, like the Pythagoreans, considered more advanced mathematical knowledge to be transcendental and esoteric; therefore, it was never committed to writing, but memorized and orally transmitted. For an analysis of some Egyptian bas reliefs which demonstrate an advanced mathematical knowledge, see Fideler, "The Science and Art of Animating Statues" in *Alexandria* 2.

4. Plato, *Laws* 656.

5. τοῦ γὰρ ἀει ἡ γεωμετρικὴ γνῶσις ἐστιν (Plato, *Republic* 527B).

6. Heath, *A History of Greek Mathematics I: From Thales to Euclid*, 24.

Xenocrates, who took over the leadership of the Academy after Plato's Pythagorean nephew Speusippus, would turn away applicants who knew no geometry with the words, "Go thy way, for thou hast not the means of getting a grip on philosophy."

7. We must remember that for Plato only unqualified, power-hungry people would tend to *voluntarily* seek political office! Those philosophers, capable of doing the best job of governance, because they are high-minded individuals devoted to the study of first principles and the pursuit of the truth, would never on their own accord wish to become involved in the dismal realm of politics when they could be studying the universe instead. Dragged screaming and kicking into office, they finally submit to the necessary evil of governing the state—not out of any personal desire, but out of civic duty, since they are the most qualified for the job.

8. *Republic* 527B (Cornford translation, 244).

9. *Republic* 526B (Cornford translation, 242).

10. *Republic* 527B (Cornford translation, 245).

11. For a discussion of the relation between justice and the principle of proportion in Pythagorean thought, see Robinson, *An Introduction to Early Greek Philosophy*, 81–83. This Pythagorean definition of justice is a given first principle in the thought of Plato.

12. *Republic* 443D–444 (Cornford translation, 142).

13. See McClain, *The Pythagorean Plato: Prelude to the Song Itself*. If someone is instructed in the principles of harmonics on the monochord in even the most rudimentary sense, it will increase his or her appreciation and understanding of the Platonic dialogues exponentially.

14. As a contemporary textbook of harmonics observes, "Acoustics teaches the need for norms—better still, the recognition that norms exist whether we like them or not. The octave is a norm. One of our colleagues, Robert Sanders, once said to a class: 'You can't argue with an octave.' The triad is a norm. There are others that emerge strongly and logically as one studies acoustics. Music cannot exist without norms. A sensible course of action is not to fight the norms but to find out how best to operate in relation to them. This is the real meaning of harmony" (Levarie and Levy, *Tone: A Study in Musical Acoustics*, ix).

15. Our modern scale sacrifices these perfect intervals so musicians can modulate or change keys without running into sonic difficulty. All keys are exactly the same, but *all* the perfect intervals are equally out of tune with the exception of the octave. The Pythagorean scale has perfect octaves, fifths, and

fourths, but sacrifices the sweeter sounding "perfect thirds" of just tuning. Just tuning maintains the perfect consonances of Pythagorean tuning and adds the better sounding "perfect third," but forces one to include two different sized whole tones!

16. Likewise, the study of the laws of harmony exposes each student to certain principles that everyone can ultimately agree on: "No one can argue with the octave." In the world of international relations, rife as it is with competing interests in need of harmonization, the value of such a common language, based on the laws of universal relation, becomes immediately obvious.

17. *Republic* 486E (Cornford translation, 192).

18. After admitting that the ideal city defined in the *Republic* is to be found nowhere on earth, Socrates remarks that "Perhaps there is a pattern set up in the heavens for one who desires to see it and, seeing it, to found one in himself. But whether it exists anywhere or ever will exist is no matter; for this is the only commonwealth in whose politics he can ever take part" (*Republic* 592B; Cornford translation, 319–20).

19. In the ideal state—whether inhabited by gods or their offspring—there would be no private property; all would be held in common and the state would be perfectly unified. Realizing that this is unattainable in the world of practical affairs, the "second best" and "third best" options must be investigated, but one should always hold fast to the absolute ideal, and "seek the constitution that is as like to it as possible" (*Laws* 739 ff; Bury translation, Loeb Classical Library).

20. *Republic* 486E (Cornford translation, 192).

21. See the Indo-European Roots Appendix, s.v. **ar-**, in the third edition of *The American Heritage Dictionary of the English Language*.

22. "The monad is the principle of numbers; and the one [= unit] the principle of numbered things" (Theon of Smyrna, *Mathematics Useful for Understanding Plato* 1.4; Lawlor translation, 13).

23. Theon of Smyrna, *Mathematics Useful for Understanding Plato* 2.40 (Lawlor translation, 66).

24. Theon, *Mathematics Useful for Understanding Plato* 2.41 (Lawlor translation, 66).

25. Cornford, "Mysticism and Science in the Pythagorean Tradition," part 2, p. 3.

26. Clement of Alexandria, *Exhortation to the Greeks* 1 (*Ante-Nicene Fathers*, II, 172).

27. Plutarch, *On Music* 1135F–1136B. See also Diodorus, *Library of History* 5.74.5.

28. Plutarch, *On the Generation of the Soul in the Timaeus* 1030A–B.

29. Hence his title *Mousêgetês* (Μουσηγέτης), "leader of the Muses." For more on the Muses, see Peter Russell, "The Muses: Archetype of the Divine Intellect in Feminine Form" and John Carey, "The Daughters of Memory."

30. For more on Delphi, see Peter Hoyle's illustrated account, *Delphi*, which also describes attempted revivals of the "Delphic Idea."

31. For the story of Deukalion and his ark, see Apollodorus, *Library of Mythology* 1.7.2, and Kerényi, *Gods of the Greeks*, 228–229.

32. For Apollo Pytios (Πύτιος) see Cook, *Zeus*, I, 730, note 6; II, 723, note 5; II, 934; Roscher, *Neue Omphalosstudien*, 19, 21. By gematria, PYTIOS is 1060, one less than APOLLO.

33. Plutarch, *The Oracles at Delphi No Longer Given in Verse* 397C–D.

34. See Hesiod, *Homeric Hymn to Apollo* 3.388ff. From his associations with dolphins, the god was also known as *Apollôn Delphinios*, which has an obvious relation to the word *Delphi*: originally the place was called *Pythô*, but with the introduction of Apollo *Delphinios*, it became *Delphoi* (Farnell, *Cults of the Greek States*, IV, 186 note A). Interestingly, dolphins are rational creatures, known to delight in music, laughter, and play; and they have, on many a recorded occasion, rescued travelers lost at sea, who otherwise would have drowned. On dolphins in Greek mythology, see Rabinovitch, *Der Delphin in Sage und Mythos der Griechen*.

35. Pausanius, *Description of Greece* 10.5.7–8.

36. Plutarch, *On the E at Delphi* 385D.

37. Apollo's role as the god of archery may be related to the need of archers to master string tension (balance, mean) and aim (foresight, prophecy). I am indebted to R. C. Hogart for bringing this symbolism to my attention.

38. In the Greek world there were numerous writings dealing with this type of number symbolism. The most complete text which survives, and the only one translated into English, is *The Theology of Arithmetic*, attributed to Iamblichus. See futher note on pp. 355–56 and 375–76.

39. See Plutarch, *On the Mysteries of Isis and Osiris* 381F and *Concerning the E at Delphi* 393C; see also Plotinus, *Enneads* 5.5.6.25.

40. Cook, *Zeus: A Study in Ancient Religion*, II, 177–78. The term *axis* was both a Pythagorean name of the Monad and a term applied to the omphalos at Delphi. By gematria, both AXIS (ἄξων) and OMPHALOS (ὀμφαλός) amount to 911. See further note on pp. 374–75.

41. Guthrie, *The Pythagorean Sourcebook and Library*, 147. Iamblichus also states that Pythagoras was named after the Pythian Apollo. He examines some accounts which state that Pythagoras was a son of Apollo, which he rejects, concluding, "However, no one will deny that the soul of Pythagoras was sent to mankind from Apollo's domain, having either been one of his attendants, or more intimate associates, which may be inferred both from his birth and his versatile wisdom" (Guthrie, *Pythagorean Sourcebook*, 58–59). Robert Eisler, in *Orpheus the Fisher*, 12, sees the name *Pythagoras* as being analogous to *Pyl-agorai*, "the messengers to the Amphictyonic assembly, held alternately at Pylae and in Delphi." Pythagoras is thus a name of Apollo, for it signifies "him who speaks in Pytho."

42. Hence, he was known as *Hebdomagetês* (Ἑβδομαγέτης) or "Seven-leading." See Cook, *Zeus*, II, 236–238 for a comprehensive listing of primary sources relating to Apollo's association with the hebdomad.

43. Hence his title *Hebdomagenês* (Ἑβδομαγενής), "Seven-born."

44. For the seven-stringed lyre as a terrestrial symbol of the celestial "harmony of the spheres," see Theon of Smyrna, *Mathematics Useful for Understanding Plato* 3.15 (Lawlor translation, 91–94); Nicomachus, chapter 3, and excerpts 3 and 6, in *The Manual of Harmonics*; Servius, quoted by Cook, *Zeus*, II, 256; Macrobius, *Saturnalia* 1.19.14; Lucian, *On Astrology*, 10; Spitzer, *Classical and Christian Ideas of World Harmony*, 8ff. The Orphic *Hymn to Helios*, the lower aspect of Apollo, states: "Yours [are] the golden lyre and the harmony of cosmic motion" (*Orphic Hymns* 8.9; Athanassakis translation, 13). See also Plato, *Cratylus* 405D. For more on *harmonia mundi* or the music of the spheres, see the works of Joscelyn Godwin: *Music, Mysticism, and Magic: A Sourcebook*; *Harmonies of Heaven and Earth*; *The Harmony of the Spheres: A Sourcebook of the Pythagorean Tradition in Music*; and "The Golden Chain of Orpheus: A Survey of Musical Esotericism in the West." Regarding the heavenly music of the spheres, Cicero writes that "Learned men, imitating this with strings and with songs, have opened for themselves a way back to this [celestial] region, even as others have done, who thanks to outstanding genius, have all their lives devoted themselves to divine studies" (*Dream of Scipio*, quoted by Guthrie, *History of Greek Philosophy*, I, 297).

45. For a comprehensive study of this topic, see Joscelyn Godwin, *The Mystery of the Seven Vowels*.

46. This is "the mystery of the hebdomad," the teaching of "Peter," set forth in *The Clementine Homilies* 17.8–10 (*Ante-Nicene Fathers*, VIII, 320–321).

47. The other two special problems are the squaring of the circle and the

trisection of any angle. For a summary, see Heath, *A History of Greek Mathematics*, I, 218–270.

48. Mathematically, this involves the problem of finding $\sqrt[3]{2}$, the cube root of two.

49. Eratosthenes, quoted by Theon of Smyrna, in Heath, *A History of Greek Mathematics*, I, 245. See also Plutarch, *Concerning the E at Delphi* 386E.

50. θεὸς ἀεὶ γεωμετρεῖ (Heath, *A History of Greek Mathematics*, I, 10).

51. *Laws* 738B.

52. *Republic* 427B.

53. Plutarch, *On the Sign of Socrates* 579D.

54. See the discussion in Robinson, *An Introduction to Early Greek Philosophy*, 81–83.

55. Plato, *Timaeus* 31B–32A (Cornford translation, 21).

56. For the names and numbers of ZEUS (612) and HERMES (353) given together in a magical formula, see *Greek Magical Papyri* 62.47–51 (Betz, 293).

57. As Heath notes in *A History of Greek Mathematics*, I, 168, the Pythagoreans discovered the existence of the irrational and proved the irrationality of $\sqrt{2}$; moreover, they showed "how to approximate as closely as we please to its numerical value." For discussion, see *History of Greek Mathematics*, I, 154–157 and 90ff. On the theory of proportion and the means, see *History of Greek Mathematics*, I, 84ff.

58. Plato, *Gorgias* 507E.

59. *The Excerpts of Theodotus* 32 (*Ante-Nicene Fathers*, VIII, 47).

60. Plato, *Laws* 657B.

61. One scholar states that Abraxas, "a name that has for its basis the numerical value 365 . . . was probably originally a secret paraphrase of the name of the Jewish God Yahweh written in four (Hebrew: *arba* = *abra*) consonants (tetragram)" (Kurt Rudolph, *Gnosis: The Nature and History of Gnosticism*, 311).

62. Iamblichus, *On the Mysteries* 6.4 (Taylor translation, 293).

63. Iamblichus, *On the Mysteries* 6.4 (Taylor translation, 293–294).

64. *Athenagoras' Plea* 18 (in Richardson, *Early Christian Fathers*, 316).

65. For sources relating to the Orphic *Hymn to Number*, see Kern, *Orphicorum Fragmenta*, 320–325. For a brief discussion, see Rohde, *Psyche: The Cult of Souls and Belief in Immortality among the Ancient Greeks*, 350, note 9.

66. Quoted by Thomas Taylor in his translation of *Iamblichus' Life of Pythagoras*, 78.

67. Guthrie, *Pythagorean Sourcebook*, 93.

68. Guthrie, *Pythagorean Sourcebook*, 94.

69. Diringer, *The Alphabet: A Key to the History of Mankind*, 458.

70. See the article on Simonides in Anthon, *Anthon's Classical Dictionary*, 1239–40. Also see the fragments in *Lyra Graeca*, vol. 2, Loeb Classical Library. See also Hyginus, *The Myths of Hyginus* 277.

71. Bond and Lea, *Gematria*, 85.

72. In their common, practical, everyday mathematics, the Greeks did not use decimal ratios. Rather, they expressed ratios as whole number fractions. For example, the string ratio of the perfect fifth was represented as 2:3, 6:9, 384:576, 486:729, or some other common value. In Pythagorean thought, however, all the phenomena of nature are related to Unity, and all these particular values express the common, underlying relationship of 666:1000. While more difficult to work with in everyday mathematics, these "decimal ratios" encapsulate the hidden, canonical essence of the other manifestations, relating them all to the Supreme Principle and reference point of ancient cosmology: the principle of Unity.

73. Technically speaking, the fact that the sphere encompassing the tetrahedron of 612 cubic units has the surface area of 1415 is a coincidence, while the other relationships are dictated by the mathematical laws of *ratio*. However, given the astonishing nature of the other relationships, we include this value here, given the possibility that it represents the work of the Far-Shooter himself!

74. For a translation of this work, see Barker, *Greek Musical Writings II: Harmonic and Acoustic Theory*.

75. As Aristides Quintilianus points out, the peculiar thing about the art of music "is that it is constituted, like the world of natural generation, out of opposites, and bears the image of the *harmonia* of the universe" (*On Music* 3.9; in Barker, *Greek Musical Writings*, II, 507).

76. For a discussion of this concept and ancient harmonic theory in general, see Nicomachus, *The Manual of Harmonics of Nicomachus the Pythagorean*, translation and commentary by Flora Levin; see also Barker, *Greek Musical Writings II*.

77. For a discussion of the Arithmetic, Harmonic, and Geometric Means, and the formation of the scale in Pythagorean science, see my introduction to *The Pythagorean Sourcebook and Library*; also see Flora Levin's translation of and commentary on *The Manual of Harmonics*. The realizations set forth in this section on the relations between harmonic science and the values of

Greek gematria were inspired by an important, unpublished work, *Means and Music*, from the corpus of the Canadian musicologist and intonation theorist Siemen Terpstra. The illustrations of the "circular graph" in this section are adapted from Terpstra's monograph on the Means.

78. Proclus, *The Commentaries of Proclus on the Timaeus of Plato*, book 3 (Taylor translation, II, 78). For the relationship between other mathematical entities and the Greek divinities, see Proclus, *Commentary on the First Book of Euclid's Elements*. For more on Proclus, his life and work, see Marinus of Samaria, *The Life of Proclus*.

79. See the discussion in Heath, *The Thirteen Books of Euclid's Elements*, II, 112.

80. Because of these perfect, symmetrical, harmonic relations, and the fact that the mathematically ordained 6:8::9:12 proportion underlies the framework of any octave and encapsulates the laws of perfect harmony, "For the Pythagoreans, this construct came to constitute the essential paradigm—of unity from multiplicity, of concinnity between opposites, in fact, of truth incarnate" (Levin, Commentary 7, in Nicomachus, *The Manual of Harmonics*). Moreover, Dr. Levin notes that when "Pythagoras found a way to express these relations in mathematical terms, he constructed a utopian ideal, a totally enclosed and self-contained cosmos in which all the parts fit together to form a perfect unity. Rooted as it was in mathematical truth, that unity was rendered explicit, coherent, knowable, and absolute" (Levin, Commentary 8, in Nicomachus, *The Manual of Harmonics*).

81. The intrinsic reciprocity between string length and tonal frequency in harmonic science recalls the words of Plato, "Good mathematicians, as of course you know, scornfully reject any attempt to cut up the unit itself into parts: if you try to break it up small, they will multiply it up again, taking good care that the unit shall never lose its oneness and appear as a multitude of parts" (*Republic* 525E; Cornford translation, 242).

82. Clement of Alexandria, *Exhortation to the Greeks* 1 (*Ante-Nicene Fathers*, II, 172).

83. Book 6, chapter 5 of Clement's *Stromata* is devoted to "the mystical meanings in the proportions of numbers, geometrical ratios, and music," in which he mentions the 6:8::9:12 harmonic proportion among other topics. The same chapter concludes with references to the mystery of the loaves and fishes, in which he says the fishes signify Greek philosophy. The "choir of mute fishes" is a fragment quoted from an otherwise lost piece of Greek tragedy (*Ante-Nicene Fathers*, II, 499–502). As the Greek poet Simonides tells

us, when Orpheus played his magical lyre, the fish jumped out of the sea to greet him; see page 352 of the present volume, where this passage is quoted.

84. Clement of Alexandria, *Exhortation to the Greeks* 1 (*Ante-Nicene Fathers*, II, 171–174).

Chapter Five

The Miraculous Feeding of the Five Thousand and Other Mysteries of the New Testament

1. Acts 14.12.

2. 2 Corinthians 5.16.

3. On the attribution of Mark, see Tyson, *A Study of Early Christianity*, 183, 190; on the attribution of Matthew, see Tyson, *Early Christianity*, 199; on the attribution of Luke, see Tyson, *Early Christianity*, 206; on the attribution of John, see Tyson, *Early Christianity*, 221.

4. For some early Christian gospels and other writings omitted from the New Testament, see Hennecke-Schneemelcher, *New Testament Apocrypha*, 2 vols., and Robinson, editor, *Nag Hammadi Library*. For an astonishing list of writings rejected as heretical by the Synod at Ariminum—most of which are now lost—see Hennecke-Schneemelcher, *New Testament Apocrypha*, I, 47–49. It is tragic to reflect upon the vast number of ancient writings, all copied by hand, which are now forever lost to us; some of them, like the lost Orphic books, would certainly offer important new insights into the thought of antiquity if they were available. The percentage of philosophical, religious, and scientific writings which has survived is, alas, infinitesimally small!

5. Irenaeus, *Against Heresies* 3.8 (*Ante-Nicene Fathers*, I, 428).

6. Origen, *Philocalia* 1.17.

7. Tyson, *A Study of Early Christianity*, 183, 190.

8. "Although he emphasizes the newness of Jesus, Matthew sees him in the light of the old. He is new, but his character is best illuminated by the Moses of ancient times. More than the other Synoptic writers, Matthew relates Jesus to the Old Testament. He looks upon the Old Testament as a set of predictions of Jesus, so he sometimes interprets his life by an Old Testament passage and sometimes molds his story so that it conforms to the predictions" (Tyson, *Early Christianity*, 202).

9. Koester, *Introduction to the New Testament*, II, 310.

10. Koester, *New Testament*, II, 311–312.

11. See, for example, Burton Throckmorton, Jr., *Gospel Parallels: A Synopsis of the First Three Gospels*. For the reader who wishes to see how little the Gospel

of John has in common with the others, see Kurt Aland, *Synopsis of the Four Gospels: Greek-English Edition of the Synopsis Quattuor Evangeliorum.*

12. See Helmut Koester's introduction to the *Gospel of Thomas* in Robinson, *The Nag Hammadi Library*, 124–125.

13. Clement of Alexandria writes that "John, the last of all, seeing that what was corporeal was set forth in the Gospels, on the entreaty of his intimate friends, and inspired by the Spirit, composed a spiritual Gospel" (Fragment from Clement of Alexandria, quoted by Eusebius, *Ecclesiastical History* 6.4; in *Ante-Nicene Fathers*, II, 580).

14. "As late as about 130, Papias of Hierapolis still placed a higher value on the oral tradition from the apostles that was passed down by their successors than on written gospels" (Koester, *New Testament*, II, 3).

15. For more on the nature of and difficulties implicit in the early Christian oral tradition, see Tyson, *Early Christianity*, chapter 5. On the development of dialogues and discourses developed from the interpretation of Jesus sayings, see Koester, *New Testament*, II, 179–180.

16. See Eisler, *Orpheus the Fisher: Comparative Studies in Orphic and Early Christian Cult Symbolism*, 125; the parallel is also drawn by Cartlidge and Dungan who, in *Documents for the Study of the Gospels*, include the tale of Pythagoras predicting the number of the fish in the net. Were there 1224 of them?

17. For the account in Porphyry's biography, see Guthrie, *Pythagorean Sourcebook*, 128; for the account in Iamblichus' biography, see *Pythagorean Sourcebook*, 64–65. These are reproduced here, in Appendix 1. For discussion see Eisler, *Orpheus the Fisher*, 121ff.

18. That is, if you ignore the feeding of the four thousand, which most scholars take to be a variant of the feeding of the five thousand.

19. Like his little brother Hermes, Apollo the Logos was also a god of shepherds. "Apollo has been called 'the God of Shepherds' . . . because the sun feeds all that the earth brings forth, so that men sing of him as the feeder of not a single kind of stock but of all kinds" (Macrobius, *Saturnalia* 1.17.43–44). Macrobius records that Apollo's titles include "Feeder of Sheep," "Guardian of Flocks," "Patron of Shepherds," and "the God with the Lamb's Fleece." These titles all point "to his function as a 'god who feeds'; so that he is recognized to be the overseer of all flocks and herds and in very truth to feed them" (*Saturnalia* 1.17.45).

20. Origen, *Philocalia* 1.8.

21. Origen, *Philocalia* 1.16.

22. By gematria, a circle with a circumference of 1224, THE NET, has a diameter of 389, THE STONE (Ὁ ΛΙΘΟΣ), one more than THE SUN (Ὁ ἫΛΙΟΣ), 388. The symbolism suggested by this arrangement is that the Foundation Stone—the solar omphalos—represents the Seed or the First Cause which transcends time and space, while the woven net represents the Veils of Manifestation which spring from it. On the cosmological symbolism of weaving and "the net of time and space," see René Guénon, *The Symbolism of the Cross* and Adrian Snodgrass, *The Symbolism of the Stupa*; both of these works discuss the symbolism of the sacred center and the related symbolism of the woven world fabric. Classical scholars such as A. B. Cook (*Zeus*, II, 169ff.) and Jane Harrison ("Aegis—ΑΓΡΗΝΟΝ") have puzzled over the mystery of the net-covered omphalos stone with unsatisfying results, but seen from a cosmological perspective, the symbolism of the net becomes intelligible. Interestingly, there was also an Orphic book which was simply entitled ΔΙΚΤΥΟΝ, "The Net," which is the same term used in John 21 (Kern, *Orphicorum Fragmenta*, 297). G. R. S. Mead in his *Orpheus* links "The Net" with another Orphic manuscript, "The Veil," and cites ancient references which suggest that these works dealt with the Veil of Nature and the mysteries of generation (Mead, *Orpheus*, 31).

Chapter 6
The Gospel of John and the Gnostic Tradition

1. *Excerpts of Theodotos* 78, quoted in Robinson and Koester, *Trajectories through Early Christianity*, 140.
2. 1 Corinthians 12.8.
3. Kurt Rudolph, *Gnosis: The Nature and History of Gnosticism*, 56.
4. *Gospel of Truth* 22.3–20 (in Robinson, *Nag Hammadi Library*, 42).
5. Irenaeus, *Against Heresies* 1.5.4 (*Ante-Nicene Fathers*, I, 323).
6. *Gospel of Truth* 31.4–17 (translation from the first edition of *The Nag Hammadi Library in English*).
7. *Gospel of Truth* 31.28–32 (in Robinson, *Nag Hammadi Library*, 46).
8. *Tripartite Tractate* 123.29–35 (in Robinson, *Nag Hammadi Library*, 97).
9. *Gospel of Truth* 18.7–10 (in Robinson, *Nag Hammadi Library*, 40).
10. See Robinson, *Nag Hammadi Library*, 220ff.
11. Hennecke-Schneemelcher, *New Testament Apocrypha*, II, 807–808.
12. As Rudolph notes, "The manner in which the redeeming function of the Logos is seen to operate without assuming any personal figure is shown in the Hermetic texts," but also impressively by a Nag Hammadi tractate, *The*

Authoritative Teaching. See Rudolph, *Gnosis*, 144.

13. Summarizing Rudolph, *Gnosis*, 131.

14. Rudolph, *Gnosis*, 132.

15. In *A Separate God: The Christian Origins of Gnosticism*, Simone Pétrement argues against the now commonly held view that Gnosis is pre-Christian. Despite the length and complexity of her argument, however, it remains unconvincing and painfully strains to account for the historical evidence to the contrary.

16. *Gospel of Philip* 67.26–27 (in Robinson, *Nag Hammadi Library*, 150).

17. *Gospel of Thomas* 108 (in Robinson, *Nag Hammadi Library*, 137).

18. "This conviction—that whoever explores human experience simultaneously discovers divine reality—is one of the elements that marks gnosticism as a distinctly religious movement. Simon Magus, Hippolytus reports, claimed that each human being is a dwelling place, 'and that in him dwells an infinite power . . . the root of the universe.' But since that infinite power exists in two modes, one actual, the other potential, so this infinite power 'exists in a latent condition in everyone,' but potentially, not actually'" (Elaine Pagels, *The Gnostic Gospels*, 134–35).

19. *Gospel of Thomas* 1 (in Robinson, *Nag Hammadi Library*, 126).

20. *Gospel of Thomas* 3 (in Robinson, *Nag Hammadi Library*, 126).

21. *Gospel of Thomas* 113 (in Robinson, *Nag Hammadi Library*, 138).

22. *Gospel of Thomas* 51 (in Robinson, *Nag Hammadi Library*, 132).

23. Koester, *Introduction to the New Testament*, II, 153.

24. Eusebius, *Ecclesiastical History* 6.14, quoting Clement of Alexandria (in *Ante-Nicene Fathers*, II, 580).

25. Koester, *New Testament*, II, 198.

26. Koester, *New Testament*, II, 179–180.

27. Koester, *New Testament*, II, 180.

28. Koester, *New Testament*, II, 181.

29. Koester, *New Testament*, II, 189.

30. Koester, *New Testament*, II, 190.

31. "Cosmos is second God, a life that cannot die" (*Corpus Hermeticum* 8.1). "Cosmos is God's Son" (*Corpus Hermeticum* 9.8).

32. Jonas, *The Gnostic Religion*, 320.

33. Rudolph, *Gnosis*, 159.

34. Rudolph, *Gnosis*, 159.

35. John 9.47.

36. John 19.28.

37. Koester notes "a section interpolated [at a later date] into the Johannine discourse about the bread of life speaks about the physical eating and drinking of Jesus' blood (6.52b–59), whereas John otherwise speaks about Jesus as the bread of life who is present in his word (6.63, 68). Obviously, a redactor speaks here who wants to insist upon a realistic interpretation of the eucharist, which was also advocated by Ignatius of Antioch around the turn of the first century" (Koester, *New Testament*, II, 187). See also Koester, *New Testament*, II, 191.

38. John 5.24. Koester points out "a number of obviously interpolated remarks about the future resurrection of the dead . . . and the future judgment" which "contradict the Johannine discourses about the presence of judgment and resurrection" (Koester, *New Testament*, II, 187).

39. John 3.3.

40. See the remarks in Rudolf, *Gnosis*, 159, in which he quotes the conclusions of L. Schottroff, *Der Glaubende und die feindliche Welt*. See also Rudolph's remarks on the Gospel of John and the Johannine Epistles (which were written by someone other than the author of the Fourth Gospel); Rudolph, *Gnosis*, 305–6. For a discussion of the "Jewish-Gnostic" background of the Gospel of John, see Werner Georg Kümmel, *Introduction to the New Testament*, 217–228; like Koester, however, Kümmel's definition of Gnosis is too limited.

41. "I am the vine, you are the branches. He who abides in me, and I in him, he it is that bears much fruit . . ." (John 15.5).

Chapter Seven

New Light on the Mithraic Mysteries

1. Vermaseren, *Mithras: The Secret God*, 36.

2. Ernest Renan, quoted by Ulansey, *The Origins of the Mithraic Mysteries: Cosmology and Salvation in the Ancient World*, 4.

3. "The rock of Mithras' birth contains both light and fire; he who is born from the rock is thus a fiery god of light. This conception is almost certainly based on a very ancient tradition dating from the time when man first discovered that both light and fire could be produced by striking a flint" (Vermaseren, *Mithras*, 76). This notion could also be compared with the Stoic idea of the fiery *spermatikos logos* hidden in matter. Because of his birth, Mithras bore the title *petrogenês* (πετρογενής), "rock born" and *theos ek petras* (θεὸς ἐκ πέτρας), "god from the rock."

4. See Justin Martyr, *Dialogue with Trypho* 78 (*Ante-Nicene Fathers*, I, 237), where the birth of Jesus in the cave is compared with the birth of Mithras. See

also Gervers, "The Iconography of the Cave in Christian and Mithraic Tradition."

5. Porphyry, in his work *On the Cave of the Nymphs* 6, notes that the cave is "an image of the cosmos that Mithras created" and that "the objects arranged symmetrically within the cave were symbols of the elements and regions of the cosmos" (Lamberton translation, 25). For more on the use of cosmological symbolism in Mithraic temples, see R. L. Gordon, "The Sacred Geography of a Mithraeum: The Example of Sette Sfere."

6. Vermaseren, *Mithras*, 37.

7. Vermaseren, *Mithras*, 103. The creative sacrifice of the bull and the creative sacrifice of Christ are related symbolically because of their common date, the vernal equinox; see Deman, "Mithras and Christ: Some Iconographical Similarities," 511.

8. Vermaseren, *Mithras*, 177; see also Burkert, *Ancient Mystery Cults*, 111–112.

9. Vermaseren, *Mithras*, 44, 103.

10. On the astronomical orientation of Mithraic temples, see Lentz, "Some Peculiarities Not Hitherto Fully Understood of 'Roman' Mithraic Sanctuaries and Representations"; Vermaseren, *Mithras*, 67; and Burkert, *Ancient Mystery Cults*, 83.

11. Symbols of the seven grades appear in a mosaic in a Mithraeum at Ostia; for reproductions and discussion, see Vermaseren, *Mithras*, chapter 14, "The Seven Grades of Initiation." For a complete illustration of "the mosaic of the seven grades," see Beck, "Mithraism Since Franz Cumont," 2012.

12. Cumont, *Mysteries of Mithra*, 131; see also illustrations in Vermaseren, *Mithras*, 73, 77.

13. Tertullian, *On Prescription Against Heretics* 40 (*Ante-Nicene Fathers*, III, 262); discussion in Weigall, *The Paganism in Our Christianity*, 133–134. Tertullian also refers to Mithraic baptism in his work *On Baptism* 5 (*Ante-Nicene Fathers*, III, 671).

14. Tertullian, *On Prescription Against Heretics* (*Ante-Nicene Fathers*, III, 262–263); discussion in Vermaseren, *Mithras*, 103.

15. Justin Martyr, *First Apology* 66 (*Ante-Nicene Fathers*, I, 185). The Christian eucharist, he writes, "the wicked devils have imitated in the mysteries of Mithras, commanding the same thing to be done."

16. Vermaseren, *Mithras*, 102–103.

17. Firmicus Maternus, *De errore profanarum religionum* 22, cited by Angus, *Religious Quests of the Graeco-Roman World*, 179.

18. Weigall, *The Paganism in Our Christianity*, 130.

19. Vermaseren, *Mithras*, 11, 103. As Cumont notes, illustrating his observation with a photograph, "The Christians, in order to render places contaminated by the presence of a dead body ever afterward unfit for worship, sometimes slew the refractory priests of Mithra and buried them in the ruins of their sanctuaries, now forever profaned" (Cumont, *Mysteries of Mithra*, 204–205).

20. Godwin, *Mystery Religions in the Ancient World*, 98.

21. See A. S. Geden, *Select Passages Illustrating Mithraism*, a mere 80 pages of large type. See also the remarks of Burkert, *Ancient Mystery Cults*, 42, on the absolute secrecy and scarcity of literary references.

22. See Hinnells, "Reflections on the Bull-Slaying Scene," 292.

23. See Gordon, "Franz Cumont and the Doctrines of Mithraism."

24. See also his later, popular article, "The Mithraic Mysteries."

25. Ulansey, *Origins of the Mithraic Mysteries*, 20.

26. See Liddell and Scott, *Greek-English Lexicon*, s.v. Περσεύς.

27. Ulansey, *Origins of the Mithraic Mysteries*, 79–80.

28. Ulansey, *Origins*, 93.

29. Ulansey, *Origins*, 40–41.

30. Ulansey, *Origins*, 93.

31. Ulansey, *Origins*, 125.

32. Plato writes that the name Apollo means *a-polos*, referring to the rotation of the cosmic spheres on the world axis which results in *harmonia mundi*: "And with reference to music we have to understand that *alpha* often signifies 'together,' and here it denotes moving together in the heavens about the poles, as we call them, and harmony in song, which is called concord; for, as the ingenious musicians and astronomers tell us, all these things move together by a kind of harmony. And this god directs the harmony, making them all move together, among both gods and men" (*Cratylus* 405D; Fowler translation, Loeb Classical Library). According to Hyginus, Apollo's maternal grandfather was Polos, the celestial pole (see *The Myths of Hyginus* 140 and Kerényi, *Gods of the Greeks*, 130, for discussion). For another ancient etymology linking Apollo with the celestial pole, see Macrobius, *Saturnalia* 1.17.7.

33. For the omphalos at Delphi as "the axis," see pp. 67, 332, 374–75.

34. Betz, *Greek Magical Papyri*, 48.

35. Betz, *Greek Magical Papyri*, 48.

36. Betz, *Greek Magical Papyri*, 50.

37. Betz, *Greek Magical Papyri*, 51.

38. For ancient sources and iconography relating to the symbolism of Aeon turning the wheel of Time (and/or the zodiac), see Levi, "Aion," 284–314.

39. *Hymn to King Helios*, in Julian, *Works of the Emperor Julian*, I, 353–435.

40. Levi, "Aion," 288–291.

41. Godwin, *Arktos: The Polar Myth in Science, Symbolism, and Nazi Survival*, 163.

42. Ulansey, *Origins*, 94.

43. Ulansey, *Origins*, 125.

44. Joscelyn Godwin, who suggested back in 1981 that the Mithraic tauroctony commemorates the passing age of Taurus (*Mystery Religions in the Ancient World*, 99), points out in a more recent work that, "Ironically enough, by the time that Mithraism was fully established, the equinoctial point was already moving out of Aries and into Pisces: an event celebrated by such words as 'Worthy is the Lamb that was slain' (Apocalypse 5.12) and 'Behold, I shall make you fishers of men' (Matthew 4.19)" (Godwin, *Arktos*, 162).

Chapter Eight
The Birth of the Aeon: Christianity and the Renewal of Time

1. Plato, *Timaeus* 37D. Plato adds that time is a moving image of eternity "according to number."

2. Franz, *Time: Rhythm and Repose*, 31.

3. See Eliade, *The Sacred and the Profane*, chapter 2 ("Sacred Time and Myths"); *The Two and the One*, chapter 3 ("Cosmic and Eschatological Renewal"); *Cosmos and History*, chapters 1 and 2 ("Archetypes and Repetition" and "The Regeneration of Time"); *Patterns in Comparative Religion*, chapter 11 ("Sacred Time and the Myth of Eternal Renewal"). For some astronomical views relating to the concept of the Great Year in traditional cultures, see B. L. van der Waerden, "The Great Year in Greek, Persian and Hindu Astronomy."

4. As one scholar notes, "The celebration of the birth of the sun god, which was accompanied by a profusion of light and torches and the decoration of branches and small trees, had captivated the followers of the cult to such a degree that even after they had been converted to Christianity they continued to celebrate the feast of the birth of the sun god" (Halsberghe, *The Cult of Sol Invictus*, 174). On the adoption of December 25 by the early church, see Excursus I, "The Origin of Christmas," in Hyde, *Paganism to Christianity in the Roman Empire*, 249–256.

5. For more on January 6 as the birthday of Aeon, see Duchesne-Guillemin,

"Jesus' Trimorphism and the Differentiation of the Magi," 93–96. Ioannes Lydus, *De mensibus* 4.1, also attests to January 6 as the birthday of Aeon; see Levi, "Aion," 278.

6. Epiphanius, *Panarion* 51.22.10 (Amidon translation, 182). We quote from Jung, *Aion*, 104.

7. Hans Leisegang, "The Mystery of the Serpent," 228–229.

8. On Nile water turning to wine on January 6, see R. A. Wild, *Water in the Cultic Worship of Isis and Sarapis*, 91, quoting the church father Epiphanius. For water turning to wine in the Dionysian festivals, see Pausanius, *Description of Greece* 6.26; Pliny, *Natural History* 2.106.231 and 31.13.16; Athenaeus, *The Deipnosophists* 1.34A. For an excellent discussion of the January 6 wine miracles and their connection with the January 6 baptism of Jesus and the January 6 wine miracle at Cana, see Arthur Weigall, *The Paganism in Our Christianity*, chapter 22, "The Origin of Epiphany." On Dionysian wine miracles, also see Martin P. Nilsson, *The Dionysiac Mysteries of the Hellenistic and Roman Age*, 97.

9. See Levi, "Aion," 278, and Aristotle, *On the Heavens* 1.279A.

10. 1 Corinthians 2.6.

11. John 3.16, 36; 4.14; 5.24; 6.27; 6.40; 12.50.

12. "There is a well known theorem which proves that the Zodiac, like the planets, moves from west to east at the rate of one part in a hundred years, and that this movement in the lapse of so long a time changes the local relation of the signs; so that, on the one hand, there is the invisible sign, and on the other, as it were, the visible figure of it; and events, they say, are discovered not from the figure, but from the invisible sign; though it cannot possibly be apprehended" (Origen, *Philocalia of Origen*, 191).

Jung notes that "Being the twelfth sign of the Zodiac, Pisces denotes the end of the astrological year and also a new beginning. This characteristic coincides with the claim of Christianity to be the beginning and end of all things, and with its eschatological expectation of the end of the world and the coming of God's kingdom" (Jung, *Aion*, 114). This conception of the precession of the ages or Aeons is also present in the thought of Origen, who writes that "as the last month is the end of the year, after which the beginning of another month ensues, so it may be that, since several ages complete as it were a year of ages, the present age is 'the end,' after which certain 'ages to come' will ensue, of which the age to come is the beginning, and in those coming ages God will 'shew the riches of his grace in kindness' (Ephesians 2.7)" (Origen, *De Oratione*, 27; Oulton/Chadwick translation, cited by Jung, *Aion*, 114).

13. See Krupp, "Astronomers, Pyramids, and Priests," 218–219.

14. Lamy, *Egyptian Mysteries: New Light on Ancient Spiritual Knowledge*, 38.

15. Lamy, *Egyptian Mysteries*, 38.

16. Santillana and Dechend, *Hamlet's Mill: An Essay on Myth and the Frame of Time*, 60.

17. For a discussion of Amen-Ra and Zeus Ammon, along with reproductions of the ram-horned Zeus, see Cook, *Zeus*, I, 346–390.

18. Santillana and Dechend, *Hamlet's Mill*, 318. *The Oxford Classical Dictionary*, in the article on the ancient constellations, confirms that the constellation Aries "was the ram with the golden fleece," whose fleece "was the object of the Argonauts' quest" (*Oxford Classical Dictionary*, 283).

19. Mark 1.17; Matthew 4.19.

20. "But we, little fishes, after the example of our 'ΙΧΘΥΣ Jesus Christ, are born in water . . ." Tertullian, *On Baptism* 1 (*Ante-Nicene Fathers*, III, 669). See also Jung, *Aion*, 92, 113. As Jung notes, "the baptismal bath was described as a *piscinia* (fish-pond) quite early" (*Aion*, 89).

21. Ἰησοῦς Χριστὸς Θεοῦ Ὑιὸς Σωτήρ = 'ΙΧΘΥΣ. One of the so-called *Christian Sibyllines* encodes the formula as an acrostic: the initial letters of the Greek phrase "Jesus Christ, Son of God, Savior, Cross" begin each line of the oracle. See Hennecke-Schneemelcher, *New Testament Apocrypha*, II, 732–733. For more on the symbolism of the fish in early Christianity and other ancient religions, see the remarkable study by Doelger, ΙΧΘΥΣ: *Das Fischsymbol in frühchristlicher Zeit*.

22. Cf. "Worthy is the Lamb who was slain" (Revelation 5.12).

23. "The advent of Christ the Fish marks our age" (Santillana and Dechend, *Hamlet's Mill*, 59). As Jung succinctly notes, "To the extent that Christ was regarded as the new aeon, it would be clear to anyone acquainted with astrology that he was born as the first fish of the Pisces era, and was doomed to die as the last ram (ἀρνίον, lamb) of the declining Aries era" (*Aion*, 90). See also the discussion in Michell, *City of Revelation*, chapter 1, "Time and Portents."

24. Franz, *Time*, 80. For the Egyptian gods and goddesses of the twelve hours of the night and the day, see Budge, *Gods of the Egyptians*, II, 300–302; for the gods of the decans (the 36 divisions, in 10 degree increments, of the celestial sphere), ibid., 304–310; for the gods of the day of the month, ibid., 320–322. The notion of "the gods of time" is reflected in the planetary names of the days of the week; see "Celestial Archetypes IV: Cosmic Cycles" in this volume, 244–245.

25. The Florentine Renaissance, as Noel Cobb observes, "saw the great flowering of soul in its time as intimately related to the return of Orpheus," especially in relation to the work of Marsilio Ficino (Cobb, *Archetypal Imagination: Glimpses of the Gods in Life and Art*, 244ff.). As Ficino himself wrote, "This age, like a golden age, has brought back those liberal disciplines that were practically extinguished, grammar, oratory, painting, sculpture, architecture, music and the ancient singing of songs to the Orphic lyre" (translation by John Warden, "Orpheus and Ficino," 88).

26. On the symbolism of the garden in the Western esoteric traditions, see Fideler, "The Rose Garden of the Philosophers."

27. Graves, *The Greek Myths* 5.B.

28. Clark, *Myth and Symbol in Ancient Egypt*, 103.

29. Richard Barber, *The Knight and Chivalry*, 77.

30. For an excellent analysis and discussion, see Irving Singer, *The Nature of Love 2: Courtly and Romantic*.

31. Quoted by G. R. S. Mead, *Fragments of a Faith Forgotten*, 4.

32. Virgil, *Eclogue* 4.

33. As one scholar notes, "There is little doubt that the three elements Virgil welded together in his fourth Eclogue, namely, the return of the golden age, the solar kingship and the infant saviour, already existed a long time before him, even if they had not yet been welded into a synthesis. The Babylonian doctrine of the Great Year and, earlier, the conception of a periodic renewal and an eternal return had spread the hope of a new era as far as Italy. This is proved by Roman coins at least since Caesar's death. . ." (J. Duchesne-Guillemin, "Jesus' Trimorphism and the Differentiation of the Magi," 94–95).

34. Jesus' birth is placed by scholars between 8 and 6 B.C.E. Due to the illusion of retrograde motion, the conjunction of Jupiter and Saturn occured three times in 7 B.C.E. in Pisces over a period of eight months. J. H. Charlesworth notes that "astrologers and astronomers eagerly anticipated the celestial wonder," which was predicted on a cuneiform tablet, "The Celestial Almanac of Sippar" (Charlesworth, editor, *The Old Testament Pseudepigrapha*, I, 479, and the accompanying notes). This discussion takes place in Charlesworth's introduction to "The Treatise Composed by Shem, the Son of Noah, Concerning the Beginning of the Year [World, Age] and Whatever Occurs in It," an ancient Jewish astrological treatise which may be "an unparalleled record of this monumental shift, the Precession of the Equinoxes," the movement of the spring point from Aries into Pisces. For a

complete study of the triple conjunction of 7 B.C.E., see David Hughes, *The Star of Bethlehem: An Astronomer's Confirmation*. See also the article by Ronald Oriti, "The Star of Bethlehem."

Chapter Nine

The Orphic Christ and the "New Song" of Christianity

1. Macchioro, *From Orpheus to Paul: A History of Orphism*, 213–214.
2. See Macchioro, *From Orpheus to Paul*, 210–211, 213–214.
3. For a discussion of the playthings of Dionysus, see Guthrie, *Orpheus and Greek Religion*, 120ff. See also Mead, *Orpheus*, 160ff.
4. For the most comprehensive account with complete citations, see Cook, *Zeus*, II, 1030–2.
5. Origen, *Contra Celsum* 5.17 (Chadwick translation, 194).
6. Clement of Alexandria, *Exhortation to the Greeks* 2 (*Ante-Nicene Fathers*, II, 176). The cauldron in which Dionysus' fragments were boiled by the Titans was symbolically identified with the Delphic Tripod. According to Tatian, the omphalos was his tomb (as it was said to be of the slain Python); see Fontenrose, *Python: A Study of Delphic Myth and its Origins*, 375ff. On the important relationship of Apollo and Dionysus at Delphi, see Plutarch, *On the E at Delphi* 388F–C.
7. For this argument at greater length, see Macchioro, *From Orpheus to Paul*, 190ff.
8. Clement of Alexandria, *Exhortation to the Greeks* 1 (*Ante-Nicene Fathers*, II, 171).
9. Clement of Alexandria, *Exhortation to the Greeks* 1 (*Ante-Nicene Fathers*, II, 172).
10. "You make everything bloom, and with your versatile lyre / you harmonize the poles . . ." (*Orphic Hymns* 34.16–17; Athanassikis translation, 47–49); see also Skythinos, frag. 1, quoted in Levin, *The Harmonics of Nicomachus and the Pythagorean Tradition*, 41. The Orphic Hymn also states that Apollo, as the harmony of the universe, holds "the master seal of the entire *kosmos*."
11. Clement of Alexandria, *Exhortation to the Greeks* 1 (*Ante-Nicene Fathers*, II, 172).
12. Clement of Alexandria, *Exhortation to the Greeks* 1 (*Ante-Nicene Fathers*, II, 172). In quoting from the *Ante-Nicene Fathers* translation I have rendered *supramundane* as "Extraterrestrial" and *Word* as "Logos."
13. Clement of Alexandria, *Exhortation to the Greeks* 1 (*Ante-Nicene Fathers*,

II, 173).

14. This symbolism is not confined to Clement. As Robert Eisler notes, "Eusebius, the friend of Constantine, in the fourteenth chapter of his panegyric on that emperor, simply compares the Logos, taming and redeeming mankind as if playing on an instrument, with Orpheus displaying his magical skill on the mystic lyre" (Eisler, *Orpheus the Fisher*, 54).

15. See discussion in Weigall, *The Paganism in Our Christianity*, 223.

16. Guthrie, *Orpheus and Greek Religion*, 23, and plate 18 a–b.

17. For the work and thought of Philo, see the two studies by E. R. Goodenough, *An Introduction to Philo Judaeus* and *By Light, Light: The Mystic Gospel of Hellenistic Judaism*.

18. Angus, *Religious Quests of the Graeco-Roman World*, 112–113.

19. Clement of Alexandria plainly tells us that he has used techniques of concealment, having "interspersed the dogmas which are the germs of true knowledge, so that the discovery of the sacred traditions may not be easy to any one of the uninitiated." For discussion of his technique, see Molland, *The Conception of the Gospel in the Alexandrian Theology*, 7ff.

20. Clement of Alexandria, *Stromata*, book 6, chaper 5, "The Mystical Meanings in the Proportions of Numbers, Geometrical Ratios, and Music" (*Ante-Nicene Fathers*, II, 499–502). Clement pleads to the reader to grant him pardon "if I shrink from advancing further" in the treatment of this subject.

21. The underlying theological bias of many scholars, based on the premise "it can't exist, therefore it doesn't," has prevented them from penetrating to the heart of these studies. Yet how can one really appreciate the thought of antiquity if you start off with the premise that ancient Greek philosophy and religion was merely "a preparation for the gospel" (*praeparatio evangelica*) or that "Christianity is a thing that is wholly *sui generis*. It is something unique and not a derivative from any cult or other institution, nor has its essential character been changed or touched by any such influence"? (Rahner, *Greek Myths and Christian Mystery*, 90, 28).

22. For the beautiful account of Jesus singing to his followers and leading them in a cosmic dance, see the *Acts of John* 94–96 (in Hennecke-Schneemelcher, *New Testament Apocrypha*, II, 227–232); for translation and commentary see Mead, *The Hymn of Jesus*. In his song, Jesus hymns, "To the Universe belongs the dancer / He who does not dance does not know what happens." The symbolism of the Choirleader of the Celestial Dance was well developed in antiquity; for a massive study (over 600 pages), see Miller, *Measures of Wisdom: The Cosmic Dance in Classical and Christian Antiquity*.

23. Walter Hyde, *Paganism to Christianity in the Roman Empire*, 198. Later, in 529 C.E., the emperor Justinian issued an edict closing down the Platonic Academy in Athens which had stood as a cultural and educational center for nearly one thousand years.

24. Hyde, *Paganism to Christianity in the Roman Empire*, 199. Hyde's chapter on "The Triumph of Christianity" offers a good picture of the anti-intellectual nature of the early church and its campaign to wipe out other forms of religious expression, which included the destruction of books and temples, the closing of schools, and killing adherents of other faiths.

25. P. Gardner, *The Growth of Christianity*, quoted in Angus, *Religious Quests of the Graeco-Roman World*, 151.

26. An edict of February 37, 391 outlawed all pagan worship in Rome and visits to pagan temples. On November 8, 392, an edict called for the severe punishment of anyone involved in the practice of pagan religions, including private devotions. See Vermaseren, *Mithras: The Secret God*, 191; for further discussion see Hyde, *Paganism to Christianity in the Roman Empire*, chapter 7.

27. Pagels, *The Gnostic Gospels*, xxiii.

Chapter Ten
The Harmony that Was, Is, and Shall Ever Be

1. See chapter 1, "The Uroboros," in Neumann, *The Origins and History of Consciousness*.

2. See Jung, *Psychology and Alchemy*, chapter 5, "The Lapis-Christ Parallel," and Edinger, *Ego and Archetype*, chapter 10.

3. See index to Jung, *Psychology and Alchemy*, s.v. *filius philosophorum*.

4. Edinger, *Ego and Archetype*, chapter 5.

5. See Clement of Alexandria, quoted on page 50 of the present work.

6. Purce, *The Mystic Spiral: Journey of the Soul*, 9–10.

7. This traditional Pythagorean understanding was set forth by the Christian gnostic teacher Monoimus who held that the Monad, the source of creation, is akin to "a certain musical harmony, which comprises all things in itself" and goes on to manifest and generate all things (Hippolytus, *Refutation of All Heresies* 8.5; in *Ante-Nicene Fathers* 5, 121).

8. "The physicist can point out that every particle of a vibrating string participates in the fundamental vibration and that a vibrating string will divide itself into any number of identical segments; each such segment produces a corresponding overtone. The musician explains the overtone series as a psychological reality which exists not only in nature but which necessarily

agrees with a particular norm of our soul. If this were not so, we would not respond to the particular character of the various tone values" (Levarie and Levy, *Tone: A Study in Musical Acoustics*, 48). This work contains an excellent discussion of the underlying principles of harmonic manifestation from which all musical expression originates and also explores the philosophical realizations which arise from a study of these principles. A lengthy chapter on the monochord describes simple experiments relating to the division of the canon.

9. Cicero wrote that "For walk where we will, we tread upon some story," and, as H. J. Rose succinctly observes, "Every spot in Greece and in the Greek colonies had its local legend" (Rose, *A Handbook of Greek Mythology*, 254). The animated and enchanted landscapes of traditional cultures when contrasted with desacralized landscape of modern civilization and its shopping malls represents a very different world indeed.

10. See John Michell and Christine Rhone, *Twelve-Tribe Nations and the Science of Enchanting the Landscape*, particularly chapter 8, summarizing the work of Jean Richer, *Géographie sacrée du monde grec* (Sacred Geography of the Greek World). An English language translation of Richer's book by Christine Rhone is forthcoming from the State University of New York Press.

11. For the underlying Pythagorean cosmological perspective which inspired the Gothic cathedrals, with special emphasis on the cathedral at Chartres, see *The Gothic Cathedral* by Otto von Simson, in which he devotes an excellent chapter to "Measure and Light."

12. See Rudolf Wittkower, *Architectural Principles in the Age of Humanism* and George Hersey, *Pythagorean Palaces: Magic and Architecture in the Italian Renaissance*.

Notes to the Documentary Illustrations

Orpheus the Theologian

ALL THEOLOGY: "All theology among the Greeks is sprung from the mystical doctrine of Orpheus. First Pythagoras was taught the holy rites concerning the gods by Aglaophamus; next Plato took over the whole lore concerning these matters from the Pythagorean and Orphic writings" (Proclus, *Commentary on Plato's Timaeus*, cited by Linforth, *The Arts of Orpheus*, 252).

THE BEASTS GATHERED ROUND: This mythic scene was depicted in the Grove of the Muses on Mount Helicon. Pausanius, who visited it, tells us that "by the side of Orpheus the Thracian stands a statue of Telete ("Initiation"), and around him are beasts of stone and bronze listening to his singing" (Pausanius, *Description of Greece* 9.30.4). The music of Apollo, with whom Orpheus was related, possessed a similar power to attract and tame beasts; see Euripides, *Alcestis* 578ff. According to a cosmological interpretation of this well-known scene, Orpheus represents the harmony of the universe: the seven strings of his lyre symbolize the planets, and the animals which surround him are the figures of the zodiac (Lucian, *On Astrology*, chapter 10).

THE FISH JUMPED OUT OF THE SEA TO GREET HIM: According to the poet Simonides (fragment 51, in *Lyra Graeca*, II, 311):

> Above his head there hovered birds innumerable,
> and fishes leapt clean from the blue water because
> of his sweet music.

Compare also the fragment about the "mute choir of fishes" preserved by Clement of Alexandria, cited on page 101 of the present work. As Dr. Eisler notes, the story of the fishes being summoned by music has an interesting historical background: the sacred, oracular fish at Apollo's sanctuaries in Lycia were known as *orphoi* (singular: *orphôs* or *orphos*). According to Pliny (*Natural History* 32.8), at the thrice-repeated call of a flute player, the oracular fish are summoned. Varro also mentions the practice of priests calling the sacred fish in Lydia to their feeding places by music (Varro, *On Agriculture* 3.17). Dr. Eisler argues that the name *Orpheus* is "an absolutely regular derivation from that old noun" *orphôs*, "and simply means 'the fisher'" (Eisler, *Orpheus the Fisher: Comparative Studies in Orphic and Early Christian Cult Symbolism*, 14, 297–298; see also plate 20). Aelian notes that "tame fish which answer to a call and gladly accept food are to be found and kept at many places," and, as one scholar notes, these sacred fish and other displays "were one of the things that caused religion to be talked about. As a wonder or a curiosity, they drew people to strange places of worship" (MacMullen, *Paganism in the Roman Empire*, 35). For other examples of fish being called or charmed by music, see Aelian, *On Animals* 6.31–32, 12.18; Pliny, *Natural History* 9.8; Plutarch, *Dinner of the Seven Wise Men* 162F.

MUSIC COULD STOP A STREAM IN ITS COURSE: Apollonius Rhodius, *Argonautica* 1.27.

"ORPHIC" AND "BACCHIC" AS "EGYPTIAN" AND "PYTHAGOREAN": Herodotus, *History* 2.81. For Orpheus bringing the rites of Isis and Osiris from Egypt, and transforming them into the Greek mysteries of Demeter and

Dionysus, see Diodorus Siculus, *Library of History* 1.96.4–6 and 4.25.

TRAVELED TO EGYPT: See Diodorus, cited above.

INVENTED THE ALPHABET: Cramer, *Anecd. Oxon.* iv. 318, 15, cited by Eisler, *Orpheus the Fisher*, 42.

TAUGHT GREECE THE MYSTERIES OF INITIATION: Guthrie, *Orpheus and Greek Religion*, 17. Other sources assembled in Linforth, *The Arts of Orpheus.*

A PRIEST OF BOTH APOLLO AND DIONYSUS: According to Aeschylus, Orpheus "neglected the worship of Dionysus who made him famous and instead worshipped the Sun . . . Apollo, as the greatest of the gods." For this he was torn to pieces by the Maenads, the female followers of Dionysus, and thus Proclus notes that "Orpheus, as the founder of the Dionysiac mysteries, is said in the myths to have suffered the same fate as the god himself" (Proclus, *Commentary on Plato's Republic*, cited in Eisler, *Orpheus the Fisher*, 12); yet, on a Thracian inscription, Orpheus is identified as a "companion of Apollo" (Guthrie, *Orpheus and Greek Religion*, 42). According to Pindar, *Pythian Ode* 4.176–177, Orpheus is the son of Apollo. For a further discussion on the relationship between Orpheus, Apollo, and Dionysus, see Guthrie, *Orpheus and Greek Religion*, 39, 42ff., 54. For an excellent discussion of Orpheus as the mediator between Apollo and Dionysus, see Lee Irwin, "The Orphic Mystery: Harmony and Mediation."

WAS THE FIRST TO GIVE GODS NAMES: *Athenagoras' Plea* 18, in Richardson, editor, *Early Christian Fathers*, 316.

ORPHEUS ON "THE ETERNAL ESSENCE OF NUMBER": Iamblichus, *Life of Pythagoras*, in Guthrie, *The Pythagorean Sourcebook and Library*, 93.

THE PYTHAGOREANS RECEIVED THE ORPHIC NUMBER THEOLOGY: Syrianus, *Commentary on Aristotle's Metaphysics*, book 13; quoted and translated by Thomas Taylor in *Iamblichus' Life of Pythagoras*, 78.

CHRIST AS ORPHEUS: The illustration reproduced is a painted ceiling from the Domitilla catacomb, third century C.E. The symbolism of Christ as Orpheus synthesizes the symbolism of the Greek bard with the Jewish theory of the Messianic age of the Peaceable Kingdom, a recapitulation of the Golden Age (for ancient sources: Eisler, *Orpheus the Fisher*, plate 28). Eisler, plate 29, reproduces a painting of "David as a lyre-playing shepherd represented in the typical attitude of Orpheus among the animals," and notes that "the Christian Orpheus among with wild and tame animals is the reborn Messianic King David." Like Pythagoras, David was an ancient "music therapist": "And whenever the evil spirit from God was upon Saul, David took the lyre and played it with his hand; so Saul was refreshed, and was well, and the evil spirit departed from him" (1 Samuel 16.23). See also Hall, *A History of Ideas and Images in Italian Art*, 65–66.

THE "TRUE GOD CRUCIFIED": "Christ crucified is the 'true Orpheus,' who carried home mankind as his bride from the depths of dark Hades—the 'Ορφεὺς Βακχικός as he is called in a famous early Christian representation of the Crucifixion" (Hugo Rahner, "The Christian Mystery and the Pagan Mysteries," 379).

ADDITIONAL NOTE: For a comprehensive introduction to the Orphic lore, see R. C. Hogart's introductory essay in *The Hymns of Orpheus*; this work also contains an extensive, annotated bibliography to Orphic studies. See also Alderink, *Creation and Salvation in Ancient Orphism*.

The Pythagorean Tradition

FIRST TO CALL THE UNIVERSE A COSMOS: "It was Pythagoras who first called heaven *kosmos*, because it is perfect, and 'adorned' with infinite beauty and living beings" (Anonymous biography of Pythagoras preserved by Photius in *The Pythagorean Sourcebook and Library*, 139).

PYTHAGORAS AND ORPHEUS: Orphism and Pythagoreanism were "believed by the ancients to be two sides of the same philosophico-religious system" (Guthrie, *Orpheus and Greek Religion*, 129). See also Guthrie, "Who Were the Orphics?", 115ff., and Guthrie, *Orpheus and Greek Religion*, 216–220. Pythagoras himself is even credited with writing some poems under the name of Orpheus; see *The Pythagorean Sourcebook*, 19, 143.

THE MEANING OF HIS NAME: *The Pythagorean Sourcebook*, 147. See further discussion in chapter 4, note 41 of the present work.

Gematria: The Sacred Language

HEBREW: Hebrew gematria figures prominently in the Jewish kabbalistic tradition. For a discussion see Gershom Scholem, *Kabbalah*, chapter 10.

ARABIC: Arabic gematria figures in the Islamic mystical tradition of Sufism and is known as *abjad*; see Laleh Bakhtiar, *Sufi: Expressions of the Mystic Quest*, 114–115, for some simple examples; see also Schimmel, *The Mystery of Numbers*, 30–34, and her bibliography, 288–290.

SANSKRIT: In Sanskrit gematria is used as a mnemonic aid in memorizing mathematical formulae; see Jagadguru Shankarachanga, *Vedic Mathematics*. For example, a Sanskrit *shloka* in addition to praising Krishna and Shiva, gives the value of π to 32 decimal places (!); for this value, and "the Vedic numerical code," see Khare, *Issues in Vedic Mathematics*, 54–56.

ORPHIC HYMN TO NUMBER: For Greek sources, see Otto Kern, *Orphicorum Fragmenta*, 320–326; for a brief discussion, see Erwin Rohde, *Psyche: The Cult of Souls and Belief in Immortality among the Ancient Greeks*, 350, note 9. There was also an Orphic book entitled *The Art of Names*; Kern, *Orphicorum Fragmenta*, 311.

THE UNIVERSE, A REFLECTION OF THE LOGOS: That's why, in the myth of the *Timaeus*, Plato depicts the World Soul as being divided according to the ratios of perfect harmony: the exemplar of the physical cosmos is itself the harmonic blueprint, "the Logos," on which all creation is based.

The One and the Many

THE TRUE GNOSTIC: "He who is to have knowledge in this manner knows where he comes from and where he is going" (*The Gospel of Truth* 22.14–15; in Robinson, *Nag Hammadi Library*, 42). See also quotation from the *Excerpts of Theodotos* on p. 125 of the present volume.

QUALITATIVE NUMBER: For a contemporary discussion of how "every number represents an individual aspect of the same primal one," see chapter 4, "Number as a Time-bound Quality of the One-Continuum," in the important study by Marie-Louise von Franz, *Number and Time: Reflections Leading Towards a Unification of Psychology and Physics*. Part one of this work discusses "Number as the Common Ordering Factor of Psyche and Matter."

Kosmos: The Ordered World

THE HARMONIA OF THE HEXAD: The gematria of the word KOSMOS = 600 was related to the harmonic nature of the hexad in ancient Pythagorean symbolism. On this topic, *The Theology of Arithmetic* notes that the hexad is called "reconciliation," for "it weaves together male and female by blending." Moreover, "it is plausibly called 'peace,' and a much earlier name for it, based on the fact that it organizes things, was 'universe': for the universe, like 6, is often seen as composed of opposites in harmony, and the summation of the word 'universe' (*kosmos*) is 600" (pseudo-Iamblichus, *The Theology of Arithmetic: On the Mystical, Mathematical and Cosmological Symbolism of the First Ten Numbers*, 80).

NICOMACHUS ON THE HEXAD: Quoted by Thomas Taylor in *The Theoretic Arithmetic of the Pythagoreans*, 192–93. This passage is from Nicomachus' untranslated *Theology of Arithmetic* which appears in Photius, *Codex* 187. Another untranslated work of Greek arithmology relating to the symbolism of the first ten numbers is Anatolius, Περὶ δεκάδος καὶ τῶν ἐντὸς αὐτῆς ἀριθμῶν, edited by Heiberg, *Annales Internationales d'Histoire* (Congrès de Paris, 1900), 5e. sect., *Histoire des Sciences*, pp. 22ff.

THE COSMOS AND WORLD SOUL, LIKENED TO A NET: See Plotinus, *Enneads* 4.3.9.

THE VEIL OF HARMONIA: See W. R. Lethaby, *Architecture, Mysticism, and Myth*, 34–35, 79, and Nonnos, *Dionysiaca* 41.295–301. According to one ancient writer, the soul descending into incarnation, through the power of *harmonia*, "weaves bonds for itself, like a net," giving birth to the physical body; see Aristides Quintilianus, *On Music* 2.17 (Barker translation, 490). According to Aristotle in his work *On the Generation of Animals* 734 A 18, Orpheus writes that "the process by which an animal is formed resembles the plaiting of a net (δίκτυον)"; for this and other classical references to this notion, see Mead, *Orpheus*, 31–32.

COSMOLOGICAL SYMBOLISM OF WEAVING: See chapter 14, "The Symbolism of Weaving," in Guénon, *The Symbolism of the Cross*; see also Snodgrass, *Symbolism of the Stupa*, 111–126; Eliade, *The Two and the One*, chapter 4.

ORPHIC WRITINGS, "THE NET" AND "THE VEIL": According to some ancient authorities, these works were written by Brontinos of Kroton or Metapontion, a Pythagorean; see Thesleff, *Introduction to the Pythagorean Writings of the Hellenistic Period*, 12, and Kern, *Orphicorum Fragmenta*, 297, 314.

The Celestial Man of Light

HUMANITY, MADE IN GOD'S IMAGE: Genesis 1.26.

IN GNOSTICISM: For the archetype of the pre-existing Man of Light in gnostic cosmology, see the excellent studies by Kraeling, *Anthropos and Son of Man: A Study in the Religious Syncretism of the Hellenistic Orient*, and Zandee, "Gnostic Ideas on the Fall and Salvation," 43–45.

IN ISLAM: For Islamic sources see Henry Corbin's *The Man of Light in Iranian Sufism*.

AS CULTURE HERO: Examples of the Cosmic Man as culture bringer include Orpheus, Prometheus (literally, "Forethought"), Atlas, Janus, Hermes Trismegistos, and Osiris.

PHANES: See the Orphic *Hymn to Protogonos* ("First-Born," a name of Phanes) in Athanassakis, *The Orphic Hymns*, 11.

THE "LIGHT-WORD" AS "SON OF GOD": *Corpus Hermeticum* 1 ("Poimandres"), 6.

ADAM KADMON: *Adam Kadmon* means, literally, "Primal Man."

THE FIGURE OF "PHOS," MAN OR LIGHT: *Zosimos of Panopolis on the Letter Omega*, translated by Howard M. Jackson.

THROUGH THE PRINCIPLE OF HUMANITY, THE UNIVERSE IS PERFECTED: See Allers, "Microcosmus," 322.

MAN, AN IMAGE OF THE SUN: *Corpus Hermeticum* 11 ("Mind unto Hermes"), 15.

KABBALISTIC SEPHIRA: Historically speaking, the development of the kabbalistic tree is later than the Hellenistic conceptions alluded to here; however, since the kabbalistic tree is based on this geometry and concurs with these ideas, we have decided to show the sephira in their proper position to help further amplify these ideas for those who are familiar with the kabbalistic tradition.

THE PLATONIC DIVISION OF THE SOUL: The Platonic division of the soul into three parts originated with the Pythagoreans. See my discussion in Guthrie, *Pythagorean Sourcebook and Library*, 30–33, and Stocks, "Plato and the Tripartite Soul."

"BRINGING INTO TUNE THOSE THREE PARTS": Plato, *Republic* 443D (Cornford translation, 142).

HUMANITY AS UNIVERSAL MEDIATOR: See Critchlow, *Time Stands Still*, 23–24, 55, 83–84, for a discussion of humanity as the mediator between heaven and earth. This traditional view is presented in Pico della Mirandola's *Oration on the Dignity of Man* and leads to a philosophy of spiritual humanism which recognizes the central, sacred, and cosmic function of humanity, poised between the angels and the beasts, as universal mediator; see Michell, *The Dimensions of Paradise*, chapter 6, and Allers, "Microcosmus," 407, for further discussion.

The God Apollo: The First "Word" of Celestial Harmony

THE COSMOS AS UNION OF IDEAL EXTREMES: For a discussion of the ancient Pythagorean view of the *kosmos* as the *harmonia* of the Limited and the Unlimited, see my introduction to Guthrie, *The Pythagorean Sourcebook and Library*, 20–28. See also the fragments of Philolaus, one of the earliest Pythagoreans: "The world's nature is a harmonious compound of Limited and Unlimited elements; similar is the totality of the world (*kosmos*) in itself, and of all it contains" and "Harmony is generally the result of contraries; for it is the unity of multiplicity, and the agreement of discordances" (*Pythagorean Sourcebook*, 168).

THE GEOMETRIC MEAN AS THE MOST PERFECT FORM OF MEDIATION:

Robinson, *An Introduction to Early Greek Philosophy*, 81–83, and Plato, *Timaeus* 31B–32A.

The Cosmic Temple I

SARGON'S GEMATRIA: Farbridge, *Studies in Biblical and Semitic Symbolism*, 94.

THE WASHINGTON MONUMENT: Tompkins, *The Magic of Obelisks*, 1, 335–336. The idea of constructing sacred and secular buildings to conform to symbolic numbers has an appeal which is eternally rooted in the human imagination. In addition to Greek temples, the practice was also frequently used in the design of Christian churches. For an analysis of a particularly interesting example, King's College Chapel in Cambridge, see Pennick, *Geomancy: Man in Harmony with the Earth*, 136–138.

DIDYMA: For more on this important Apollo temple and oracular site, see the excellent study by Joseph Fontenrose, *Didyma: Apollo's Oracle, Cult, and Companions*.

THE GREEK FOOT: The length of the ancient Greek foot is 1.01367 English feet (Michell, *Ancient Metrology*, 16–17). The dimensions of the stylobate at Didyma are 167.7 x 358.7 English feet (Dinsmore, *The Architecture of Ancient Greece*, 340).

The Cosmic Temple II

PARTHENON: The temple was also known as the Hecatopompedon or "hundred foot" temple and defines the length of the Greek foot, which is equivalent to 1.01376 English feet. This defined value of the Greek foot stands in harmony with the reports of ancient writers who record a 24:25 ratio between the length of the Roman and Greek feet (Michell, *Ancient Metrology*, 16–17). The width of the stylobate, 100 Greek feet, is precisely one second of arc in the circumference of the earth, of which there are 1,296,000 parts in a circle. One circle equals:

360 degrees (360 = 6x60)
21,600 minutes (2,160 = 6x60x60)
1,296,000 seconds (1,296,000 = 6x60x60x60)

This number, 1,296,000, is analogous to the enigmatic "marriage number," 12,960,000, referred to in the *Republic* of Plato; see Adam, *The Nuptial Number of Plato*.

ATHENA, BORN FROM THE HEAD OF ZEUS: Hesiod, *Theogony* 886ff., 935ff.; Hesiod, *Homeric Hymn* 28; Apollodorus, *Library of Mythology* 1.3.6.

The Music of the Sun I

THE GODS OF MUSIC: "The theologians of ancient times, who were the oldest of philosophers, put musical instruments into the hands of the statues of the gods, with the thought, I presume, not that they [do play] the lyre and the pipe but that no work is so like that of gods as concord (*harmonia*) and consonance (*symphonia*)" (Plutarch, *On the Generation of the Soul in the Timaeus* 1030B).

HERMES' GIFT OF THE LYRE TO APOLLO: See Hesiod, *Homeric Hymn to Hermes* and Apollodorus, *Library of Mythology* 3.10.2. For discussion, see Brown, *Hermes the Thief: The Evolution of a Myth*, chapter 5.

MUSICAL TIMBRE DEPENDENT ON AN INSTRUMENT'S OVERTONE CONSTELLATION: See Levarie and Levy, *Tone*, 63–65

The Music of the Sun II

OLEN, APOLLO'S FIRST PROPHET: Pausanius, *Description of Greece* 10.5.7–8. See also *Anthon's Classical Dictionary*, s.v. Olen.

Helios: The Image of the One

"GOD IS A SPHERE": On the sources and influence of this aphorism, see Wind, *Pagan Mysteries in the Renaissance*, 227, note 30.

THE DIVISIONS OF THE CUBIT: For a listing of the twenty-eight Egyptian gods associated with the divisions of the cubit, see Budge, *Gods of the Egyptians*, II, 291.

⊙ ON A DELPHIC COIN: "Early autonomous coins of Delphi in bronze and silver have *obv*. the tripod, *rev*. the Omphalos symbolized by a circle with a dot in the middle ⊙" (Middleton, "The Temple of Apollo at Delphi," 300). For a photograph of this coin, see Roscher, *Omphalos*, plate 1, figure 6.

In Greek sacred geography, the symbol ⊙ represents the central omphalos and the bounds of the circular earth. The circumference of the circle is represented in Greek mythology by the figure Okeanos, the swift spinning circular stream whose waves encircle the earth. Appropriately, Okeanos was associated with the letter *O-mega*, the "great circle," which begins his name (see Zosimos, *On the Letter Omega*, 17). Okeanos represents the power of motion and source of genesis or manifestation: in Homer he is the source of all life, including the gods. On the shield of Achilles, Okeanos was represented encircling its periphery, while the central knob of a Greek shield was called the *omphalos*: the Greeks envisioned the earth in identical fashion. According to the Orphic *Hymn to Okeanos*, he is "the earth's own end, the pole's beginning," for the perfectly circular motion of the equator describes the location of the central pole, axis, or omphalos. If the outer circle of ⊙ is Omega, moving and manifest creation, then the central omphalos is *Alpha*, the cosmic seed of infinite potentiality at the "unmoved axis" of the sacred center (see also following note). In the same way that Apollo's Delphic omphalos is the navel of the earth "below," Helios the sun is described as the "mid-omphalos" (μεσομφαλός) of the seven planets "above" in Nonnos, *Dionysiaca* 41.347. Thus, in the symbolism of Delphi we have a clear synthesis of "polar" (Hyperborean) and "solar" traditions, for which see Joscelyn Godwin, *Arktos*, especially chapters 11–13. For the *Hymn to Okeanos*, see Athanassakis, *The Orphic Hymns*, 104–105. For a relief of Okeanos and his identification with the ouroboros, see von Franz, *Time*, plate 2, and 66–67. For more on the ouroboros and its relation in antiquity with the symbols A and Ω, see Hans Leisegang, "The Mystery of the Serpent."

THE GEMATRIA OF THETA, Θ = ⊙: This gematria throws light on an esoteric cosmological passage in Philo of Byblos' *Phoenician History*, keeping in mind that the letter Theta is derived from the Phoenician/Hebrew letter Teth which means "snake" and is represented as an ouroboros, a circular tail-biting serpent: ט (see Philo of Byblos, *The Phoenician History*, 67). In connection with the note above, a fragment of the Greek writer Agatho describes the dot in the center of Θ as the "mesomphalos," a name also of the omphalos at Delphi (see Liddell and Scott, *Greek-English Lexicon*, s.v. μεσομφαλία).

PLUTARCH ON HELIOS AS A LOWER MANIFESTATION OF APOLLO, THE ONE: Plutarch, *The Obsolesence of Oracles* 433E.

Hermes, the Logos

HERMES = LOGOS: For the relation between Hermes *Logios* (god of speech) and ratios (*logoi*) and proportions (*analogiai*), see Aristides Quintilianus, *On Music* 2.17 (Barker translation, 491). For Hermes as Logos see also Plutarch, *On the Mysteries of Isis and Osiris* 373B.

THE NAASSENES ON HERMES AS LOGOS: Hippolytus, *Refutation of All Heresies*, quoted by Jean Doresse, *Secret Books of the Egyptian Gnostics*, 84.

MANETHO ON THE BOOKS OF HERMES: Iamblichus, *On the Mysteries* 7.1 (Taylor translation, 300).

QUOTATION FROM FOURTH GOSPEL: John 21.25.

BUDGE ON THE NATURE OF THOTH: Budge, *Gods of the Egyptians*, I, 407–408.

JESUS ENCOUNTERS THE 365 STATUES AT HERMOPOLIS: Hennecke-

Schneemelcher, *New Testament Apocrypha*, I, 412–413. Interestingly, in late Egyptian mythology, the cosmic mound at Hermopolis was "the place where Ra appeared on the first occasion . . ." (Saleh, "The So-called 'Primeval Hill' and other Related Elevations in Ancient Egyptian Mythology," 118).

EPITHETS OF THOTH: The epithets of Thoth in hieroglyphic script are taken from Patrick Boylan, *Thoth: The Hermes of Egypt*.

Hermes, the Good Shepherd

HERMES PSYCHOPOMPOS: See Kerényi, *Hermes: Guide of Souls*.

CHRIST AS GOOD SHEPHERD: Art historians are unanimous that the early Christian iconography of Jesus as Good Shepherd was influenced by the earlier representations of Hermes Kriophoros ("Ram-bearer"). For an early representation, see Hall, *A History of Ideas and Images in Italian Art*, 74. For the sanctuary of Hermes Kriophoros at Tanagra, see Pausanius, *Description of Greece* 9.22.1–2. For the Logos as Good Shepherd in Philo, see *On Husbandry* 49ff.; for Apollo as Shepherd see the present work, p. 338, note 19.

THE NAME POIMANDRES: While the name of the Hermetic Revealer *Poimandres* probably meant "Shepherd of Men" (*poimên andrôn*) to most Greek speaking readers of the Hermetic writings, it seems to be derived from an Egyptian name, "The Knowledge of the Sun" or "The Knowledge of Ra." As one scholar notes, the designation Poimandres "is not very different from what a Christian might have understood by the Word (λόγος) or Spirit (πνεῦμα) of the supreme God. It is probably incorrect to derive the name Poimandres from the Greek ποιμήν (shepherd), ἀνήρ (man). It is rather a Greek form of the Coptic *p-eimi-n-re*, 'the knowledge of the [sun-] God.' For such a name cf. Manda dHaiyê, 'the knowledge of life' (or salvation), the name given by the Mandaeans to the saviour and revealer" (Barrett, *The New Testament Background: Selected Documents*, 95). For more on the Egyptian background of Poimandres, see the article by Ralph Marcus in the *Journal of Near Eastern Studies*, "The Name Poimandrês."

"THE WAY," A NAME OF CHRISTIANITY: Acts 9.2.

THE KNOWLEDGE OF THE LOGOS AS "THE PATH BETWEEN OPPOSITES": This is suggested by a saying of the Logos in the *Gospel of Thomas*. When asked by the disciples when they would enter the Kingdom, Jesus replied: "When you make the two one, and when you make the inside like the outside, and the above like the below, and when you make the male and the female one and the same . . . then you will enter [the Kingdom]" (*Gospel of Thomas*, 22).

"TOOL OF PEACE," A TITLE OF THE CADUCEUS: *Orphic Hymns* 28.7

(Athanassakis translation, 41). On the caduceus and its relation to shamanism and the *axis mundi*, see Butterworth, *The Tree at the Navel of the Earth*, 214.

Thrice-Greatest Hermes: The Triple Logos

THE POWER OF HERMES, COMMON TO ALL PRIESTS: Iamblichus, *On the Mysteries* 1.1 (Taylor translation, 17–18).

HERMES AS GNOSTIC REVEALER: "Among the Mandeans the redeeming knowledge has become an independent person called 'knowledge of life' (*manda dehaijî*). In the Hermetic texts the 'thrice great Hermes' or 'shepherd of men' (*Poimandres*) is the redeemer or revealer. Christian Gnosis naturally sets Christ in this position . . ." (Rudolph, *Gnosis: The Nature and History of Gnosticism*, 131–132). See also his comments on the Logos personified as Revealer, pages 121 and 144.

"THE SOURCE OF ALL KNOWLEGE": Quotation from Tamara Green, *The City of the Moon God: Religious Traditions of Harran*, 85.

For more on the Egyptian Hermetic writings, see Mead, *Thrice-Greatest Hermes* (texts and commentary); Mead, *The Hymns of Hermes* (texts and commentary); Scott, *Hermetica* (texts and commentary); Keizer, *The Eighth Reveals the Ninth* (text and commentary); Fowden, *The Egyptian Hermes: A Historical Approach to the Late Pagan Mind.* For additional bibliography with discussion, see Blanco, "Hermetism: A Bibliographical Approach."

The Emerald Tablet of Hermes Trismegistos

THE RELATIONS OF ALCHEMY AND GNOSTICISM: See Sheppard, "Gnosticism and Alchemy"; Sheppard, "The Origin of the Gnostic-Alchemical Relationship"; Jung, *Psychology and Alchemy*, 295–316. On the differences between the "transcendental Hermeticism" of Corpus Hermeticum and the "incarnational Hermeticism" of medieval alchemy, see Fideler, "The Path Toward the Grail: The Hermetic Sources and Structure of Wolfram von Eschenbach's *Parzival*," 210–211.

THE "REDEMPTION OF MATTER" THROUGH CONSCIOUSNESS: The conception of humanity as microcosm leads to the notion that "man participates by his being and doing in the maintenance of the universe and, eventually, the perfection of the whole" (Allers, "Microcosmus," 322). See also the comments in Faivre, "Ancient and Medieval Sources of Modern Esoteric Movements," 6, 32.

THE TRUE CHRISTIAN, OR GNOSTIC, BECOMES A CHRIST: *Gospel of Philip* 67.26 (in Robinson, *Nag Hammadi Library*, 150); see also Origen, *Contra*

Celsum 6.79.

JESUS, ON BECOMING "THE MIDST": *The Books of Ieou*, quoted in Hennecke-Schneemelcher, *New Testament Apocrypha*, I, 262 (= MacDermot, *Books of Jeu*, 46). See also the *logion* preserved in *Gospel of Thomas* 28: "I took my place in the midst of the world."

TEXT OF THE EMERALD TABLET: Burckhardt, *Alchemy: Science of the Cosmos, Science of the Soul*, 196–197.

The Elemental Continuum of Hellenistic Cosmology

THE GEOMETRICAL STAGES OF EXISTENCE: See Critchlow, "The Platonic Tradition on the Nature of Proportion."

THE PLATONIC SOLIDS: The so-called regular solids are first described by Plato in his dialogue the *Timaeus* where they are associated with the elemental continuum of Greek cosmology and form the basis of his "molecular theory." See discussion in Critchlow, cited above. For the knowledge of the Platonic solids a millennium before Plato, see Critchlow, *Time Stands Still: New Light on Megalithic Science*, chapter 7.

PSYCHOLOGICAL FUNCTIONS: Jung's theory of psychological types conforms very closely to the Platonic theory of knowledge described by the famous "divided line" in the *Republic*; for discussion, see the Cornford translation, 221–223. Plato's four cognitive states are: sensation, opinion, scientific analysis, and direct knowledge.

THE THREE PARTS OF THE SOUL: See discussion in Guthrie, *Pythagorean Sourcebook and Library*, 30–33, and Stocks, "Plato and the Tripartite Soul." For the three parts of the soul in Plato, see *Republic* 434D–441C.

QUOTATION FROM THEAGES: Theages, *On the Virtues*, in *Pythagorean Sourcebook*, 225–228.

THE TETRAKTYS: See discussion in *Pythagorean Sourcebook*, 28–30, and also Theon of Smyrna, "How Many Tetraktys are There?", in *Pythagorean Sourcebook*, 317–319.

The Astral Spheres

ORIGEN ON HUMANITY AS MICROCOSM: Origen, *Homiliae in Leviticum* 5.2, quoted by Moore, *The Planets Within: The Astrological Psychology of Marsilio Ficino*, 4.

CHALDEAN ARRANGEMENT OF THE PLANETS: The so-called Chaldean or Babylonian arrangement of the planets is based on the orbital periods of the planets as viewed from the earth: Saturn (29.46 years), Jupiter (11.86 years),

Mars (686.98 days), Sun (365.26 days), Venus (224.70 days), Mercury (87.97 days), Moon (29.53 days). This arrangement arose in the second century B.C.E.; see Zerubavel, *The Seven Day Circle*, 14–15.

"THE WORLD IS FULL OF GODS": Thales, one of the very earliest Greek philosophers, is famous for saying that "all things are full of gods"—in other words, even matter has life and soul. See Zeller, *Outlines of the History of Greek Philosophy*, 27.

For more on the archetypal symbolism of the seven planets, see Moore, *The Planets Within*.

Celestial Archetypes I: Planetary Squares

MORAN QUOTE: Moran, *The Wonders of Magic Squares*, 6.

FORMULATING NAMES OF PLANETARY SPIRITS: See "Celestial Archetypes: Planetary Signatures." In Arabic, the name for Saturn, Zuhal, amounts to 45, the sum of all numbers in the magic square of Saturn (Calder, "A Note on Magic Squares," 198).

DETERMINING DIMENSIONS OF TEMPLES: For example, in ancient China the 3x3 magic square, known as the "Lo-shu," was endowed with extraordinary significance. It served as the groundpland of the Ming-T'ang temple, the "Hall of Brightness," which was a model of the entire universe in the Later Han dynasty. "By carrying out the appropriate rituals in the Ming T'ang, the Emperor's rule and virtue would radiate, by resonance, to every part of the empire" (Moore, *The Trigrams of Han*, 54; see also von Franz, *Number and Time*, 22–26).

For more on magic squares in traditional symbolism, see Schimmel, *The Mystery of Numbers*, 29–34. For magic squares in Islam, see Schimmel, ibid.; Bakhtiar, *Sufi: Expressions of the Mystic Quest*, 114–115; Nasr, *Islamic Science*, 79ff. For magic squares as the basis of projective ornament in design, see Bragdon, *The Frozen Fountain*, chapter 7.

Celestial Archetypes II: Planetary Numbers

THE NUMBER 666: Most commentators have failed to recognize that .666 is the most powerful harmonic ratio, the ratio of the perfect fifth in music. For some other interesting properties of 666, see Michael Keith's article on 666 in the *Journal of Recreational Mathematics*. For the gematria of 666 in Revelation 13, see Michell, *City of Revelation*, chapter 13.

Illustration adapted from Anonymous, *Magickian's Desk Reference*.

Celestial Archetypes III: Planetary Signatures

TECHNIQUE OF SIGIL CONSTRUCTION: See Nowotny, "The Construction of Certain Seals and Characters in the Work of Agrippa of Nettesheim" and McLean, *The Magical Calendar*.

Celestial Archetypes IV: Cosmic Cycles

THE PLANETARY WEEK: On its history, see Colson, *The Week: An Essay on the Origin and Development of the Seven-Day Cycle*, chapter 3, "The Planetary Week," and Zerubavel, *The Seven Day Circle: The History and Meaning of the Week*, 12–26. For a listing of the planets in both their "weekly" and "celestial" order, see *Greek Magical Papyri* 13.210ff (Betz, 178). Each of the twelve hours of the day and the night is also associated with a particular planet, a scheme which harmonizes with the planetary days; see Critchlow, *Time Stands Still*, 62, and Zerubavel, *The Seven Day Circle*, 18.

TIME, A MOVING IMAGE OF ETERNITY: Plato, *Timaeus* 37D.

THE CELESTIAL DANCE: For the geometrical divisions of the zodiacal circle by the planetary dance, see Critchlow, *Time Stands Still*, chapter 8, "The Planets as Time Keepers: Patterns in Space and Time."

Illustration from Anonymous, *Magickian's Desk Reference*.

The Solar Heart

Illustration from Godwin, *Robert Fludd: Hermetic Philosopher and Surveyor of Two Worlds*, 73.

Heliopolis: The City of the Sun

GREEK PHILOSOPHERS AT HELIOPOLIS: There are many references from the ancient world relating to the travels of Greek philosophers and scientists in Egypt. For Pythagoras at Heliopolis, see Plutarch, *On the Mysteries of Isis and Osiris* 354E; for Plato at Heliopolis, see Clement of Alexandria, *Stromata* 1.15 (in *Ante-Nicene Fathers*, II, 315). Regarding the mathematician and astronomer Eudoxus (fl. *circa* 368 B.C.E.), Thomas Heath notes that "when in Egypt Eudoxus assimilated the astronomical knowledge of the priests of Heliopolis and himself made observations. The observatory between Heliopolis and Cercesura used by him was still pointed out in Augustus' time" (Heath, *History of Greek Mathematics*, I, 322). See also the account in Strabo, *Geography* 1.96ff. and 1.98ff., in which he tells how Greek sculptors assimilated the Egyptian canon of proportion, a fact that has now been verified by archaeologists (see Eleanor Guralnick, "Proportions of Korai").

BIRTHPLACE OF MOSES: Some ancient writers identify Moses as a priest from Heliopolis. See Gager, *Moses in Greco-Roman Paganism*, 40, 123.

ANU: *Anu* means, literally, "City of the Pillar," a reference to the *ben-ben*/obelisk. Historically speaking, the *ben-ben* at Heliopolis is the most ancient omphalos in the Western world of which we know.

BUDGE ON THE BENNU OR PHOENIX: Quotation from Budge, *Tutankhamen: Amenism, Atenism and Egyptian Monotheism*, 63–64. *Bennu* and *ben-ben* are derived from the Egyptian word *uben*, "to rise" or "shine" like the sun; see Budge, *Egyptian Hieroglyphic Dictionary*, 159, for *uben* and cognates. The figure of the Phoenix is associated with the cosmic cycles and the renewal of time. One Egyptologist notes that "when the Phoenix gave out the primeval call it initiated all these cycles"; moreover, the Egyptians anticipated the landing of the Phoenix at "Heliopolis, the symbolic center of the earth where it will announce the new age" (Clark, *Myth and Symbol in Ancient Egypt*, 246–247). On the *Bennu* and Egyptian creation myth, see also Saleh, "The So-called 'Primeval Hill' and other Related Elevations in Ancient Egyptian Mythology."

QUOTATION FROM PYRAMID TEXTS: Pyramid Texts 1652, quoted by Lamy, *Egyptian Mysteries*, 8.

LAKE OF RA AT HELIOPOLIS: Budge, *Gods of the Egyptians*, I, 328.

AIN SHEMS/FOUNTAIN OF THE SUN: See René Francis, *Egyptian Aesthetics*, 85ff. *Ain Shems* can also be translated as "Eye of the Sun."

THE HOLY FAMILY AT HELIOPOLIS: See the Arabic Infancy Gospel in Hennecke-Schneemelcher, *New Testament* Apocrypha, I, 409.

ON/HELIOPOLIS = "BEING": ὤν (being) in Greek is the masculine present participle of the irregular verb εἰμί, "I am." In the Septuagint, the Greek translation of the Old Testament, the statement of Yahweh, "I am who I am" (Exodus 13.14), is given a Platonic twist: in Greek it is rendered Ἐγώ εἰμι ὁ ὢν, literally, "I am Being." For On/Heliopolis as a symbol of the Logos in Philo of Alexandria, see Philo, *On Dreams* 1.77ff.

Nile: The Celestial Stream

EGYPT, "IMAGE OF THE SKIES": Lamy, *Egyptian Mysteries*, 5. See also the Hermetic tractate *Asclepius* 24 in which Egypt is discussed as "the image of Heaven" and "temple of the world."

SENECA ON THE NILE: Quoted by Wild, *Water in the Cultic Worship of Isis and Serapis*, 93.

HELIODORUS ON THE TITLES OF THE NILE: From Wild, *Water*, 88.

LIBANIUS ON ABOLISHING FOOD OFFERINGS TO THE NILE: Wild, *Water*, 93.

THE NILE AS "THE YEAR," THE RECURRENCE OF THE FLOOD, ETC.: Wild, *Water*, 89.

THE NILE, "THE EXACT COUNTERPART OF HEAVEN": "The Egyptians apotheosize the Nile and consider it the greatest of all divinities, hallowing the river as the exact counterpart of heaven. . ." (Heliodorus, *An Ethiopian Story* 9.9).

THE NILE, "THE YEAR INCARNATE": Heliodorus, *An Ethiopian Story* 9.22.

NEILOS = 365: Heliodorus, *An Ethiopian Story* 9.22. See also Eustathinus, quoted by Wild, *Water*, 89.

Syene: The Place of Heavenly Alignment

THE MEASUREMENT OF THE EARTH: For a description of how the earth was measured in antiquity, see Berriman, *Historical Metrology: A New Analysis of the Archaeological and the Historical Evidence Relating to Weights and Measures.*

KHEKH, THE EGYPTIAN NAME OF SYENE: The hieroglyphic names of Syene are taken from Budge, *An Egyptian Hieroglyphic Dictionary*, 1028.

HELIODORUS ON THE GEMATRIA OF NEILOS: Heliodorus, *An Ethiopian Story* 9.22. The fact that SYENE = 666 was noted by the present writer.

Osiris: The Cosmic Seed

THE GRAIN OF MUSTARD SEED: Matthew 13.31–32; Mark 4.30–32; Luke 13.18–19. On the gematria of the grain of mustard seed, see Michell, *The New View Over Atlantis*, chapter 5; *City of Revelation*, chapter 8; *The Dimensions of Paradise*, 178–198.

PARABLE OF THE SOWER: Matthew 13.1–9; Mark 4.1–9; Luke 8.4–8.

"THE SEED IS THE LOGOS OF GOD": ὁ σπόρος ἐστὶν ὁ λόγος τοῦ θεοῦ (Luke 8.11).

PAUL ON THE MYSTERY OF THE SEED AND THE SPIRITUAL RESURRECTION: 1 Corinthians 15. As one writer points out, it's probably not coincidental that Paul teaches the mystery of the resurrection—"the first fruits of those who have fallen asleep"—to the inhabitants of Corinth, located a mere forty miles from Eleusis, where the Eleusinian Mysteries of Demeter, the grain mother, were celebrated (Elderkin, *Related Religious Ideas of Delphi, Tara, and Jerusalem*, 49).

THE SPERMATIKOS LOGOS IN STOIC PHILOSOPHY: For an excellent discussion, see Witt, "The Plotinian Logos and its Stoic Basis."

THE SPIRITUAL SEED OR LIGHT SPARK: On the importance of the Spiritual Seed or Light Spark which the savior awakens in gnostic thought, see Zandee, "Gnostic Ideas on the Fall and Salvation," 41–43.

THE WORD "INITIATION": See Hogart, *The Hymns of Orpheus*, 17; see also Liddell and Scott, *Greek-English Lexicon*, s.v. τελέω and τελειόω.

BUDGE ON OSIRIS-NEPRA: Budge, *Osiris and the Egyptian Resurrection*, I, 58. For the British, the word *corn* denotes wheat. For more on Osiris-Nepra and the mystery of resurrection in Egypt, see Lamy, *Egyptian Mysteries*, 22.

THE "RE-MEMBERED" MAN OF LIGHT: See, for example, the fragment of a gnostic hymn preserved in MacDermot, *The Books of Jeu*, 79–82, which contains the formula: "Save all my members which have been scattered since the foundation of the world . . . gather them together and take them to the light."

Abraxas: The Demiurgic Sun

ABRAXAS: On the origin of the name, see Rudolph, *Gnosis*, 311.

IAO: The mystic name IAO seemingly originated as a Hellenistic "translation" of the name of Yahweh, but thereafter took on a life of its own and became assimilated to speculations relating to vowel magic, etc. It appears with great frequency in gnostic writings, in the Greek magical papyri, and on magical gems and amulets. In Greek cosmology, IAO easily symbolizes the nature of the All, for Iota is the middle vowel—the vowel of the Sun—flanked by Alpha and Omega. The name IAO was used in gnostic rituals (Irenaeus, *Against Heresies* 1.21.3) and in *Pistis Sophia*, the resurrected Jesus leads the disciples in a ritual based on the mystic name: "And Jesus cried out as he turned to the four corners of the world with his disciples, and they were all robed in linen garments, and he said: 'IAO. IAO. IAO. This is its interpretation: Iota, because the all came forth; Alpha, because it will return again; Omega, because the completion of all completions will happen'" (*Pistis Sophia*, MacDermot translation, 707). On vowel names of the gods, see Joscelyn Godwin, *The Mystery of the Seven Vowels*. For an oracle of Apollo at Claros concerning the name IAO, see Cook, *Zeus*, I, 234.

HIS WHIP: In the case of Sol Invictus, by showing the sun god with a whip in his hands, the emperors Maximian and Diocletian "evidently wished to emphasize the dominance and invincibility of this god" (Halsberghe, *The Cult of Sol Invictus*, 166).

"365 HEAVENS": For the numbers 360 and 365 in gnostic writings, see Pryzybylski, "The Role of Calendrical Data in Gnostic Literature." For references to ABRAXAS = 365 in the church fathers, see chapter 2, note 13. See also *Greek Magical Papyri* 13.155 (Betz, 176) for the statement "You are the number of [the days of] the year, ABRASAX."

THE ANGUIPEDE: See Nilsson, "The Anguipede of the Magical Amulets," where he argues that Abraxas symbolizes the god of the entire cosmos: the cock's head denotes him as god of the sun, light, and the heavens; the military costume denotes rulership of the world and terrestrial life; the snake legs symbolize the underworld. For the figure on magical gems, see the examples and discussion in Bonner, *Studies in Magical Amulets*, chapter 9, "The Snake-Legged God with the Cock's Head."

Mithras: "The Invincible Sun"

HIS AEONIC ASPECT: On the identification of Mithras and Aeon in antiquity, see Ulansey, *Origins of the Mithraic Mysteries*, 120–124; Vermaseren, *Mithras: The Secret God*, 127–128; Godwin, *Arktos*, 162–163.

MITHRAS AS MEDIATOR: Cumont, *Mysteries of Mithra*, 127–128.

ROCK FROM WHICH HE SPRANG: Mithras was known as *petrogenês*, or the "rock born" god. See Cumont, *Mysteries of Mithra*, 130–131.

MITHRAS AS LOGOS: Cumont, *Mysteries of Mithra*, 140.

ANCIENT CAMEO STONE: Reproduced from Cumont, *Textes et monuments figurés relatifs aux mystères de Mithra*, II, 452.

"THE AEONIC MITHRAS": The figure shown has been identified as Phanes Cosmocrator—Phanes as source and lord of the cosmos—a representation of the "Celestial Man of Light." Later, this relief was taken over and used by a Mithraic congregation, a fact indicated by the inscription "Felix Pater" and an erased female name. See Godwin, *Mystery Religions in the Ancient World*, 170, in which he refers to the relief as "the ultimate in Mystery iconography." As Levi notes, "The youthful image of the Modena relief is at the same time Mithras and Phanes" (Levi, "Aion," 300). For more on Mithras, Aeon, and Phanes, see my discussion in chapter 7.

Janus: The Roman God the of Year

TWO FACES: Because of his knowledge of past and future (Macrobius, *Saturnalia* 1.9.3); because he is the sun, and his two faces suggest his lordship over the two heavenly gates (ibid., 1.9.9); because he is the doorkeeper of both heaven and hell (ibid., 1.9.13); because he "looks back to the year that is past and forward to the beginnings of the year to come" (ibid., 1.13.3).

OLDEST GOD OF ITALY: Macrobius, citing Xenon's *Italian Antiquities*, tells us that King "Janus was the first to build temples to the gods and ordain religious ceremonies" (*Saturnalia* 1.9.3).

GOD OF GATES AND DOORWAYS: Macrobius, *Saturnalia* 1.9.7.

GOD OF TIME: Sources cited by Cook, *Zeus*, II, 336–337.

TWELVE ALTARS: Varro, *Antiquities of Religion*, cited by Macrobius, *Saturnalia* 1.9.16.

THE FATHER OF AEON, OR AEON'S VERY SELF: Ioannes Laurentius Lydus, *De mensibus* 4.1, cited in Cook, *Zeus*, II, 337.

FICINO ON JANUS, AS IMAGE OF SOUL: Moore, *The Planets Within*, 44.

FOUR-HEADED JANUS: The quadriform figures "show that his greatness embraces all the regions of the world" (Macrobius, *Saturnalia* 1.9.13, citing Gavius Bassus' book on the gods). "The temples of Janus Quadrifrons were built with four equal sides, each side containing a door and three windows. The four doors were emblematic of the four seasons of the year, while the three windows on a side represented the three months in each season" (*Anthon's Classical Dictionary*, s.v. Janus).

HANDS OF JANUS REPRESENT 365: Macrobius, *Saturnalia* 1.9.10 and Pliny, *Natural History* 34.16.33. Translation from Menninger, *Number Words and Number Symbols*, 210.

DOORS OPEN IN TIMES OF WAR, CLOSED IN TIMES OF PEACE: Macrobius, *Saturnalia* 1.9.16ff.

For more on Janus, see Macrobius, *Saturnalia* 1.9. The article on Janus in *Anthon's Classical Dictionary* is outstanding, and the entry in Seyffert's *Dictionary of Classical Antiquities* is good.

Harpocrates: The Infant Sun

ISIS AND HARPOCRATES AS A PRECURSOR OF "MADONNA AND CHILD": "There is little doubt that in her character of the loving and protecting mother she appealed strongly to the imagination of all the Eastern peoples among whom her cult came, and that the pictures and sculptures wherein she is represented in the act of suckling her child Horus formed the foundation for the Christian figures and paintings of the Madonna and Child" (Budge, *Gods of the Egyptians*, II, 220).

HARPOCRATES ON A LOTUS FLOWER: See El-Kachab, "Some Gem-Amulets Depiciting Harpocrates Seated on a Lotus Flower." See also Bonner, *Studies in Magical Amulets*, chapter 10, "The Young Sun." Why a flower? Perhaps because it is both an "image of the sun" or wholeness and ascends towards its "maker." Writing of the symbolism of Apollo, Macrobius notes that "the likeness of a flower represents the flowering of all that the god sows and engenders and fosters, nourishes and ripens" (*Saturnalia* 1.17.68). As El-Kachab notes, in Egyptian symbolism the lotus represents the sun god emerging from the primordial sea.

JESUS DEPICTED AS HARPOCRATES, SEATED ON THE LOTUS: El-Kachab, "Some Gem Amulets," 136. For more sources relating to the figure of Horus used as an ancient symbol of Christ, see Barb, "Three Elusive Amulets," 15–16.

THE FORMULA OF HARPOCRATES = 9999: See Bonner, "The Numerical Value of a Magical Formula" and *Studies in Magical Amulets* 141–142. The formula appears on over a dozen ancient amulets which have come down to us, most of which show Harpocrates.

THE NAME OF AGATHOS DAIMON: *Greek Magical Papyri* 4.2428 (Betz, 82).

THE ADDRESS TO APOLLO: *Greek Magical Papyri* 2.128 (Betz, 17).

Jesus Christ: The Solar Logos

"I AM THE LIGHT OF THE WORLD": Ἐγω εἰμι τὸ φῶς τοῦ κόσμου, John 8.12, literally reads "I am the light of the *kosmos*." "Light of the world," like "light of life," is also a title given to Helios; see the hymn quoted in Macrobius, *Saturnalia* 1.23.21, cited by Rahner, "The Christian Mystery of Sun and Moon," 123; for the companion title "light of life" in the Orphic *Hymn to Helios*, see *Orphic Hymns* 8.18 (Athanassakis translation, 15). The fact that these two titles of Helios the sun are attributed to Jesus in John 8.12 is a clear example of earlier "pagan" symbolism being assimilated to the new faith within the framework of the canonical gospels themselves.

"ENLIGHTENED": The baptism ceremony of the early Christians which took place on Easter Eve, the festival of the resurrected spring sun, was called *photismos* (φωτισμός) or illumination "from the very earliest beginnings of the Church" (Rahner, "The Christian Mystery of Sun and Moon," 123).

SPIRITUAL SUN OF THE LOGOS: "The Savior, however, being the 'light of the world,' does not illuminate corporeal natures. He illuminates the incorporeal spirit with an incorporeal power in order that each of us, being illuminated as though by the sun, may also be able to see the other spiritual beings" (Origen, *Commentary on John* 1.164).

JESUS, "A NAME ABOVE ALL NAMES": Philippians 2.9.

THE MAGICAL POWERS OF THE NAME JESUS: "The name of our Jesus is also connected with the same [magical] philosophy of names . . ." (See Origen, *Against Celsus* 1.24–25; Chadwick translation, 23–26). Because the name of

Jesus was esteemed as possessing magical efficacy, it sometimes appears in ancient magical papyri along with the names of other divine powers; see, for example, Betz, *Greek Magical Papyri* 4.1227–64 (Betz, 62), 4.3007–86 (Betz, 96), 12.190–92 (Betz, 160). On the incorporation of Christian elements on ancient, magical amulets, see for example Barb, "Three Elusive Amulets."

JESUS, "AN ARTIFICIAL AND IRREGULAR GREEK TRANSLITERATION": Eisler, *Orpheus the Fisher*, 120. Simcox Lea also concludes that "the argument for contrivance of number in the spelling of these names [IÊSOUS and CHRISTOS] is so strong as to be irresistible" (Lea and Bond, *Materials for the Study of the Apostolic Gnosis* I, 24–25).

ON THE MULTIPLES OF 37 AND 74 IN GREEK GEMATRIA: See Bond and Lea, *Gematria*, 65–73; Lea and Bond, *Materials for the Study of the Apostolic Gnosis* I, 64–106; II, 133–201.

ADDITIONAL NOTE: For further depictions of Jesus as the Spiritual Sun in early Christianity, see also the notes below to "Jesus, the Sun Behind the Sun."

Jesus Christ: The Harmony of the Sun

The longer axis of the *vesica* formed by the interpenetrating circles of circumference 4440 measures 1224 units in length. Therefore, this geometry intersects with the geometry of the 153 fish in the net and the feeding of the five thousand.

Jesus Christ: The "Word" of Life and Light

THE EMANATION OF LIFE: The philosophical perspective of the traditional Logos teaching summarized here—"emanationism"—provides a solution to the warring, contemporary dogmas of "creationism" and "evolutionism." The Logos philosophy represents an eminently scientific perspective, worthy of the name; and while it does away with the crude, exoteric literalism of a thinking and planning creative divinity, it stresses the universal, sacred, and theophanic dimensions of life and consciousness.

Jesus: The Sun Behind the Sun

THE SYMBOLISM OF 6 AND 8 IN EARLY CHRISTIAN COSMOLOGY: Bond and Lea, *Gematria*, 24–25.

THE CHRISTIAN SYMBOLISM OF SUNDAY, THE "EIGHTH DAY": See discussion in chapter 2, pages 31-32, and the corresponding notes.

THE SYMBOLISM OF THE "SEVEN STARS" AND THE SPIRITUAL SUN: Bond and Lea, *Gematria*, 24–30.

JESUS, THE ARCHETYPE OF THE SUN: "When thou seest the sun, think of its Lord. . . . If the sun shines in so beneficent a fashion, though it is but a part of nature and must share its fate, how lovely must be Christ, the Sun of Righteousness!" (Ambrose, cited in Rahner, "The Christian Mystery of Sun and Moon," 91–92). Synesius, the Bishop of Cyrene, in his hymn on "Christ's Ascension through the Spheres," tells us that "the Son of God / the all-creating Spirit," is the very archetype of the sun's fire (translation in Godwin, *Music, Mysticism, and Magic: A Sourcebook*, 32–33). Father Rahner, in "The Christian Mystery of Sun and Moon," quotes ancient writers to show us that, among the early Christians, Jesus was known as the "Sun of Righteousness" (91, 119), "the only True Helios" (115), "Sun and God" (117), "a greater light than Sol" (122), the "true Apollo" (122), "Sun of the Resurrection" (125), "Dayspring upon High" (132), and so forth. See also note C, "Le Soleil Symbole du Christ," in Cumont, *Textes et monuments figurés relatifs aux mystères de Mithra*, I, 355–356. For the tradition that Jesus "had twelve apostles according to the number of solar months," see *Clementine Homilies* 2.23 (in Hennecke-Schneemelcher, *New Testament Apocrypha*, II, 547). For an ancient tradition that Jesus' body was deposited in the sun, see *Excerpts of Theodotos* 56 (*Ante-Nicene Fathers*, VIII, 49). In the Latin infancy gospel preserved in the Arundel manuscript, according to the midwife's account, when Jesus was born "the child shone brightly round like the sun, and was pure and most beautiful to behold, since he alone appeared as peace everywhere." This light, which was greater than the sun, filled the cave at Bethlehem along with a sweet odor; see Hennecke-Schneemelcher, *New Testament Apocrypha*, I, 414.

PHILO ON GOD, "THE SUN BEHIND THE SUN": *The Special Laws* 1.279, quoted in this volume, note 9 to chapter 3, p. 325.

MITHRAS, "THE SEVEN-RAYED GOD": Julian, *Hymn to the Mother of the Gods* 172D.

Alpha and Omega: The First and Last Mysteries

ALPHA AS ARCHÊ: For the Pythagoreans, the Monad, the source of all things was represented, by α, Alpha, which also stands for 1, unity, and is the first letter of the word *archê*, beginning or Source. See pseudo-Iamblichus, *The Theology of Arithmetic*, 39.

AΩ, SYMBOLS OF AEON: Leisegang, "The Mystery of the Serpent," 228–229.

THE GEM OF HARPOCRATES: From King, *The Gnostics and Their Remains*, plate C.4.

JESUS ON THE "FIRST AND LAST MYSTERIES": See MacDermot, *Pistis Sophia*, especially book 1.

FIRST MYSTERY IS LAST MYSTERY, "FROM WITHIN OUTWARDS": MacDermot, *Pistis Sophia*, 19, 411.

APOLLO, HOLDS THE BEGINNING AND THE END: ". . . you hold the bounds of the whole world (*kosmos*). Yours, too, are the beginning and end to come" (*Orphic Hymn* 34.14–15; Athanassakis translation, 49).

APOLLO, HARMONIZES THE POLES WITH HIS LYRE: *Orphic Hymns* 34.16–17 (Athanassakis translation, 49). This line in the Orphic Hymn has a double meaning: on one hand, Apollo harmonizes the poles of the seasons, summer and winter; in a cosmic sense, he harmonizes "beginning and end," the polarities of *all* creation. The same symbolism appears in fragment 1 of Skythinos (translated by Flora Levin, *The Harmonics of Nicomachus and the Pythagorean Tradition*, 41):

> Zeus' [lyre], which has as a shining
> plectrum the light of the Sun, fair
> Apollo set all in harmony, bringing
> its beginning in tune with its end.

INHERITANCE OF LIGHT: Mead translation of *Pistis Sophia* in his *Fragments of a Faith Forgotten*, 479 (= MacDermot, *Pistis Sophia*, 415).

Omphalos: The Philosophical Stone in Antiquity

EAGLES OF ZEUS MET AT DELPHI: See the scholion on Pindar, in Cook, *Zeus*, II, 179. According to Plutarch, *On the Obsolescence of Oracles* 1, the birds were eagles or swans; swans are sacred to Apollo. For a comprehensive study of Apollo's swan symbolism and its Hyperborean dimensions, see Ahl, "Amber, Avallon, and Apollo's Singing Swans."

OMPHALOS = NAVEL: The Greek word *omphalos* is cognate to the Latin *umbilicus*. Both are related to the Sanskrit *nābhis* ("navel," "knob," etc.). See Liddel and Scott, *Greek-English Lexicon*, s.v. omphalos.

AXIS MUNDI, THE CENTER OF SACRED SPACE: See Eliade, *Patterns in Comparative Religion*; *Cosmos and History*; *The Sacred and the Profane*; see also Cook, *The Tree of Life*.

OMPHALOS AS "MID-NAVEL AXIS": Nonnos, in his *Dionysiaca*, applies the following titles to the omphalos at Delphi: "mid-navel axis" or μεσόμφαλος ἄξων (2.696); "mid-navel axis of Pythô [or Delphi]" (4.290); "Pythian axis"

(4.291); "oracular axis" (7.71 and 27.252). In several places, for example 13.132, he makes the omphalos-axis speak on its own accord, without the Pythia being present; Nonnos also draws a connection between the Greek word *omphê*, "divine or oracular voice," and omphalos. Likewise, the Latin poet Claudianus also refers to the omphalos at Delphi as *Pythius axis* (Claudian, preface to *The Panegyric on the Consulship of Flavius Manlius Theodorus*, line 16). In Greek gematria, AXIS and OMPHALOS amount to exactly the same value. Omphalos stones were present at other Apollo temples, for example, Apollo's temple at Didyma, where the Pythia was said to sit on an "axis" before delivering oracles (for discussion, see Roscher, *Omphalos*, 36ff.).

THE VEIL OF HARMONIA: Nonnos, *Dionysiaca* 41.294ff.; see translation in Lethaby, *Architecture, Mysticism, and Myth*, 34–35.

OMPHALOS, THE TOMB OF DIONYSUS: Tatian, cited by Fontenrose, *Python*, 376 n. 16.

OMPHALOS, THE TOMB OF PYTHON: Varro, *On the Latin Language*, 7.17; see also Hesychios, cited by Fontenrose, *Python*, 374–375.

SERPENT AND THE OMPHALOS: The conjunction of serpent and omphalos or *axis mundi* is a universal symbol: Python guards the sacred center in the same way that the dragon surrounds the "primordial Pearl of Beginning, from which all things come forth" in Oriental iconography (von Franz, *Time*, 32–33). In metaphysical terms, the omphalos is "the Center in the midst of conditions," while the serpent or dragon represents the coils of manifestation (cf. Purce, *The Mystic Spiral*, 16–18). The Center, guarded by the serpent, represents "the treasure hard to obtain": in Greek mythology, this symbolism is implicit in the story of Python, who guards the omphalos; the dragon who guards the Golden Fleece, which is nailed to a great oak; and the serpent Ladon, who guards the Golden Apples of the Hesperides, which bestow immortality. This symbolism is also reflected in the celestial vault, for these mythic serpents were identified with constellation Draco, the dragon, who is entwined about the pole star—the celestial omphalos-axis—around which the heavenly spheres revolve (*Oxford Classical Dictionary*, 284; cf. also Godwin, *Arktos*, 145).

OMPHALOS, EMBLEM OF THE MONAD: See A. B. Cook, quoted in this work, p. 67. Pythagorean titles of the Monad include "the Axis," "Apollo" (Unity), "the Seed," "the Sun," "Space-Producer," "Atlas" (for upholding creation), etc. For Pythagorean titles of the first ten numbers, see pseudo-Iamblichus, *The Theology of Arithmetic*; Taylor, *Theoretic Arithmetic of the Pythagoreans*,

168–207; Theon of Smyrna, *Mathematics Useful for Understanding Plato*, 66–70; Stanley, *Pythagoras*, 525–529; Guthrie, *Pythagorean Sourcebook*, 321–323; see also Aristides Quintilianus, *On Music* 3.6 and 3.11–12 (Barker translation, 502–504 and 511–514).

OMPHALOS AT HELIOPOLIS (EGYPT): See discussion in "Heliopolis: The City of the Sun," 248–249.

OMPHALOS AT JERUSALEM (ISRAEL): See Roscher, *Der Omphalosgedanke bei verschiedenen Völkern, besonders den semitischen*; Elderkin, *Related Religious Ideas of Delphi, Tara, and Jerusalem*; Lethaby, *Architecture, Mysticism, and Myth*, 87ff.; and Michell and Rhone, *Twelve-Tribe Nations and the Science of Enchanting the Landscape*, 166, in which the Dome of the Tablets is now identified as the Rock of Foundation.

OMPHALOS AT TARA (IRELAND): Giraldus Cambrensis quoted by Elderkin, *Related Religious Ideas of Delphi, Tara, and Jerusalem*, 2; see also Rees and Rees, *Celtic Heritage*, chapter 7; Michell and Rhone, *Twelve-Tribe Nations*, 49–56.

For more on the omphalos and the omphaloi of the ancient world, see the works of Wilhelm Roscher: *Omphalos*; *Neue Omphalosstudien*; and *Der Omphalosgedanke bei verschiedenen Völkern, besonders den semitischen*. The widespread iconography of the omphalos collected by Roscher amply testifies to the importance of this central symbol of traditional cosmology.

Simon Petros: The Omphalos of Christianity I

SIMON PETER AS OMPHALOS: This symbolism has also been noted by Lethaby, *Architecture, Nature, and Magic*, 103, and by Elderkin, *Related Religious Ideas of Delphi, Tara, and Jerusalem*, 42, who asks in his discussion, "Was the pagan rock at Delphi to be superseded by the Christian?"

PETER = PETROS / PETRA: Matthew 4.18.

CEPHAS = PETER: John 1.42.

729, THE CUBIC FOUNDATION STONE: See Bond and Lea, *Gematria*, 112–113.

GOD'S SHAPE, THE FOUNDATION STONE AT THE CENTER OF CREATION: For this "mystery of the hebdomad," which is the teaching of "Petros," see *The Clementine Homilies* 17.8–10 (*Ante-Nicene Fathers*, VIII, 320–321); for an alternate translation and additional material, see Lea and Bond, *Materials for the Study of the Apostolic Gnosis*, part 2, 104–115, which also gives the Greek text.

729/486: Another dimension to the "metacube" of Cephas is the unique harmonic relation between its volume (729) and surface (486), for 729:486 is the perfect fifth in music, the most powerful harmonic *logos*, and one which was associated in antiquity with the most powerful celestial body, the sun. If one expresses the Pythagorean diatonic scale described in Plato's *Timaeus* in the smallest possible set of whole numbers, the rising tone numbers are: 384 (C) – 432 (D) – 486 (E) – 512 (F) – 576 (G) – 648 (A) – 729 (B) – 768 (C). In order to bring out this scale on the monochord, however, again using the smallest possible set of whole numbers, the string needs to be divided into 972 parts to bring out the above tones; in terms of string divisions we arrive at the following values: 972 (C) – 864 (D) – 768 (E) – 729 (F) – 648 (G) – 576 (A) – 512 (B) – 486 (C). As can be seen, 729 and 486, separated by a fifth, appear in this central harmonic configuration of the scale both as tonal frequencies and string divisions, thus confirming their canonical stature in ancient tuning theory. This arrangement can be studied in the polychord photograph which appears on page 58.

Simon Petros: The Omphalos of Christianity II

729 IN PLATO: Plato, *Republic* 587E–588A.

THE MAGIC SQUARE OF 729: This fabulous 27x27 magic square was noted by C. A. Browne, Jr., "Magic Squares and Pythagorean Numbers," and is also described by Jim Moran in his book *The Wonders of Magic Squares*, 85–105. Moran notes, "The numbers in the rows, columns, and corner-to-corner diagonals of the central 3x3 square add up to 1,095, or the days of a three-year period, those of the 9x9 central square add up to 9,855, the days of a twenty-seven-year period—in other words, periods of years corresponding to 1,3,9,27" (*Wonders of Magic Squares*, 89). Since each horizontal, vertical, or diagonal line of the complete square amounts to 9,855 (27x365), the sum of *all* the numbers comprising this magic square is 266,085 or 729x365. Hence, not only is 729 the number of days and nights in a year (365+364), but the sum of 1–729 is itself 729x365—the number of days in 729 years—thus truly confirming this value's solar character!

729, A NUMBER OF THE SUN: Plutarch, *On the Generation of the Soul in the Timaeus*, 1028B. Noting that 729 is both a square and a cubic number, Plutarch remarks that "this is why they [the Pythagoreans] sometimes call the sun too a square and a cube."

619 = DELPHI: 619 is also the value of PYTHION (ΠΥΘΙΟΝ), a temple of Apollo Pythios. Apollo's Pythion in Athens housed a replica of the omphalos at Delphi: see Roscher, *Omphalos*, 85–86, and Cook, *Zeus*, II, 184.

SOLAR FOUNDATION STONE: According to a scholiast on Pindar's first

Olympian Ode, the ancient "naturalists, speaking of the Sun, often call him a stone, or petra" (Greek text, translation, and discussion in Bryant, *Antient Mythology*, I, 366–367).

The Symbolism of the Cross

A UNIVERSAL ARCHETYPE: See Cook, *The Tree of Life: Image for the Cosmos* and Guénon, *The Symbolism of the Cross.*

EARLY CHRISTIAN SYMBOLISM OF THE CROSS: See the many sources collected in Rahner, *Greek Myths and Christian Mystery*, chapter 2, "The Mystery of the Cross." For the cross prefigured by the tree of Paradise, see ibid., 61–63.

HIPPOLYTUS ON THE CROSS: *De Pascha Homilia* 6, translated in Rahner, *Greek Myths and Christian Mystery*, 67–68.

MYSTERY OF THE CROSS IN THE ACTS OF JOHN: Hennecke-Schneemelcher, *New Testament Apocrypha*, II, 232–233.

EARLY REPRESENTATIONS OF THE CROSS FROM THE CATACOMBS: From Lehner, *Symbols, Signs, and Signets*, 110.

Jerusalem: The Spiritual Center

ROCK OF FOUNDATION HOLDS DOWN WATERS OF THE FLOOD: Raphael Patai, *Man and Temple*, cited in Michell, *Dimensions of Paradise*, 18–9.

CROSS OF JESUS ATOP SKULL OF ADAM: Rahner, *Greek Myth and Christian Mystery*, 64.

ROCK OF FOUNDATION IN ISLAM: Landay, *Dome of the Rock*, chapter 4.

DOME OF TABLETS, THE TRUE ROCK OF FOUNDATION: See Kaufman, "Where the Ancient Temple of Israel Stood: Extant 'Foundation Stone' for the Ark of the Covenant is Identified."

THE GEOMETRICAL ALIGNMENT OF JERUSALEM'S SACRED SITES: Michell and Rhone, *Twelve-Tribe Nations and the Science of Enchanting the Landscape*, 164–183.

Jesus the Fish

THE VESICA: See Lawlor, *Sacred Geometry*, 32–35; Michell, *Dimensions of Paradise*, 70–73.

CATHEDRALS BASED ON GEOMETRY OF VESICA: A clear example is Saint Mary's Chapel at Glastonbury, illustrated in the next section. See also Kerrich, "Observations on the Use of the Mysterious Figure, Called the Vesica Piscis, in the Architecture of the Middle Ages, and in Gothic Architecture" and Pennick, *Geomancy*, 137. For the use of $\sqrt{3}$ by medieval architects, see also Frankl and Panofsky, "The Secret of the Mediaeval Masons with an Explanation of Stornaloco's Formula."

Illustrations F and G are from Bragdon, *The Beautiful Necessity: Architecture as Frozen Music*, 69, which contains other examples.

Glastonbury Abbey

GLASTONBURY: All these themes and more are discussed in John Michell's beautifully written *New Light on the Ancient Mystery of Glastonbury*. See also his *City of Revelation*, chapter 4, "The Twelve Hides of Glaston," and *New View Over Atlantis*, chapter 6. All three volumes discuss the unusual relationship between Saint Mary's Chapel, the first Christian sanctuary in England, and the dimensions of nearby Stonehenge.

AVALON: On the relationship between Avalon and the Hyperborean Apollo, see Ahl, "Amber, Avallon, and Apollo's Singing Swan."

The Cosmic Tree: Reading a Symbol of Nature's Book

THE SYMBOL OF THE COSMIC TREE: Jung, "The Philosophical Tree," in *Alchemical Studies*, 251–349; Cook, *The Tree of Life: Image for the Cosmos*; Guénon, *Symbolism of the Cross*, chapter 9, "The Tree in the Midst"; Butterworth, *The Tree at the Navel of the Earth*.

THE FORMULA OF MARIA PROPHETISSA: Jung, *Psychology and Alchemy*, 160.

Appendix 1
The Miraculous Catch of the 153 Fishes in the Unbroken Net

1. Michell, *The Dimensions of Paradise*, 178.

2. See Plato, *Timaeus* 50A–53C.

3. Plato describes the Receptacle as "filled with powers that were neither alike nor evenly balanced," being "everywhere swayed unevenly and shaken" by the forces of disequilibrium. See *Timaeus* 52E.

4. Plotinus, *Enneads* 4.3.9 (MacKenna translation, 307).

5. "The way in which he makes these assumptions, without explanation of any kind, shows that they were common in his day, and much ingenuity has been spent in devising the processes by which they may have been reached" (Thomas, *Greek Mathematical Works*, I, 323).

6. See Eisler, *Orpheus the Fisher: Comparative Studies in Orphic and Early Christian Cult Symbolism*, chapter 14, for a discussion of the Orphic-

Pythagorean background of the New Testament account.

7. Guthrie, *The Pythagorean Sourcebook and Library*, 128.

8. Guthrie, *The Pythagorean Sourcebook and Library*, 64–65.

Descriptive List of Ancient Authorities

Aristides Quntillianus (3rd or 4th century C.E.) The Neopythagorean author of a work *On Music*; it deals with tuning theory (harmonics), the value of music in education, psychotherapy, music and metaphysical knowledge, and other topics.

Basilides (fl. 120–130 C.E.) Important gnostic teacher and Christian theologian of Alexandria. He taught an emanationist cosmology in which the figure of Abraxas was identified as the Demiurge, the fabricator of the physical universe.

Clement of Alexandria (*c*. 150–216 C.E.) Early church father and head of the Cathetical School of Alexandria. Widely read in Greek literature, philosophy, and knowledgable about the mystery religions, Clement refers in his writings to the mysteries of the early church which he describes as being similar to those of the Greek philosophers. For Clement, the true Christian is a gnostic, and he fought to defend the traditions of Christian gnosis within the framework of developing orthodoxy. He presented Christianity to his Hellenistic readers as "The New Song," a new manifestation of the preexisting Logos.

Eratosthenes (*c*. 275–194 B.C.E.) Keeper of the Library at Alexandria and writer in the fields of literary criticism, chronology, mathematics, astronomy, geography, and philosophy. He is famous for measuring accurately the dimensions of the Earth, based on the difference in the shadows cast by the sun at Syene and Alexandria on the summer solstice.

Heliodorus (fl. 220–50 C.E.) Author of the ancient Greek novel *An Ethiopian Romance* which contains interesting fragments of esoteric lore. He was a priest of Helios from Emesa in Syria.

Heraclitus (fl. *c.* 500 B.C.E.) One of the earliest Greek philosophers. Heraclitus wrote a book of gnomic aphorisms which he deposited in the temple of Artemis at Ephesus. His philosophy revolves around the nature of change ("All is flow"), the identity of opposites ("The way up and the way down are the same"), and the nature of the Logos ("Listening not to me but to the *logos*, it is wise to acknowledge that all things are one").

Hermes Trismegistos. Thrice-Great Hermes, the mythical revealer of all the arts and sciences. The reputed author of the Egyptian Hermetic writings and all priestly knowledge, Hermes Trismegistus is a personified representation of the Logos as Gnostic Revealer. Many of his attributes are based on those of the Egyptian god Thoth, the so-called "Hermes of Egypt."

Hippolytus (*c.* 170–*c.* 236 C.E.) A bishop in Rome and early chuch father. His chief writing, *The Refutation of All Heresies*, attempts to show that the teachings of the Christian gnostics are the offspring of Greek philosophical systems. This book, along with *Against Heresies* by Irenaeus, is one of the most valuable sources on gnostic beliefs written from a polemical perspective.

Iamblichus of Chalcis (*c.* 250–*c.* 325 C.E.) A Neoplatonic philosopher who wrote a ten-volume encyclopedia of Pythagorean philosophy which included *The Life of Pythagoras*; *The Exhortation to Philosophy*; *On the Common Mathematical Science*; *Commentary on Nichomachus' Introduction to Arithmetic*; three books *On the Natural, Ethical, and Divine Conceptions which are Perceived in the Science of Numbers* (of which the anonymous *Theology of Arithmetic* is based on the third book); and three lost works on Pythagorean harmonics, geometry, and astronomy.

Irenaeus (*c.* 130–*c.* 202 C.E.) Born in Asia Minor, Irenaeus became the bishop of Lyons in Gaul *circa* 178. He is the author of a massive work entitled *Against Heresies*, a polemic directed against the early Christian gnostic schools.

Jesus (*c.* 6 B.C.E–*c.* 30 C.E.) A spiritual teacher and reformer who was seen by his followers as a revealer of saving knowledge and personification of the Logos at an early point after his death. The details of his life and teachings were orally transmitted and first set into a narrative framework in the gospel attributed to Mark, written around the year 70 C.E.

Julian (332–363 C.E.) Though educated as a Christian when a youth, this Roman emperor was devoted to classical culture and became a defender of pagan philosophy and religious beliefs. A Neoplatonist and initiate into the mysteries of Mithras, when "Julian the Apostate" became Augustus, he proclaimed toleration for all religions and attempted to reverse the policies of Constantine that officially embraced Christianity and rejected paganism. His beautiful *Hymn to King Helios* is an important exposition of late classical solar monotheism.

Macrobius (fl. 410 C.E.) His *Saturnalia* is an important source for antiquarian details of Greek and Roman religion and the allegorical interpretation of myth. His writings, which include a philosophical and cosmological *Commentary on the Dream of Scipio* by Cicero, reveal no influence of Christianity.

Maximus of Tyre (*c.*125–85 C.E.) A Platonist and sophist who lived the life of a traveling lecturer. Forty-one of his lectures are extant.

Nicomachus of Gerasa (fl. 140–150 C.E.) Mathematician and Neopythagorean. His works include an *Introduction to Arithmetic*, *The Manual of Harmonics*, *The Theology of Arithmetic* (fragments survive), *Introduction to Geometry* (lost), and a *Life of Pythagoras* (lost). His *Introduction to Arithmetic* was translated into Latin and remained a definitive handbook up until the Renaissance.

Nonnos of Panopolis (5th century C.E.) His *Dionysiaca*, the last great epic poem of antiquity, consists of forty-eight books. Written in an extravagant and unrestrained style, the poem details the expedition of Dionysus to India, and contains some interesting details of mystic and cosmological lore.

Origen (185/86–254/55 C.E.) Born in Alexandria of Christian parents, Origen studied under Clement in the Alexandrian Cathetical School. He was a scholar, teacher, theologian, and prolific writer. Like Clement, Origen was a Christian Platonist with a profound interest in the mystical traditions of the early church, including the Christian traditions of hidden knowledge.

Orpheus (before Homer) An ancient, mythical (?) poet, bard, and musician, who was held to be the founder of the Greek mysteries and a revealer of esoteric knowledge concerning the structure of the cosmos and the nature and fate of the soul.

Paul (active 35–60 C.E.) The earliest New Testament writer. Paul, whose primary language was Greek, grew up in the university town of Tarsus.

Philo Judaeus (*c.* 30 B.C.E.–45 C.E.) Jewish theologian of Alexandria who was heavily influenced by Platonic and Neopythagorean ideas. He interpreted Jewish scripture allegorically in the light of Greek philosophy and cosmology and sets forth a fully developed Logos doctrine in his writings. He depicts the nature of the Logos in allegorical terms, presenting it as "the Son of God," "the Good Shepherd," etc.

Plato (*c.* 429–347 B.C.E.) Aside from Pythagoras himself, the most influential Pythagorean philosopher in the history of Western civilization. His dialogues reveal an outstanding artistic ability and a genius for expressing the insights of the Orphics and Pythagoreans within the context of philosophical debate.

Plotinus (205–269/70 C.E.) Greek philosopher who is generally described as the founder of Neoplatonism. His description of reality is hierarchical, moving from the absolute unity of the First Cause (the One) to the multiplicity of the phenomenal world. For Plotinus, the four levels of reality are the One; Nous (Intelligence); Soul; and Nature. Born in Egypt, he held philosophical seminars in Rome. Like Plato, his conceptions have exerted influence in every succeeding age.

Plutarch of Chaerona (*c.* 45–*c.* 125 C.E.) This philosopher, scholar, and prolific essayist is well-known for his *Parallel Lives*. But Plutarch was also a keen student of Greek religion, myth, cosmology, and esoteric traditions. A Pythagorean and a Platonist, he was a priest of Apollo at Delphi during the last thirty years of his life. His "Delphic essays" are indispensible reading for anyone interested in the esoteric dimensions of Greek thought.

Posidonius of Apamea (*c.* 135–*c.* 51 B.C.E.) Stoic philosopher, scientist, and cosmologist. He was extremely influential in promulgating the idea that humanity is the bond between spirit and matter and that the different parts of the cosmos are related to one another through the power of universal sympathy.

Proclus (*c.* 410–485 C.E.) One of the last heads of the Platonic Academy in Athens before the teaching of pagan philosophy was outlawed by Justinian in 529 C.E. Philosopher, scientist, and poet, this prolific Neoplatonist was a great expositor of the Greek esoteric traditions. He was described by his student and biographer, Marinus of Samaria, as a "truly blessed man" and "a priest of the entire universe."

Ptolemy (fl. 127–148 C.E.) This Alexandrian astronomer, mathematician, and geographer is also the author of a book *On Harmonics*, one of the most important works on tuning theory to survive from the ancient world.

Pythagoras of Samos (*c.* 570–*c.* 496 B.C.E.) The first man to call himself a philosopher, this Greek cosmologist and mathematician was a religious reformer in the Orphic tradition. He taught that Number is a universal archetype which underlies the structure of reality. He is said to have traveled widely, visiting priests and scholars in distant lands, before founding his own philosophical school at Croton in southern Italy.

Sallustius (fl. 360 C.E.) This Neoplatonist and friend of the Emperor Julian wrote a cosmological and theological treatise *Concerning the Gods and the Universe*.

Simonides (*c*. 556–468 B.C.E.) Poet, devotee of Dionysus, and inventor of the art of memory (*memoria technica*), Simonides is said to have introduced several of the long vowels into the Greek alphabet that was being used in Athens.

Thales (fl. 580 B.C.E.) This very early Greek scientist and philosopher lived near Miletus in Asia Minor. He predicted a solar eclipse based on Babylonian astronomical data, introduced an important geometrical theorem (the theorem of Thales), and is famous for his saying "All things are full of gods."

Theon of Smyrna (fl. *c*. 115–140 C.E.) This Pythagorean philosopher and Platonist wrote a work entitled *Mathematics Useful for Understanding Plato*; it deals with arithmetic, number symbolism, harmonics, and astronomy.

Valentinus (*c*. 100–180 C.E.) The most famous and influential gnostic teacher of Alexandria who was well-known for his emanationist cosmology described in chapter 6. Some scholars attribute the beautiful *Gospel of Truth* to Valentinus. At one point he was nearly elected the Bishop of Rome.

Zosimos of Panopolis (fl. 300 C.E.) An Egyptian alchemical writer who drew upon gnostic, Hermetic, pagan, and Christian mystical traditions.

Bibliography of Works Cited

Acts of John. In Hennecke-Schneemelcher, *New Testament Apocrypha*, II, 215–258.

Acts of Thomas. In Hennecke-Schneemelcher, *New Testament Apocrypha*, II, 425–531.

Adam, James. *The Nuptial Number of Plato*. 1891. Reprint. London: Kairos, 1985.

Aelian. *On the Characteristics of Animals*. 3 vols. Loeb Classical Library. Cambridge: Harvard University Press, 1958–1959.

Ahl, Frederick M. "Amber, Avallon, and Apollo's Singing Swan," *American Journal of Philology* 103 (1982), 373–411.

Aland, Kurt. *Synopsis of the Four Gospels: Greek-English Edition of the Synopsis Quattuor Evangeliorum*. Eighth corrected edition. Stuttgart: German Bible Society, 1987.

Alderink, Larry J. *Creation and Salvation in Ancient Orphism*. American Classical Studies 8. Chico: Scholars Press, 1981.

Allers, R. "Microcosmus from Anaximandros to Paracelsus," *Traditio* 2 (1944), 319–407.

American Heritage Dictionary of the English Language. Edited by Anne H. Soukhanov. Third edition. Boston: Hougton Mifflin, 1992.

Angus, S. *The Religious Quests of the Graeco-Roman World: A Study in the Historical Background of Early Christianity*. London: John Murray, 1929.

Anonymous. *Magickian's Desk Reference*. Berkeley: Beth-Shin-Tau, 1978.

Ante-Nicene Fathers. See Roberts and Donaldson, editors, *The Ante-Nicene Fathers*.

Anthon, Charles. *Anthon's Classical Dictionary*. New York: Harper, 1851.

Apollodorus. *The Library of Mythology*. Translated by J. G. Frazer. 2 vols. Loeb Classical Library. Cambridge: Harvard University Press, 1921.

Apollonius Rhodius. *Argonautica*. Loeb Classical Library. Cambridge: Harvard University Press, 1912.

Aristides Quintilianus. *On Music*. In Barker, *Greek Musical Writings II:*

Harmonic and Acoustic Theory, 392–535.

Aristotle. *Works*. 23 vols. Loeb Classical Library. Cambridge: Harvard University Press, 1926–1970.

Athanassakis, Apostolos M., translator. *The Orphic Hymns*. Graeco-Roman Religion 4. Missoula, MT: Scholars Press, 1977.

Athenaeus. *The Deipnosophists*. 7 vols. Loeb Classical Library. Cambridge: Harvard University Press, 1921–1941.

Athenagoras. *Athenagoras' Plea*. In Richardson, *Early Christian Fathers*, 300–340.

Bakhtiar, Laleh. *Sufi: Expressions of the Mystic Quest*. London: Thames & Hudson, 1976.

Barb, A. A. "Three Elusive Amulets," *Journal of the Warburg and Courtauld Institutes* 27 (1964), 1–22.

Barber, Richard. *The Knight and Chivalry*. London: Cardinal, 1974.

Barker, Andrew. *Greek Musical Writings II: Harmonic and Acoustic Theory*. Cambridge: Cambridge University Press, 1984.

Barnabas. *The Epistle of Barnabas*. In *Ante-Nicene Fathers*, I, 137–149.

Barnstone, Willis, editor. *The Other Bible: A Collection of Ancient, Esoteric Texts from Judeo-Christian Traditions, Excluded from the Official Canon of the Old and New Testaments*. New York: Harper & Row, 1984.

Barrett, C. K. *The Gospel of John*. New York: Macmillan, 1955.

———. *The New Testament Background: Selected Documents*. Revised and expanded edition. New York: Harper & Row, 1989.

Beck, R. "Mithraism since Franz Cumont," in *Aufstieg und Niedergang der Römischen Welt* 2 (1984), 17.4, 2002–2115.

Berriman, A. E. *Historical Metrology: A New Analysis of the Archaeological and the Historical Evidence Relating to Weights and Measures*. London: J. M. Dent & Sons, 1953.

Betz, Hans Dieter, editor. *The Greek Magical Papyri in Translation*. Vol. 1, *Texts*. Chicago: University of Chicago Press, 1986.

Bianchi, Ugo. *The Greek Mysteries*. Iconography of Religions 17, 3. Leiden: E. J. Brill, 1976.

Blanco, Antonino González. "Hermetism: A Bibliographical Approach," *Aufstieg und Niedergang der Römischen Welt* 2 (1984), 17.4, 2240–2281.

Bond, F. B., and Lea, T. S. *Gematria: A Preliminary Investigation of the Cabala Contained in the Coptic Gnostic Books and of a similar Gematria in the Greek Text of the New Testament*. Oxford: Basil Blackwell, 1917.

Reprint. London, Research into Lost Knowledge Organization, 1977. (*See also* Lea and Bond.)

Bonner, Campbell. "The Numerical Value of a Magical Formula," *Journal of Egyptian Archaeology* 16 (1930), 6–9.

———. *Studies in Magical Amulets, Chiefly Graeco-Egyptian*. University of Michigan Studies Humanistic Series 49. Ann Arbor: University of Michigan Press, 1950.

Book of Thomas the Contender. Translated by John D. Turner. In Robinson, *The Nag Hammadi Library in English*, 199–207.

Books of Ieou. See entry under MacDermot.

Boylan, Patrick. *Thoth, the Hermes of Egypt: A Study of Some Aspects of Theological Thought in Ancient Egypt*. London, 1922. Reprint. Chicago: Ares, 1987.

Bragdon, Claude. *The Frozen Fountain: Being Essays on Architecture and the Art of Design in Space*. New York: Alfred A. Knopf, 1932.

———. *The Beautiful Necessity: Architecture as Frozen Music*. New York: Alfred A. Knopf, 1939. Reprint. Wheaton: Quest, 1978.

Brown, Norman O. *Hermes the Thief: The Evolution of a Myth*. Madison: University of Wisconsin Press, 1947. Reprint. Great Barrington: Lindisfarne Press, 1990.

Browne, C. A. "Magic Squares and Pythagorean Numbers." In *Magic Squares and Magic Cubes*, edited by W. S. Andrews. 1917. Reprint. New York: Dover, 1960.

Bryant, Jacob. *A New System or an Analysis of Antient Mythology*. Third edition. 6 volumes. London, 1807.

Budge, E. A. Wallis. *The Gods of the Egyptians*. 2 vols. London, 1904. Reprint. New York: Dover, 1969.

———. *Osiris and the Egyptian Resurrection*. 2 vols. London, 1911. Reprint. New York: Dover, 1973.

———. *An Egyptian Hieroglyphic Dictionary*. 2 vols. London, 1920. Reprint. New York: Dover, 1978.

———. *Tutankhamen: Amenism, Atenism and Egyptian Monotheism*. London: M. Hopkinson, 1923.

Burckhardt, Titus. *Alchemy: Science of the Cosmos, Science of the Soul*. Translated by William Stoddart. London: John M. Watkins, 1967.

Burkert, Walter. *Ancient Mystery Cults*. Cambridge: Harvard University Press, 1987.

Butterworth, E. A. S. *The Tree at the Navel of the Earth*. Berlin: de Gruyter,

1970.

Calder, I. R. F. "A Note on Magic Squares in the Philosophy of Agrippa of Nettesheim," *Journal of the Warburg and Courtauld Institutes*, 12 (1949), 196–199.

Campbell, Joseph, editor. *The Mysteries: Papers from the Eranos Yearbooks*. Princeton: Princeton University Press, 1955.

Carey, John. "The Daughters of Memory," *Temenos* 7 (1986), 223–230.

Cartlidge, David, and Dungan, David. *Documents for the Study of the Gospels*. Philadelphia: Fortress, 1980.

Charlesworth, James H., editor. *The Old Testament Pseudepigrapha*. 2 vols. Vol. 1, *Apocalyptic Literature and Testaments*. Vol. 2, *Expansions of the "Old Testament" and Philosophical Literature, Prayers, Psalms and Odes, Fragments of Lost Judeo-Hellenistic Works*. New York: Doubleday, 1983–1985.

Clark, R. T. Rundle. *Myth and Symbol in Ancient Egypt*. London: Thames & Hudson, 1959.

Claudian. *Works*. 2 vols. Loeb Classical Library. Cambridge: Harvard University Press, 1922.

Clement of Alexandria. *The Exhortation to the Greeks*. In *Ante-Nicene Fathers*, II, 171–206.

———. *The Stromata, or Miscellanies*. In *Ante-Nicene Fathers*, II, 299–402.

———. *On the Salvation of the Rich Man*. In *Ante-Nicene Fathers*, II, 591–604.

———. *The Exhortation to the Greeks*. Translated by G. W. Butterworth. Loeb Classical Library. Cambridge: Harvard University Press, 1919.

Clementine Homilies. In *Ante-Nicene Fathers*, VIII, 223–346.

Cobb, Noel. *Archetypal Imagination: Glimpses of the Gods in Life and Art*. Hudson: Lindisfarne Press, 1992.

Colson, F. H. *The Week: An Essay on the Origin and Development of the Seven-Day Cycle*. Cambridge: Cambridge University Press, 1926.

Cook, Arthur B. *Zeus: A Study in Ancient Religion*. 3 vols. in five. Vol. 1, *Zeus God of the Bright Sky*. Vol. 2, *Zeus God of the Dark Sky (Thunder and Lightning)*. Vol. 3, *Zeus God of the Dark Sky (Earthquakes, Clouds, Wind, Dew, Rain, Meteorites)*. Cambridge: Cambridge University Press, 1914–40.

Cook, Roger. *The Tree of Life: Image for the Cosmos*. London: Thames & Hudson, 1974.

Copleston, Frederick. *A History of Philosophy: Greece and Rome*. 2 vols. New York: Doubleday, 1962.

Corbin, Henry. *The Man of Light in Iranian Sufism*. Boulder: Shambhala, 1978.

Cornford, Francis M. "Mysticism and Science in the Pythagorean Tradition," *Classical Quarterly* 16 (1922), 137–150; 17 (1923), 1–12.

Critchlow, Keith. "The Platonic Tradition on the Nature of Proportion," *Lindisfarne Letter* 10, 11–32.

———. *Time Stands Still: New Light on Megalithic Science*. New York: St. Martins Press, 1982.

Cumont, Franz. *Textes et monuments figurés relatifs aux mystères de Mithra*. 2 vols. Bruxelles, 1896–1899.

———. *The Mysteries of Mithra*. Second revised edition. 1903. Reprint. New York: Dover, 1956.

———. *Astrology and Religion Among the Greeks and Romans*. New York: G. P. Putnam's Sons,1912. Reprint. New York: Dover, 1960.

Deman, A. "Mithras and Christ: Some Iconographical Similarities." In Hinnells, *Mithraic Studies*, 507–517.

Dinsmore, W. B. *The Architecture of Ancient Greece: An Account of its Historic Development*. New York: Norton, 1975.

Diodorus Siculus. *Library of History*. 12 vols. Loeb Classical Library. Cambridge: Harvard University Press, 1933–1967.

Diringer, David. *The Alphabet: A Key to the History of Mankind*. New York: Philosophical Library, 1948.

Doelger, Franz Joseph. ΙΧΘΥΣ: *Das Fischsymbol in frühchristlicher Zeit*. 2 vols. Münster: Verlag der Aschendorffschen Verlagsbuchhandlug, 1922–28.

Doresse, J. *The Secret Books of the Egyptian Gnostics*. New York: Viking Press, 1960.

Duchesne-Guillemin, J. "Jesus' Trimorphism and the Differentiation of the Magi." In *Man and His Salvation: Studies in Memory of S. G. F. Brandon*, edited by Eric Sharp and John Hinnells, 91–98. Manchester: Manchester University Press, 1973.

Edinger, E. F. *Ego and Archetype: Individuation and the Religious Function of the Psyche*. Baltimore: Penguin, 1973.

Eisler, Robert. *Orpheus the Fisher: Comparative Studies in Orphic and Early Christian Cult Symbolism*. London: J. M. Watkins, 1921.

El-Kachab, A. M. "Some Gem-Amulets Depicting Harpocrates Seated on a Lotus Flower," *Journal of Egyptian Archaeology* 57 (1971), 132–145.

Elderkin, George W. *Related Religious Ideas of Delphi, Tara and Jerusalem: A*

Study of the Dionysiac Tradition. Springfield, Mass.: Pond-Ekberg, 1961.

Eliade, Mircea. *The Sacred and the Profane*. New York: Harcourt, Brace, and World, 1959.

———. *Cosmos and History: The Myth of the Eternal Return*. New York: Harper & Row, 1959.

———. *The Two and the One*. New York: Harper & Row, 1965.

———. *Patterns in Comparative Religion*. New York: Meridian, 1974.

Epiphanius. *The Panarion of St. Epiphanius, Bishop of Salamis: Selected Passages*. Translated by Philip R. Amidon. New York: Oxford University Press, 1990.

Euclid. *On the Division of the Canon*. In Barker, *Greek Musical Writings II: Harmonic and Acoustic Theory*, 190–208.

Euripides. *Works*. 4 vols. Loeb Classical Library. Cambridge: Harvard University Press, 1912.

Faivre, Antoine. "Ancient and Medieval Sources of Modern Esoteric Movements." In *Modern Esoteric Spirituality*, edited by Antoine Faivre and Jacob Needleman, 1–70. World Spirituality 21. New York: Crossroad: 1992.

Farbridge, M. H. *Studies in Biblical and Semitic Symbolism*. New York: Dutton, 1923.

Farnell, L. R. *The Cults of the Greek States*. 5 vols. Oxford: Oxford University Press, 1896–1909. Reprint. New Rochelle: Caratzas Brothers, 1977.

Fideler, David. "The Passion of Sophia: An Early Gnostic Creation Myth," *Gnosis* 1 (Fall/Winter 1985), 17–22.

———. "A Comparison of the Prayer of the Apostle Paul with the Hymns of Corpus Hermeticum and Some Greek Magical Papyri," *The Hermetic Journal* 34 (Winter 1986), 4–17.

———. "Introduction." In Guthrie, *The Pythagorean Sourcebook and Library*, 19–54.

———. "The Voice from the Center: The Oracle of Apollo and the Oracle of the Heart," *Gnosis* 5 (Fall 1987), 23–27.

———. "The Rose Garden of the Philosophers: A Compendium of Diverse Observations Concerning Spiritual Horticulture, Alchemystical Gardening, and the Glades of Divine Inspiration," *Gnosis* 8 (Summer 1988), 40–44.

———. "The Path Toward the Grail: The Hermetic Sources and Structure of Wolfram von Eschenbach's *Parzival*." In *Alexandria* 1, edited by

David Fideler, 187–227. Grand Rapids: Phanes Press, 1991.

———. "The Science and Art of Animating Statues." In *Alexandria* 2, edited by David Fideler. Grand Rapids: Phanes Press, 1993.

———. "The Gematria of the Parthenon and Some Other Greek Temples." In *Alexandria* 3, edited by David Fideler. Grand Rapids: Phanes Press, 1994.

Fontenrose, Joseph. *Python: A Study of Delphic Myth and Its Origins*. Berkeley: University of California Press, 1959.

———. *Didyma: Apollo's Oracle, Cult, and Companions*. Berkeley and Los Angeles: University of California Press, 1988.

Fowden, Garth. *The Egyptian Hermes: A Historical Approach to the Late Pagan Mind*. Cambridge: Cambridge University Press, 1986.

Francis, René. *Egyptian Aesthetics*. London, 1911. Reprint. New York: Benjamin Blom, 1972.

Frankl, Paul, and Panofsky, Erwin. "The Secret of the Medieval Masons with an Explanation of Stornaloco's Formula," *Art Bulletin* 27 (1945), 46–60.

Franz, Marie-Louise von. *Number and Time: Reflections Leading Towards a Unification of Psychology and Physics*. Evanston: Northwestern University Press, 1974.

———. *Time: Rhythm and Repose*. London: Thames & Hudson, 1978.

Frazer, James G. *The Golden Bough: A Study in Magic and Religion*. 12 vols. Third edition. London: Macmillan, 1911–1915.

Gager, John G. *Moses in Greco-Roman Paganism*. Society of Biblical Literature Monograph Series 16. Nashville: Abingdon Press, 1972.

Geden, A. S. *Select Passages Illustrating Mithraism*. New York and London: Society for Promoting Christian Knowledge, 1925. Reprinted as *Mithraic Sources in English*. Hastings: Chthonios Books, 1990.

Gervers, Michael. "The Iconography of the Cave in Christian and Mithraic Tradition." In *Mysteria Mithrae: Proceedings of the International Seminar on the 'Religio-Historical Character of Roman Mithraism, with Particular Reference to Roman and Ostian Sources,' Rome and Ostia 1978*, edited by Ugo Bianchi, 579–596. Leiden: E. J. Brill, 1979.

Godwin, Joscelyn. *Robert Fludd: Hermetic Philosopher and Surveyor of Two Worlds*. London: Thames & Hudson, 1979. Reprint. Grand Rapids: Phanes Press, 1991.

———. *Mystery Religions in the Ancient World*. London: Thames & Hudson, 1981.

———. "The Golden Chain of Orpheus: A Survey of Musical Esotericism in the West," *Temenos* 4 (1984), 7–25; *Temenos* 5 (1984), 211–239.

———. *Music, Mysticism and Magic: A Sourcebook*. London: Routledge & Kegan Paul, 1986.

———. *Harmonies of Heaven and Earth*. London: Thames & Hudson, 1987.

———. *The Mystery of the Seven Vowels in Theory and Practice*. Grand Rapids: Phanes Press, 1991.

———. *Arktos: The Polar Myth in Science, Symbolism, and Nazi Survival*. Grand Rapids: Phanes Press, 1993.

———. *The Harmony of the Spheres: A Sourcebook of the Pythagorean Tradition in Music*. Rochester: Inner Traditions, 1993.

Goodenough, Erwin R. *By Light, Light: The Mystic Gospel of Hellenistic Judaism*. New Haven: Yale University Press, 1935.

———. *An Introduction to Philo Judaeus*. Second edition. Oxford: Basil Blackwell, 1962.

Gordon, R. L. "The Sacred Geography of a Mithraeum: The Example of Sette Sfere," *Journal of Mithraic Studies* 1 (1976), 119–165.

———. "Franz Cumont and the Doctrines of Mithraism." In Hinnells, *Mithraic Studies*, 215–248.

Gospel of Philip. Translated by Wesley W. Isenberg. In Robinson, *The Nag Hammadi Library in English*, 139–160.

Gospel of Thomas. Translated by Thomas O. Lambdin. In Robinson, *The Nag Hammadi Library in English*, 124–138.

Gospel of Truth. Translated by Harold W. Attridge and George W. MacRae. In Robinson, *The Nag Hammadi Library in English*, 38–51.

Grant, F. C. *Hellenistic Religions: The Age of Syncretism*. Indianapolis: Bobbs-Merrill, 1953.

Graves, Robert. *The Greek Myths*. 2 vols. in one. New York: George Braziller, 1959.

Green, Tamara. *The City of the Moon God: Religious Traditions of Harran*. Leiden: E. J. Brill, 1992.

Guénon, René. *The Symbolism of the Cross*. London: Luzac, 1958.

Guralnick, Eleanor. "Proportions of Korai," *American Journal of Archaeology* 85 (1981), 269–280.

Guthrie, Kenneth Sylvan, compiler and translator. *The Pythagorean Sourcebook and Library: An Anthology of Ancient Writings Which Relate to Pythagoras and Pythagorean Philosophy*. Edited and introduced by David Fideler. Grand Rapids: Phanes Press, 1987.

———. *The Message of Philo Judaeus of Alexandria*. London: Luzac, 1909.

Guthrie, W. K. C. "Who Were the Orphics?" *Scientia* 61 (1937), 110–20.

———. *Orpheus and Greek Religion: A Study of the Orphic Movement*. Second edition. London: Methuen, 1952.

———. *A History of Greek Philosophy*. Vol. 1, *The Earlier Presocratics and The Pythagoreans*. Cambridge: Cambridge University Press, 1971.

———. *A History of Greek Philosophy*. Vol. 4, *Plato, The Man and his Dialogues: Earlier Period*. Cambridge: Cambridge University Press, 1975.

Hall, James. *A History of Ideas and Images in Italian Art*. New York: Harper & Row, 1983.

Halsberghe, Gaston H. *The Cult of Sol Invictus*. Leiden: E. J. Brill, 1972.

Hamilton, J. D. B. "The Church and the Language of the Mystery: The First Four Centuries," *Ephemerides Theologicae Lovanienses* 53, 479–494.

Harrison, J. E. "Aegis—ΑΓΡΗΝΟΝ," *Bulletin de correspondence hellénique* 24 (1900), 254–262.

Heath, Thomas L. *A History of Greek Mathematics*. Vol. 1, *From Thales to Euclid*. Vol. 2, *From Aristarchus to Diophantus*. Oxford: Clarendon Press, 1921. Reprint. New York: Dover, 1981.

———. *The Thirteen Books of Euclid's Elements*. 3 vols. Cambridge: Cambridge University Press, 1926. Reprint. New York: Dover, 1956.

Heliodorus. *An Ethiopian Story*. Translated by J. R. Morgan. In *Collected Ancient Greek Novels*, edited by B. P. Reardon, 349–588. Berkeley and Los Angeles: University of California Press, 1989.

Hennecke–Schneemelcher. *New Testament Apocrypha, 1: Gospels and Related Writings*. Philadelphia: Westminster Press, 1963.

———. *New Testament Apocrypha, 2: Writings Relating to the Apostles; Apocalypses and Related Subjects*. Philadelphia: Westminster Press, 1965.

Herodotus. *Histories*. 4 vols. Loeb Classical Library. Cambridge: Harvard University Press, 1920–1924.

Hersey, George L. *Pythagorean Palaces: Magic and Architecture in the Italian Renaissance*. Ithaca: Cornell University Press, 1976.

Hesiod. *The Homeric Hymns and Homerica*. Loeb Classical Library. Cambridge: Harvard University Press, 1914.

Hillman, James. *Re-Visioning Psychology*. New York: Harper & Row, 1975.

Hinnells, John R., editor. *Mithraic Studies: Proceedings of the First International Congress of Mithraic Studies*. 2 vols. Manchester: Manchester University Press, 1975.

Hinnells, John R. "Reflections on the Bull-Slaying Scene." In Hinnells,

Mithraic Studies, 290–312.

Hippolytus. *The Refutation of All Heresies*. In *Ante-Nicene Fathers*, V, 9–153.

Hoeller, Stephan A. "Our Hermetic Heritage." In G. R. S. Mead, *The Hymns of Hermes*, 7–26.

Hogart, R. C., translator. *The Hymns of Orpheus*. Grand Rapids: Phanes Press, 1993.

Hornum, Michael. "A Plotinian Solution to a Vedantic Problem." *Alexandria* 1, edited by David Fideler, 293–306. Grand Rapids: Phanes Press, 1991.

Hoyle, Peter. *Delphi*. London: Cassell, 1967.

Hughes, David. *The Star of Bethlehem: An Astronomer's Confirmation*. New York: Walker, 1979.

Hyde, Walter. *Paganism to Christianity in the Roman Empire*. Philadelphia: University of Pennsylvania Press, 1946.

Hyginus. *The Myths of Hyginus*. Translated by Mary Amelia Grant. Lawrence: University of Kansas Press, 1960.

Iamblichus. *Iamblichus' Life of Pythagoras*. Translated by Thomas Taylor. London, 1818. Reprint. Rochester: Inner Traditions, 1986.

———. *On the Mysteries of the Egyptians, Chaldeans, and Assyrians*. Translated by Thomas Taylor. London, 1821. Reprint. London: Stuart and Watkins, 1968.

——— [Pseudo-Iamblichus]. *The Theology of Arithmetic: On the Mystical, Mathematical and Cosmological Symbolism of the First Ten Numbers*. Translated by Robin Waterfield. Grand Rapids: Phanes Press, 1988.

Ifrah, Georges. *From One to Zero: A Universal History of Numbers*. Translated by Lowell Bair. New York: Viking, 1985.

Irenaeus. *Against Heresies*. In *Ante-Nicene Fathers*, I, 315–567.

Irwin, Lee. "The Orphic Mystery: Harmony and Mediation." *Alexandria* 1, edited by David Fideler, 37–55. Grand Rapids: Phanes Press, 1991.

Jonas, Hans. *The Gnostic Religion: The Message of the Alien God and the Beginnings of Christianity*. Revised second edition. Boston: Beacon Press, 1963.

Julian. *Works of the Emperor Julian*. 3 vols. Loeb Classical Library. Cambridge: Harvard University Press, 1913–1923.

———. *Hymn to King Helios*. In Julian, *Works of the Emperor Julian*, I, 353–435.

———. *Hymn to the Mother of the Gods*. In Julian, *Works of the Emperor Julian*, I, 443–503.

Jung, C. G. *Aion: Researches into the Phenomenology of the Self.* Collected Works 9, II. Princeton: Princeton University Press, 1959.

———. *Psychology and Alchemy*. Collected Works 12. Princeton: Princeton University Press, 1968.

———. *Alchemical Studies*. Collected Works 13. Princeton: Princeton University Press, 1967.

Justin Martyr. *First Apology*. In *Ante-Nicene Fathers*, I, 163–193.

———. *Dialogue with Trypho*. In *Ante-Nicene Fathers*, I, 194–270.

Kaufman, A. S. "Where the Ancient Temple of Israel Stood: Extant 'Foundation Stone' for the Ark of the Covenant is Identified," *Biblical Archaeological Review* (March-April 1983), 40–59.

Keith, Michael. "The Number 666," *Journal of Recreational Mathematics* 15 (1982–83), 85–87.

Keizer, Lewis S. *The Eighth Reveals the Ninth: A New Hermetic Initiation Discourse (Tractate 6, Nag Hammadi Codex VI)*. Seaside, California: Academy of Arts and Humanities, 1974.

Kerényi, C. *The Gods of the Greeks*. London: Thames & Hudson, 1951.

———. *Hermes: Guide of Souls*. Translated by Murray Stein. Dallas: Spring Publications, 1986.

Kern, Otto. *Orphicorum Fragmenta*. Berlin: Weidmann, 1922.

Kerrich, T. "Observations on the Use of the Mysterious Figure, Called the Vesica Piscis, in the Architecture of the Middle Ages, and in Gothic Architecture," *Archaeologia* 19 (1821), 353–68.

Khare, H. C., editor. *Issues in Vedic Mathematics: Proceedings of the National Workshop on Vedic Mathematics, 25–28 March, 1988 at the University of Rajasthan, Jaipur*. Delhi: Motilal Banarsidass, 1991.

King, C. W. *The Gnostics and Their Remains, Ancient and Medieval.* Second enlarged edition. London, 1887. Reprint. Savage, Minnesota: Wizards Bookshelf, 1973.

Knox, W. L. *Some Hellenistic Elements in Primitive Christianity*. London: The British Academy, 1944.

Koester, Helmut. *Introduction to the New Testament*. Vol. 1, *History, Culture, and Religion of the Hellenistic Age*. Vol. 2, *History and Literature of Early Christianity*. Berlin and New York: Walter de Gruyter, 1982.

———. *Ancient Christian Gospels: Their History and Development*. Philadelphia: Trinity Press International, 1990.

Kraeling, Carl H. *Anthropos and Son of Man: A Study in the Religious Syncretism of the Hellenistic Orient*. New York: AMS Press, 1966.

Krupp, E. C. "Astronomers, Pyramids, and Priests." In *In Search of Ancient Astronomies*, edited by E. C. Krupp, 203–239. New York: McGraw Hill, 1978.

Kümmel, Werner George. *Introduction to the New Testament*. Nashville: Abingdon, 1975.

Lamy, Lucie. *Egyptian Mysteries: New Light on Ancient Spiritual Knowledge*. London: Thames & Hudson, 1981.

Landay, Jerry M. *Dome of the Rock*. New York: Newsweek, 1972.

Lawlor, Robert. *Sacred Geometry: Philosophy and Practice*. London: Thames & Hudson, 1982.

Lea, Simcox, and Bond, Bligh. *Materials for the Study of the Apostolic Gnosis*. Part 1. Oxford: Basil Blackwell, 1919. Reprint. London: Research into Lost Knowledge Organization, 1979.

———. *Materials for the Study of the Apostolic Gnosis*. Part 2. Oxford: Basil Blackwell, 1922. Reprint. London: Research into Lost Knowledge Organization, 1985.

Lehner, Ernst. *Symbols, Signs, and Signets*. New York: Dover, 1950.

Leisegang, Hans. "The Mystery of the Serpent." In Campbell, *The Mysteries: Papers from the Eranos Yearbooks*, 194–260.

Lentz, W. "Some Peculiarities not Hitherto Fully Understood of 'Roman' Mithraic Sanctuaries and Representations." In Hinnells, *Mithraic Studies*, 358–377.

Lethaby, William. *Architecture, Mysticism, and Myth*. London, 1891. Reprint. New York: George Braziller, 1975.

———. *Architecture, Nature, and Magic*. New York: George Braziller, 1956.

Levarie, Siegmund, and Levy, Ernst. *Tone: A Study in Musical Acoustics*. Second edition. Kent: Kent State University Press, 1980.

Levi, Doro. "Aion," *Hesperia* 13 (1944), 269–314.

Levin, Flora R. *The Harmonics of Nicomachus and the Pythagorean Tradition*. American Classical Studies 1. New York: Interbook, 1975.

Liddell, Henry George, and Scott, Robert. *A Greek-English Lexicon*. Unabridged edition. Oxford: Oxford University Press, 1983.

Linforth, I. M. *The Arts of Orpheus*. Berkeley: University of California Press, 1941.

Lucian. *Works*. 8 vols. Loeb Classical Library. Cambridge: Harvard University Press, 1913–1967.

Lyra Graeca. 3 vols. Loeb Classical Library. Cambridge: Harvard University Press, 1924–1927.

Macchioro, Vittorio D. *From Orpheus to Paul: A History of Orphism*. New York: Henry Holt, 1930.

MacDermot, Violet, translator. *Pistis Sophia*. Nag Hammadi Studies 9. Leiden: E. J. Brill, 1978.

———. *The Books of Jeu and the Untitled Text in the Bruce Codex* (= *Books of Ieou*). Nag Hammadi Studies 13. Leiden: E. J. Brill, 1978.

MacMullen, Ramsay. *Paganism in the Roman Empire*. New Haven: Yale University Press, 1981.

Macrobius. *Saturnalia*. Translated by Percival Vaughn Davies. New York: Columbia University Press, 1969.

Marcus, Ralph. "The Name Poimandrês," *Journal of Near Eastern Studies* 8 (1949), 40–43.

Marinus of Samaria. *The Life of Proclus, or Concerning Happiness: Being the Biographical Account of an Ancient Greek Philosopher Who Was Innately Loved by the Gods*. Translated by Kenneth Sylvan Guthrie. Grand Rapids: Phanes Press, 1986.

McClain, Ernest G. *The Pythagorean Plato: Prelude to the Song Itself*. York Beach, Nicolas-Hays, 1978.

McLean, Adam, editor and translator. *The Magical Calendar: A Synthesis of Magical Symbolism from the Seventeenth Century Renaissance of Medieval Occultism*. Grand Rapids: Phanes Press, 1993.

Mead, G. R. S. *Orpheus*. London, 1896. Reprint. London: J. M. Watkins, 1965.

———. *The Hymns of Hermes*. London, 1898. New edition, with introduction by Stephan A. Hoeller. Grand Rapids: Phanes Press, 1991.

———. *Fragments of a Faith Forgotten: The Gnostics, A Contribution to the Study of the Origins of Christianity*. Second edition. London, 1906. Reprint. New Hyde Park: University Books, 1966.

———. *Thrice-Greatest Hermes: Studies in Hellenistic Theosophy and Gnosis, Being a Translation of the Extent Sermons and Fragments of the Trismegistic Literature with Prolegomena, Commentaries and Notes*. 3 vols. London, 1906. Reprint. 3 vols. in one. York Beach: Samuel Weiser, 1992.

———. *The Hymn of Jesus*. London, 1907. Reprint. Wheaton: Quest, 1973.

Menninger, Karl. *Number Words and Number Symbols: A Cultural History of Numbers*. Cambridge: M.I.T. Press, 1969.

Michell, John. *City of Revelation: On the Proportions and Symbolic Numbers of the Cosmic Temple*. London: Garnstone, 1972.

———. *Simulacra: Faces and Figures in Nature*. London: Thames & Hudson, 1979.

———. *Ancient Metrology*. Bristol: Pentacle Books, 1981.

———. *The New View Over Atlantis*. San Francisco: Harper & Row, 1983.

———. *The Dimensions of Paradise: The Proportions and Symbolic Numbers of Ancient Cosmology*. San Francisco: Harper & Row, 1988.

———. *New Light on the Ancient Mystery of Glastonbury*. Glastonbury: Gothic Image, 1990.

Michell, John, and Rhone, Christine. *Twelve-Tribe Nations and the Science of Enchanting the Landscape*. Grand Rapids: Phanes Press, 1991.

Middleton, J. H. "The Temple of Apollo at Delphi," *Journal of Hellenistic Studies* 9, 282–322.

Miller, James. *Measures of Wisdom: The Cosmic Dance in Classical and Christian Antiquity*. Toronto: University of Toronto Press, 1986.

Molland, Einar. *The Conception of the Gospel in the Alexandrian Theology*. Oslo: Jacob Dybwad, 1938.

Moore, Steve. *The Trigrams of Han*. Wellingborough: Aquarian Press, 1989.

Moore, Thomas. *The Planets Within: The Astrological Psychology of Marsilio Ficino*. Lewisburg: Bucknell University Press, 1982. Reprint. Great Barrington: Lindisfarne Press, 1990.

Moran, Jim. *The Wonders of Magic Squares*. New York: Vintage Books, 1982.

Nasr, S. H. *Islamic Science: An Illustrated Study*. London: World of Islam Festival Publishing Company, 1976.

Needleman, Jacob, and Appelbaum, David. *Real Philosophy: An Anthology of the Universal Search for Meaning*. New York: Arkana, 1990.

Neugebauer, Otto. *The Exact Sciences in Antiquity*. Second edition. Providence: Brown University Press, 1957. Reprint. New York: Dover, 1969.

Neumann, Erich. *The Origins and History of Consciousness*. Princeton: Princeton University Press, 1954.

Nicomachus. *The Manual of Harmonics of Nicomachus the Pythagorean*. Translated by Flora Levin. Grand Rapids: Phanes Press, 1993.

Nilsson, Martin P. "Early Orphism and Kindred Religious Movements," *Harvard Theological Review* 28 (1935), 181–230.

———. "The Anguipede of the Magical Amulets." In Martin P. Nilsson, *Opuscula Selecta*, III, 228–232. 3 vols. Lund: C. W. K. Gleerup, 1951–60.

———. *The Dionysiac Mysteries of the Hellenistic and Roman Age*. Lund: C. W.

K. Gleerup, 1957.

———. "The High God and the Mediator," *Harvard Theological Review* 56 (1963), 101–20.

Nonnos. *Dionysiaca*. 3 vols. Loeb Classical Library. Cambridge: Harvard University Press, 1940.

Nowotny, Karl Anton. "The Construction of Certain Seals and Characters in the Work of Agrippa of Nettesheim," *Journal of the Warburg Institute* 12 (1949), 46–57.

Origen. *The Philocalia of Origen: A Compilation of Selected Passages from Origen's Works Made by St. Gregory of Nazianzus and St. Basil of Caesarea*. Translated by George Lewis. Edinburgh: T. & T. Clark, 1911.

———. *Contra Celsum*. Translated by Henry Chadwick. Cambridge: Cambridge University Press, 1980.

———. *Commentary On the Gospel According to John, Books 1–10*. Translated by Ronald E. Heine. Fathers of the Church 80. Washington, D.C.: Catholic University of America Press, 1989.

Oriti, Ronald. "The Star of Bethlehem," *Griffith Observer* 39 (1975), 9–14.

Oxford Classical Dictionary. Edited by N. G. L. Hammond and H. H. Scullard. Second edition. Oxford: Clarendon Press, 1970.

Pagels, E. *The Gnostic Gospels*. New York: Random House, 1979.

Parsons, E. A. *The Alexandrian Library: Glory of the Hellenic World; Its Rise, Antiquities, and Destructions*. New York: Elsevier, 1952.

Pausanias. *Description of Greece*. 5 vols. Loeb Classical Library. Cambridge: Harvard University Press, 1918–1935.

Peck, Russell. "Number as a Cosmic Language." In *Essays in the Numerical Criticism of Medieval Literature*, edited by Caroline Eckhardt, 15–64. Lewisburg: Bucknell University Press, 1980.

Pennick, Nigel. *Geomancy: Man in Harmony with the Earth*. London: Thames & Hudson, 1979.

Pétrement, Simone. *A Separate God: The Christian Origins of Gnosticism*. San Francisco: HarperSanFrancisco, 1990.

Philo of Alexandria. *Works*. 10 vols. Loeb Classical Library. Cambridge: Harvard University Press, 1929–1962.

———. *On Husbandry*. In Philo, *Works*, III, 109–203.

———. *On the Confusion of Tongues*. In Philo, *Works*, IV, 9–119.

———. *On Dreams*. In Philo, *Works*, V, 295–579.

———. *On the Special Laws*. In Philo, *Works*, VII, 101–606; VIII, 7–155.

Philo of Byblos. *The Phoenician History*. Translated by Harold W. Attridge and Robert A. Oden. Washington: Catholic Biblical Association of America, 1981.

Pico della Mirandola, Giovanni. *Oration on the Dignity of Man*. In *The Renaissance Philosophy of Man*, edited by Cassirer, Kristeller, and Randall, 223–254. Chicago: University of Chicago Press, 1948.

Pindar. *The Odes of Pindar Including the Principal Fragments*. Loeb Classical Library. Cambridge: Harvard University Press, 1915.

Pistis Sophia. See entry under MacDermot.

Plato. *Works*. 12 vols. Loeb Classical Library. Cambridge: Harvard University Press, 1914–1927.

———. *The Collected Dialogues, Including the Letters*. Edited by Edith Hamilton and Huntington Cairns. New York: Pantheon, 1961.

———. *The Republic of Plato*. Translated by Francis M. Cornford. London: Oxford University Press, 1941.

———. *Plato's Timaeus*. Translated by Francis M. Cornford. Indianapolis: Bobbs-Merrill, 1959.

Pliny. *Natural History*. 10 vols. Loeb Classical Library. Cambridge: Harvard University Press, 1938–1962.

Plotinus. *The Enneads*. Translated by A. H. Armstrong. 7 vols. Loeb Classical Library. Cambridge: Harvard University Press, 1966–1988.

———. *The Enneads*. Translated by Stephen MacKenna. Burdett: Larson Publications, 1992.

Plutarch. *Moralia*. 16 vols. Loeb Classical Library. Cambridge: Harvard University Press, 1927–1969.

———. *The Dinner of the Seven Wise Men*. In Plutarch, *Moralia*, II, 349–449.

———. *On the Mysteries of Isis and Osiris*. In Plutarch, *Moralia*, V, 7–191.

———. *The E at Delphi*. In Plutarch, *Moralia*, V, 199–253.

———. *The Oracles at Delphi No Longer Given in Verse*. In Plutarch, *Moralia*, V, 259–345.

———. *The Obsolescence of Oracles*. In Plutarch, *Moralia*, V, 351–501.

———. *On the Sign of Socrates*. In Plutarch, *Moralia*, VII, 373–509.

———. *On the Generation of the Soul in the Timaeus*. In Plutarch, *Moralia*, vol. XIII, pt. 1, 159–345.

Porphyry. *Porphyry on the Cave of the Nymphs*. Translated by Robert Lamberton. Barryhill, New York: Station Hill Press, 1983.

———. *Porphyry's Letter to His Wife Marcella: Concerning the Life of Philosophy and the Ascent to the Gods*. Translated by Alice Zimmern. Grand Rapids: Phanes Press, 1986.

———. *Launching-Points to the Realm of Mind: An Introduction to the Neoplatonic Philosophy of Plotinus*. Translated by Kenneth Sylvan Guthrie. Grand Rapids: Phanes Press, 1988.

Proclus. *The Commentaries of Proclus on the Timaeus of Plato*. Translated by Thomas Taylor. 2 vols. London, 1820. Reprint. Hastings: Chthonios Books, 1988.

———. *Commentary on the First Book of Euclid's Elements*. Translated by Glen R. Morrow. Princeton: Princeton University Press, 1970.

———. "On the Sacred Art." Translated by Stephen Ronan. In Iamblichus of Chalcis: *On the Mysteries*, edited by Stephen Ronan, 146–149. Hastings: Chthonios, 1989.

Przybylski, Benno. "The Role of Calendrical Data in Gnostic Literature," *Vigiliae Christianae* 34 (1980), 56–70.

Ptolemy. *On Harmonics*. In Barker, *Greek Musical Writings II: Harmonic and Acoustic Theory*, 270–391.

Purce, Jill. *The Mystic Spiral: Journey of the Soul*. London: Thames & Hudson, 1974.

Rabinovitch, Melitta. *Der Delphin in Sage und Mythos der Griechen*. Dornach: Hybernia-Verlag, 1947.

Rahner, Hugo. *Greek Myths and Christian Mystery*. London: Burns and Oates, 1963.

———. "The Christian Mystery of Sun and Moon." In Rahner, *Greek Myths and Christian Mystery*, 89–176.

———. "The Christian Mystery and the Pagan Mysteries." In Campbell, *The Mysteries: Papers from the Eranos Yearbooks*, 337–401.

Rees, B. R., editor and translator. *Papyri from Hermopolis and Other Documents of the Byzantine Period*. Graeco-Roman Memoirs 42. London: Egypt Exploration Society, 1964.

Rees, Alwyn and Brinley. *Celtic Heritage: Ancient Tradition in Ireland and Wales*. London: Thames & Hudson, 1961.

Reitzenstein, R. *Hellenistic Mystery-Religions: Their Basic Ideas and Significance. Translated by John Steely*. Pittsburgh Theological Monograph Series 15. Pittsburgh: Pickwick Press, 1978.

Richardson, Cyril C., editor and translator. *Early Christian Fathers*. New York: Macmillan, 1970.

Richer, Jean. *The Sacred Geography of the Greek World*. Translated by Christine Rhone. Albany: SUNY Press, 1994.

Roberts, Alexander, and Donaldson, James, editors. *The Ante-Nicene Fathers:*

Translations of the Writings of the Fathers down to A.D. 325. 10 vols. Edinburgh, 1868. Reprint. Grand Rapids: William B. Eerdmans, 1981.

Robinson, James M. and Koester, Helmut. *Trajectories through Early Christianity*. Philadelphia: Fortress Press, 1971.

Robinson, James M., editor. *The Nag Hammadi Library in English*. Third revised edition. San Francisco: Harper & Row, 1988.

Robinson, John. *An Introduction to Early Greek Philosophy*. New York: Houghton-Mifflin, 1968.

Rohde, Erwin. *Psyche: The Cult of Souls and Belief in Immortality Among the Greeks*. London: Routledge, 1925. Reprint. Chicago: Ares, 1987.

Roscher, W. H. *Omphalos*. Leipzig: Teubner, 1913.

———. *Neue Omphalosstudien*. Leipzig: Teubner, 1915.

———. *Der Omphalosgedanke bei verschiedenen Völkern, besonders den semitischen*. Leipzig: Teubner, 1918.

Rose, H. J. *A Handbook of Greek Mythology*. New York: E. P. Dutton, 1959.

Rudolph, Kurt. *Gnosis: The Nature and History of Gnosticism*. San Francisco: Harper & Row, 1983.

Russell, Peter. "The Muses: Archetype of the Divine Intellect in Feminine Form," *Temenos* 13 (1992), 112–128.

Saleh, A. A. "The So-called 'Primeval Hill' and other Related Elevations in Ancient Egyptian Mythology," *Mitteilungen des Deutschen Archäologischen Instituts Abteilung Kairo* 25 (1969), 110–20.

Sallustius. *Concerning the Gods and the Universe*. Translated by A. D. Nock. Cambridge: Cambridge University Press, 1926.

Santillana, Giorgio de, and Dechend, Hertha von. *Hamlet's Mill: An Essay on Myth and the Frame of Time*. Boston: Gambit, 1969. Reprint. Boston: David R. Godine, 1977.

Schimmel, Annemarie. *The Mystery of Numbers*. New York: Oxford University Press, 1992.

Scholem, Gershom. *Kabbalah*. Jerusalem: Keter Publishing House, 1974.

Scott, Walter. *Hermetica: The Ancient Greek and Latin Writings which Contain Religious or Philosophic Teachings Ascribed to Hermes Trismegistus*. 4 vols. Oxford: Oxford University Press, 1924–1936. Reprint. Boston: Shambhala, 1985.

Seyffert, Oskar. *A Dictionary of Classical Antiquities, Mythology, Religion, Literature and Art*. Revised and edited by Henry Nettleship and J. E. Sandys. London: William Glaisher, 1894.

Shankarachanga, Jagadguru. *Vedic Mathematics*. Delhi: Motilal Banarsidass, 1975.

Sheppard, H. J. "Gnosticism and Alchemy," *Ambix* 6 (1957), 86–101.

———. "The Origin of the Gnostic-Alchemical Relationship," *Scientia* 97 (1962), 146–149.

Simson, Otto von. *The Gothic Cathedral: Origins of Gothic Architecture and the Medieval Concept of Order*. New York: Pantheon, 1956.

Singer, Irving. *The Nature of Love*. 3 vols. Vol. 1, *Plato to Luther*. Vol. 2, *Courtly and Romantic*. Vol. 3, *The Modern World*. Chicago: University of Chicago Press, 1984–1987.

Snodgrass, Adrian. *The Symbolism of the Stupa*. Ithaca: Cornell Southeast Asia Program, 1985.

Spitzer, Leo. *Classical and Christian Ideas of World Harmony: Prolegomena to an Interpretation of the Word "Stimmung."* Baltimore: Johns Hopkins Press, 1963.

Stanley, Thomas. *Pythagoras: His Life and Teachings; Being a Photographic Facsimile of the Ninth Section of the 1687 Edition of The History of Philosophy*. Los Angeles: Philosophical Research Society, 1970.

Stocks, J. L. "Plato and the Tripartite Soul," *Mind*, new series, 24 (1915), 207–21.

Strabo. *Geography*. 8 volumes. Loeb Classical Library. Cambridge: Harvard University Press, 1917–1932.

Taylor, Thomas, translator. *The Hymns of Orpheus*. London, 1792. Reprint. Los Angeles: Philosophical Research Society, 1981.

———. *The Theoretic Arithmetic of the Pythagoreans*. London, 1816. Reprint. New York: Samuel Weiser, 1972.

———. *The Eleusinian and Bacchic Mysteries: A Dissertation*. New York, 1875. Reprint. San Diego: Wizards Bookshelf, 1980.

Terpstra, Siemen. *Means and Music: The Generation of the Consonant Ratios of Music Through the Application of Means*. Unpublished.

Tertullian. *On Prescription Against Heretics*. In *Ante-Nicene Fathers*, III, 243–265.

———. *On Baptism*. In *Ante-Nicene Fathers*, III, 669–679.

Theodotus. *The Excerpts of Theodotus*. In *Ante-Nicene Fathers*, VIII, 43–50.

Theon of Smyrna. *Mathematics Useful for Understanding Plato*. Translated by Robert and Deborah Lawlor. San Diego: Wizards Bookshelf, 1979.

Thesleff, Holger. *An Introduction to the Pythagorean Writings of the Hellenistic Period*. Åbo: Åbo Akademi, 1961.

Thomas, Ivor. *Greek Mathematical Works*. Vol. 1, *From Thales to Euclid*. Vol. 2, *Aristarchus to Pappus of Alexandria*. Loeb Classical Library. Cambridge: Harvard University Press, 1951.

Throckmorton, Jr., Burton. *Gospel Parallels: A Synopsis of the First Three Gospels*. Nashville: Thomas Nelson, 1979.

Tompkins, Peter. *The Magic of Obelisks*. New York: Harper & Row, 1981.

Tripartite Tractate. Translated by Harold W. Attridge and Dieter Mueller. In Robinson, *The Nag Hammadi Library in English*, 58–103.

Tyson, Joseph B. *A Study of Early Christianity*. New York: Macmillan, 1973.

Ulansey, David. *The Origins of the Mithraic Mysteries: Cosmology and Salvation in the Ancient World*. New York: Oxford University Press, 1989.

———. "The Mithraic Mysteries," *Scientific American* (December 1989), 130–135.

UNESCO. "Bibliotheca Alexandria: The Revival of the First Universal Library." *Alexandria* 2, edited by David Fideler. Grand Rapids: Phanes Press, 1993.

Varro. *On the Latin Language*. 2 vols. Loeb Classical Library. Cambridge: Harvard University Press, 1951.

———. *On Agriculture*. In Cato and Varro, *On Agriculture*. Loeb Classical Library. Cambridge: Harvard University Press, 1934.

Vermaseren, M. J. *Mithras: The Secret God*. London: Chatto and Windus, 1963.

Virgil. *The Eclogues and Georgics of Virgil*. Translated by T. F. Royds. New York: Dutton, 1924.

Waerden, B. L. van der. *Science Awakening I: Egyptian, Babylonian and Greek Mathematics*. Fourth edition. Dordrecht: Kluwer Academic Publishers, 1975.

———. "The Great Year in Greek, Persian and Hindu Astronomy," *Archive for the History of the Exact Sciences* 18 (1978), 359–384.

———. *Geometry and Algebra in Ancient Civilizations*. Berlin and New York: Springer-Verlag, 1983.

Warden, John. "Orpheus and Ficino." In *Orpheus: The Metamorphoses of a Myth*, edited by John Warden, 85–110. Toronto: University of Toronto Press, 1982.

Weigall, Arthur. *The Paganism in Our Christianity*. London: Hutchison, 1928.

Westerink, L. G., translator. *The Greek Commentaries on Plato's Phaedo*. 2 vols. Amsterdam: North Holland Publishing Company, 1977.

Wheelwright, Philip. *Heraclitus*. New York: Atheneum, 1964.

Wiens, D.H. "Mystery Concepts in Primitive Christianity and in Its Environment," *Aufstieg und Niedergang der Römischen Welt* 2 (1980), 23.2, 1248–84.

Wild, R. A. *Water in the Cultic Worship of Isis and Sarapis*. Leiden: E. J. Brill, 1981.

Wind, Edgar. *Pagan Mysteries in the Renaissance*. New York: W. W. Norton, 1968.

Witt, R. E. "Plotinus and Posidonius," *Classical Quarterly* 24 (1930), 198–207.

———. "The Plotinian Logos and its Stoic Basis," *Classical Quarterly* 25 (1931), 103–111.

Wittkower, Rudolf. *Architectural Principles in the Age of Humanism*. New York: Norton, 1971.

Zandee, J. "Gnostic Ideas on the Fall and Salvation," *Numen* 2 (1964), 13–74.

Zeller, Eduard. *Outlines of the History of Greek Philosophy*. 13th edition. London: Routledge and Kegan Paul, 1931. Reprint. New York: Dover, 1980.

Zerubavel, Eviatar. *The Seven Day Circle: The History and Meaning of the Week*. New York: The Free Press, 1985.

Zosimos. *Zosimos of Panopolis On the Letter Omega*. Translated by Howard M. Jackson. Graeco-Roman Religion 5. Missoula, MT: Scholars Press, 1978.

Acknowledgment of Illustrations

American Oriental Society (Cuneiform tablet showing Babylonian value of $\sqrt{2}$, page 55; from *Mathematical Cuneiform Texts*, edited by Otto Neugebauer and A. Sachs, New Haven, 1945) • Beth-Shin-Tau Publishing (pages 241 and 245) • E. J. Brill (Gnostic diagrams, page 15; from *The Books of Jeu and the Untitled Text in the Bruce Codex* translated by Violet MacDermot, Leiden, 1978) • British Museum (Star map on front cover, engraved by Philip Lea, London *c.* 1686; Greek coin Apollo seated on the omphalos, pages 65 and 302; Orphic-Christian signet ring, page 203) • Chatto and Windus (*Mithras petrogenês*, page 144; Mithraic sanctuary in Sofia, page 145; Mithras on coin, page 163; from *Mithras: The Secret God* by M. J. Vermaseren, London, 1963) • Galerie e Museo Estense, Modena, Italy (*Phanês kosmokratôr* or the Aeonic Mithras, page 259) • Inner Traditions International (Bennu bird, page 249; drawing by Lucie Lamy from *Symbol and the Symbolic: Ancient Egypt, Science, and the Evolution of Consciousness* by R. A. Schwaller de Lubicz, published by Inner Traditions International © 1978, 1 Park Street, Rochester, VT 05767) • Wahlström och Widstrand (Jerusalem depicted as a chalice holding a stone, page 283; from *Graltempel und Paradies* by Lars Ivar Ringbom, Stockholm, 1951) • U. S. Games Systems ("The Sun" on front cover; from 1JJ Swiss Tarot Deck, © 1970 by Stuart R. Kaplan; further reproduction prohibited.)

Index of Names and Topics

Index of Gematria: Numerical Values

The following gematria numbers are referred to in this study. Those values indicated in **bold** correspond with the primary ratios of geometry and musical harmony. For the discussion of these values and their properties in the text, see the index of words and titles.

769 = PYTHIOS

800 = LORD

801 = AΩ
= DOVE

815 = LIFE (*Zôê*)

849 = MACROCOSM
= OMEGA

888 = JESUS
= OLEN

891 = HEAVEN

911 = AXIS
= OMPHALOS

1040 = MICROCOSM

1059 = PLEROMA

1060 = PYTIOS
= THE FISHER'S COAT

1061 = APOLLO

1110 = THE MICROCOSM

1111 = IOTA

1179 = FIRST MYSTERY

1224 = FISHES
= THE NET

1332 = ALPHA-OMEGA

1414 = THE GOD PYTIOS

1415 = THE GOD APOLLO

1480 = CHRIST

1925 = SIMON PETER

2368 = JESUS CHRIST

9999 = CHABRACHPHNESÊRPHICHROPHNYRÔPHÔCHÔBÔCH
= PHRÊANÔIPHÔRCHÔPHUUUURORPSISOROCHÔÔI

Index of Gematria: Names and Words